# IN THE RING

# IN THE RING

## THE TRIALS

### of a Washington Lawyer

## ROBERT S. BENNETT

CROWN PUBLISHERS

*New York*

Copyright © 2008 by Robert S. Bennett

Published in the United States by Crown Publishers, an imprint of
the Crown Publishing Group, a division of Random House, Inc., New York.
www.crownpublishing.com

Photographs are courtesy of the author unless otherwise noted.

Library of Congress Cataloging-in-Publication Data
Bennett, Robert S.
In the ring : the trials of a Washington lawyer / Robert S. Bennett.—1st ed.
Includes index.
1. Bennett, Robert S.    2. Lawyers—Washington (D.C.)—Biography.    I. Title.
KF373.B446A3 2007
340.092—dc22
[B]        2007023035

ISBN 978-0-307-39443-9

Printed in the United States of America

*Design by Leonard W. Henderson*

10 9 8 7 6 5 4 3 2 1

First Edition

*To Ellen, Catherine, Peggy, and Sarah,*
*the loves of my life*

# CONTENTS

# INTRODUCTION

**CHIEF JUSTICE REHNQUIST:** We will hear argument now in No. 95-1853, *William Jefferson Clinton v. Paula Jones,* Mr. Bennett.

**MR. BENNETT:** Mr. Chief Justice and may it please the Court: I am here this morning on behalf of the . . . President of the United States, who has asked this Court to defer a private civil damage suit for money damages against him until he leaves office.

IT WAS A FEW MINUTES after 10:00 A.M. on January 13, 1997. This was a lawyer's fantasy—the stuff of dreams. But here I was, a kid from Brooklyn standing at the podium in this marble palace, arguing before the United States Supreme Court on behalf of our forty-second president, William Jefferson Clinton.

A chill ran up my spine, and I was nervous and thrilled as I looked at the black-robed justices. I wished for a moment that my parents were alive to see this day but was happy and proud that my wonderful wife, Ellen, and daughters, Catherine, Peggy, and Sarah, were there to watch this special moment in my life.

The law has been good to me. As a child I had read *The Arabian Nights* and was fascinated by the magic carpet that could transport its rider to a variety of wondrous places. The law has been my magic carpet. It has allowed me to work with, meet, and represent many interesting people, from bookies to corporate titans, public figures of all stripes, even a president of the United States. I have learned from them all. Some of the lessons were positive; others, not. I have written this book because I want to share the ride with you and so that someday when I am gone, my children's children and their children will know who I was and what I did, and hopefully they and the many young lawyers to come will learn some lessons from my exciting and interesting life in the law.

This is a memoir and not an autobiography. I will tell you about myself and my family, but only to give background and context to my story. This is not about me. I am simply not important enough or exceptional enough to waste time focusing on each event in my life or nuance of my personality. I have had an interesting life in the law and have learned much about life as a result of it, and I want to share it with you, but to appreciate the message and properly evaluate it, you should know at least something about the messenger. So here goes.

# THE CARDS YOU'RE DEALT

O N AUGUST 2, 1939, I was born in Brooklyn, New York. I was the first child of Nancy Walsh Bennett and F. Robert Bennett. Mother was a housewife and Dad worked for a bank. We lived at 698 St. Marks Avenue in what is now known as the Bedford-Stuyvesant section. It was much different in the thirties and forties than it is today. Then, it was a safe and secure neighborhood consisting of middle- and upper-middle-class homes. The house was a large brownstone that was owned by my grandmother Irene Szalay and my step-grandfather, Dr. Stephen Charles Szalay.

My brother, Bill, was born on July 31, 1943. While I am sure that it was quite a shock to no longer be the center of attention, it didn't take me long to realize how wonderful it was to have a brother. From the very earliest of days, I felt a strong protective instinct toward him, which has continued to this day. While now he is very able to take care of himself, in his early years he was shy, quiet, and nonaggressive. My, how time changes things. It was standard fare for me to return from grade school and be given a list of neighborhood bullies who had mistreated Bill, then I did my brotherly duty of evening the score. No one was going to hit my little brother. That was a privilege I reserved for myself. From his early years, Bill was a great student and an avid reader. I am sure we read many of the same things, but unlike me, he remembers everything he reads. More about Bill later.

Grandmother Irene Szalay, my mother's mother, was born in Budapest, Hungary, and came to the United States as a very young child.

She was married three times and gave birth to four children. Gladys and John were born of the first marriage, Bill and my mother, Nancy, were born of a marriage to an Irishman, Dr. Joseph Walsh, a prominent doctor who at nineteen was the youngest person ever to receive a medical degree in the United States. Their marriage ended in a bitter divorce, the reports of which filled the newspapers. While the Irish genes and mannerisms from Joe Walsh, my mother's dad, seem to have taken over in my case and Bill's, the only grandfather we knew was our Hungarian step-grandfather, Dr. Szalay. Unfortunately, very little is known about my father's side of the family, but I do understand that we have English and German ancestry on his side.

Dr. Szalay was an old-school doctor. He saw as many as fifty patients a day and made house calls. The ability of a patient to pay made no difference to him. He felt that one does not go into a profession to make money, but to serve. When he received money for his services, he had the unusual habit of washing it. This was not the type of money laundering that would engage my legal expertise in the future; he always told me that money carries germs. "Bobby, you never know where it has been. It's been in lots of places." This is one lesson I have never followed. I can still see him sitting at his desk, after all his patients had left and after he had washed the money, playing classical records with baton in hand following the music as if he were conducting the world's great orchestras.

Dr. Szalay was a true renaissance man. He spoke several languages, was an engineer, a first-class photographer, and a superb musician. In his early teens, he played the cello in an orchestra in Budapest. He was a man of strong opinion and when discussing politics, he had a quick temper. He was very good to me, helping with my studies, covering my school books with strong brown paper and doctor's adhesive tape to protect the corners. When he died, I was about ten. I felt a great loss and was worried about his soul. As far as I could tell, he was not a religious man in any way. If he did believe in God, I saw no evidence of it, which caused me great concern. I recall placing a set of rosary beads in his hand as he lay dying hoping that this would allow him to go in the right direction. Because Dr. Szalay wanted me to play the cello, it was an enormous disappointment to him when, after a few lessons, I told him it was not for me. I had a tin ear and found lessons painful. Some fifty years later, I was invited to sit with the National Symphony Orchestra for a special event. When I was asked which section I wished to sit in, I said the cello section. I sat next to Glenn Garlick, the assistant principal cellist for the orchestra, and tears formed in my eyes as I thought about Grandpa Szalay and whispered under my breath, "Grandpa, this is the best I can do."

Grandmother was a strong-willed woman who was very loving and caring. Not a day went by that I was not on the receiving end of her age-old maxims, which she believed were the formula for a successful and honorable life: "Be on time." "People will not respect you if you dress like a bum." "The lazy man pays twice," etc. These and many other sayings were given to me by her throughout her life. Most important of all to her was honesty. Grandma did not accept the notion that little white lies were all right. There was nothing worse than telling a lie—big or small. While my brother, Bill, didn't know it at the time, the seeds for his *Book of Virtues* were planted in those early years.

Dad never talked much about either of his parents although I was told that his father had died when he was quite young. My father's parents lived in Northport, Long Island. I was told that my paternal grandmother felt very attached to me when I was an infant, but I have absolutely no recollection of her. She became a recluse in my infancy and would sit long hours, probably in a seriously depressed state, in a dark room in her Northport, Long Island, home. What put her there was a particularly tragic event. As she was returning home from her husband's funeral (my grandfather), she observed the family bull break loose from his chain. My father's younger brother had been near the bull and the broken chain wrapped around his neck and he was dragged to his death. Apparently, this was too much for my grandmother to absorb. I am told that my dad was very devoted to her and cared for her until she died.

Dad was a handsome and athletic man. He stood about six feet tall and was about 175 pounds of solid muscle. My mother told me he had been offered an acting job in Hollywood, but his mother objected, believing it was sleazy work. Dad was quiet and introverted. I have no recollection of him ever expressing an opinion or raising his voice. I don't think the poor guy ever had a chance with my mother, grandmother, and grandfather, all of whom were extroverts.

My mother was an attractive, outgoing, personable, and intelligent woman who always supported the underdog. She was smart and quick-witted. Had she been born twenty-five years later, she probably would have been enormously successful in whatever field she chose. In those days, her brothers, Bill and John, went to medical school because, after all, they would have to support a family. Mother, on the other hand, went to what was called a finishing school. It was appropriately named because it almost finished her. This woman of great natural talent never had the opportunity to spread her wings. However, she was a wonderful mother. In our teenage years, after she and my father were divorced, she worked two jobs so that Bill and I would have a comfortable life.

Everyone in life is dealt some good cards and some bad ones. One of my not-so-good cards was the divorce of our parents. At the time, I was about seven, and Bill, three. We all lived in my grandparents' house and I was oblivious to any strains in the marriage. In those days I was focusing on those great Brooklyn games of stickball—I was working hard on becoming a three-sewer-hitter—punchball, and a variety of high-risk games involving Bill, which usually involved no risk to me. A favorite game of mine, which was not a favorite of Bill's, was Rocket Ship. This required Bill to get to the top of the staircase, place his arms to his sides, and, under my direction, often accompanied by a push, travel down the stairs headfirst. It is amazing that he is still alive, functioning at a very high level, and still loves me.

Throughout the years, I thought the tension in my parents' marriage was Dad's fault, but years later, when he was on his deathbed at the young age of sixty-four, I realized that was probably not the case. Living in my grandmother's house was not a good situation. She often spoke disparagingly of my father, objected to him enjoying the simple pleasures of reading a newspaper after work, and always reminded my mother and him how much she was doing to help out the family in a financial way. Moreover, my mother was emotionally dependent on her mother, who was not hesitant to interfere with Mom and Dad's marriage. Also, Grandma was not shy in recommending how my mother and father should be raising us. She frequently made comparisons between her successful doctor sons and my not-so-financially-successful father. Early in his career, Dad worked at Chase bank and then at Manufacturers Trust Co. in New York. Eventually, Manufacturers Trust merged with Hanover. Although, at the end of his career, he had the title of assistant vice president, he did not make very much money.

Drs. John and William Walsh, on the other hand, would become very prominent doctors. John became the physician to Jacqueline Kennedy and delivered Patrick, who died shortly after birth, and John, Jr., who many years later died in a plane crash. He also delivered several of the children of Bobby and Ethel Kennedy. Bill Walsh left his successful practice in internal medicine and founded Project Hope, the hospital ship that brought care to the needy all over the world. He and my aunt Helen devoted their lives to making it the success that it was. How could Dad, a working stiff, compare to this? My mother and father should have rounded us up, moved into an apartment Dad could afford, and gone on with our lives. It is hard to know what would have happened—how things would have worked out—but I sometimes wonder. I am sure that the decision to stay was based on many factors—a better life for Bill and me, but also my mother's emotional dependency on my grandmother, and my father's nonaggressive approach to life all played a part.

One evening, when I was about seven, I recall seeing my Dad packing a bag. I can still picture him standing by a chest of drawers, placing his socks in a suitcase. I asked him where he was going—Dad didn't travel for his work, so I was curious. He told me he and Mother were splitting up and he was leaving. I was devastated. I did not know what it all meant, but I knew it wasn't good. I recall being hysterical and lashing out. How could they do this to Bill and me? There had been no warning, no preparation. I recall the feeling that I must protect Mother and Bill, a daunting task for a seven-year-old.

Mother, Bill, and I moved a few years later to 350 Parkside Avenue, in Flatbush, New York. My grandparents bought a duplex house there, and again we moved in with them. Mother had remarried a big tough Irishman, Michael Walsh, who joined us. Dad, following the divorce, rented a depressing room in someone's house in Brooklyn not too far from where Bill and I lived with our mother. I recall visiting him and later crying about his situation. It would soon change as he, too, remarried. Mike Walsh was a heavy drinker and he and my mother fought constantly. Walsh and my grandparents disliked each other intensely. We all lived in a duplex house with a connecting door. Bill and I would go back and forth from one section to the other. Following an argument with Grandma, Walsh told us that we could no longer go to their side of the house. The connecting door was locked. I was crushed.

Walsh was so physically intimidating and so violent when he got drunk that I slept with a baseball bat under my bed in case I needed it to protect my mother. Of course, little Bobby Bennett was no match for Mike Walsh, who stood six foot three and 240 pounds. He and Mother would eventually divorce only to be remarried again, then finally separated. Mike Walsh was not all bad. When he was not drinking, he could be thoughtful and generous, and I liked the feeling of having a strong male figure around. It was Walsh who, some years later, gave me a book about Clarence Darrow, the famous criminal lawyer. This probably planted the seed for my future work.

My parents' divorce was civilized. Every Sunday, Dad would come to the house—he was not invited in—and Bill and I would spend the day with him, usually at the movies. I looked forward to his visits and was deeply troubled that he was not invited into the house. In the summers, Dad would take Bill and me to North Conway, New Hampshire. As a result, I fell in love with New England.

While in Flatbush, two great things happened to me. James Typond, our next door neighbor, came into my life, and the Brooklyn Dodgers captured my heart and soul.

When we moved to Parkside Avenue, our next-door neighbors were James and Lonnie Typond. They had two daughters—Patty and Carol. Jim was a Chinese businessman who ran an insurance company and owned Shavey Lee's, a restaurant in Chinatown. He was an important link between the Chinese community and the city of New York, helping Chinese merchants with their personal and business affairs. Jim, known as the unofficial mayor of Chinatown, was very successful. A wise and generous man, he helped me through my younger years as a father substitute. Both Jim and I loved to fish; on weekends we would drive to New Jersey and fish in a lake where he kept his boat. The day would be topped off with a sumptuous meal at his restaurant. In many ways, he filled the gap missing from my relationship with my own father. And Patty, Jim's youngest daughter, was my first girlfriend—that is, until we both hit the age of about fourteen. She was then and still is a beautiful and charming lady. I owed Jim a great deal, as he was a comforting and guiding hand at an important time in my life. How could I ever repay him?

About thirty years later, the opportunity presented itself. I learned that Jim's grandson, Douglas Chu, a young lawyer and the son of his oldest daughter, Carol, had recently passed the bar and was looking for work in a tight market. I arranged a meeting with Douglas, liked him immediately, and offered him a job. He joined me at Dunnells, Duvall, Bennett and Porter, my firm until I joined Skadden. It has always been important to me to pay people back, as best I could, for kindnesses shown to me.

The second great thing, the Brooklyn Dodgers, was the center of my life in the 1950s. In those days the ballplayers were much more accessible to fans than they are today and were active participants in the local community. My aunt Gladys, who passed away at ninety-nine in 2005, was married to the sportswriter Bill McCullough, who was a writer for Jimmy Powers, the famous sportswriter for the *Brooklyn Eagle*. In its day, the *Eagle* was a great sports paper. McCullough gave me a season pass to Ebbets Field, and I made much more use of it than I should have, since I was often at the ballpark rather than in school. I knew everything about the players and was an autograph hound. When the players exited the ballpark, they would often run to their awaiting buses. If they stopped to give autographs, they would be mobbed. I decided that if I gave them a self-addressed postcard as they ran for their buses rather than fighting the mob, I had a better chance of getting autographs. Since they could sign my postcards during their long bus, plane, and

train trips to the next city, it worked out well and I was very successful.
On the back of each postcard I would write, "Autograph Please. Please
ask your mates to sign." I don't know how many postcards were lost in
the mail or taken by postal workers, but a good number were sent back.
I can recall rushing home from school every day in anticipation of
whose autograph would have arrived that day. Leo Durocher, then of
New York Giants fame, took the "mates" language literally and sent back
the postcard with his autograph as well as that of his wife, Larraine Day,
a television personality. While that is not what I had in mind by "mates,"
I was glad to have it. I still have a collage of postcards with autographs of
many of baseball's greats.

Frankly, I hated the Yankees and loathed the Giants. In 1951, when
the Giants's Bobby Thomson hit his famous home run—the shot heard
round the world—to beat the Dodgers for the pennant, I was depressed
for days. When I read recently that the Giants may have cheated by having someone in the stands reading signals, I felt relieved—it was almost
fifty years later, but it still felt good. I knew they couldn't beat my "bums"
fair and square.

Once, when the St. Louis Cardinals were visiting Ebbets Field, a few
buddies and I managed to secrete ourselves in a visiting-players-only area.
When Enos Slaughter approached the gate, I ran up to him and asked for
his autograph. "Get away from me, you little S.O.B.," he shouted. I was
crushed. Many years later, I felt joy whenever his baseball career took a
bad turn. On the other hand, when Dick Williams, who originally came
up through the Brooklyn Dodgers and later became a successful manager of several teams, was approached by me in similar circumstances, he
asked me who I was and spoke kindly. He even let me hold his glove. I was
a fan of his forever.

Once, at the ballpark, Bill McCullough introduced me to an elderly
gentleman named Harry M. Stevens. He was probably a lot younger than
I am now, but he seemed old at the time. Stevens's story is one of those
great American rags-to-riches tales. Starting with a pushcart outside of
Ebbets Field, Stevens became a corporate powerhouse. He became the
principal concessionaire in ballparks all over the country. I can recall sitting on his lap as a youngster and meeting the ballplayers as they would

come in to see him. This was before players had agents, and Stevens would freely give business advice and guidance to the players. I could not believe my good fortune as I met many baseball greats.

I sometimes read articles that comment upon my brother Bill's and my successes as rags-to-riches stories, which are greatly exaggerated. We were not Horatio Alger figures. Bill and I had all that we needed—and most of what we wanted—but most important, we were raised in a family that impressed upon us the importance of hard work, personal honesty, and integrity. Moreover, ours was a culturally rich environment where great conversation and appreciation of the important things in life were emphasized. Material things were never focused upon, but the importance of education was a constant theme. There was never an issue in our family as to whether Bill and I would go to college, but rather whether we would be doctors, lawyers, or professors.

To the best of my recollection, we were happy kids. These were not "touchy feely" times. We did not evaluate our happiness each day and we played the cards we were dealt. I always felt we had much more than others, even if that may or may not have been the case.

One Sunday morning, when I was in the seventh or eighth grade, Dad picked Bill and I up and took us to the movies. After the movies, he seemed nervous. "Bobby, I have met somebody, and would like to marry her—her name is Lois. I am sure you will like her—is it all right with you and Bill?" My immediate reaction was one of joy. Clearly, Dad was relieved when I said okay. Bill looked at me for my reaction. He would follow my lead. He would not always agree with my positions in future years, but I am still working on him.

After securing our approval, Dad proposed to Lois and she accepted. (She could never quite get over the fact that before proposing, he sought our permission, but she was pleased we gave the go-ahead.) For months Dad and Lois were busy making plans for their upcoming marriage in New York. On one of his weekly visits, he asked me if I would be his best man. What a wonderful request to make of a son. I was thrilled, proud, and happy, and readily said yes. This pleased him. As silly as it sounds today, there was a big problem, however. Dad, who was a Methodist, was going to marry Lois, a Presbyterian, in a Protestant church service. When

Dad and my mother Nancy were married, he promised to raise Bill and me as Catholics. Dad honored his commitment. But the church, speaking through a not-so-thoughtful priest, told me I could not be a participant in a non-Catholic church service as this could bring scandal to the church. While this seems absurd today, I was tormented. My father was important to me, but so was my religion. I decided the right thing to do was serve as best man, and I did so to the delight of my father. I was much relieved that the newspaper blip referring to the wedding did not include a caption along the following lines, "Bobby Bennett, 12, a Catholic, brings disgrace to his church by attending Protestant service."

Shortly after the wedding, I went to confession. I recall Father Kiernan, a priest in the parish, who was known as a soft touch, telling me that he did not think God would be too terribly troubled about a twelve-year-old boy serving as best man in his father's wedding. After that, Father Kiernan became my confessor of choice.

Lois, forty-eight, worked for the New York Infirmary, a hospital for women, and was in charge of the Debutante and Cotillion Ball held each year at the Waldorf-Astoria when she met my dad. He had been sent over by the bank to assist with the charity auction part of the ball. Lois, never married before, told me, "I saw the most handsome man I ever saw. I introduced myself and said I hope you and Mrs. Bennett will come to the ball. When he said there was no Mrs. Bennett, I grabbed his arm, invited him for a drink, and never let go." They had sixteen wonderful years together before Dad died of cancer in 1971. Dad had the body and cardiovascular system of an athlete. Unfortunately, he smoked several packs of unfiltered cigarettes a day. Because of his athlete's body, he lingered on and on as cancer ravaged his body. I spent a lot of time with him in his final days and we became closer than we had ever been before. I realized he loved me, but simply had trouble expressing it, and the circumstances following the divorce with my mother did not permit him to be the father he wanted to be or the one I wished for. Poor Dad, he was very careful with money and never dared splurge on anything he wanted. He was a superb golfer and always wanted to play the golf courses in Ireland and England, but he put that off for retirement. Lois and he always wanted to buy a little house in North Carolina, where she was from, but he put that off for retirement. He even said that he wanted a Cadillac, but that, too, had to wait for retirement. Just before he retired, a nurse at Manufacturers Hanover Trust Company, where he worked, told him he should get his annual physical before he left, as this would save him some money. Well, the physical showed a spot on the lung. He died a year later. He never got to Europe and never got the Cadillac, and his trip to North Carolina was not to buy a house, but to be buried in Lois's family plot in Warsaw. I recall thinking that I would do it differently. I would live my life and do the things my family and I wanted to do, not putting things off to retirement.

Lois and Dad had a wonderful marriage, and I am happy that the both of them experienced that fulfillment and joy. Lois often commented that it was a good thing I approved of the marriage and wondered what would have happened had I said no. I can hear her now with her heavy Southern drawl, "It's the damnedest thing I ever heard, a grown man asking a twelve-year-old boy if he could get married."

During these early years when I attended the Holy Cross Boys School, the teachers whacked you in class and your fellow students whacked you after. Since I started at this tough school in the seventh grade, following public school, I was an unwelcome outsider. I had to prove myself. In those days, that meant duking it out after school. After a few reports of bullies giving me trouble, Michael Walsh, my mother's second husband, taught me how to box. I became pretty good. In fact, he created a monster. After squaring-off repeatedly at even the slightest of insults, my mother and Walsh agreed to pay me a nickle a day for every day I did not get in a fight at school. Additionally, they tried to channel my aggressiveness by enrolling me in the Flatbush Boys Club boxing program. Over a few years time I had innumerable fights both in the ring and in the streets. I won every fight in the Boys Club program—eighty-eight— except for one, which was called a draw. I say *called a draw* because I think my opponent clearly beat me. His name was Howard and he was fighting his way out of the ghetto. I realized as a result of this fight that my future lay elsewhere, and I would earn my living with my brain. Years later, when some of my high-profile cases got my name in the paper, reporters loved to tell of my boxing history as it fit well with the image of being a tough trial lawyer. The stories did not usually report that I was only a kid at the time and that I did not really give up a career in the ring for the law. But some reporters never let the facts get in the way of a good story.

1953 was a very important year of my life. I was fourteen years of age and about to start high school at Brooklyn Prep. "The Prep" was a Jesuit school of very high academic standards. It was the same school my uncle Dr. William Walsh had attended many years before. It no longer exists. Frankly, I was not a particularly good student during my years at Prep, and I only did what I had to do to get by and little more. Most of the teachers in those days were either Jesuit priests or young men who were studying to become Jesuit priests. They were smart and dedicated and didn't let kids fall through the cracks. They were constantly on me for not producing the work they thought I was capable of. Rather than focusing on my studies, I was concentrating more on sharing my opinions on all sorts of issues with my teachers, and was determined to make my mark on the athletic field. I joined the junior varsity football team at the position of center. Although I was strong and aggressive and did pretty well, I lacked speed. However, I was determined that I would be a football star. But, fate disrupted my plans—it was hardly a tragedy, except in the mind of a young teenager. While playing in a pickup basketball game, I broke my ankle—it was a bad break and my football career was over. However, as things turned out, it might have been a very lucky break.

My mother and stepfather, Michael Walsh, consoled me. Walsh suggested that since I was always arguing with everyone, I should join the debate team. This sounded like a terrible idea. There were no stud points for debating. However, I agreed to give it a try, and it changed my life. I became fully engaged with the intellectual challenges of debate, which taught me lessons that would be important for my life as a trial lawyer. It was there that I developed analytical thinking, logical argument, and clear expression. Debating at Brooklyn Prep was not simply an extracurricular activity; debating in those days was well organized and highly competitive. Particular emphasis was placed upon it in Catholic schools. They had their own organization called the CFL, the Catholic Forensic League. In terms of time commitment, training, instruction, and fighting spirit, it ranked with professional sports. There were innumerable local and regional tournaments throughout the country. Each day when classes were done, we would spend hours working on our debating skills and mastering the subject matter of the national debate topic. Brooklyn Prep was at the top of the heap. It had a long tradition, both before and after I attended, as being the very best.

We were very fortunate to have dedicated and selfless faculty advisors who worked with us late into the night. Most important was Father Owen Daley, S.J., who at the time was a Jesuit scholastic. A *scholastic* is a young man studying for the priesthood. Owen, who had no family to go home to at night, would work with us for endless hours on our communications skills. In addition to Owen, Reverend Jim Dolan, S.J., guided and supported us. This was serious business for us, and we won tournament after tournament, including the New York State Finals in 1957. Just before I was to invite him to my fiftieth reunion at Brooklyn Prep, Father Daley died of a massive coronary on April 10, 2007. On April 14, my daughter Catherine and I attended the funeral mass in remembrance of Owen at the magnificent St. Ignatius Church at Eighty-fourth Street and Park Avenue. It was a beautiful ceremony and a fitting departure for this good and honorable man.

While a senior debater at Brooklyn Prep, I noticed a young fourteen-year-old on our team who seemed to have some real potential. His name: John Sexton. John went on to become a national college debating champion and today he is the president of New York University. Several years ago, when my daughter Peggy went to NYU Law School, John and I renewed our friendship. Before becoming president, John was the dean of NYU Law School and turned it into one of the very top law schools in the country. John and I have often talked about how Brooklyn Prep—particularly the debate program—taught us lessons and skills for life and helped us reach our goals.

An unusual feature of high school debating in those days was cross-examination. Following a direct presentation, a debater would be cross-examined by an opposing debater. Before I ever went to college, much less law school, I had conducted hundreds of cross-examinations. Of course, at the time I was not thinking about how this skill would be helpful in the law because my grandmother had pretty much decided that, like her sons, I would be a doctor.

In addition to debating, many local and national organizations would sponsor public-speaking tournaments. I became an accomplished public speaker. Tournaments were sponsored by organizations such as the Knights of Columbus and the American Legion. At one such tournament, I had survived the elimination rounds and was to speak in the finals. This was a big deal. I invited my dad and stepmother, Lois, who wanted to see me in action. As the day approached, one of the priests at the Prep approached me and told me that while my father and stepmother were welcome to attend, it would be necessary for them to sit in the back. This was because Dad was divorced. Again, the fear of scandal to the church. My father and Lois graciously obliged and sat in the back beaming with pride, but they never completely forgot the insult. Can't you see the front page of the *New York Times* reporting: "Divorced father of Bobby Bennett sits in front row with wife to watch son prevail in tournament. Those attending were shocked." Many years later I would serve on the National Review Board of the United States Conference of Catholic Bishops to assist the church in dealing with the devastating sexual abuse scandal facing it. As I will discuss later, it was this almost paranoid fear of scandal that would plant the seeds for a real crisis.

Through debating, I found something that I was good at and which brought me recognition and self-respect. I no longer cared about becoming a great athlete, an impossible goal given my talents, and focused more on matters of the mind. I graduated from the Prep in 1957, and while I had received my letter in sports, what was more important to me were the medals and awards I received for debating and public speaking.

About forty years after graduating from the Prep, I was told that I had been selected as the alumnus of the year. To this day, it is the award I most cherish. The award was made at the Church of St. Vincent Ferrer on the

Upper East Side of New York. While the school has been closed for well over a quarter of a century, the alumni is active and raises substantial sums for scholarships for needy students to attend Catholic high schools. It speaks volumes of Brooklyn Prep that each year hundreds of alumni attend the affair.

When I accepted the award, I thanked them for not kicking me out of the school, as they so often threatened, and sticking with me. I turned to give special thanks to Father Owen Daley and Reverend Jim Dolan, who were sitting on the altar behind me. Also, that evening an award was given to a former faculty member, Fr. Daniel Berrigan, S.J. He began his brief remarks by saying, "This is the first time this award has been given to a felon." You may recall that Dan Berrigan and his brother Phil were nationally known protestors against the war in Vietnam and each had been arrested several times for civil protests. Embarrassingly, several of the alumni walked out of the church when he received his award. As far as I was concerned, I didn't care if they ever came back. Dan Berrigan was one of my teachers. I have no recollection of seeing any signs of his future rebellion and civil disobedience. He was an extremely thoughtful and gentle man who enriched the school and those who came in contact with him.

As a result of my debating skills, I was offered a scholarship to St. Peter's College in Jersey City, New Jersey. I turned down the scholarship because my heart was set on Georgetown University in Washington, D.C. My uncle Dr. William Walsh encouraged me to go to Georgetown, and while I was at Brooklyn Prep, he arranged for me to meet Father Edward Bunn, S.J., who was the president of the university. During my last two years at Prep, Father Bunn took the time to correspond with me—complimenting me on my debating successes, but always encouraging me to improve my grades so that I would qualify for admission to Georgetown. Our team had won Georgetown's Annual Cherry Blossom debating tournament and this certainly was a plus in the eyes of Father Bunn. When I was accepted, it was one of the happiest days of my life.

As I reflect on my early years in Brooklyn, I believe I learned many valuable lessons. I learned at an early age that life has its ups and downs and you shouldn't whine or complain but do the best you can with the cards you have been dealt. I am sure that I developed a streak of independence because of the frequent turmoil I was faced with at home. Also, at a very early age I developed a sense of responsibility toward others. I felt that my mother and Bill needed me, and I learned that it is a good feeling when you are protective of others. This feeling would follow me throughout my personal and professional lives. Clients need not only sound legal advice but also protection.

# CHAPTER TWO

# A LESSON FROM A GOOD OL' BOY

THE MAJOR OBSTACLE to my attending Georgetown was the cost. I had no money. Fortunately, I was given a grant by a wonderful Catholic institution—the Bill Raskob Foundation. The grant paid room, board, and tuition. Together with jobs during summers and part-time jobs during the school year, I was able to attend Georgetown full time. Under the terms of the grant, I had a moral obligation, but not a legal one, to repay the money, but that was a distinction without a difference to me. As soon as I was able to repay their generosity, I did so in full.

Many of my jobs during my college years were not intellectually challenging, nor did I expect them to be, but I learned from each of them. During the summer after my first year of college, I worked as a moving man for a franchise of North American Van Lines. This was hard work, but kept me in shape. My fellow workers were tough guys with little education. I am sure they never had the nourishing background or opportunities I had. They were unmerciful in their harassment of me as a college punk. One fellow, Joe, was a bully. He was clearly the meanest and toughest guy of the bunch. Sick and tired of his harassing me, on one particular day I foolishly stood up to him. This outraged him and he came after me. My boxing skills came in handy in street fights with my equals, but this guy was an animal. As he charged like a raging bull, I picked up a two-by-four and hit him squarely in the face. He fell to the ground, blood pouring from his nose and mouth. He gave me a toothless smile and said, "Kid, you're okay." From that day forward, I was accepted by the group and no one would dare touch me as Joe became my protector. The harassing stopped. I am sure I was quite obnoxious with my college-boy opinions, which I expressed often. One night I learned a valuable lesson. Because I was low man on the totem pole at the company, one of my jobs was to assist long-distance drivers who came into town. When a cross-country driver arrived in the Washington area, he would call the local franchise and ask for a helper to assist in unloading. As a result, I would work all hours of the night.

One night I was instructed to help on a particularly hard move. An army colonel was moving into a townhouse somewhere in Virginia and the good-ol'-boy driver picked me up at the company in Arlington. As we headed toward the colonel's home, I was at my opinionated best and raised questions about how anyone like the driver could be part of a union like the Teamsters and allow the likes of Jimmy Hoffa and the union to engage in questionable activities and do so on the backs of the working man. (Years later I would represent Frank Fitzsimmons, the president of the Teamsters.) The good ol' boy said nothing and let me mouth off. When we got to the colonel's house, after midnight, we began the long night's move. The colonel had an enormous freezer that he wanted carried up to the third floor. We suggested that the basement would be a better place, but he insisted. As the good ol' boy and I carried this monster upstairs, he said to me, "Kid, how much are you making?" He was making many times more than I was. Since I was making peanuts compared to him, he said, "Isn't your end just as heavy as mine?" When I confirmed that he was making much more than I was, he said, "That, kid, is why I'm in the union and don't give a damn what Hoffa takes. If it wasn't for Hoffa, I'd be making what you make."

Another job I had while at Georgetown was as a janitor for an air conditioning company. Each night I would go to their offices in Georgetown and wax the floors and clean the toilet. The good thing about the job was that as long as the offices were spotless in the morning, I could do the cleaning anytime—8:00 P.M. or 2:00 A.M., it made no difference. This fit in well with my schedule. I can remember thinking that I better study hard and make a success of myself because I didn't want a permanent job cleaning floors and bathrooms. It was honest work, but work I would just as well avoid in the future.

While I was not embarrassed about the job, I am sure I did not tell my dates from Georgetown Visitation or Trinity College that before meeting them I was cleaning a bathroom. While most were not, a few of my jobs were intellectually challenging. I had agreed to be the debating coach at Gonzaga College High School, a Jesuit school in Washington. Before I began, the headmaster, Fr. Tony McHale, told me that the baseball coach, who also taught American history, had left and asked if I would teach his history course. Since I didn't know as much about American history as I should for this job, I worked hard at it and managed to stay a few lessons ahead of the students.

What I did not realize when I started Georgetown was that I had already begun my training to be a trial lawyer. With hundreds of cross-examinations and final arguments behind me, I nevertheless thought I wanted to be a doctor. I did not want to disappoint my grandmother. My grades were not good enough at the Prep to be admitted to the very demanding premed program at Georgetown, but I was assured that if I did well my first year, I could apply. I continued my debating and at long last got more serious about my academic studies. I did well my first year and was admitted into the premed program. I found the hard sciences to be boring, and, frankly, I had little interest or aptitude for them.

One day while visiting my mother and grandmother, who were now living in Arlington, Virginia, I met a young lawyer named—no joke— Lewis Carroll. Lew was an assistant United States attorney for the District of Columbia. He lived with several other lawyers in a large multibedroom apartment on the top floor of the building where my mother and grandmother lived. He told me about his work and invited me down to his office to meet his colleagues. I learned that the courts were open to the public and that for no charge at all, you could watch criminal trials play out in the courtroom. During these days, there was no Court TV. I found myself going down to the United States District Court at Third Street and Constitution Avenue on a fairly regular basis to watch murder, robbery, and rape trials. It intrigued me. All of a sudden, a light went off in my head, "Bob, you are in premed, but you are not hanging around George-town Hospital—you are hanging out in the courts." I knew for the first time in my life what I really wanted to do.

I graduated from Georgetown in the spring of 1961 with a B.A. degree and was headed the following fall to the University of Virginia Law School. With a partial scholarship, summer earnings, and a little help from my grandmother, I was able to devote full time and attention to my studies. I looked forward to Virginia because for the very first time, I would be away from home.

Brother Bill left for Williams College that same fall. Mother, Bill, and I, with a loaded car, drove to Williamstown, Massachusetts. I had encour-aged Bill to get away from Washington because Mother's drinking—the curse of the Irish—was getting worse. While a fabulous and loving mother for the formative years of our lives, she now felt unneeded. Once Bill and I left and were independent, Mother fell apart. She felt she had done her job and was no longer useful. The air went out of her balloon and drinking became the focus of her life. It was a tragedy that this beau-tiful and intelligent woman saw little purpose for herself. I felt somewhat guilty leaving, but the University of Virginia was only a few hours away and I could come home if needed. It was important to me that Bill be in-sulated as much as possible from family problems. Following my parents' divorce, I continued to feel that I had to protect Bill at all costs. I was far more assured of his ultimate success than my own and I didn't want him to be affected adversely in any way. I was the older brother and it was my responsibility to deal with family problems, which included pro-tecting both Mother and Bill.

Sometimes my brotherly advice was not appreciated, at least not when it was given. While at Williams College, Bill called me one evening and told me he was about to join SDS—Students for a Democratic Soci-ety. This was an extremist group and I didn't want Bill to go near them. Bill asked me why and when I explained, he told me that my arguments were no good. Finally, I said, "Bill, I'm your older brother, please do it for me—don't join." Bill angrily agreed and suggested that this was a chit I shouldn't call in again. SDS was a left-wing radical organization and I was afraid that if its members moved from lawful protest to unlawful activity, which some did, Bill would be tarnished by his membership. I would have been equally opposed to his joining a right-wing radical organization.

Many years later, Bill was nominated to be the chairman of the National Endowment for the Humanities. This was a wonderful opportunity for Bill, but he had to get Senate approval. Prior to his confirmation hearing, he was asked to visit Senator Jesse Helms, who had a great interest in the appointment. During his meeting, Senator Helms asked Bill if he had ever been a member of certain "subversive organizations," and leading the list was SDS. Bill answered, "Oh no, Senator." Helms approved Bill and the Senate confirmed him. Immediately after his meeting with Helms, Bill called and said, "Bob, I owe you a lot, you really saved me." This position would bring Bill to national attention and the rest is history. He would become President Reagan's secretary of education and the "drug czar" under the first President Bush.

Bill never asked me for advice regarding his social life, and that is probably why he actually went on a date with Janis Joplin, who *Rolling Stone Magazine* described as the "greatest white female blues singer." When I heard about it, I asked him how it went. Bill, who is discrete, told me very little, but he did say candidly, "Bob, let me put it this way, we were both disappointed." I didn't ask any more questions.

The University of Virginia Law School is one of the best. The professors were outstanding. One in particular I will never forget is Hardy Cross Dillard, who taught a first-year contracts class on Saturday mornings. He was such a brilliant communicator that his early-morning class was packed not only with his students but also weekend dates. Although I did very well during my first year, I had some family trouble. Mother was not doing well and my elderly grandmother could not deal with the situation. I decided to return to Washington and transfer to Georgetown Law School. Apart from Mother's situation, I also felt poor at Virginia. I had very little extra money and no car. There were only a handful of women in the school and the nearest girls' school was many miles away. Fortunately, one of my friends had a car, so I didn't always feel isolated. Charlottesville was an idyllic place, but I was a city boy and felt that it would be easier to make some extra money in a city, as I had in the past.

In the summer after my first year of law school, I received a big break.

I was hired as a law clerk at the firm of Corcoran, Foley, Youngman and Rowe. The lead partner was Thomas G. Corcoran, known around Washington as "Tommy the Cork." Corcoran was the most influential lobbyist in town, and the firm was a Democratic powerhouse. I spent a lot of time with him—driving him to appointments, answering his calls, and handling his files. This was a man at the center of power in Washington and it was interesting to watch him work. He had been an outstanding student at Harvard and became a law clerk to Justices Oliver Wendell Holmes and Felix Frankfurter.

Corcoran later joined the Roosevelt administration and together with his sidekick, Benjamin Cohen, wrote much of the New Deal legislation, such as the securities laws, which he helped push through Congress. Corcoran has been described as President Franklin Roosevelt's personal hatchet-man, and the president relied on Corcoran to get things through Congress. He was often described as a "Washington Institution." Corcoran was a force of nature, and I only hoped some of it would rub off on me. His front office was run by two wonderful and capable women. Anneta Behan was his girl Friday and Frances Melvin was her sidekick. I got along well with the both of them. Anneta and I became good friends and she always encouraged me to spend time with the boss. Corcoran was on a first-name basis with most of the senior members of Congress and members of the Supreme Court. He was the ultimate insider. When I was with him, I would take the opportunity to ask lots of questions, and learned a great deal from the answers. When my friend Anneta became ill, I spent even more time with Corcoran.

Corcoran had many gifts. He was well versed in the classics, was a wonderful musician, and could tell stories with the best of them. One gift he had was quite unusual. He could fall asleep by willing it. Several times a day, in between appointments, he would lie on his couch in a conference room adjoining his office and fall asleep for fifteen or twenty minutes at a time. "Bob," he would say, "wake me up in twenty minutes." At the end of the day, well rested, he was ready to work until late into the night when everyone else was tired and wanted to go home. He would often tell me that he won many arguments at 2:00 A.M. because "guys with a family and who were tired will give up their positions just to get home and get some sleep."

Corcoran's principal competitor as the go-to lobbyist was Clark Clifford. The two men were enormously talented, but very different. They did not like each other. I would later represent each of them when they got into trouble in separate matters, but that was many years down the road.

When Corcoran asked me to work full time for him following my summer job, that was the clincher. For all the many reasons I mentioned, I returned to Washington, got an apartment in nearby Arlington, went to law school at night at Georgetown, and worked full time for Corcoran. I have always been able to keep a lot of balls in the air, but even for me this year was a challenge. In addition, I joined the moot court program at Georgetown to try to develop my advocacy skills.

My principal job at Corcoran's office was to run a staff of about nine office boys. This was an incredible number of office boys given that the firm was a loose-knit organization of twelve to fifteen lawyers. Corcoran had a big heart and would never say no to a friend, many of whose children were office boys. I often handled the phones for Corcoran and was absolutely amazed at all the powerful figures who called him. Everett Dirksen, the influential senator from Illinois would call frequently and would use a fictitious name. Usually, he would say something like, "This is Mr. Burns." What was funny was that Dirksen had a deep, gravelly voice that was one of the most recognizable in town. Occasionally I would slip up and answer the phone and say, "Yes, Senator, I'm sorry, Mr. Burns, I will connect you with Mr. Corcoran."

After my year of night school at Georgetown, I decided to transfer to day school so that I could complete my law school education in three years. My schedule at the firm was flexible so I was able to make the change. Full-time law school, full-time working, moot court, and a relatively active social life had me running very hard. Fortunately, I have always done best when I am under a lot of pressure, and still do.

On November 22, 1963, I went to work after a morning class. President John F. Kennedy was in Dallas. The office, because it was a major player in Democratic politics, followed closely the travels of the president. In addition to Tommy Corcoran, Jim Rowe, Ed Foley, and Dick O'Hare, all had ties in one way or another to the president and his senior staff. As I passed one of the offices, I heard the news report that President Kennedy had been shot. My heart sank. I could not believe it. I quickly ran to each office reporting the tragic news. Everyone was devastated. There were screams and tears and feelings of total disbelief. I remember driving over the Fourteenth Street Bridge to my apartment in Virginia that evening. Everyone in my generation remembers exactly where they were and what they were doing on that day. My uncle Dr. John Walsh was First Lady Jacqueline Kennedy's doctor and flew to her side. Neither I nor anyone else will ever forget the deeply moving photograph of young John John all dressed up saluting as the riderless horse passed by. The most accurate and chilling record of the assassination was captured on film by Abraham Zapruder, an amateur photographer who lived and worked in Dallas. Like all Americans, I watched and rewatched that film. Little did I know that almost thirty-five years later, I would be representing the Zapruder family in a fascinating case involving that very film (for that story, see chapter 15, "A Death on Film"). To a great extent, the old feelings and heartache would come back as I prepared the case and watched the film again and again.

In May of 1964, I graduated from law school. I felt well prepared since Georgetown is a great law school. My mother and grandmother attended the graduation. Grandmother was very proud of her first grandson and I'm sure was relieved that I graduated. Since I never had the scholarly interest of Bill, she was always a little bit worried that I would do something crazy like joining the French Foreign Legion. I recall, after receiving my diploma, she said, "Bobby, I'm very proud of you. If you couldn't be a doctor, this is okay." I told you she was brutally honest—perhaps to a fault. Frankly, her comment weighed heavily on me over the years as I desperately wanted to please her.

In the summer of 1964, Corcoran asked me to go to the Democratic National Convention with him in Atlantic City. The place was mobbed. Mr. Corcoran said he had made the arrangements and I would be staying with him. No cramped quarters for us. We shared a lovely suite with all the amenities.

It was a heady and wonderful few days. I met everybody. I could not believe my good fortune. Jim Rowe, one of Corcoran's partners, handed me a fistful of bills and told me to take a group of young Democrats out on the town. I was in seventh heaven and knew that I had made the right choice in moving back to Washington.

After graduation from Georgetown, I worked for Mr. Corcoran in the summer, then attended Harvard Law School for a master of laws degree in the fall. Frankly, I had had little interest in more school and was anxious to get started as a lawyer, but late one evening I drove Mr. Corcoran to the apartment of Anna Chennault. Anna, the widow of the famous Gen. Claire Chennault of Flying Tiger fame, was a beautiful and exotic-looking woman and an accomplished person in her own right. I had given Anna, at Corcoran's request, some very low-level assistance when she wrote her own book. During that evening, as Corcoran and I were driving to her apartment, he said he thought I should go to Harvard for a graduate degree. He thought a Harvard degree would be a good thing for me to have on my résumé. I remember him telling me that he admired how hard I had worked at both my job and law school. He acknowledged my loyalty to him, and said he wanted to do something special for me. I could never have afforded Harvard, especially without working. Corcoran said he would pay my way by keeping me on the payroll and suggested that I could continue doing research on his matters. I'm sure this suggestion was to make me feel like I was not a charity case. Also, Margaret, Tommy's oldest daughter, was in her final year at Harvard Law School and Tommy liked the idea of having me around Harvard for Margaret's final year.

In September, I headed for Cambridge for what would be a very interesting year. While I was anxious to start working as a lawyer, I realized this was a great opportunity. Having passed the Virginia bar during my final year at Georgetown, there was little pressure on me. Moreover, for the first time in a long time I would be able to study without having the distractions of family and work.

In those days, Harvard had a master of laws program in which they admitted seventy-five students—fifty foreigners and twenty-five Americans. You could pretty much decide what you wanted to take provided it made sense and was approved by your faculty advisor. Rather than focusing on any particular subject matter, I decided I would study areas that I knew little about and would also select courses, whatever they were, if they were taught by one of the great Harvard professors. Each student, in order to get this treasured graduate degree, had to write a master's thesis.

My master's thesis was in a course called constitutional litigation, taught by the great Paul Freund. I also took jurisprudence with Lon Fuller and legal process with Henry Hart. These were legendary scholars and teachers, and I am grateful for the opportunity to have taken their courses. Two of the areas in which I had no background were tax and government regulation such as antitrust and federal trade regulation. A young professor, Derek Bok, taught a course called economic regulation, which covered these areas. Bok was an excellent teacher and communicator. He later would become dean of the law school and president of the university.

Paul Freund was a legendary figure, and deservedly so. He was a big but gentle bear of a man. I did very well in his course and became friendly with him. There was nothing he did not know in the field of constitutional law and his dream was to be on the Supreme Court. He never got there. I was told by both Tommy Corcoran and Joe Rauh, the great civil rights lawyer, that he would have been put on the court had he accepted President Kennedy's offer to be the solicitor general of the United States. Ironically, Tommy Corcoran wanted to be solicitor general years before, but the position was never offered to him. Justice Felix Frankfurter undercut him with President Roosevelt. What made Corcoran quite bitter about this was that as a key adviser to Roosevelt, Corcoran was instrumental in Frankfurter being named to the Supreme Court. When it was his turn to help Corcoran, Frankfurter pulled the rug out from under him. Corcoran vowed then to use his talents to represent private interests and not give his heart and soul to government service any longer.

One day in class I can recall Freund looking at me and asking, "Mr. Bennett, what do you think are the constitutional implications of . . ." He was really interested in what his students thought and acted like we might have some insight he had never thought of. I am sure that the chances of me coming up with a bright idea he hadn't thought of was impossible. He was a brilliant man and my exposure to him alone was worth my year at Harvard. It was a real loss to our country that someone of the caliber of Paul Freund never made it to the Supreme Court.

Margaret Corcoran, Tommy's daughter, and I spent a lot of time together at Harvard but both looked forward to returning to Washington. I would become a law clerk to her uncle, United States District Court Judge Howard Corcoran, and she would become a law clerk to Hugo Black, associate justice of the Supreme Court. Life was good and we were both looking forward to bright futures and good times in Washington.

Margaret was a fun companion and, like her father, a ball of energy. She was always on the go and often asked me to join her. A few years after her clerkship, Margaret would die an untimely and mysterious death. I was devastated.

# CHAPTER THREE

# A FRONT-ROW SEAT

WHILE I WAS AT Harvard, Howard F. Corcoran, Tommy's younger brother and a member of the firm of Corcoran, Foley, Youngman and Rowe, was nominated by President Lyndon Johnson to be a United States District Court judge for the District of Columbia. I had done work for Howard at the firm and we had a great relationship. After his confirmation, he called and asked me if I would join him as his law clerk when my year at Harvard was over. The handiwork of Tommy was clearly present in both job opportunities. Tommy was close to President Johnson and secured the appointment for Howard, and Tommy Corcoran, who was always looking out for me, believed that there was no better way for me to start my career than by being a law clerk to a federal judge and put the word in with his brother Judge Corcoran. Also, he trusted me and thought I could be helpful to Howard.

I was absolutely thrilled with Judge Corcoran's offer and readily accepted. I could hardly wait to tell my graduate-school colleagues. Each afternoon the graduate students in the masters program at Harvard would gather for tea and coffee. It was fun and interesting. Since most were graduates of foreign law schools, it was an opportunity to meet others who would become important lawyers and leaders in their countries. We would compare notes and discuss our futures. I vividly recall going to the afternoon tea the day I accepted Judge Corcoran's offer and hoping that I would be asked what was new or what I would be doing next year. I was asked, and beaming with pride, I answered and enjoyed the congratulatory remarks of my colleagues. A few minutes later one of my friends from an African nation came into the tea and proudly announced that he had just been appointed attorney general of his country. Another lesson in life—everything is relative.

While at Harvard, I met a beautiful, charming young woman who was a whirlwind. Her name was Elizabeth Hanford. Liddy, as she was called, asked me to campaign for her among the graduate students in an upcoming election at the law school. After Harvard, we both came to Washington to begin our careers and would continue our friendship. Liddy would later marry former Senator Robert Dole, head the Red Cross, and become a United States senator from North Carolina. We all knew she would make it big.

Howard Corcoran was a delight to work for. He had a wonderful judicial temperament and was by nature a fair man blessed with a great deal of common sense. Prosecutors, defense lawyers, and plaintiffs lawyers all liked to appear before him. That is a true test of a first-rate trial judge. While he was not a trial lawyer, it never interfered with his running an outstanding courtroom in which all litigants felt that they had had their day in court. Judge Corcoran understood that his was not an appellate court and felt it was important to decide cases promptly.

Clerking for a brand-new judge was a particularly wonderful experience because we were learning together. Everything was new and had to be learned from the beginning. As a result, I had much greater responsibility than I would have had if I worked for a judge who had done it all before and used his clerks solely for research outside of the courtroom. Make no mistake about it, he was the judge and made the decisions, but still he gave me a lot of running room and fully involved me in the decision-making process. The one area that he kept to himself, seeking little input from me, was sentencing. He felt that this was his job and his job alone and that only he could weigh the many factors and nuances in a defendant's life so as to be sure that he applied individualized justice. Were he on the bench today, Judge Corcoran would be very troubled by current sentencing practices that have taken away much of a judge's independence and discretion. I believe that when she looks at our sentencing practices today, Lady Justice covers both of her eyes. The problem at its core is that we have taken discretion away from the one independent person in the process and handed it over to the prosecutor. We have given the keys to the jailhouse to the prosecutor and have left judges with much less power than they should have.

Judge Corcoran wanted me to be in the courtroom with him and even allowed me to participate in bench conferences with counsel, which took place out of earshot of the jury. We would go back to his chambers during recesses and at the end of the court day and we would discuss the evidence and issues. Judge Corcoran and I would discuss the lawyers who appeared before him and what they did right and what they did wrong. This was an incredible learning experience for a newly minted lawyer. I saw it from the inside and learned many valuable lessons that I have followed throughout my life as a trial lawyer. I learned that a trial lawyer must always be prepared. In presenting your case, you should be simple and direct. Sometimes I feel lawyers are masters of the art of making simple things complicated. It should be just the opposite. The best trial lawyers have the ability of taking complex facts and issues and making them understandable to everyone. Also, I learned that jurors watch everything that goes on in the courtroom and make judgments about which lawyers they can trust and which ones they can't.

One day a federal prosecutor filed a pleading that, while good, had several grammatical errors and misspellings. Judge Corcoran looked at me and said, "Never hand a judge a piece of paper like this." His view was that if the prosecutor did not exercise the care to catch these errors, "Why should I have confidence in his arguments and conclusions given his sloppiness?" This was a great lesson; nothing is ever filed in a court under my name that I have not reviewed carefully.

Since I had to read all of the pleadings that were filed with the judge, I learned that short and clearly written pleadings were the way to go. Lawyers who think that theirs is the only case the judge has to deal with and that the judge has all the time in the world to read their lengthy and laborious pleadings are sadly mistaken. Trial lawyers should remember that they are not writing for history—they are writing to persuade and win the case. Another very valuable lesson I learned was that while lawyers are expected to be advocates and persuasively present their clients' positions, they are also officers of the court and must never mislead a court by misstating the facts or the law. Also, a lawyer should never fail to cite a relevant case even if it is against his or her position. If you can distinguish a harmful case, that's fine, and if you can't, it is appropriate to argue it was wrongly decided, but don't hide it. As a law clerk, when I found an important and relevant case that a lawyer failed to cite, that undercut his or her position, the judge lost confidence and trust in that attorney.

For me, being in the courtroom was the best part of the job. I learned what worked with judges and juries and what did not. The most important of the lessons I learned as a law clerk was the importance of being candid and straight with the court. A lawyer's reputation for honesty and integrity is the coin of the realm. Once lost, it can never be regained. This lesson, learned early on, has been confirmed time and again over the past forty years. These were all lessons I learned before I ever handled a case as a lawyer. Another lesson I learned is that the single biggest tactical mistake a trial lawyer can make is to overtry the case. Put in the important evidence, not all the evidence. Make the essential arguments, not every one that pops into your head.

The United States District Court for the District of Columbia was a very unique court until court reorganization took place in the early seventies. Because Washington is a federal city and there was no counterpart state system, all of the serious common-law crimes were tried in federal court, not state courts as would be the case in other jurisdictions. While misdemeanors were tried in a local court known as the Court of General Sessions, the common law felonies like murder, rape, robbery, and serious narcotic offenses were tried before federal judges in the federal courts.

Judge Corcoran occasionally complained that the heavy load of street-crime cases distinguished his court from other federal courts. A few times I heard him comment that federal judges in other jurisdictions are "real" federal judges and don't have to hear these street-crime cases.

After reorganization of the District of Columbia Court system, these local and common law felony cases were tried in the Superior Court of the District of Columbia, and the United States District Court became just like every other federal court regarding the cases they handled.

Howard and Esther Corcoran were devoted to each other. They had a long and successful marriage. Esther was a very accomplished woman. She served with distinction as an officer in the United States Army during the Second World War. Judge and Mrs. Corcoran had no children and so the law clerks became their children. Over time, Judge Corcoran had many law clerks, and we held an annual dinner in honor of Judge and Mrs. Corcoran. At one of the dinners, Judge Corcoran told me how much he missed the good old days. "Bob, do you remember that murder case I tried . . ." etc., and ". . . Bob, if I hear one more complex regulatory case, I'll go crazy." He went on to comment on how painful it was to hear the lengthy testimony of some economist knowing that later in the case another economist with equally lengthy testimony but taking the other side would be testifying before him. We laughed about the old cases and agreed that in many ways those early years were more interesting and fun.

THE TOWPATH ALONG the canal that runs through Georgetown is a favorite spot for Washingtonians to walk, jog, ride bikes, or simply enjoy nature.

On October 12, 1964, Mary Pinchot Meyer, just shy of her forty-fourth birthday, went walking on the towpath. She was the divorced wife of Cord Meyer, a former CIA official and the sister-in-law of Ben Bradlee, the well-known journalist. Bradlee would become world famous as the tough and hard-charging editor of the *Washington Post* overseeing coverage of the Watergate and Pentagon Papers stories. Mary was well connected with the Kennedy administration and was a well-liked member of Washington's upper crust. Sometime after noon, while walking on the towpath, Mary was brutally murdered by a gunshot wound to her head. Her death sent shock waves through Washington. Within a few hours the police arrested Raymond Crump Jr. and a grand jury would later indict him on charges of first-degree murder.

Every law clerk at the court hoped that their judge would draw the case. When I mentioned it to Judge Corcoran, he said that there was no way it would be assigned to him because Chief Judge Matt Maguire promised him that he would only assign him smaller criminal matters until he got his feet wet as a new federal judge. Corcoran, an accomplished corporate lawyer, had little criminal experience, so the last thing he wanted was the most high-profile criminal case in the country.

Within the hour, a clerk from the criminal division entered chambers and handed us a jacket entitled *United States of America v. Raymond Crump Jr.* I was ecstatic. It was the hottest case in the court and the city, indeed the country, and I would not only have a front-row seat, but would be working closely with Judge Corcoran on it. I was the envy of all of my fellow law clerks.

Judge Corcoran was not as happy. He was on the shy side and had no ego. Having a big, high-profile case did not mean much to him. Judge Corcoran thought that maybe it was a mistake given the earlier assurances of the chief judge. Louise Cooper, his wonderful and devoted secretary, and I assured the judge it was no mistake and that the chief knew what he was doing. We were soon proved right.

On July 20, 1965, the trial began. The lead prosecutor on the case was Al Hantman. Al was a very senior and experienced prosecutor, but lacked the jury skills of some of his colleagues. The defense counsel was Dovey Roundtree, an experienced defense lawyer who related well to juries. She had a motherly warmth and her low-key, casual style concealed a very bright and aggressive advocate. When not defending criminal cases, she was a preacher in her church. She was well known in legal circles as a formidable defense attorney.

The prosecution had a strong case including the eyewitness account of a Mr. Wiggens, a gas station employee, who testified that when he heard a gunshot and scream, he ran to a wall overlooking the towpath some forty yards away and saw a man he identified as Raymond Crump Jr., standing over the body of Ms. Meyer. In addition, the government had substantial circumstantial evidence tying Crump to the location of the murder. Clothes identified as his were found near the scene. Upon his arrest, Crump told the police that he had been fishing, but fell asleep and fell in the water along with his fishing equipment, which was never recovered at the scene. The police, for good reasons, believed this was a phony alibi. Hantman would present evidence from a neighbor that when Crump left the house that morning, Crump was not carrying fishing equipment.

Throughout the trial, there was a very subtle racial overtone. Was this poor African-American man a scapegoat for the murder of an establishment white woman? Would the justice system be fair to Crump or was the deck stacked against him because of her high-profile friends? Dovey Roundtree was masterful in raising such issues at the trial without offending anyone.

I sat next to the jury box, as if I was the thirteenth juror. Frankly, I would have convicted Crump because of the overwhelming evidence. While Hantman did a first-rate job in his closing argument, pulling together the evidence in support of his claim that Crump was guilty of first-degree murder, he did not do a particularly good job at various points in the trial. Helping the prosecution was the fact that Crump, who did not testify at trial, gave the police an unbelievable explanation of why he was on the towpath—that he went fishing—especially since his fishing tackle was never located. Nevertheless, the jury returned a not guilty verdict.

While heartsick because I believed that justice was not done, I could understand the jury's verdict. Hantman had overtried his case and thereby gave Dovey Roundtree the opportunity to raise reasonable doubt in the minds of the jurors. By *overtried*, I mean he took a vacuum cleaner approach to presenting evidence. He put it all in no matter how insignificant, and this diluted the impact of his strong evidence.

Again, if there is one lesson above all others I have learned as a trial lawyer, it is that while you should overprepare your cases, you should always undertry them. A trial lawyer always does better when he sticks to a few basic themes and supports them with his strongest evidence. However, in the preparation stage, there is no issue or fact that should be ignored.

At the start of the trial, Hantman, with great fanfare, had put up on the wall of the courtroom a topographical map of the canal area where the murder occurred. The map appeared to be thirty or forty feet in length. It was the prosecution's theory that the police quickly responded to the towpath after receiving a report of the shooting and that all of the exits from the towpath were promptly sealed off, thereby preventing the escape of the murderer. With military precision, Hantman showed minute by minute the arrival time of the police at each exit. The map made the area look very large and dense. I remember asking myself, If someone else committed the murder, couldn't the murderer hide behind some tree in the area? Weren't there ways to exit the towpath area not reflected in the map? Initially, Ms. Roundtree objected to the map being left on the wall for the jury to see unless it was actually the subject of testimony. So it repeatedly went up and then it came down and then it went up again. As a result, the map received a lot of attention. At some point Dovey Roundtree realized that the map helped her because of the sheer size of the area it covered and she withdrew any objection to it being displayed. On cross-examination of a representative from the U.S. Department of the Interior, she elicited damaging testimony that the map only showed official exits. The witness then acknowledged that it did not show unofficial exits and walkways out of the area. Moreover, the witness testified that he had never been to the area, but had prepared the map from other documents. Thus, the map was effectively turned against the prosecution.

One of the major problems with the government's case was that they never recovered the murder weapon. Here is how Dovey Roundtree in her closing argument, turned the tables on the prosecutor, who had gone as far as to present evidence of a recovered button from the scene, but could not produce the gun:

> We had the Marines, Army, and Navy personnel out there— not to play. They were given specific instructions.
>
> If the policeman were able to find for you a button not as large as the thumbnail of my finger, rest assured if there resided in this area the .38 caliber revolver, they would have had it here during this trial.
>
> It simply left the park. It left the area. If it were there, these fine officers would have had it here for you.
>
> Now, not only did they take men into the area—in one

instance, you know, they drained the canal. They withdrew and sifted mud by mud, and that is the way it should have been done.

They did that and they found no weapon.

Not only did they do that, but one officer testified there came a time when officers went four abreast walking down—down the towpath, down the canal area, looking for the gun.

And I believe—I believe and I say to you I believe you must be convinced that if the gun were still in the area, it would have been found.

The witnesses called by the government were too good to be true. The next-door neighbor who observed Crump leaving his apartment that morning without any fishing equipment later identified Crump's fishing equipment that was found in his closet. When I heard this testimony, I recall thinking that my best friends and closest relatives couldn't identify my fishing equipment, but Hantman's witness did. To appeal to the jury emotionally, Hantman went to great lengths to show that a bloody massacre occurred on the towpath. Roundtree turned that appeal against him in her final argument emphasizing that no blood was found on Crump or his belongings.

A good trial lawyer must appeal not only to the mind but also the heart and soul of the jurors. You must get in their gut and get them to want to decide in your favor. It is important that they like you, think you are fair, and respect you. On all these counts, Dovey Roundtree succeeded, and in several Hantman failed. Dovey was warm and motherly. It was as if she was pleading for her own son, not a guilty defendant. She communicated well with the largely African-American jury, many of whom, especially the women, identified with her. Hantman, on the other hand, was cold and arrogant at times and overreaching. Moreover, throughout the trial he chewed gum. His gum chewing became the subject of discussion in chambers, and Judge Corcoran told me never do that in a courtroom. It was disrespectful to the court and the jury. I am sure the jury noticed.

Nothing is missed by twelve jurors. What one misses, another sees, and before long all of them know everything. Moreover, jurors watch the lawyers before them—what they wear, who they talk to in the courtroom, who they are friendly with in the audience, and who they are rude to. Perhaps it should not be that way, but it is.

In her closing argument, Roundtree, referring to Crump, spoke in motherly tones and humanized her client while at the same time pointing out discrepancies in the prosecutor's case based on earlier descriptions given the police.

> So I say to you that you must consider this. He is a man of peace and good order, not given to assaulting anyone, not known to be violent. That is this man, who is not five feet eight and does not weigh 185 pounds. . . .
>
> I leave this little man in your hands, and I say to you fairly and truly, if you can find that he is five feet and eight inches tall, that he weighs 185 pounds, irrespective of what he wore that day—if you can find—I cannot from this evidence—and I say you must have a substantial and a reasonable doubt in your minds, and until the government proves its case beyond such doubt, then you must bring back a verdict of not guilty.

The jury did what was asked of them by Dovey Roundtree. Both Judge Corcoran and I were surprised at the verdict, but understood how it happened. It was not easy for Judge Corcoran to look directly at Crump and tell him that he was a free man and could leave the courtroom, but that was his duty and that is how the system works.

I am told that the D.C. police escorted Raymond Crump Jr. to the city limits and told him never to return, but he did return. This so-called little, nonviolent man of peace and good order, as he was described by Dovey Roundtree, would over the years assemble a rap sheet of violent crimes, including assault and arson for which he would spend substantial time in prison.

A number of interesting facts about the life of Mary Pinchot Meyer came to light after her death. In fact, her brutal murder and the high-profile case resulted in the life of a very private person becoming very public.

According to several writings that came out after her death, Mary kept a private diary, which was known by only a few of her friends. On the night of her murder, Anne Truitt, a close friend who was an artist and sculptor, called Ben Bradlee from Tokyo and told him that Mary had asked her to take possession of her diary should anything happen to her. When Bradlee and his wife at the time, Tony, Mary's sister, went in search of the diary before receiving the call, they found that James Jesus Angleton, the senior counterintelligence official of the CIA, had apparently picked the locks and searched for the diary in both her home and studio. Angleton was a friend of Mary's. Was this just an act of friendship or was there more to it? What was in the diary? Ben Bradlee revealed in his own book that it appeared that Mary Meyer was having an affair with the president of the United States, John F. Kennedy. Who was Angleton protecting? Of course, none of this was testified to at trial, but it has added to the mystery surrounding the life and death of Mary Pinchot Meyer, and this relationship fed conspiracy theories over the years.

After the Meyer case, Judge Corcoran would go on to serve many more years on the bench. He proved himself to be a first-class jurist of even temperament and total fairness. Once, after I left my clerkship, I brought my then-young daughter Catherine to watch the judge in court. She was about six years old. I said, "Cat, that's Judge Corcoran, I worked for him, doesn't he look like a judge?" She answered, "Daddy, he looks like God."

Being a law clerk to a good federal judge can be, as it was in my case, a life-changing experience. I learned what worked and what did not. I saw the system from the inside, observed hundreds of jurors, read their notes to the judge, and occasionally heard their explanations after the verdict. This was the best preparation in the world for someone who wanted to make his mark as a trial lawyer.

But for me one of the greatest rewards was the relationships I developed as a law clerk. Being a judge is a lonely job. The judges, law clerks, and court personnel were like a family. One judge with whom I became very close was United States District Court Judge William B. Jones. Judge Jones was a friend of my aunt and uncle, Helen and Dr. William B. Walsh, and I actually met him when I was about twelve years old.

The first time I encountered Judge Jones after being hired by Judge Corcoran, we had a good laugh about our earlier meeting when I was a boy. Judge Jones was a fabulous trial judge and a warm and gregarious person. His law clerks were his extended family. His daughter Barbara, a charming and accomplished businesswoman, has been a friend for years. When Judge Jones had a gathering of his law clerks for dinner, I was often invited and a few of his clerks became friends. David Barrett, an attorney in Washington, would later become a partner of mine, and Tommy Hogan would become chief judge of the United States District Court for the District of Columbia. This is the same court in which Judge Jones sat. Tom Hogan is a superb jurist, and I know that Bill Jones is beaming with pride at his accomplishments. Years later I would help found a lecture series at the University of Montana School of Law in honor of Judge Jones and another Washington judge, Ed Tamm—both of whom had strong Montana ties.

In the early seventies I began fly-fishing in Montana, and Ellen and I bought a home on the Yellowstone River in Paradise Valley a few miles outside of Livingston. Over the years, my friends Lenny Gregrey, a retired New York City policeman and longtime resident of Livingston; Judge Jack Shanstrom; and I caught many trout, which we released to live another day. I would later be admitted to the Montana Bar and have the distinct honor of successfully representing the federal district court judges in Montana in a controversial lawsuit with the Department of Justice.

Because of my strong Montana ties, I was asked to serve on the Board of Visitors at the University of Montana law school. At one board meeting I suggested to Dean Ed Eck that the law school sponsor a judicial lecture series in honor of Judges Tamm and Jones. The series has been remarkably successful. Each year we invite a prominent speaker who gives the annual lecture and teaches a few classes. The list of our speakers says it all. To date, our speakers have been:

THE HONORABLE SANDRA DAY O'CONNOR
*Justice*
*United States Supreme Court*

THE HONORABLE CLARENCE THOMAS
*Justice*
*United States Supreme Court*

LLOYD N. CUTLER
*Senior Counsel*
*Wilmer, Cutler & Pickering, and*
*Former White House Counsel*

LOUIS J. FREEH
*Director*
*Federal Bureau of Investigation, and*
*Former Federal Judge*

WILLIAM J. BENNETT
*Former Secretary of Education*
*Former Director of the Office of National Drug Policy*

THE HONORABLE STEPHEN G. BREYER
*Justice*
*United States Supreme Court*

THEODORE B. OLSON
*Solicitor General of the United States*

THE HONORABLE THOMAS F. HOGAN
*Chief Judge*
*United States District Court for the District of Columbia*

THE HONORABLE JOHN ROBERTS
*Chief Justice*
*United States Supreme Court*

The lecture series is a wonderful event for the students, law school, and legal community. The presence and participation of the chief justice was extra special. Chief Justice Roberts, in addition to giving the annual lecture, spent hours with the students answering their questions. It was a memorable event. Chief Judge Don Molloy of the federal district court in Montana and his wife, Judy, host a small dinner party in honor of each year's speaker, and the law school hosts a dinner so that our guest speaker has the opportunity to meet the federal judiciary. Most important, however, is that the students have an opportunity to hear and meet with some of our country's leading jurists and public figures. It is a wonderful event and I must confess I usually bring my fly rod with me.

# CHAPTER FOUR

# THE BEST JOB IN THE WORLD

B Y  THE  COMPLETION of my clerkship with Judge Corcoran, I knew that I wanted to be a federal prosecutor more than anything in the world and applied for a position as an assistant United States attorney. By this point I had watched hundreds of proceedings and trials and believed that I could do it and do it well. I was not lacking for confidence.

On April 11, 1967, my dream came true. I was sworn in as an assistant United States attorney for the District of Columbia in the Chambers of Judge Corcoran. April 11 was important to me because it was the day that Judge Corcoran was sworn in as a federal judge.

I could hardly believe my good fortune and felt I was on my way to fulfilling my dream of being a trial lawyer. I knew that I was about to embark on an interesting and fulfilling period of my life. I was not disappointed. The U.S. Attorney's Office was a wonderful and life-changing experience. I learned about the interaction of law with the real world and about people, their strengths, their weaknesses, and what motivates them. I learned that whether a prostitute or a corporate executive, most people have secrets and pick and choose the things they will be honest about.

In 2003, the assistant United States attorneys for the District of Columbia held a reunion. We honored Thomas A. Flannery, who had been the U.S. attorney and our boss and who later had a distinguished career as a federal judge. (Unfortunately, Judge Flannery passed away in September 2007. We will miss him.) I was flattered that my colleagues asked me to deliver a few remarks at the reunion on what the office meant to me. Here is what I said:

I very much appreciate being asked to comment upon "What the Office Meant" because it has—and continues to mean—a great deal to me.

Last night and tonight we have gathered again to celebrate a wonderful and special time in our lives—a time that has never really ended.

Our conversations picked up where they left off as if a quarter of a century and more never intervened.

The cases, the stories of the old days, are still fresh in our minds—in fact, like a good wine, they have greatly improved with age.

In that wonderful time we learned our profession, and there is no doubt that we produced some of the best and most sought-after lawyers in the country and distinguished members of the judiciary.

We learned how to do it right with a strong sense of professionalism, ethics, and decency.

As young women and men, we shared a passage of trial and error. We won cases—we lost cases—we did justice, and sometimes we did not but we always tried. We laughed and we cried together.

My only regret—one which we could do nothing about—is that we were so young and inexperienced in life and yet we were making crucial decisions that dramatically affected the lives of people with whom we dealt. But notwithstanding our youth we did exceedingly well.

This is so because we had great teachers and mentors like Judge Flannery, Frank Nebeker, Don Smith, and Vic Caputy and others.

And on those occasions when we—in our youthful enthusiasm forgot what was at stake—judges like Bill Bryant firmly but ever so gently reminded us that ours was not a game of wins and losses but rather a mission of justice to be tempered with compassion.

And we did well because we bonded together in a cause we deeply believed in. We generously and selflessly shared with each other our knowledge, experience, and skills. As a result there was wisdom, knowledge, and skill beyond our tender years.

Today in the District of Columbia, juries are far more integrated than in the late sixties and early seventies. That is because most of the white people, who for the most part lived in the more affluent parts of the city, found it easy to be excused from jury duty. Fortunately, this shameful practice is no longer the norm.

Most of the juries I tried cases before were African-American, as were the overwhelming number of victims and defendants. My conviction rate was over 95 percent. One important reason for this was that the African-American jurors wanted the bad guys off the streets because they were a real threat to them and their families. Law-abiding African-American citizens who worked hard to raise their families wanted law and order and protection from the thieves, drug dealers, and armed criminals.

During my first year, I was assigned to the Court of General Sessions. This was basically a police court. Initially, prosecutors were "at the counter" where we made decisions on who would be charged and what the charges would be. The police who made arrests the night before would come to the counter—later we had cell-like offices, a big "improvement"—"to paper the cases." We would decide whether to charge a felony or misdemeanor or whether to dismiss the charges altogether because of a lack of evidence or because of an illegal arrest or search. Here we were, the most inexperienced of prosecutors exercising substantial discretion that had huge impact on the lives of real human beings. The responsibility was awesome.

The wise exercise of discretion is the most important quality a prosecutor possesses. I remember one day a police officer came into my office requesting me to file charges against a juvenile who had stolen a neighbor's property. The property was of minimal value and well under the amount required for a felony charge. No weapon or threat of violence was involved. I decided that before filing a charge that I would hold an informal meeting with the young man, his attorney, and his family. While I made it clear that none of them had any obligation at all to speak with me, I thought it might be helpful in making the right charging decision, since it was pretty clear-cut that the young man had stolen the property.

The young man readily admitted his guilt and expressed his remorse for what he had done. His parents, who both worked for the government, pleaded with me not to charge their son. They explained how difficult it was to raise a young man in a law-abiding way because in their neighborhood the other young men, who had fancy cars and clothes, were looked up to even though it was well known that these material things were the fruits of crime. They explained that their son had never before been in trouble and they were concerned that a criminal charge would be an albatross for the rest of their son's life. After arranging for the return of the property to its rightful owner, I decided to give the young man a break and "no papered" the case, meaning I dropped the matter. I made it clear that if I ever saw him again under similar circumstances I would not be so lenient. As far as I know, my approach worked, and this young man went on with his life.

In another case, a near-poverty-stricken mother, who we will call Mary and who was the sole caretaker of her quadriplegic son, was charged with larceny. Had she been incarcerated, her son would have become a ward of the city, which did not have the resources to care for the young man. Again, I gave her a break. I simply did not have it in me to deliver a devastating blow to her life as well as that of her helpless son. For many years after, each Christmas I would receive a small gift from Mary with a scrawled note of thanks and an update on her son. The gifts were themselves very inexpensive, but the spirit behind them was rich. My colleagues made similar decisions every day. Who is to say that we were not doing real justice?

Very often the police, rather than making an arrest, would tell victims to go to the U.S. Attorney's Office and get a warrant. This situation most

typically involved husband-and-wife or girlfriend-boyfriend disputes. In
those days the police, prosecutors, and courts were quite insensitive and
callous when women complained of assault or harassment. I recall as a
young assistant U.S. attorney being told that it was a waste of time charging the offending husbands and boyfriends because "they would kiss and
make up" before the trial, that we would only clog the courts with cases
that go nowhere. Also, we believed that many women were using the system to get even or cause trouble for their boyfriends and husbands.
While abuse of the system was a fact, there occasionally were disastrous
consequences to our inaction. Not infrequently, we would refuse a warrant if the woman had not taken some positive steps to help herself, such
as leaving the house. We did not always appreciate that very often she was
financially or emotionally incapable of doing this because of long-term
psychological and physical abuse. We did not always take the time to distinguish between the cases where we were being used and those where
the risk of real harm was great. While it is fair to criticize us for not being
sufficiently sensitive, it is also true that in those days, mere threats in a do-
mestic situation were not an adequate basis for a charge that would hold
up in court. Many a wife or girlfriend would ask, "So before you do anything, I have to be shot or beaten?" Unfortunately, the answer we most
often gave was, "Yes."

I recall one Saturday morning when I had desk duty and was in
charge of the office for the very first time. Police Officer Jones, a giant
of a man, was assigned to our desk and his job was to screen the many
citizens who were told by the police to go to the U.S. Attorney's Office
for a warrant. Officer Jones told me that a lady wanted a warrant for the
arrest of her husband. I asked Officer Jones to bring her to my office—
by this time we had gotten rid of the counter—and I was prepared to
repeat the litany of why I could not issue a warrant. Officer Jones escorted a thirtyish, well-dressed, African-American lady into my office.
She was sad and obviously distressed. I began to explain why I could not
issue a warrant and asked her why she believed her husband would
carry out his threat. The following dialogue, as well as I remember it,
occurred:

**MR. BENNETT:** Why do you think he will carry out his threat?
**COMPLAINANT:** Because after threatening me, he stabbed me.
**MR. BENNETT:** When did that occur?
**COMPLAINANT:** A little while ago.
**MR. BENNETT:** Where did he stab you?
**COMPLAINANT:** Here, let me show you.

With that she lifted up her arm, and I observed her gray suit soaked with blood. I was astonished.

**MR. BENNETT:** You mean you came here for a warrant before you went to the hospital?
**COMPLAINANT:** Yes, because if you don't arrest him, he will kill me.

I remember calling Officer Jones and telling him, "She's got the warrant, but please, get her to the hospital."

I was not about "to join the club." This was a very insensitive phrase we used when a prosecutor turned down a woman for a warrant, because of a threat, who was then later killed by her husband or boyfriend. This was a club no one wanted to join.

While we did not often issue warrants in these cases, we would often hold informal hearings in which we would exercise authority that we never really had, such as granting informal, and frankly, legally baseless, "separations." I suppose we operated on the premise that since we could charge an offending husband or boyfriend with a crime, we could impose lesser sanctions such as warning an individual to stay away from his wife or girlfriend. I am quite sure that many lives were saved by our extrajudicial approach. Fortunately, today's law enforcement is much more sensitive to the plight of abused women.

Another group of citizens who were treated poorly by the police was the gay community. In those days, many police officers did not want to deal with them or did not care what happened to them. Whatever their problem, they would be sent down to the U.S. Attorney's Office for legal assistance. I was always troubled by this obvious discrimination and found myself resolving many disputes between gay friends and lovers. Apparently, the word got around that Mr. Bennett would be fair, and I was frequently the prosecutor requested by members of the D.C. gay community.

One of the lessons I learned in dealing with citizens who walk in off the street is that you have to be careful of first impressions. One day an elderly woman came in to complain about the kids in her neighborhood. She was oddly dressed and her mannerisms were strange. While I was anxious to get rid of her, I asked her what the kids were doing. She said she had sixteen cats in her house on U Street, N.W., and the neighborhood kids would throw things at the windows and door of her house, which upset the cats. When I told her that there was nothing I could do, she got quite upset with me. "Mr. Bennett, I helped the government break a big counterfeiting case some years ago and now its your turn to help me." I disregarded her comment as the fantasy of a troubled individual; to get her out of my office, I said I would ask the police patrol in her area to keep an eye on her house. She left unhappy and frustrated. I didn't give her another thought until about a year later when a Secret Service agent came to the office for the purpose of having me review a search warrant application for presentation to a judge. When he gave me his name, I smiled. He asked me why I was smiling, and I told him it reminded me of a crackpot I talked to a long time ago who had a cat problem. Before I could finish, he knocked me off my feet with the following, "Oh, let me tell you, Mr. Bennett, it was the strangest thing that ever happened to me as an investigator. This old lady—the one with the cats—was in a market and someone grabbed her purse. She tripped the woman with her cane and the security guard detained the thief and turned her over to the police. The police upon searching the thief found several counterfeiting plates in her possession. It broke one of the biggest cases I ever worked on." I sat there dumbfounded. So much for my judgment. This was a valuable lesson—listen carefully and don't draw conclusions too quickly.

In case you are wondering, after talking to the agent, I did locate my notes and called her to see how she and the cats were doing. They were all doing fine.

Assistant United States attorneys covering the Court of General Sessions served another important function that really was not in their job description. We were in a sense a safety valve to help citizens who could not get help elsewhere. There was a steady stream of dysfunctional and often-times mentally ill people. They were shunted from one agency to another. Often they just needed someone to talk to. While you tried your best to steer people to the right professionals, the sad fact was that the resources were usually not available. Of course, none of these sad souls would voluntarily commit themselves to a mental health facility and it was all but impossible to get them committed without their consent.

A few funny stories arose out of these tragic tales. A common complaint presented by many troubled souls was that the Russians, or some alien force, were directing rays into their brains that caused them all sorts of problems. Believe it or not, we would occasionally suggest that they role up a ball of aluminum foil and carry it with them at all times. We suggested that the foil would stop the rays from penetrating their bodies. Many of these folks would call back and thank us. Often they would say the foil was working and they were getting a good night's sleep for the first time in years.

One day a woman came to the office and complained that there was a serious problem in her neighborhood and that no one would help her or even talk to her about it. As I was on the citizen's counter that day, I asked her to sit down and assured her I would try to help. While I no longer remember the exact words, something along the following lines occurred:

**CITIZEN:** Mr. Bennett, I am a God-fearing woman but I must tell you that Jesus has been causing a lot of problems in our neighborhood. He is loud and causes all sorts of trouble and no one will help me.
**MR. BENNETT:** Well, I don't know what I can do about it. I am quite sure we don't have the authority to prosecute Jesus.
**CITIZEN:** You are giving me the runaround just like everyone else. I can't sleep and unless you do something, I don't know what will happen.

**MR. BENNETT:** I will tell you what I'd do, but you can't tell anyone about it.

**CITIZEN:** I promise it will be between us.

**MR. BENNETT:** I will call a police friend and we will lock Jesus up and put him someplace so he will never bother you again.

This lady, while sick, was no fool.

**CITIZEN:** How will I know when you arrest him and it will be safe to go outside?

**MR. BENNETT:** Call me later today.

She called me later that day and I told her that Jesus was locked up in a secret place and her problems were over. She thanked me for being a "man of action." It must have worked because we never heard from her again.

My legal education at the University of Virginia, Georgetown, and Harvard did not prepare me for these real-life experiences, nor could they be expected to. The world of the classroom is far different than what occurred on the streets. I was receiving a top-notch education in the real world of crime and justice.

Another wonderful real-world experience was accompanying the police on their nightly patrols. These were called ride-alongs and they introduced me to a world that I had seen only in the movies and on television. Spending many nights on the street made me a better prosecutor. And the cops liked it because they believed we would better understand the challenges that they faced.

On one occasion I was riding with Detective Jose Estrada, of the vice squad and his partner. Jose was a great detective who had lots of common sense. Jose could see and understand things happening before him that most of us would miss. Good cops have a sixth sense, an intuition, that is very reliable but not always easy to articulate in terms understandable to a judge. On one particular night I was riding with Jose in an unmarked vehicle when he pointed out an obvious "mark" who had just left his hotel on Fourteenth Street. I saw a gentleman who appeared to be tipsy following close behind a known pimp. We followed them in our car. It was obvious the pimp was leading the mark to a promised rendezvous. Jose said, "He probably promised him a woman who doesn't exist." The pimp entered a building on N Street with the mark a short distance behind him. As the two of them went up the stairs, Jose, his partner, and I followed closely. We heard a scream and the pimp came running down the stairs. Before anything registered with me, Jose and his partner had the pimp against the wall, patted him down for a weapon, handcuffed him, and escorted him out of the building. I was no more than three feet away. Within a minute the mark came strolling down the stairs bleeding from the head having been struck by a fire extinguisher.

As was the routine, the arrested pimp appeared in arraignment court the following day. Quite by coincidence, I was the assistant handling the arraignments that day. Sure enough, the pimp was brought before the court for the setting of bail. He looked at me a few times and then whispered something to his court-appointed lawyer. After he was escorted to the cell block, his lawyer commented, "This fool told me you were one of the arresting officers, what a nut." I looked at him innocently and shrugged my shoulders.

On another occasion, while riding with the vice squad in the inner city, we observed a well-known transvestite escorting a distinguished-looking and well-dressed gentleman into a building on Fourteenth and U Streets. Before we entered the hallway, we heard a scream and the transvestite came running out the door into the arms of the officers. On the pat down for weapons, the wallet and money of the victim were found. An arrest was made and the victim was given a summons to appear the next morning at the United States Attorney's Office. The victim was a well-known educator at one of our country's most prestigious Ivy League universities. He had an outstanding reputation for integrity and good character and was thought of as a devoted family man. When I was "papering the case," he explained to me that he had been drinking and the desire for sex overcame him. He was embarrassed and mortified. He pleaded with me to drop the case as his personal and professional lives would be destroyed if he appeared as a complaining witness in this case. The fact that he had been kissing and fondling a man he thought was a woman disgusted him and he readily acknowledged that he should not have done what he did.

What was I to do? Once I placed charges, it was all but certain the matter would become public. Reporters assigned to the court were looking for just this kind of matter to write about. By dropping the case, I would save the man's reputation, but I would be allowing a criminal to go free. It weighed heavily on me that by pursuing the case, which I clearly had reason to do, I would destroy the victim and do great harm to his family. After confirming that the defendant had no gun or knife and after determining he was not a violent person, I dropped the case. I knew that we could arrest our transvestite friend any night of the week for similar conduct. Was I right or wrong in exercising my discretion this way? Shouldn't a prosecutor, in the exercise of his discretion, think of the consequences of his or her actions? I think I was right, but you decide.

My good friend David C. Acheson, one of the most erudite and witty human beings on earth, writes about the occasion of his appointment as the United States attorney for the District of Columbia in 1961. The oath of office was administered by Justice Felix Frankfurter in his chambers at the Supreme Court. Justice Frankfurter was a very close and dear friend of David's father, former Secretary of State Dean Acheson, and the Acheson family. At the swearing in, Justice Frankfurter observed, "Always remember that you carry a great power to ruin people's lives and livelihoods and exercise that power with care and conscience." David followed that advice as the U.S. attorney, and I only wish that more prosecutors followed that advice today.

The very best part of the job was when I was in court. In my first year alone, I had thirty-two jury trials, about one hundred nonjury trials, and hundreds of other kinds of hearings. While a few of the judges were good, most were not. After my experience at the Court of General Sessions, no judge anywhere will ever intimidate me. I might lose, but I will not be intimidated.

Being in court every day in our overloaded court system had its pluses and minuses. For a young lawyer, it was great experience. I learned how to think on my feet. My mouth and brain eventually started working as a team. I developed the confidence that I could handle any situation thrown at me no matter what the circumstances.

On the downside, because of the enormous workload, there was little time to prepare your cases. Rarely did you have time to spend more than a few minutes with your witnesses. Sometimes, in a more serious case, you might get a few hours, but that was the exception. I recall one day when I had preliminary hearing duty, a clerk in the U.S. Attorney's Office handed me the "files" in about fifteen cases. A preliminary hearing is a proceeding to determine if there is sufficient evidence to hold over a defendant for the action of the grand jury. The files included a cover sheet that provided general information about the defendant and the police report—called a PD 163. This one sheet, or at most two, contained all the information available to the prosecutor. The clerk was supposed to give you the files in the order in which the cases were called in court. But in this busy court, things did not always work the way they were supposed to.

The clerk of the court called the first case—a preliminary hearing in a robbery case—and the judge told me to proceed. I called the arresting officer to the stand and the following transpired:

> **MR. BENNETT:** Officer, directing your attention to the date of March 15 at three in the morning, where were you?
> **OFFICER:** *(With a perplexed look)* Well, actually, sir, I was home in bed.
> **MR. BENNETT:** Your Honor, I'm sorry I pulled the wrong file.

Fortunately, this kind of mistake didn't happen often, but in the hurried atmosphere of the court, it sometimes did.

I do recall one case in which I had a lot of time to prepare. Two intoxicated college students from a local university had managed to enter the grounds of the Russian Embassy on Sixteenth Street, N.W., in the early hours of the morning and removed from the front of the building a heavy bronze plaque that bore the name of the embassy. It was quite an accomplishment considering the plaque was bolted to the wall.

As they left the embassy grounds, they were promptly arrested and the plaque, rather than adorning their dormitory room, was taken to the police property clerk. The case was assigned to me.

After making inquiry into the facts, I determined that it was a foolish college prank and should not be treated as a criminal matter, at least not a very serious one. Since we couldn't keep up with an overwhelming number of serious crimes, why should we spend our limited resources on this kind of case? Also, why should we make criminals out of two college kids who acted stupidly? I was overruled. Because the case involved a foreign embassy, the State Department became involved. The Soviets were outraged by what occurred and demanded prosecution. The State Department officer made it clear that the case had to be prosecuted and, if it wasn't, our own embassies abroad would be at risk. I was ordered to proceed and larceny charges were placed against the students.

This should have been an easy case to prosecute, or so I thought, but it wasn't. The Soviet officials refused to make any witness available to testify that the plaque belonged to them, that it had been on the wall of their building, and that it had been taken without their permission. I guess they felt that if one of their employees took the stand, I would ask them to identify all their spies in the United States or might question them about their totalitarian regime. No witness would be provided but the case could not be dropped. I thought all of this was pretty foolish. The case was assigned to Tim Murphy, an excellent judge. While I believe he shared my view of the case, he nevertheless made clear that I would be required to present proof on all of the elements of the offense.

I looked forward to the challenge. I obtained land records to show the ownership of the building, obtained photographs of the building to show the plaque was on the wall, and obtained invoices to show that the Soviet Embassy had purchased the plaque.

After one week of trial, Judge Murphy found the defendants guilty, but showed leniency to them in sentencing. He required them to spend a few weekends in jail and suspended the rest of the sentence.

By the end of the year, I was ready to move on. My goal was to prosecute serious felonies in the "Big Court," the United States District Court for the District of Columbia, but I realized that before I got that assignment, if I got it at all, I would have to spend a minimum of several months in the appellate section.

On April 4, 1968, my transfer to appellate was put on hold. The April riots turned Washington into a war zone. Following the assassination of Dr. Martin Luther King, the city of Washington was in a state of siege. The outbreak of violence was frightening, as stores and buildings in certain parts of the city went up in flames and the looters destroyed what they could not steal. Because I had seniority—I had been at the Court of General Sessions for one year—I could not be spared until the riot cases were largely resolved. A court system that could barely handle a few hundred cases a day now had many times that. It was reported that approximately 7,600 persons were arrested in riot-connected charges, which resulted in almost 1,700 being brought before the court on felony and misdemeanor charges. The remainder were released after being held in custody for a short period of time. I can recall working around the clock during the first few days of the riots, including one thirty-six-hour stint. I will never forget riding with the police watching parts of the city burn. The sight of armed soldiers on street corners only blocks away from the nation's Capitol is forever seared in my memory.

My tour of duty at the Court of General Sessions was extended a few months, but finally the day arrived when I was transferred to the appellate section of the United States Attorney's Office.

The next nine months would be a stark contrast to the preceding fifteen. The frantic pace and hustle and bustle of the police court was replaced by a calm and deliberative atmosphere where one could think, research, and write. My responsibility as a member of the appellate section was to write and argue briefs on behalf of the United States in both the United States Court of Appeals for the District of Columbia Circuit and the District of Columbia Court of Appeals. This was a different world from the police court. Each day I would read transcripts of the trials, analyze legal issues, research the law, read and write briefs, and a few times each month, I would argue appeals. In the course of only nine months, I wrote innumerable briefs and argued approximately thirty-five cases. This was a fabulous experience, which polished my writing skills and taught me how to protect a record in the trial courts. For me the most enjoyable part of the appellate experience was arguing cases before the judges.

What made my appellate experience particularly interesting was that during my time there, a criminal law revolution was taking place in the District of Columbia.

The United States Court of Appeals for the District of Columbia Circuit is considered by many to be the most influential court in the country, after the United States Supreme Court. The chief judge of the Court of Appeals at that time was David Bazelon, an extremely liberal jurist. He and his colleague Judge Skelly Wright, who we prosecutors called Skelly Wrong, were always on the alert to use the cases that came before them to expand the rights of defendants. When representing the government before them, there was always a good chance the conviction in the trial court would be reversed. On the same court there were strong conservatives who were pro-government on criminal law matters such as Warren Burger, who later became the chief justice of the United States Supreme Court. It was exciting and interesting to argue cases before them. Judge Bazelon would focus on the weaknesses in your case, and Judge Burger, the strengths. Whether you won or lost usually depended on the third member of the panel. If you drew Carl McGowan or Harold Leventhal, both excellent jurists, the final outcome was unpredictable.

This was a wonderful experience and taught me valuable lessons in appellate advocacy:

- Always be fully candid with the court—this is true of all courts.
- If you don't know the answer to a question, say so and don't waffle.
- Do your homework and master the trial court record.
- Anticipate the questions and the concerns of individual jurists.
- Remember, the oral argument is the judges' time, not yours. This is their opportunity to ask you questions that are not answered in the briefs or to resolve issues or concerns that they have.
- Never, never exaggerate or misrepresent the facts or the law.

WHILE APPELLATE COURT judges realize that you are advocating a position, they look at the prosecutor less as an advocate and more as an officer of the court helping them to reach the right decision.

When trying cases, you must always have one eye on the court of appeals. What is obvious to a participant in the trial court is not always obvious to an appellate judge who was not present and who must rely on a cold transcript. Often trial judges will make rulings, the reasons for which are unclear or confusing. It is an important part of being a trial lawyer to be sure that the reasons for the rulings in your favor are clear in the record.

After nine months in the appellate section, I was ready for the big time—the United States District Court for the District of Columbia. Unlike the Court of General Sessions, these cases were the more serious felonies, and I had more time to prepare. I was in heaven.

I found that I had a knack for jury trials and understood what was important to jurors. I won most of my cases, and after a short while I was rewarded by being one of three prosecutors assigned to practice before the entire federal bench in Washington. This meant that I would be trying the most serious cases and was not limited to trying cases before any single judge. Before this promotion, I was assigned to one judge, District Court Judge Oliver Gasch. When a new assistant appeared before him, he always told them that brevity was a virtue. "Mr. Bennett," Judge Gasch said on my first day before him, "do you know who also spoke at Gettysburg when Abraham Lincoln gave his Gettysburg address?" I said, "Yes, Your Honor, I believe it was Edward Everett, the former president of Harvard." Gasch was impressed. Of course, I had done my homework on the judge and learned that he might ask this question. The judge's point was that everyone remembered Lincoln's Gettysburg address, which lasted a little over two minutes, whereas Everett spoke for hours and no one remembered him or what he said. One day when I was giving a closing argument, Judge Gasch was getting impatient and stared at me. I said, "Judge, I am almost finished." He replied, "Oh, Mr. Bennett, I know that but I'm not sure you do." He was a first-rate judge and I have fond memories of him and the cases I tried before him.

I remember many of the cases I prosecuted as if they happened yesterday. One case I will never forget was billed by the press as the "Good Samaritan" murder case.

On March 14, 1969, Donald C. Schreiber and his girlfriend, Margaret Tuttle, both college students, left the Biograph Theatre at the edge of Georgetown. After walking a brief distance, they observed a young man— later identified as Anthony H. Coleman—who appeared to be ill and staggering. They went to his aid. A second man—later identified as Derek C. Bigesby—approached and asked what was going on, making believe that Coleman was a stranger and that he just happened to be passing by. Schreiber explained that they were helping the young man to his apartment nearby. What Schreiber and Ms. Tuttle did not know was that the men were cousins and that this was all a ploy to rob them. When they got to a landing in the apartment building, Coleman pulled a gun and a brief struggle ensued, a shot was fired, and Donald Schreiber was killed by a bullet that went through his heart. Coleman and Bigesby fled the scene, leaving Donald Schreiber to die. Whenever the cause of death is described in a murder case, it always sounds so cold and clinical. This is how the cause of death was described at trial by the medical examiner, Dr. Lynwood L. Rayford Jr., when I questioned him:

> **MR. BENNETT:** Will you tell the ladies and gentlemen of
> the jury what the results of your autopsy were in the case of
> Mr. Schreiber?
> **DOCTOR:** The external examination showed the decedent
> looked like his stated age of twenty-two years, was six feet tall,
> weighed 195 pounds; he was a well-built and well-nourished
> male who was rigorous at the time of examination.
> **MR. BENNETT:** What does that mean, Doctor?
> **DOCTOR:** Rigor mortis had set in.
> This autopsy was performed, incidentally, at 1:30 P.M. on
> March 15.
>
>        Now, there was a half-inch irregular circular hole located two
> and a half inches to the left of the midline, and three and a half
> inches down from the sternal notch. If you place your fingers in

the midline of the lower part of your neck, you will feel right at the top of your collarbone the sternal notch.

Now, three and a half inches down from the sternal notch and two and a half inches to the left was this entry wound of a bullet.

The direction of this track went from front to back, slightly left to right and downward to go across the upper lobe of the left lung, to go across the heart, to go across the diaphragm, the muscle between the chest and the abdomen, and across the liver, and the slug was lodged in the abdomen.

As a result of the bullet going through the heart, there was a massive amount of blood in the chest cavity and in the abdominal cavity.

**MR. BENNETT:** What was the cause of death?

**DOCTOR:** The cause of death was a gunshot wound of the chest.

Following a thorough investigation by the homicide squad of the Metropolitan Police Department, both Coleman and Bigesby were arrested. And on July 15, 1969, a grand jury returned an indictment against Anthony H. Coleman and Derek C. Bigesby for first-degree murder and several related counts. In the District of Columbia, a killing in the course of a robbery constituted felony first-degree murder. In those days, upon conviction the penalty was death by electrocution or life imprisonment to be determined by the jury.

I drew the case, which was assigned to District Court Judge Oliver Gasch. I was fortunate in that the homicide squad detectives Clarence Day and William Manning were the investigators. They were first-rate detectives, and I had the pleasure of working with them on other cases. Day, who had a bit of the Baptist preacher in him, acting on what he and Manning heard on the street, brought Bigesby to the police station, where Bigesby asked for his mother. His mother came to the station and Day convinced her that it would be best if Derek told him the truth. "You tell Detective Day what happened!" Derek spilled the beans—at least in substantial part. He tried to protect his cousin, Coleman, by claiming that he had the gun.

Because no one saw the gun go off and because Tuttle did not make a positive identification of them at the lineup, I had a strong case against Bigesby because of his confession, but not against Coleman, who we were convinced was the shooter. Bigesby eventually admitted that he was protecting his cousin by claiming that he had the gun.

I told Bigesby's lawyer that I was prepared to prosecute his client for first-degree murder and would undoubtedly get a conviction because of the confession, but indicated that I would accept a plea to a lesser felony count of the indictment if he agreed to testify truthfully against his cousin. A deal was reached.

Mr. Bigesby entered his guilty plea. This plea subjected him to a sentence as high as life imprisonment, but what it really meant was that after serving fifteen years, he could be eligible for parole.

The trial of Anthony H. Coleman was set for February 24, 1970, before Judge Gasch. During my final preparation on the day before the trial, Detectives Day and Manning came to see me. They told me that the witness, Ms. Tuttle, was having second thoughts about identifying Coleman at trial. While she had not previously identified him at a lineup, she had identified him in a photo lineup and at the preliminary hearing. They believed strongly that she could identify him since she had been in his presence for a period of thirty to forty-five minutes, but that she was concerned about Coleman's welfare and that she did not want to identify him and "mess his life up." The detectives and I were incredulous that she felt this way since it was her boyfriend who was murdered by Coleman.

I spoke with her in my office and tried to convince her that it was her obligation to tell the truth, that she should not be less than truthful because of her concerns for Coleman. When she left my office, I did not know what she would do, but I did know that if she did not identify Coleman before the jury, there could be a real problem with the case. A second problem would develop when Bigesby would try to back away from his agreement to testify against Coleman, but more on that later.

Bill Garber and Jim Durkin, two experienced criminal lawyers, were representing Coleman. Garber, his lead lawyer, knew about Tuttle's shaky identification of Coleman and tried to prevent her from identifying Coleman at trial. He argued that if Coleman was the only person at the defense table other than the lawyers, the circumstances were too suggestive and any identification would be unfair. After hearing about the circumstances of her weak identification, Judge Gasch suggested that we hold a lineup in court and sent his marshal, Ricky Griffiths, to locate four other young men of similar appearance to come to the courtroom. After they were seated at counsel's table with the defendant, Tuttle was brought in. The tension in the courtroom was high and my stomach was in knots. Fortunately for my case and for the sake of justice, she positively identified the defendant. Would the court allow the identification under all of the circumstances? Here is how the judge ruled:

> The court believes that in view of the lineup held in the courtroom in which the marshals secured the presence of four other young men, the court observed they had comparable complexions, were of the same general age group, two of them had mustaches, one had some chin hair, they all appeared to be the same height while seated, and they were all dressed in coats, ties, and similar-wearing apparel.
>
> The court is convinced beyond a reasonable doubt that there is an appropriate basis on the decided case law to permit the witness Tuttle to make an in-court identification.

The next problem that developed, which could have been devastating, was the refusal of Bigesby to testify against his cousin, Coleman, at the trial. I had asked the marshals to keep Coleman and Bigesby away from each other in the cell block. While separated by bars, they were still able to speak to each other. Bigesby had a change of heart and told his lawyer that he would not testify. When this was reported to me, my heart sank. I had no doubt that Coleman threatened Bigesby to change his mind. I told his lawyer that if he reneged on his deal, I would prosecute his client on the more serious first-degree murder charge. I reminded him that I had a solid confession and that while I wanted the shooter, I would settle for his client Bigesby, if I had to. This is a tough business and I wasn't going to let the murderer of Schreiber go free without giving it my all. I advised the court that Bigesby wanted to renege and asked that he be called into court so he could be questioned. It was touch and go. When he took the witness stand, he folded and agreed to testify. I now knew I had a good shot at a conviction. Fearing that he might again change his mind, I asked the court to keep him on the stand, call the jury into the jury box, and allow me to get his testimony immediately. This was done and I breathed a great sigh of relief when he positively identified Coleman as the shooter in the presence of the jury.

Eventually, the evidence was completed, and it was time for closing arguments. As I got out of my chair and looked toward the back of the courtroom, Mr. and Mrs. Schreiber, the victim's parents, were in the same seats they had been in for every moment of the trial. I knew that I could not bring their son back, but I could give them everything I had to see that they received some justice.

In every jury trial, you must find a way to get into the gut of a jury. You must appeal to them intellectually as well as emotionally. When you are finished arguing, you want them to be with you.

In this case, as in every case I try, I am always thinking about my closing argument from the very beginning. Where do I want to be when all the evidence is in? This helps me in developing the case and deciding what evidence I will use. Early on I decided that the parable of the Good Samaritan said it all.

On the witness stand a Bible is always present so witnesses can place their hands on the Good Book and swear to tell the truth when they are sworn in before the court and jury.

As I stood in front of the jury, without notes, I began my closing argument. I first appealed to their intellect explaining why the evidence justified a conviction of first-degree murder under the law. I then turned to their gut, their heart, their soul. I walked slowly to the witness stand and picked up the Bible and reminded them of the parable of the Good Samaritan. Here is what transpired:

Ladies and gentlemen, somehow I feel at this point that talking about the law and the specifics is important, but somehow something is missing. I mean, there is something about this case that really doesn't lend itself to—it doesn't lend itself to legal terms.

Do you remember in the beginning of the case you took an oath? And you placed your hand on the Bible, and in this Bible, ladies and gentlemen of the jury, there is a section of Luke, Chapter 10, and in that, ladies and gentlemen of the jury—

At this point, Garber, Coleman's lawyer, made an objection. Bill would later tell me that the minute the objection came out of his mouth, he wished he could pull it back.

**MR. GARBER:** Your Honor, I am going to object.
**THE COURT:** Come to the bench, please.
*(At the bench)*
**MR. GARBER:** I am going to object to the prosecutor reading passages from the Bible to possibly appeal to any religious convictions that the jury might have.
**THE COURT:** I don't know what Chapter 10 says.
**MR. BENNETT:** It is the Good Samaritan.
**MR. GARBER:** It appeals to passion and prejudice. As I understand, the Good Samaritan is a parable, and the Good Samaritan came along and tried to help this man, and he was set upon.
**MR. BENNETT:** I will make that applicable. . . . This is a fair argument.
**MR. GARBER:** I object to it. It is an appeal to passion and prejudice and religious convictions that this jury might have. I think we should concern ourselves here with the evidence at this trial.
**THE COURT:** I think that is right. I would suggest you not read any passage. You can say this man was a Good Samaritan.

**MR. BENNETT:** I will make reference to it.

**THE COURT:** Yes, you may make reference to it.

**MR. GARBER:** I object to it.

**THE COURT:** All right.

I then closed the Good Book and placed it back on the witness stand.

*(In open court)*

**MR. BENNETT:** Luke in Chapter 10 talks about a Good Samaritan. Briefly, it says that there was a lawyer. The lawyer asked Jesus, he said how do I gain the eternal life, and Jesus said, well, you are a lawyer. What does the law say; and the man says, love Him and love your neighbor.

The lawyer said, Lord, excuse me, what do you mean by love your neighbor? What is a neighbor?

That is when, ladies and gentlemen of the jury, Jesus said to him about the man who came to Jerusalem to Jericho, and the man fell among a group of thieves who robbed him and took his clothes and wounded him and left him for dead. And when the man was lying half dead in a ditch, a priest comes along. And he looks at the man and he walks on. He crosses to the other side of the road.

Then a Levite comes along, and he sees the man in the ditch and he crosses over and goes down the other side of the street.

Then a third man came, and put his arm around him, and helps him and bathes his wound in wine and oil, gave him money, and put him up and then clothed him.

And Jesus said to the man, that is what a neighbor is. You go forth and do likewise, and you shall reach the eternal life.

Ladies and gentlemen of the jury, the guts of this case, the heart and soul of this case is that.

Donald Schreiber did likewise when he saw Mr. Coleman in need of help. The easiest thing in the world would have been to cross the street to the other side and not get involved; but he didn't do that. He went forth and did likewise like the Good Samaritan. He put his arm around him and he helped him; and what did he get for his trouble? He got a bullet in his chest.

When I looked at the jury, I knew I had them—some were crying and others were nodding approval.

Judge Gasch, I later learned, did not think I knew the parable as well as I did and he thought I would have to read from the Good Book to use the parable. Actually, I anticipated that Garber might make such an objection, so I made sure that I knew it cold. Garber's objection and Judge Gasch's ruling helped me with the jury, who I later learned were impressed with my knowledge of Scripture. A trial lawyer must anticipate every possibility and be prepared for it.

Waiting for a jury's verdict, especially in a murder case, is agony. On February 26, 1970, the jury convicted Mr. Coleman of first-degree murder and other related counts and recommended that he serve a term of life imprisonment. I was relieved. I looked at Mr. and Mrs. Schreiber and they nodded their appreciation and later thanked me.

I was, of course, satisfied with the verdict. It was the policy of the United States Attorney's Office not to ask for the death penalty, but to leave it to the jury. This was fine as far as I was concerned. As a general rule, I am not in favor of the death penalty. My major objection to it is that too many mistakes are made. With the science of DNA, we frequently learn that defendants are wrongfully convicted. It is only wishful thinking to believe that only guilty persons have been sentenced to death. Death is irreversible. A tragic mistake cannot be rectified.

One reason why some innocent people are convicted of crime is the impact on a jury of eyewitness identification. I have always been struck by the confidence most juries place on eyewitness testimony. When a sympathetic victim testifies that a defendant is the perpetrator, there is a strong likelihood of conviction even in the absence of other evidence. As a prosecutor, I was always more comfortable when I had strong circumstantial evidence supporting an eyewitness identification such as fingerprints or other scientific data. The unreliability of eyewitness identification is well known, but in the real world, it has a powerful impact on a jury. I was not at all troubled with the eyewitness identification of Coleman by Ms. Tuttle. Hers was not an in-court identification after only a fleeting glance. She had been in Mr. Coleman's presence, under good lighting conditions, for over half an hour. Moreover, we had strong corroborating evidence.

Most Americans favor the death penalty, but with the revelations of the last few years that innocent people can be convicted, the support for the death penalty is decreasing. I believe that what bothers most people and encourages support for the death penalty is when serious offenders who have received lengthy sentences are released after serving only a small part of their sentence. If a life sentence really meant a life sentence, many more people would support the abolition of the death penalty.

Unfortunately, meaningful public debate on this issue by our political leaders is virtually impossible. I have personally spoken to political figures, including at least one presidential candidate, who while personally opposed to the death penalty, will not publicly say so because to do so is political death. Any public figure who publicly opposes the death penalty will be branded as "soft on crime," which is political suicide. It has always amazed me that often the political figures who talk most about God and the value of human life are the first ones who support the taking of life. In my opinion, the taking of a human life should be left to God.

Following the return of the Coleman verdict, I felt physically and emotionally drained. While I could not bring back the Schreibers' son or return joy to their life, I at least played a part in bringing some closure to the tragic death of their son and giving them a feeling that in an unjust world, at least a little justice came their way.

Many of Ellen's and my closest friends and their spouses are graduates of the United States Attorney's Office. One of them, Judge Paul Friedman, a distinguished federal judge, recently officiated at the weddings of my daughters, Catherine and Peggy. They have all enriched our lives.

# CHAPTER FIVE

# THE LOVE OF MY LIFE

I N AUGUST OF 1968, The Almighty looked favorably on me. Carl Rauh, the son of Joe Rauh, invited me to a potluck dinner party in our building where we both had apartments. At the party was a tall and strikingly beautiful woman, Ellen Gilbert, from Columbus, Ohio. Ellen was living in Southwest Washington with a few friends who were also at the party. I was smitten. The guys brought the booze, and each of the women brought a dish. While I do not remember this, I am told that I so enjoyed a broccoli dish that I said, "I will marry whoever made the broccoli." I am also told that none of the women admitted to making the dish. Since I hate broccoli, I am quite certain that I had been tipped off in advance that Ellen prepared it. Following the dinner party, I called Ellen nine times to ask her out. Each time she was busy. Her excuses were varied. She was the busiest person in the world, always taking one class or another. On the ninth call, she said she was taking a welding class and could not go out until she finished her project. I felt rejected. I decided to give it one more try. On the tenth call, she said yes. We hit it off and were married a year later, on September 20, 1969, at the Catholic Parish of Saint Dominic in Washington, D.C. Marrying Ellen was the best decision I have ever made in my life. We have had a wonderful marriage. After thirty-eight years and three grown children, Catherine, Peggy, and Sarah, I love Ellen more today than ever.

Because we were married while I was in the middle of several active cases and because Ellen, a high school teacher, had just begun the school year, we were unable to take a long honeymoon. Sandy Frankel, a fellow assistant United States attorney and now a first-rate trial attorney in New York, drove us to the Mayflower Hotel in Washington, D.C., dropped us off at the front entrance, and gave us a gigantic bottle of champagne. It was a short but great honeymoon.

By the way, Ellen's "welding class" excuse was the truth. When we moved into our first apartment, it took four of our friends to lift and carry a gargantuan iron coffee table that felt like it weighed 800 pounds. The table became known as "the monster" as it moved with us from apartment to apartment and house to house. Many of my friends, Carl included, have awful memories of it.

After three and a half years of nonstop work in the U.S. Attorney's Office, I became restless. Also, Ellen and I wanted to start a family, and it seemed like a good time to go into private practice. Where should I go? What should I do? I spoke with the people I most respected, including Judge Howard Corcoran, Judge Bill Jones, and Tommy Corcoran. Tommy offered me about $50,000 a year and "a piece of the action," which was a lot of money in those days, to join his firm Corcoran, Foley, Youngman and Rowe but was quick to add, "Bob, we are not a trial shop. Why don't you speak to my friend John Wilson. I want to do what is best for you."

I made an appointment with John Wilson. He was a small man, with white hair and thick glasses. He was known as a lawyer's lawyer and was one of the most sought after attorneys in Washington. His office was right out of the *Saturday Evening Post*—old prints on the wall and a desk totally covered with papers and documents. As we were talking, several dignitaries and high government officials called him; I was impressed. I told Mr. Wilson about Corcoran's offer and that Hogan and Hartson, a first-rate firm in Washington, had offered me a position in their litigation section. Wilson asked me what I wanted to do as a lawyer. My answer was simple, "I want to try cases." Wilson said, "I love Tommy, but you should go somewhere like Hogan and Hartson, where you will be in court."

At about this time, a dramatic change was occurring in the District of Columbia court system as a result of the Court Reorganization Act. A new court was created: the Superior Court, which would handle many of the cases that were handled previously in the federal court. The Superior Court is akin to a state court of general jurisdiction. In my opinion, the Superior Court of the District of Columbia is now one of the best courts in the country. At the time, the United States attorney was Thomas A. Flannery. Tom offered me a very senior position in the office if I stayed, but it would have required more administration and less trial work. I decided it was time to move on. My time in the U.S. attorney's office had been a wonderful experience, which I would never forget.

Hogan and Hartson offered me the opportunity to do trial work and I decided to join them, even though I made much less money than I would have at Corcoran's office. After a short time at Hogan, a magnificent event occurred: Catherine Gilbert Bennett, our first child, was born on November 17, 1972, at 11:15 P.M. Since Ellen had had five miscarriages and laid flat on her back for almost two months before Catherine's birth, she was a very special gift.

Some years before I joined Hogan and Hartson, several big-name trial lawyers had left Hogan and formed the firm of Williams and Connolly. Edward Bennett Williams, who had been at Hogan and Hartson, was the leading criminal lawyer in Washington, and Paul Connolly was a leading civil litigator. In the void created by their departure, I saw a real opportunity at Hogan and I was hopeful of starting a white-collar criminal practice. I believed that it was just a matter of time before it became a hot area, and I felt Hogan was a good platform on which to build such a practice. At Hogan there was very little white-collar work and most of my time was spent on civil litigation matters, a great experience. I worked on libel matters for the old *Washington Star* newspaper, handled a wide variety of commercial cases, and defended insurance companies on a daily basis. As great as it was, I missed the criminal work.

Many people believe, and I am one of them, that Watergate was a seminal event. While we have always had scandals, Watergate put new life in the scandal machine. Following the break-in at the Democratic headquarters by the "plumbers," a group of political dirty tricksters working on behalf of the Nixon White House, the scandal machine went off the charts, resulting in multiple indictments of high-level White House officials. Ultimately the break-in and subsequent cover-up caused President Nixon to resign.

At the very beginning of Watergate, I received a call from Donald Santarelli, a well-known Washington lawyer, who was then a high-level official at the Department of Justice. He asked me if I would be willing to represent one of the principal defendants in the Watergate case. I was ecstatic. Unfortunately, I did not get the case. I was later told that Robert Mardian, a high-level official of the DOJ, who himself was indicted and convicted, was concerned that there were too many high-powered Democrats at Hogan for one of its lawyers to handle such a sensitive case involving high-level Republican officials. This was foolish thinking, but there was nothing I could do. Mardian's conviction would later be reversed on appeal. He dropped out of sight until his death in 2006.

Sometime after Don's call, Bill Bittman, who had recently become a partner at Hogan, was retained to represent Watergate defendant Howard Hunt. Bill had been a prosecutor at the Department of Justice. He successfully prosecuted Jimmy Hoffa and Lyndon Johnson's chief of staff, Bobby Baker.

Some of Bill Bittman's conduct in his representation of Hunt came under inquiry, causing embarrassment to the firm. Bittman had accepted a fee in cash, which was left in a phone booth in the lobby of the building where Hogan and Hartson had its offices. Also, there was evidence that envelopes containing cash were given to Bittman, who passed them on to his client Hunt. The government believed that Hunt passed the money on to his fellow coconspirators. Bittman denied that he knew what was in the envelopes. While there was great concern at the Department of Justice about his conduct, Bittman was not charged but was named as an unindicted coconspirator. All of this caused a furor at the firm and Bittman (now deceased) fell out of favor.

One of the most interesting and unique cases I handled at Hogan was with Barrett Prettyman Jr., a first-rate lawyer, and Sandy Berger, who would later become the national security advisor under President Clinton. Barrett, who was many years senior to both Sandy and myself, had a significant First Amendment practice, so it was no surprise when the pub-

lisher of the *Boston Globe* called Barrett and asked him to represent a
young reporter, Tom Oliphant, who had been charged in connection
with the insurgency at Wounded Knee, South Dakota. Barrett asked
Sandy and me to work with him on the case.

Beginning on February 27, 1973, "Indian insurgents" occupied the
village of Wounded Knee. After a forty-nine-day siege, efforts at negotiating a peaceful resolution fell apart when shooting began and it was reported that a United States marshal was seriously hurt. Prior to the
shooting, three private planes flew over Wounded Knee and the government claimed that weapons were dropped to the insurgents. A reporter
on the plane, Tom Oliphant, told fellow reporters that he had observed
what he believed to be packages of food being dropped and that no
weapons or ammunition had been dropped as far as he knew.

Nevertheless, on April 18, 1973, the *New York Times* reported:

> An occupier of Wounded Knee was shot in the head and crit-
> ically wounded today as a fierce battle erupted between govern-
> ment forces and insurgent Indians holding the village, shattering
> a three-week-old cease-fire . . . according to the Government
> the shooting started sometime after three light planes dropped
> seven packages into the village by parachute. The packages were
> said by a newspaper reporter aboard one of the plans to have con-
> tained food.

Tom had been asked by the *Globe* to cover the story. Being the ener-
getic, hands-on reporter that he is, he accepted the invitation by supporters of the Indians to join them on their flights to drop food.

The government didn't see it that way, and on April 21, 1973, the
Federal Bureau of Investigation announced that a warrant for Tom's arrest had been issued. He was charged with conspiring to violate antiriot
provisions of the 1968 Federal Crime Control Act. Tom voluntarily sur-
rendered on April 23, and was arraigned before a federal magistrate in
Washington, D.C. We were able to obtain his release on personal bond
for a removal hearing set for May 8. The burden on the government at

the hearing was to show that there was probable cause to believe that he conspired to aid those helping the insurgents. If the government carried that burden, he would be sent to South Dakota, where the warrant for his arrest originated. Tom said he had gone to South Dakota solely to cover a news story and adamantly denied knowledge of any firearms.

In May, Tom was indicted by a federal grand jury in South Dakota on charges connected with the transporting of supplies to insurgents at Wounded Knee. Barrett, Sandy, and I believed that any objective analysis of the situation would result in the conclusion that Tom had done nothing wrong. Unfortunately, objectivity was not something that existed in South Dakota in the middle of an "Indian insurgency." We had to do all that we could to keep Tom in Washington, because we had no confidence that he would receive fair treatment in South Dakota. Tom, at the time, had shoulder-length hair and always wore sneakers and a bow tie. Frankly, I believed he would be dead meat in South Dakota. Usually challenges to removal are unsuccessful, but we were fortunate in that Magistrate—now Judge—Arthur Burnett was not a jurist who would rubber-stamp any request of the government and would give us a fair hearing. Also, if we could delay the removal, it would give us time to convince the higher-ups at the Department of Justice to drop the case.

We filed our papers objecting to removal, which the government vigorously opposed. Fortunately for Tom, we prevailed.

Barrett, Sandy, and I were ecstatic, but we knew that our success was only temporary and that we still had to do all that we could to get the charges dropped. We made calls, wrote letters, and gathered opposition to Tom being sent to South Dakota. Finally, on July 6, 1973, the Department of Justice dropped all charges against Tom, stating that they did so for "lack of sufficient evidence." Again, Barrett, Sandy, and I were thrilled. Tom, when asked by fellow reporters how he felt, commented that he was "elated," but the fighter in him added "my elation has been moderated a trifle by the somewhat cowardly way the Department of Justice got rid of [the case] yesterday." He then added that the explanation of "lack of sufficient evidence" was really "lack of any evidence." We lawyers cringed at this, but there was no stopping Tom.

Today Tom's hair is moderately short, he has gotten rid of his trademark sneakers, but he continues to wear a bow tie. He is one of the country's best political reporters. He is a good friend and I am grateful that I had the opportunity to work on this fascinating case for a truly honorable and talented reporter. Years later Tom would write a great book about what it meant to be a Brooklyn Dodger fan. The book *Praying for Gil Hodges: A Memoir of the 1955 World Series and One Family's Love of the Brooklyn Dodgers* touched me, particularly since Hodges was one of my childhood heroes.

While at Hogan, I met an able, young antitrust lawyer, Tim Bloomfield, who became a good friend. Tim decided to leave the firm and join a small boutique, Dunnells, Duvall and Porter. The Porter was Steve Porter, who had previously been at both Hogan and Hartson and Williams and Connolly. He was an outstanding real estate, commercial, and tax lawyer. A few months later, I was ready to leave Hogan myself and asked Tim if his firm would be interested in a young trial lawyer who wanted to develop a white-collar practice.

My primary reason for leaving was that I wanted to be my own boss. Also, it would take years for Hogan and Hartson to overcome the Bittman fiasco—I couldn't wait—and that year I was passed over for partnership. When I learned that the partner who was supposed to be my primary advocate didn't attend the partner selection meeting to argue my case, I was furious. I marched into the office of Ed McDermott, a member of the firm's executive committee, and told him I would leave. Ed, a wonderful guy, urged me to stay and told me that he was sure I would get a partnership the next year. But, all things considered, I felt my future was elsewhere. My only regret, leaving Hogan, was that I would miss my daily chats with George Wise, a kind and helpful mentor. George and his wife, Lillian, would always remain close to our family and would serve as godparents to our daughter Sarah.

I would be less than honest if I didn't acknowledge that I was very pleased, years later, when Hogan approached me and asked if I had any interest in rejoining the firm as a key partner. I happily declined. After meeting and talking to other partners at Dunnells, Duvall and Porter, I was impressed and enthusiastic about joining them. However, I was a bit scared. Ellen was about to give birth to our second child, Peggy, and we had little money and a big mortgage. I had no transferable clients and the new firm, given the nature of their practice, had no work for me. We were all taking a chance that I would build a successful practice. On January 13, 1975, our second child, Peggy, was born. On the day we brought Peggy home from the hospital, I signed the partnership papers with the Dunnells firm. Within a few days, my new partners had a dinner party for Ellen and me. I will never forget our new baby laying in the lap of Dick Dunnells. She was the star attraction at the dinner party.

Steve Porter and I hit it off immediately. He and his wonderful wife, Susan, would become very close to Ellen and me. They and their family have enriched the lives of all the Bennetts.

By the way, Peggy's name is really Peggy. This is not short for Margaret. When Ellen was a child, for no good reason her nickname was Peggy and so we decided to name our second child Peggy. When Peggy was about five, she told us she was tired of being called Peggy and wanted a "real name." Teachers would frequently ask her if her real name was Margaret, and this annoyed her. True to form, I made some incorrect assumptions—not a good quality for a lawyer—and turned this simple request into a learning experience. I explained to Peggy that we could consider changing her name if she wanted, but it was a serious business: "Daddy is a lawyer and he can arrange for your name to be changed." I then explained how we could file a petition with the court for a name change. We could still call her Peggy, but that since this was typically a nickname for Margaret, I would start preparing a petition changing her name to Margaret Bennett. Peggy began to cry. She said she didn't like the name Margaret. She wanted me to change her name to Heather. It seems that one of her best friends at that moment in time was a Heather. I felt stupid and told her under the circumstances, she would be stuck with the name Peggy for the rest of her life. Today Peggy is a federal prosecutor serving as an assistant U.S. attorney in Washington, D.C. It seems that whatever trial lawyer genes I passed on, Peggy got them. I know she is great because I never won an argument with her in thirty-plus years.

CHAPTER SIX

# NOT AN EDUCATIONAL EXPERIENCE

WHILE AT HOGAN and Hartson, I worked on a case for BDM, a defense contractor with offices in Northern Virginia. They would later become an important client of Dunnells, Duvall, Bennett and Porter. The firm was founded by three brilliant young men, Joe Braddock, Bernie Dunn, and Dan MacDonald. Knowing that they were engineering types who needed someone on their team with strong business skills, they recruited Earle Williams, who became president of BDM. A few years ago I attended Earle and June Williams' fiftieth wedding anniversary. Earle told the guests who filled the ballroom that I was in attendance and said that he was the first president I ever represented. Earle himself was never in trouble, but I handled several matters for BDM with great results. BDM was an important building block for my practice because the company gave our small firm a great deal of credibility. They were a first-class group of people who have remained good friends throughout the years. Because of my connection with them, I would get hired in an important case: *United States of America v. Dominic Paolucci,* which would prove to be a real break in my career.

Dominic Paolucci was born in Buffalo, New York, of Italian immigrants. He was the oldest child and grew up in poor conditions in city streets best described as a slum. Dom was very bright and hardworking and after high school won a competitive appointment to the Naval Academy, which he entered in 1940. At the time, he was one of the very few Italian-Americans to have been accepted. Following graduation, he had a distinguished career as a naval officer. He took satisfaction in the fact that he did not look or act like the typical Navy officer and took pleasure that a "street kid" could accomplish what he did in the Navy.

Shortly after leaving the academy, Dom was assigned to the North Atlantic patrol and convoy duty and served on the United States destroyer *Doyle,* which was one of the ships that lead the invasion forces onto Omaha Beach on June 6, 1944. Dom volunteered for submarine duty and over the years became one of the Navy's leading experts on submarine warfare. Before he retired, he would command a submarine flotilla consisting of twenty-five ships. On shore he became one of the Navy's acknowledged leaders in mathematical analysis and served in the Office of Naval Research, the Office of the Chief of Naval Operations, and in the Office of the Secretary of the Navy. During the time he was at OPNAV, he headed the Submarine Policy and Training Section, which was responsible for planning and arranging the training of foreign submarine crews. In addition to all of this, the poor kid from Buffalo earned advanced degrees in philosophy and mathematics from the University of Indiana.

On January 1, 1970, after twenty-six years of service, Dom started his career as a private citizen in the defense business. Col. Norair Lulejian, the chairman of Lulejian and Associates, hired Dom to open a Washington office specializing in marketing operations analysis and planning. The firm was a think tank that had contracts with the U.S. military. Dom became its president.

In his unpublished book about his ordeal entitled *The Day of the Prosecutor: A Day of Abuse,* Paolucci explained that a special agent of the FBI contacted his office requesting an interview. Because of his military background and high-level security clearances, he had spoken many times to government investigators and was not concerned about the request; he agreed to meet with the agent on August 26, 1976. The agent explained that the FBI was conducting an investigation of the activities of retired Navy Vice Adm. Malcolm Cagle during the period of 1973–74. The inquiry focused upon Cagle's relationship with Lulejian and Associates, where Dominic was president. Cagle had recommended the company for a sole source contract to train the Iranian Navy. After his retirement,

Cagle became a part-time consultant with the company. Subsequently, Dominic received a subpoena to appear before a grand jury and again, knowing of no wrongdoing by Cagle or anyone else, he saw no need to bring a lawyer with him. On the day of his grand jury appearance, he was advised that the prosecutor had overextended himself and that his grand jury appearance would be rescheduled.

Before he was recalled to the grand jury, Dominic received a call from a friend at BDM, the company I had done work for, who told him that the they had received a subpoena regarding the Cagle matter, which asked specifically for documents relating to Dominic and others. Dominic told his friend about his earlier appearance and asked if the company lawyers, Hogan and Hartson, could find out whatever they could about the government's interest in him. A few days later, Dominic learned from a lawyer at Hogan and Hartson that he was a focus of the grand jury's investigation into the hiring of Cagle. The lawyer suggested that Dom get his own counsel. The Hogan and Hartson lawyer gave Dominic my name.

I met Dominic Paolucci for the first time on June 15, 1977, at a restaurant in Northern Virginia. I would later learn that Dom believed that by breaking bread and drinking wine with someone, he could best judge the person's character. Dom was a short, stocky ball of energy. He was incredibly smart. After a few hours of background about him and my explaining the grand jury process, he asked me if I would represent him. I recall saying, "Dom, this is an interesting case, the issues are challenging, I would be happy to represent you." He leaned forward, put his arm around me, and said, "Bob, this is not an educational experience for me or for you. They want to put my ass in jail." I learned a valuable lesson. Dom reminded me that a case is not about the lawyer but the client. We must always check our egos at the door. I got up the courage to ask for a $3,000 retainer, to which Dominic agreed.

July 1, 1977, only a few weeks after meeting Dom, was another big day. Our third daughter, Sarah, was born at Georgetown University Hospital. Currently, Sarah is a postgraduate student in the doctoral program in psychology at George Washington University. She is wise beyond her years and I often talk with her about human behavior as it relates to matters of interest to me.

After being retained, I called the prosecutor, who indicated that Dominic was a target and that in all likelihood would be indicted. I don't know if I could have stopped an indictment had I gotten in the case earlier, but at the eleventh hour it was impossible. When I failed to move the lead prosecutor handling the case, Jim Hubbard, I appealed to Bill Cummings, the United States attorney. I knew Bill and had high regard for him. I thought we had a shot, but realized that U.S. attorneys give great deference to their line assistants.

Neither Bill nor the Department of Justice wanted to review the case, but eventually Bill agreed to do so. Just as United States attorneys give great deference to their line assistants, so do the officials at the Justice Department give great deference to the United States attorneys. The Department of Justice will not, except in the most unusual circumstances, substitute its judgment on the facts and evidence for that of the United States attorneys. They will review cases where there is a claim that the United States attorney is departing from the established policy of the department, where there is a claim of prosecutorial misconduct, or if a prosecution will have a nationwide impact. These criteria did not apply to Dom's case.

Unfortunately, but as expected, our requests were rejected and on the morning of August 31, 1977, a Special Grand Jury sitting in Alexandria, Virginia, returned an indictment. The indictment charged Dominic A. Paolucci, Adm. Malcolm Cagle (Ret.), and Capt. James Hooper (Ret.) with engaging in conspiracy to defraud the United States government. According to the indictment, Cagle and Hooper used their influence to persuade naval officials in Iran to provide a contract to the Lulejian company, where Paolucci was president, to train the Iranian Navy. It was alleged that in return for their efforts on behalf of Lulejian, Cagle and Hooper would be hired by the company. This was a very high profile case, particularly in Washington, since a very high ranking admiral was indicted.

The federal court in the Eastern District of Virginia is known as the rocket docket. They set an early trial date, set early and strict guidelines for motions practice, and rarely grant continuances. This gives the government a tremendous advantage because it can investigate a case for years and once an indictment is returned, the court pushes you promptly to trial.

Until an indictment, the information available to the defense is very limited and only after indictment can you, through the discovery rules, gain access to the government's evidence. As we received the evidence, my earlier suspicions were confirmed that this was a highly circumstantial case and that the government did not have a smoking gun. I always believed that Dominic would be a highly attractive defendant to a jury because of his background and rags-to-riches story. Nevertheless, I was worried because juries in the Eastern District were very pro-prosecution, and Judge Oren Lewis, to whom the case was assigned, was an irascible old jurist who repeatedly intervened in the case. Since jurors look to a judge for direction, he presented a wild card, which had all defense counsel worried.

Over the next few months, I would immerse myself in the case and, with David Martin, a talented associate, would prepare Dom's defense. The trial began at 10:00 A.M. on November 15, 1977. As lawyers go into battle, they should always remember that they will go on to another case, but the case at hand will forever change and impact the life of the client and his family. Dom believed this trial shortened the life of his wife, Dailey. Dr. Paolucci recalls in his book:

> As Hubbard started his summary, the reality of the nightmare became a little more vivid to me and to my wife, Dailey. Despite the fact that she is a cardiac case in critical condition, with a diagnosis of coronary insufficiency and high blood pressure, having had two open-heart surgeries and being under constant doctor's care, she insisted that she be in court each day, every day. She missed about three minutes of testimony during the entire trial, when she felt woozy after having ingested, sublingually, a nitroglycerine tablet to relieve heavy chest and arm pain. She recognized the

danger to her health by being present but chose to accept the risk. On the second day, one of my friends properly sized up the situation and called my middle daughter, a school teacher in Illinois, who showed up in court the morning of the third day and was at my wife's side throughout the remainder of the trial.

Paolucci's defense was simple: He had never entered into an illicit arrangement with his codefendants; and while he was deferred to on technical matters, his superior, the chairman of the company, Colonel Lulejian, handled consultants and high-level personnel decisions. Moreover, at the critical time, Paolucci was on his way out of the company because of his displeasure with Lulejian and how he operated.

Admiral Cagle was represented by Brian Gettings, the former United States attorney for the Eastern District of Virginia, and Captain Hooper was represented by Alfred Swersky, now a Circuit Court Judge in Alexandria, Virginia. These were able and experienced attorneys; we made a good team and worked well together. All of the defendants testified and made a favorable impression on the jury. In my opinion, we won our case on our cross-examination of the government witnesses, who fell apart under our questioning. For example, a key witness for the government was Charles Norman Goodale. Goodale testified about his communication with Cagle regarding Lulejian's interest in getting into the field of naval training and the efforts made to hire him.

Both Gettings and Swersky had done an excellent job in showing that Goodale was confused as to what occurred with their clients. Since he did not score any direct hit on Paolucci, I had to decide whether or not to question him at all. I decided to cross him because there were a few important points I had to nail down.

Goodale was a company employee involved in the transactions under scrutiny. While he never specifically tied Paolucci to any wrongdoing, he did, if believed, make a connection between the company and its desire to get involved in training the Iranian Navy and hiring Cagle. Since Paolucci was the president of the company, this testimony was harmful. If the jury erroneously concluded that Paolucci was involved with these efforts, it would be a big problem. It was important on cross-examination to cut through the fog and innuendo brought forth by the prosecutor. Also, I wanted to lay the groundwork for my closing argument. I wanted to show that government witnesses like Goodale, who were not prosecuted, were given white hats by the government even though they had much greater involvement with the transactions under scrutiny than did Paolucci.

My approach to cross-examination is akin to being a guerrilla fighter. You go in quickly, establish the points you need for closing, and get out as soon as you get what you need. Also, because witnesses will almost always try to help the side that called them, you always cross-examine a witness tightly with no broad, open-ended questions. In other words, keep the witness on a tight leash with leading questions. Here is how I handled Goodale:

**MR. BENNETT:** Mr. Goodale, you testified about three or four people at different times being active in which proposals were discussed?

**MR. GOODALE:** Yes, sir.

**MR. BENNETT:** Just so it is absolutely certain, Dr. Paolucci was not one of those four, isn't that correct?

**MR. GOODALE:** That is correct. . . .

**MR. BENNETT:** Isn't it a fact that Dr. Paolucci to your knowledge, did not make the decision to focus in on Iranian training?

**MR. GOODALE:** That is correct. . . .

**MR. BENNETT:** Isn't it a fact that Dr. Paolucci was not concerned about training?

**MR. GOODALE:** Yes, that is correct.

**MR. BENNETT:** Isn't it a fact that Dr. Paolucci did not have anything to do with the writing of the new proposals, that you prepared?

**MR. GOODALE:** That is correct. . . .

**MR. BENNETT:** Isn't it a fact that to your knowledge

Dr. Paolucci didn't even read them?

**MR. GOODALE:** That is correct.

**MR. BENNETT:** Isn't it a fact that you never discussed them with Dr. Paolucci?

**MR. GOODALE:** That is correct. . . .

**MR. BENNETT:** Well, isn't it a fact that because you felt that Dr. Paolucci was not interested in foreign training that you spoke directly with Colonel Lulejian, the chief executive officer of the company, about opening up the Pensacola office?

**MR. GOODALE:** Well, yes, I had a conversation with Colonel Lulejian, yes, sir. . . .

**MR. BENNETT:** . . . during the period of time that we are talking about, you weren't talking to Dr. Paolucci at all, were you?

**MR. GOODALE:** No, no, sir.

**MR. BENNETT:** It was your suggestion, wasn't it, that a Pensacola office be opened?

**MR. GOODALE:** Yes. . . . I pointed out to him that if we were going to get involved in training, that one of the things I suggest was that an office be opened in Pensacola.

**MR. BENNETT:** And it was Dr. Paolucci's lack of interest in this that caused you to discuss this matter with Colonel Lulejian, isn't that correct?

**MR. GOODALE:** No, no, that is not correct.

Goodale obviously tried to help the prosecution by minimizing Lulejian's role. However, I knew every word of his prior grand-jury testimony and confronted him with his June 20, 1977, grand-jury testimony:

**MR. BENNETT:** *(Reading)*

QUESTION: How did it come about what we were talking about, the Pensacola office, how did it come about, what generated it. I understand that there was some—

ANSWER: Well, I hope it was the talk I had with Colonel Lulegian at that time. I, I was, I had given notice.

**QUESTION:** Did you tell him you wanted to open a Pensacola office?

**ANSWER:** Well, I did tell him that it would make a lot of sense, you know, it made a lot of sense.

**QUESTION:** What did he say, sir, about it? Paolucci say?

**ANSWER:** I wasn't, well, I wasn't talking to Paolucci at the time. I was in with the chairman of the board.

**MR. BENNETT:** *(Resuming questioning)* Remember those questions?

**MR. GOODALE:** Yes, sir.


This short cross-examination torpedoed the government's case against Dr. Paolucci, the decorated submariner.

I had gotten what I wanted from Goodale for my closing argument. I was the last defense lawyer to argue and here is how I used my cross-examination of Goodale in my closing:


Ladies and gentlemen of the jury, this is a very difficult time to be last at this late hour. I promise you I'll be brief. . . . Ladies and gentlemen, at the very beginning of this case, I said to you that this was a mountain out of a molehill and I stand by that. I think the evidence shows that.

Before talking about what the case is, let me just talk briefly about what the case is not. Dr. Paolucci is charged in one, and only one count. And that is the charge of conspiracy. And in that charge, the government has to prove beyond a reasonable doubt each and every essential element.

We are not talking about mistakes. We are not talking about poor judgment. We are not talking about the most perfect of all [the science of hindsight]. We are talking about these men getting together and deciding to break the law of the United States of America.

This case is not a fraud case against Dr. Paolucci. He is not charged with bribery. . . .

. . . Dr. Paolucci is not charged with conflict of [interest], not charged with any of that. So this mountain of government testimony is a molehill. . . .

A second point that is of primary importance in this case, is that you cannot find Dr. Paolucci guilty of conspiracy because you may find—and I don't think the evidence even supports that—that someone at Lulejian and Associates did something wrong. In this era of post-Watergate morality referred to my brother, Gettings, we, thank heavens, have not as yet reached the point that merely because a man has a title in a company [he can be] found guilty of crimes if they were committed by [other] people in that company.

Dr. Paolucci cannot be responsible for the acts of other persons. You must judge his guilt or innocence based on his own acts, upon his own actions, and that is your oath to do that.

Now, it is indeed ironic, ladies and gentlemen of the jury, that the key witnesses that the prosecution have offered in this case are people who . . . admitted more involvement than . . . my client.

Mr. Goodale, for example, was a one-man army. He was down there working on these proposals all the time. This is the star witness that the prosecution has put forward.

What does Mr. Goodale say? He says Dr. Paolucci wasn't even interested in training. Wasn't even interested. He said, "I never talked to him once." Never talked to him once on these briefings and these proposals.

Who did he talk to? He said, "I wasn't talking to Paolucci. I was talking to the chairman of the board, Colonel Lulejian."

And we're not saying Colonel Lulejian did anything wrong, either. But we certainly are saying that Dr. Paolucci had minimal involvement in this, if he had any involvement at all.

At 11:15 A.M. on Wednesday, November 23, 1977, following jury instructions from Judge Lewis, the jury returned to the jury room to consider its verdict. This is a period of agony for lawyers and worse for the defendants and their families. Will the lives of the Paolucci family, as they knew it, be over? Will Dr. Paolucci go to jail? If so, how will the family survive? Will a magnificent reputation go down the drain? Will the company close and the employees lose their jobs? And for the lawyers, it's almost as bad. Should I have called X or Y as a witness? Should I have asked this or that question? Did I argue the right points? Should I have been less aggressive? Should I have been more aggressive? As we waited for the verdict, I looked at Dom and his family and wondered if I had let them down. Could I have done better? Was there something I missed? Dom must have read my mind because he came up to me and said, "Bob, no matter what happens, I want to thank you, you did a great job for me. Thanks." We then hugged. He was a classy guy. At about 1:15 P.M. the jury asked for sandwiches and for some exhibits.

At around 5:15 P.M. the judge decided that if the jury had not reached a verdict, he would adjourn court until Friday as the next day was Thanksgiving. I did not like the idea of an adjournment. The sheer agony of having to wait was too much for all of us. Also, I wanted a Thanksgiving verdict. I have had considerable success with verdicts right before holidays. Maybe some of the goodwill and cheer spills over into the jury's deliberations.

Over defense objections, the judge told the marshal to bring in the jury and have them assembled at the door. The following occurred:

**THE COURT:** Just stand right there, all of you, where you can hear. As I told you good folks, I do not want to rush you. I don't intend to rush you. In fairness to yourselves, more than anyone else, I don't think you should deliberate any longer. It's Thanksgiving, I've and you have all got families the same as other people.

**THE FOREMAN:** Sir, we are—

**THE COURT:** (*Interposing*) I forgot to tell you or ask you—I'm going to ask you now. I didn't ask you in the beginning. I can and should—if you have reached a verdict, members of the jury,

a unanimous verdict as to any defendant or as to any of the
counts, I will be glad to take it now in open court. If you
haven't—I mean as to anyone, if you have reached a verdict as to
any of them.

**THE FOREMAN:** Sir, could we have fifteen more minutes?

**THE COURT:** No, I won't give you fifteen. I'll give you a little
more time. The only reason I won't—I don't want to put this on
a time clock where you have got to vote—

**THE FOREMAN:** *(Interposing)* A little more time.

**THE COURT:** I'll give you just a little more time, but
no fifteen minutes, and certainly no hour or anything.
Because in fairness, what I don't want—I don't want to
say somebody is—well, I just don't want to say it's got to
be done by then. Now—

**THE FOREMAN:** *(Interposing)* Okay.

**THE COURT:** In fairness to all, if you've got a verdict,
Mr. Foreman or Mrs. Foreman, whoever it is, write your
verdict out on that as to the counts you have. If you don't have
it as to the others, Friday, you've got plenty of time. So I'll give
you a few minutes to write your verdict up. If you get it all
done, fine.

*(Whereupon, the jury retired to the jury room to consider its verdict.)*

**THE COURT:** You all know as well as I do what they wanted.
We're not going to run this by a clock. I have asked them to
do that. So, I don't know how long it will take me to take off this
coat and put it back, but that's what I'm going to do.

*(Whereupon, the proceedings were adjourned to await the verdict of
the jury.)*

After only a few minutes, the jury notified the marshal that they had
a verdict.

**THE COURT:** Mr. Marshal, I understand the jury has a verdict.

**THE MARSHAL:** Yes, sir.

**THE COURT:** Knock on the door and bring them in and put
them in the box.
*(Whereupon, the jury returned to the jury box.)*
**THE CLERK:** Mr. Foreman, has the jury agreed upon a verdict?
**THE FOREMAN:** We have.
**THE CLERK:** May I have them please?
*(The clerk takes the verdicts and hands them to the court.)*
**THE COURT:** The clerk will read the verdicts.
**THE CLERK:** Will the defendants please stand.

When the jury entered the room, there was total silence; you could almost hear the defendants' hearts beating. One of the jurors looked directly at me and smiled and gave an indescribable facial gesture, which
told me everything would be okay. Seconds before the verdict was read, I
leaned over to Dom and said, "Dom, if you go down, can I have your
Arena Stage theater tickets?" A look of disbelief appeared on his face, but
before he could say anything he heard "Not guilty." He smiled, hugged
me, and then called me a "no good son-of-a-bitch for asking for the tickets." Dom, Ellen, Dailey, and I had enjoyed evenings at the Arena Stage
and now we could do so again.

The courtroom burst into sounds of joy and relief. The court sternly
admonished those in the courtroom:

**THE COURT:** Wait a minute. The verdict is not over.

The clerk then read the remaining verdicts—all defendants were acquitted. Then the court continued:

Let the defendants come forward. Admiral Cagle and Captain
Hooper and [Dr.] Paolucci, in accordance with the verdict
of the jury, the clerk is hereby directed to enter up a verdict
of not guilty on each of the counts for which you stood
charged. You are each released. Your bond is released and
you are free to go.

Any trial lawyer will tell you that the time it takes for the foreman to hand the verdict to the clerk, who then gives it to the judge for review, then announces it in open court is agonizing. Everything seems to be in slow motion. One minute feels like forever. But when the words *not guilty* are heard, you explode, you cry, you hug and kiss. It is the greatest feeling in the world.

When we were selecting the jury, there was a gentleman with an Italian surname. All other things being equal, I wanted him on the jury because I knew that in a corruption case the defendant named Paolucci might be subject to prejudice. I believed that an Italian on the jury would prevent that from happening. To my surprise, the prosecutor did not strike him from the jury. While the jury was deliberating, I asked the prosecutor why he let the gentleman stay on the jury. He candidly told me what he had been heard to say in another case "where there is smoke there is fire," and so the prosecutor felt he had at least one juror on his side.

As Dom asked sarcastically, "On such factors justice rides?"

This case brought my name to national attention, particularly in the defense industry. It was great timing because the Department of Justice over the next several years would aggressively pursue defense contractors. Carl Rauh and I together with our team of first-rate lawyers—which eventually would include Alan Kriegel, Mitch Ettinger, Saul Pilchen, Amy Sabrin, among others—would become heavily engaged in defending major companies, including Boeing, Northrop, and SAIC.

Other great cases came our way as a result of this win. We developed a thriving practice. When I left Hogan, I gave up the guaranteed income of a big firm. Before joining the Dunnells firm, Ellen and I had worked out a budget assuming I would make less than my salary at Hogan. As it worked out, I made more in my first year and every year thereafter. By being on my own, I was able to spread my wings and really fly. I knew I had the skills, but also I was very lucky because the post-Watergate-scandal mentality was taking hold and there was an increasing demand for white-collar lawyers. Most big firms did not offer these services, but found that more and more of their corporate clients were getting embroiled in matters that required the skills of a criminal lawyer. Joining

Dunnells, Duvall, and Porter at the right time and having a high-profile victory such as the Paolucci case helped make me a lawyer in demand. As a result of my successes, my fellow partners decided to include me in the firm's name.

A good defense lawyer must be like a holistic physician. You must care for and protect your clients and guide them and their families through the worst times of their lives. You must never forget that a case is not about you but is about your client's life, freedom, reputation, and financial security.

# AN ASSASSINATION IN BELGIUM

I N  T H E  F A L L  of 1978, I received a call from someone in the defense industry, a friend of Paolucci, who told me that he had recommended me to Dr. Gerald Bull, the president of Space Research
Corporation (SRC), who was under investigation by the Customs Service
and Department of Justice for the sale of arms to South Africa in violation of an arms embargo. My friend told me that Dr. Bull was the world's
leading expert in the research, design, and development of military ordnance and that his armaments and projectiles far exceeded in distance
and quality those of the United States military and other world powers.
He said that Bull, a Canadian by birth, was so highly regarded by the
United States defense establishment and had made so many contributions to our national security that he was given United States citizenship
by a Special Act of Congress. This put Bull in the company of Sir Winston
Churchill and only one or two others in the history of the United States.
I was impressed.

Shortly after this conversation, I spoke by phone with Dr. Bull and
Col. Rodgers L. Gregory (Ret.), who worked closely with Bull at Space
Research, both of whom asked me to represent them in connection with
the investigation. It was agreed that Colonel Gregory would come to my
office in Washington to brief me on the case and work out the details of
the representation.

When I met Gregory in Washington, I was very impressed by him. He
had a military background, was a man of few words, but was precise and
detail oriented.

Like a good doctor, there is nothing more important than getting a good history from your client. What I learned was a fascinating story that would involve me in one of the most interesting cases of my career.

During his visit to Washington, Gregory asked me to accompany him to a nondescript film studio in Northwest Washington. My first thought on entering was that this was not an ordinary studio. It had "spook" written all over it. Bull had given an interview to a British broadcasting company which had investigated the sale of arms to South Africa, and I sat in silence as I watched a tape of the broadcast. As cargo labeled "agricultural equipment" was being hoisted on a ship, the hoist broke and the crates broke open on the deck below. Instead of agricultural equipment, long-range armaments were clearly visible. Bull agreed to be interviewed and professed ignorance of how and why guns and related equipment were in his company's shipment.

Space Research Corporation was located on eight thousand acres near the Vermont town of North Troy, which straddles the Canadian border. Gregory explained that he was the administrative assistant to Dr. Bull and said that Lt. Gen. Arthur Trudeau (Ret.) was instrumental in bringing together Gregory and Bull. The general became a director at SRC following his forty-year career in the military. Trudeau served as the chief of Research and Development, Department of the Army, and chief of Army Intelligence. He was a much decorated military officer who was an early supporter of SRC and was instrumental in helping SRC get military contracts.

Gregory himself had a distinguished military career. He was wounded in combat during the Korean War, for which he received the Purple Heart. He was also awarded the bronze star. Gregory was a devoted husband, father, and grandfather.

Bull was born in Ontario, Canada, on March 9, 1928, to a middle-class family. One of ten children, his early life was marked by the tragedy of his mother dying when he was three. His father never recovered from the death, and Bull was raised by an adoptive mother. Bull showed early signs of having a special intellect and thirst for knowledge. In 1951, he would become the youngest student to receive a doctorate of science degree from the University of Toronto. He received other advanced degrees including a doctorate in aerodynamics. He was married and had several children.

Gregory told me that Bull was an absolute genius and visionary in his chosen field of artillery and ballistics and that because of this, there was a steady stream of official and unofficial visitors to the company. It was clear to me that Space Research, Bull, and Gregory involved themselves in sensitive, intelligence-related activities.

Shortly after being retained, I visited SRC on the Vermont-Canadian border. It was out of a James Bond movie. I was shown Bull's most famous weapon, the long-gun, which was capable of shooting a projectile into space without the benefit of a rocket. Prior to visiting the facility, I was asked to recommend a lawyer for another SRC official who was also under investigation. I recommended Arnold Weiner, a prominent white-collar lawyer in Baltimore. Arnold joined me on my visit to Bull's home adjoining the SRC facility, as did Kirk Karaszkiewicz, who was asked to represent the company.

During a break in our debriefing of our clients, Arnold and I decided to take a walk in the wooded grounds of the facility. But when we cut through some thick woods hoping to find our way back, we got hopelessly lost. One problem was that I was wearing a suit and Arnold was wearing a dark velvet sport coat. We nevertheless eventually made our way through the brush. We later learned that we had unknowingly crossed over the Canadian border. I can still recall Arnold's velvet coat covered with burrs and other forest debris.

All of the lawyers believed that this was a very defensible case.

The defense could show clearly that SRC had a close working relationship with Israel and that Israel had a close working relationship with South Africa. Moreover, we would have little difficulty in showing that it was known by intelligence officials of the U.S. government that whatever was given to Israel would in all likelihood be given by them to South Africa. Had there been a full-blown trial, this relationship—which was sensitive, classified, and largely unknown—would have seen the light of day.

It was agreed that I would schedule an early meeting with the government attorneys in the hopes of getting this resolved quickly.

Bob Trout, who worked with me at Dunnells, and I met with United States Attorney Bill Gray, Assistant United States Attorney Jerome Niedermeier, and other representatives of the government in Vermont.

Gray suggested that if the case was not resolved before indictment, the indictment would charge a broad conspiracy, with hundreds of counts, and that other colleagues of Bull and Gregory would also be indicted. I made it clear at the meeting that I thought it was a tough case for the government and suggested that this was not the kind of case the feds would want to try in a public forum given the potential defenses.

While Gray indicated he was not at all concerned about our raising issues of national security and classified matters and that we would show that our clients' activities were known and approved by various government agencies, I could tell he was bothered by it. On the other hand, it was clear that the Customs Service wanted blood and would push for maximum charges and penalties. Nothing got resolved at this meeting and U.S. Attorney Gray made it clear that it was his intention to go forward with an indictment.

Under the circumstances, we had little choice but to appeal to officials higher up in the Justice Department. I was hopeful that the senior officials at the Justice Department in Washington would take a broader view of what was in the national interest and encourage a resolution short of trial. Accordingly, I communicated with Assistant Attorney General Philip B. Heymann on March 12, 1980, and laid out my case to him. Phil is now a professor at Harvard Law School.

In addition to arguing to the Department of Justice that the facts did not warrant an indictment, we contacted other government agencies and other interested persons who might not want this case to go forward because it would put into the public forum matters that were sensitive. I knew that no other agency in the federal government could stop the Department of Justice, and I did think if the right buttons were pushed, it could only help us to get the case resolved on a favorable basis. One such entity was the government of Israel, which recognized that its relationship with South Africa was a sensitive one. Through an intermediary, a meeting was scheduled in Washington with a senior Israeli general.

The plan was for me to meet the Israeli general at Washington

National Airport, brief him on the matter, and drive him to the Embassy of Israel, where he had other meetings scheduled. The real world often intrudes at the most unwelcome times. Ellen and I had two cars then—one was okay; the other was a real clunker in the truest sense of the word. Its primary use was to take our dog to the park. It looked like it and smelled like it. As I turned the ignition in the good car to head for my important pickup at the airport, nothing happened—dead. I nearly panicked. It was too late to arrange for other transportation, so I took the clunker. I met the general at the designated place. He looked at the car and almost didn't get in. As we drove to the embassy, we discussed the case over the various weird sounds coming from the engine and the exhaust. I could see the general becoming concerned. He asked me questions about me and my practice. I am sure, at least for a moment, he thought he was being kidnaped by a terrorist or a nut job. I, in turn, got nervous that he might overreact and kill me. Fortunately, I think he concluded that I was legitimate if eccentric. By the time we got to the embassy, we had had a fruitful talk and the general seemed to appreciate our mutual concerns and promised me that the issues would be fully considered. It was our hope that the Israeli government would communicate to the appropriate persons that it was not in the interests of U.S.–Israeli relations for this case to go trial.

While we all believed that we had an excellent chance at trial, it was understood by all concerned that we should explore the possibility of a plea deal before any indictment was returned. Our intelligence was that U.S. Attorney Gray was preparing a broad indictment with as many as two hundred counts against the company, Dr. Bull, Colonel Gregory, and others. As any defense lawyer knows, such an indictment could have a devastating impact on a client's many business ventures and relationships, and, if convicted, would have in all likelihood resulted in a substantial prison sentence for the client.

I have never had a client serve more than a minimal jail sentence, and I didn't want Bull or Gregory to be the first. I was prepared to pull out all the stops in making the decision to go forward as difficult as possible for the government.

A public trial could be a fiasco for the government and notwithstanding their protestations to the contrary I knew they were bluffing.

When a client's reputation and freedom is on the line, it is the attorney's obligation to do all he can for the client. The only limit is that what you do must be legal and ethical.

I never learned for sure which of the many buttons that we pushed was the one that worked, but over time it became clear that the United States Attorney's Office realized that it was in their interest to resolve the case without a trial. In his book, *Bull's Eye: The Assassination and Life of Supergun Inventor Gerald Bull*, James Adams observes:

> Gray repeatedly told Bennett that none of this "outside shit" was going to enter into the case because it was irrelevant to the charges that were going to be filed. But that tough stance against the opposition was belied by serious doubts that the prosecution would be successful. Gray knew that Judge James Holden, who had been slated to try the case, was both tough and fair. In fact, Gray actually believed that Holden would require the CIA to be represented at the trial in order to protect Bull's and Gregory's rights as defendants.
>
> "I can see Holden saying to me, 'Mr. Gray, can you assure me that this is every single document from the U.S. government on this case?' and it would have been very difficult for me to make that assurance."

While we were desirous of a plea deal, we were not prepared to accept a tough one. If I could obtain a deal that would cause minimum damage to my clients, I was prepared to recommend that our clients accept it.

With Bull's and Gregory's permission, we approached Bill Gray about a deal. After the usual back-and-forth advocacy, we found Gray to be very receptive. After some hard bargaining, we agreed that Dr. Bull and Colonel Gregory would each enter a plea of guilty to one count charging a licensing violation and that the company would enter a plea of guilty to one count charging a licensing violation and four counts of false shipping declarations. The maximum possible penalty for the plea was two years imprisonment or a $100,000 fine or both.

This was, under all the circumstances, a very favorable plea deal for Bull and Gregory. They both were very appreciative and thanked me for my efforts. On March 21, 1980, four days before we were to appear before Judge Holden to enter the plea, Bull wrote a letter to a friend and a business colleague explaining in detail why it made sense for him to enter the plea arrangement. He asked his friend to gather together other colleagues to read the letter. Bull wanted his colleagues to know that by entering the plea, there would be less damage done to them and others he cared about.

On March 25, 1980, Bull and Gregory appeared before Judge James Holden in the United States District Court for the District of Vermont. The clerk of the court read the charge to which Bull, Gregory, and the company would plead guilty. Before accepting the guilty pleas, Judge Holden questioned each of the defendants to ensure that they fully understood the charges, that the plea was voluntarily entered, that they were mentally able to enter the plea, and that they were satisfied with the services of their counsel and that they understood all of the rights they were waiving by entering the plea.

The court required the U.S. attorney to spell out what the government would prove if the case went to trial. When the court was fully satisfied that there was a voluntary admission of guilt, he accepted the pleas and referred the matter to the probation office for a presentence report. The defendants were released pending sentence.

Bull and Gregory and their families felt a great sense of relief, and they and all the lawyers were pleased with the day's proceedings.

Some of a lawyer's most important work occurs after a plea. You have an important opportunity to affect the sentencing. It has always been my practice to file with the court extensive presentencing memoranda. This is particularly important when there has been no trial, a judge knows very little about your client other than that he has pled guilty to a criminal offense and whatever other information has been provided by the probation department. Much of what finds its way into a presentence report comes from the prosecutor, so it is important that all relevant and favorable information is presented to the court by way of a defendant's presentencing memorandum. We submitted to Judge Holden a detailed presentencing memorandum on behalf of Bull and Gregory which included much of their life histories. We included letters from family, friends, and colleagues. Moreover, we put the offense in context so that the judge would conclude he was dealing with good and honorable men who were not evil.

On June 16, 1980, we again appeared before Judge Holden. Our presentencing memorandum clearly had an impact on the judge, as he sentenced Bull and Gregory to one year but suspended six months of the sentence. They would each serve six months in jail with time off for good behavior, which meant that both Bull and Gregory would serve four and a half months in a minimum-security prison.

Sometime after the case was over, I received a March 30, 1982, report from the House Committee on Foreign Affairs' Subcommittee on Africa and Global Health. Congressman Howard Wolpe chaired the subcommittee. He conducted a thorough investigation of the shipment of arms to South Africa. The committee reported in part as follows:

[Finding] 1. From 1976–78, Space Research Corporation of Vermont broke the US and UN arms embargoes against South Africa by selling and shipping to the South African government approximately 50,000 155-mm extended-range artillery shells, at least four 155-mm guns including three advanced prototypes, technology and technical assistance to establish its own 155-mm gun and ammunition manufacturing and testing capability, and other military equipment. Almost all of the equipment sent to South Africa was acquired in the US, mainly from US Army plants and supply stock.

. . . .

[Finding] 6. According to the preponderance of evidence, it is probable that a US defense consultant who was assisting the CIA's covert action program in Angola—and was under the supervision of a CIA officer—planned with South African government officials shipments of US-origin arms to South Africa for use in Angola. He also informed the South Africans (representatives of Armscor, the state defense production and procurement agency) that they could obtain superior 155-mm artillery from SRC. Much of this planning and discussion took place after the US government had decided not to ship arms for Angola via South Africa and not to respond to an official South African request for 155-mm artillery from SRC. At the very least, this episode suggests serious negligence on the part of the Agency. At most, there is a possibility that elements of the CIA purposefully evaded US policy. Although the probable CIA agent was one channel of information about SRC to South Africa and was subsequently approached by Armscor to act as an intermediary in concluding a deal with SRC, there were two other channels which seem even more important.

. . . .

[Finding] 8. The poor performance of US foreign policy agencies in the SRC case seriously weakened the Justice Department's 1980–81 criminal case against SRC, the First Pennsylvania Bank, and their officers and associates. Of particular concern to government lawyers in a potential trial was the appearance of possible US government authorization of SRC shipments to South Africa. The upshot was Justice's acceptance of a plea bargain in which only the two top officers of SRC paid a price—four and four-and-a-half months at a minimum security prison—for a $19 million illegal arms deal.

Upon his release, Gregory returned home to his role as a loving husband, father, and grandfather until he died of cancer.

Bull, who felt both the United States and Canada had betrayed him, decided to move to Belgium following completion of his sentence in prison. He had friends and business contacts there. Bull continued to work in the field of ordnance and, according to public reports, had dealings with China, Libya, Iraq, and others. This was a dangerous and cutthroat world he chose to operate in. It was a far cry from the kind of work that enabled him to receive U.S. citizenship for his research contribution to national security.

On March 22, 1990, as Jerry Bull was about to enter his Brussels apartment, someone approached him from behind and pumped bullets into his head, neck, and back. It is not known who was responsible. Some think it was the Mossad, Israel's secret intelligence service, because of Bull's dealings with Iraq. Bull had been working with the Iraqi government, helping them to develop a more sophisticated long-range artillery system. But it could have been others who were concerned about his dealings with China or Libya. It seems clear that the motive for his killing was not robbery since the assassin left $20,000 in cash in Bull's pocket.

Of Bull's assassination, James Adams wrote:

> Bull flew to the United States in February 1990, one month before his assassination. He had told his family that he was following a lead in his investigation of the CIA, but he would not tell them whom he intended to see. He met Mimi at Mardi Gras in New Orleans. They then flew to Washington, D.C., where they stayed for three days. Later investigations show that he saw a number of people who were central to SRC's involvement in South Africa in the late 1970's, including one of South Africa's key contacts in the U.S. Government.
>
> When he returned to Brussels, he seemed satisfied, even elated, at the way the trip had gone, but he still refused to reveal whom he had seen or what he had learned. All he would [say] was that he had eaten a meal with someone in Washington who had told him that if he had not pleaded guilty at his trial ten years earlier, orders had been given to assassinate him. He was shocked, he said, but the news confirmed to him that he had been used as a scapegoat.

Bull was killed on the third day after his return to Brussels from the American trip.

As I thought about his death, I could not help but think of the irony that Bull, who may well have been the greatest designer of guns in the twentieth century, would die at the wrong end of one.

# CHAPTER EIGHT

# TOMMY THE CORK—MY MENTOR IN JEOPARDY

ARLY ON IN the life of Dunnells, Duvall, Bennett and Porter, we held a reception. We invited clients, prospective clients, and leading members of the bar. We wanted everyone to know that we were around and ready for business. I invited Tommy Corcoran to the reception. And as usual, he captivated the crowd with his charm and wit. He was a legend of the bar and was still one of the most powerful go-to guys in Washington. When he left the reception, I escorted him to the elevator and asked, "Mr. Corcoran, how do young lawyers get business?" He answered, "Old lawyers die." I would also learn that young lawyers get business when old lawyers get into trouble.

On December 21, 1979, the *Washington Post* reported the following, in a major story by Morton Mintz:

> Prominent Washington attorney Thomas G. (Tommy the Cork) Corcoran faces an ethics investigation because of the recent disclosure of his apparently unprecedented lobbying of two Supreme Court justices in 1969 in connection with a pending case.
>
> The investigation will be conducted by the board on professional responsibility of the District of Columbia bar. The result could be exoneration, disbarment; or any of several in-between actions.

At seventy-eight years of age with over half a century at the bar, Tommy Corcoran was at risk. If the Disciplinary Board found that Corcoran violated rules by communicating with the Supreme Court on the merits of a case, he could be disbarred from practice. Given his age and years of practice, the real threat was not to his livelihood, but to his reputation. He did not want to leave practice in disgrace. Corcoran had been investigated before for his lobbying activities, but he always prevailed. He often said that when he went to lobby on behalf of a client, he "would go in the front door with a brass band following behind him." This was different. The allegation here was that he quietly visited two Supreme Court justices and lobbied them on behalf of the El Paso Natural Gas Company. Corcoran asked me to represent him. "Bob, I need a street fighter on this. Will you help me?" I gladly said yes, as Corcoran had been so good to me, and this gave me an opportunity to do something for him.

While Corcoran's partner, Jim Rowe, liked me, he felt that the team needed some "gray hair." I have lots of it now, but at the time had none. He recommended one of the most distinguished lawyers in Washington, John Douglas at Covington and Burling. John was the son of the respected Illinois senator Paul Douglas. Corcoran agreed that the both of us would represent him. I welcomed the opportunity to work with someone with the stature of Douglas, and we got along exceptionally well. Also on our team was John Kelly, an associate in Corcoran's firm. Here is how the case came about.

In 1979, reporters Bob Woodward and Scott Armstrong released their book, *The Brethren: Inside the Supreme Court*. They asserted in the book that in October of 1969 Corcoran separately visited Justices Hugo L. Black and William J. Brennan and lobbied them to grant a rehearing in the case of *Utah Public Service Commission v. El Paso Natural Gas*. While Corcoran was not counsel of record in the case, it was reported that he made the request on behalf of El Paso's lawyer, a friend of Corcoran's, John Sonnett, who was deathly ill. The apparent source for this report was a former law clerk to one of the justices.

In an earlier decision, the Supreme Court in an antitrust case against El Paso, the world's largest pipeline owner at the time, affirmed a decision that El Paso had established a monopoly and must divest itself of many of its holdings. This decision threatened the life of El Paso; it was critical, if at all possible, to get a rehearing. On June 29, 1970, the court announced that the petition for a rehearing was denied.

Until Woodward and Armstrong published their book, Corcoran's meetings with the justices, if they occurred at all, were not publicly known. While *The Brethren* was of historical interest to most, to Admiral Hyman Rickover, it was much more. Rickover intensely disliked Tommy Corcoran. They had crossed swords in the past when Corcoran represented the defense industry. Moreover, Rickover believed that Corcoran used his considerable influence in Washington to get Rickover reassigned and put out to pasture. Even though Rickover had nothing to do with the El Paso case, on reading about Corcoran's alleged efforts to lobby the court, he filed a formal complaint with the District of Columbia Bar asking them to take action against his nemesis Corcoran.

After I conducted a preliminary investigation, it was clear that the only three people who had any knowledge about the allegations were Justices Black and Brennan and Tommy Corcoran. Tommy denied that he lobbied either of them. He readily acknowledged that he could have met with them on a variety of subjects—all proper—since he knew them well. Also, Corcoran's daughter, Margaret, had clerked for Justice Black after law school. They had been friends since the New Deal and had worked together. Corcoran also knew Justice Brennan, and they often shared a love and pride for their Irish heritage over song and stories. Given that many years had passed, Corcoran could not recall if he had met with them in the time frame referred to in the book or what was discussed.

It clearly would have been improper for a member of the bar to meet privately with a justice to discuss a pending case. However, I felt it was reasonable to argue that if such a breach occurred that the justices would have done something about it when it occurred. No report or criticism was ever made by the justices. Justice Black had passed away in 1971, and so Justice Brennan was the only living witness, other than Corcoran, to any conversation. It was therefore essential that I contact Justice Brennan and get his side of the story. On January 15, 1980, I wrote him the following letter:

The Honorable William J. Brennan Jr.
Justice, Supreme Court
Of the United States
1 First Street, N.W.
Washington, D.C. 20543

*My dear Mr. Justice:*

I represent Thomas G. Corcoran, Esquire, a member of the New York, District of Columbia and Supreme Court bars, in connection with an inquiry being conducted by District of Columbia Bar Counsel with regard to conduct attributed to Mr. Corcoran in a <u>Washington Post</u> article . . . based upon an excerpt from a recently published book, <u>The Brethren</u>. Basically, the article and book allege that during the Fall of 1969, Mr. Corcoran, on separate occasions, had <u>ex</u> <u>parte</u> contact with the late Mr. Justice Black and you during which attempts were made to influence the Court's disposition of a pending petition for rehearing in <u>Utah Public Service Commission v. El Paso Natural Gas Co</u>.

Mr. Corcoran was advised by letter of December 11, 1979, of Bar Counsel's view that such conduct, if true, might violate Disciplinary Rule 7-110(B) of the Code of Professional Responsibility, and of his inquiry into the truth or falsity of the charges. Mr. Corcoran's written response is due on or before January 21, 1980.

I have spoken with Mr. Corcoran at length on several recent occasions concerning these allegations. Mr. Corcoran has told me that he cannot remember having met with you during the period alleged, but that, if he did so, his purpose was not to influence the outcome of any pending case.

Because Mr. Corcoran cannot recall circumstances which may have given rise to the allegations in the <u>Post</u> article and in <u>The Brethren</u>, I am writing to request an opportunity to discuss with you your recollection of the details of such circumstances.

I am, of course, aware that the subjects involved are sensitive and confidential, and I appreciate that, for this reason, you may not wish to discuss them. At the same time, I trust you will understand that, in the interest of effectively assisting my client, I am obliged to make this inquiry.

I look forward to your reply at your earliest convenience.

Respectfully yours,

Robert S. Bennett

Fred Grabowsky, Bar Counsel, wrote the justice shortly after I did. Justice Brennan never responded directly to me, but he did respond to the Bar Counsel two weeks after receiving my letter and told him that he had no independent recollection of being lobbied by Corcoran in the El Paso case.

*January 30, 1980*

Mr. Fred Grabowsky, Esq.
Bar Counsel
The Board on Professional Responsibility
1426 H Street, N.W.
Washington, D.C. 20005

Re: Corcoran/Bar Counsel
Docket No.: 230-79

*Dear Mr. Grabowsky:*

This is in response to your letter of January 24.

Although I have read published reports to the effect that over 10 years ago Mr. Corcoran approached me and another member of the Court concerning a petition for rehearing in the El Paso Natural Gas case, I am afraid I no longer have any independent recollection of the incident. I do recall seeing Mr. Corcoran in my chambers during that time period, but I made no record of the espisode [sic] and despite efforts to refresh my recollection am simply unable at this point to remember what transpired.

Sincerely,
Justice Wm. J. Brennan, Jr.

Given Corcoran's denial, the death of Justice Black, and Justice Brennan's lack of recollection, Bar Counsel had little choice but to drop the case. I got a call from Bar Counsel telling me of the decision to drop the matter. I was ecstatic, and when I told Corcoran, he was extremely grateful. A few days later, on March 6, 1980, Bar Counsel sent me a letter which said in pertinent part:

*Dear Mr. Bennett:*

We have completed our investigation of this matter and have been unable to establish that the contacts described in the book entitled The Brethren actually occurred, or that Mr. Corcoran otherwise sought to communicate with a Justice of the Court in a manner which could be considered a violation of a Disciplinary Rule. This office is, therefore, terminating its inquiry.

I was delighted that I could finally do something for a man who had done so much for me. I have never been so happy not to send a bill in my whole life.

TOMMY CORCORAN HAD a substantial impact on my life. I learned from him the importance of friendship and loyalty. He was never too busy for his friends and the children of his friends. He was a master at finding solutions to problems. I saw firsthand how he pulled together a team of lawyers to achieve the desired result. Finally, and perhaps most important, he gave me confidence in myself. If a man of such enormous talent, experience, and stature thought so highly of me, I must be all right. This was validation from a strong male mentor that I very much needed.

One of my prize possessions is a signed photograph of this great Irishman which reads: "To Bob Bennett who left this nest to fly to fame with affection and pride"

Corcoran and I would remain close until his death. Tommy died on December 6, 1981, at the age of eighty. His funeral was held at Saint Matthew's Cathedral in Washington, D.C. It was attended by the legions of people who Tommy helped over the years, many of whom would not be recognized by anyone. In addition, many of the most powerful leaders of our country came to say good-bye to this man who was the most interesting, talented, and brilliant person I ever met.

CHAPTER NINE

# THE SENATOR AND THE SHEIK

**M**Y REPUTATION WAS GROWING in Washington, and in 1980, I was retained by the Senate Ethics Committee to handle a matter that would catapult me into the national spotlight.

In February 1980, in connection with reports of an undercover operation run by the Department of Justice known as ABSCAM, the news media reported allegations of misuse of public office by Senator Harrison A. ("Pete") Williams Jr. of New Jersey. The Senate Ethics Committee notified Senator Williams that it would conduct a preliminary inquiry into the allegations.

These allegations arose out of an undercover sting operation conducted by the Department of Justice against certain members of Congress. On October 30, 1980, Senator Williams was indicted on a nine-count indictment for bribery, conspiracy, and related counts. At the heart of the indictment was the allegation that Senator Williams agreed to use his influence to assist an Arab businessman to obtain government contracts and, in return, he would get a one-hundred-million dollar loan and an interest in a titanium mine. Also, Williams pledged to do everything in his power to arrange permanent residence for the phony sheik. Unfortunately for Senator Williams, the Arab businessman was really an undercover FBI agent.

Senator Williams's trial was set for March 30, 1981, in the United States District Court for the Eastern District of New York. Prior to the indictment, the committee requested the Department of Justice to provide evidence relating to Senator Williams so it could proceed in the matter, but the department refused. They did, however, agree to provide evidence after the indictment, but then only with strict limitations on its use. Under the circumstances, the committee decided to defer action in the matter so as not to interfere with the government's prosecution of the case and to avoid any possible prejudice to Senator Williams. In those days, congressional committees would typically defer to the Department of Justice and delay their proceedings until justice completed its work. This is no longer the case.

The senator's trial began on March 30, 1981, and a guilty verdict was returned on all nine counts on May 1, 1981. A few days later, on May 5, the Senate Ethics Committee adopted a resolution authorizing a formal investigation. Simply because Williams was convicted of a crime, it did not mean that he would be removed from the Senate. Since Williams would appeal his conviction, which could take a long time, you could have the unseemly prospect of having a convicted felon serving in the Senate. This was not acceptable to most in the Senate and they had to act independently.

In early May, I was contacted by Malcolm Wallop, a Republican from Wyoming, the chairman of the ethics committee, who asked me if I would be interested in serving as special counsel to the committee. I was excited to get the call, and a meeting was scheduled with both Senator Wallop and the vice chair of the committee, Senator Howell Heflin of Alabama. They both assured me that they wanted a thorough and fair investigation, and I agreed to handle the matter. This would begin my long relationship with the Senate Ethics Committee, which would involve three high-profile matters over a number of years.

Since Wallop was the chairman, he took the lead on the committee and I dealt primarily with him. We were in close contact, often speaking or meeting several times a day. Wallop was deeply troubled by Williams's conduct but was determined to give the senator a fair hearing. Under his leadership, there was not a hint of partisanship. I recall one meeting early on when all of the committee members were present. One Republican senator made a partisan comment as to what it would mean politically if Williams was no longer in the Senate. Wallop, in stern tones, reprimanded the senator and emphasized that this was the ethics committee and that "partisanship stops at the door to this room." I was impressed and delighted that I would be working closely with this fine gentleman.

On May 28, 1981, the committee informed Senator Williams of its intention to hold a hearing. Senator Malcolm Wallop, with Heflin's concurrence, wanted to follow a trial format at the hearing with opening and closing statements and direct and cross-examination of witnesses. He felt that this model would best get at the truth. Senator Williams was represented by Kenneth Feinberg, a former aide to Senator Ted Kennedy. While I knew of Ken, I did not know him personally. After meeting with him, it was clear to me that he was a first-rate lawyer. Ken would later become one of the country's outstanding arbitrators and be chosen as the special master handling the distribution of funds for the families of the victims of 9/11.

On June 12, 1981, I sent a letter to Ken advising him of the allegations the committee was investigating, which would be the focus of the hearing. The essential allegations against Williams were as follows:

1. that he brought discredit upon the United States Senate by obtaining money for a business in which he had a financial interest;
2. that he used his position as a United States Senator to assist a company to receive government contracts in which he had a future financial interest;
3. that he used his official position to influence legislation to assist on an immigration matter;
4. that he failed to report an offer of a bribe;
5. that he concealed his receipt of a finders fee; and
6. that he lied to the FBI.

The hearing was held on July 14, 15, and 28, 1981.

In a detailed opening statement, I laid out the case and focused the senators' attention on the video- and audiotape of Senator Williams's meeting and speaking with his supposed coconspirators, which included undercover agents of the FBI.

While the senators on the committee, as well as most of the senators in the chamber, were deeply troubled about the allegations against Williams, there was great anger toward the Justice Department for conducting an undercover operation against members of Congress. They felt that this was a violation of the separation of powers and also was entrapment. While I did not believe there was much legal merit to these arguments, I was very concerned that some senators might disregard the evidence because they did not like the conduct of law enforcement.

Unquestionably, the strongest evidence against Senator Williams were the videotapes. I arranged for all senators to see the tapes if they chose to do so. The tapes were devastating to Williams because the senators could see for themselves how he engaged in clearly improper conduct. Several senators commented to me, after observing the meeting between Senator Williams and the phony Arab sheik, that had Williams thought he was doing something appropriate in meeting with the sheik, "he would have had an aide with him." The absence of an aide suggested to many that he was up to no good. The absence of aides would figure prominently in another Senate ethics case, the Keating Five, but more about that later.

At the hearing I presented the tapes as well as substantial other evidence. My role in this proceeding was more like the role of a prosecutor since the committee had decided to file allegations against Senator Williams. During the investigation stage, I was more like a neutral investigator simply trying to find the facts. But now the proceeding would follow a trial-like proceeding.

In Senator Williams's defense at the hearing, Mr. Feinberg, as any defense lawyer would, attacked our investigation, trying to undercut the reliability of the evidence. He presented two witnesses, G. Robert Blakey, a well-known criminal law professor at Notre Dame Law School and a former staffer on the Hill, as well as Senator Williams himself.

Professor Blakey was called by Mr. Feinberg for the purpose of presenting his expert opinion as to the reliability of the evidence I presented. Not surprisingly, he testified that he thought it was unreliable. He went on to say that when all the tapes are viewed together, they were not sufficient "to resolve in a reliable way" the ultimate question of Senator Williams's state of mind. Blakey based many of his conclusions on technical points of the law of evidence such as the "doctrine of completeness," which means that you must consider the entirety of things, not simply bits and pieces.

In cross-examining any witness, it is critical to understand your goals. I believed Blakey was going out of his way to help a United States senator. I also knew that if I challenged him on technical points of the law of evidence, I would bore the committee members and I would be playing to Blakey's strength. Moreover, since I didn't think the strict rules of evidence were applicable, I didn't want to waste valuable time dealing with them. Finally, I knew Blakey to be an honest man who would not jeopardize his reputation, even for Senator Williams. I figured that he would only help him if he did not get hurt in the process. Since I knew that many senators were troubled about ABSCAM and that Blakey believed in strong and creative law enforcement, I felt that I could make him a valuable witness for me. Also, I felt he was probably vulnerable as to the extent of his preparation for his testimony. Finally, I knew he was vulnerable on the intent issue. Here is how I achieved these objectives:

> **MR. BENNETT:** Professor, I don't think I will be very long. Let me just see if I understand your testimony, . . . [f]irst of all, . . . you said that it is your understanding of the senator's defense that he does not claim that he was induced or entrapped. Is that correct?
> **MR. BLAKEY:** Yes.
> **MR. BENNETT:** Second, . . . you generally endorse the ABSCAM-type of enterprise to get at political corruption?
> **MR. BLAKEY:** Yes. I think it is the least intrusive and the most productive of reliable evidence.

At this point, Blakey started to lecture and I thought it was a good idea to step him back a bit. I had to show him I was in control. He was answering my questions, not lecturing to a class.

**MR. BENNETT:** Let me ask the questions. With all due respect, you can answer and explain your answer. Today you are a witness and I am not a student and perhaps tomorrow you will be the professor and I will be a student. You made the statement during your direct examination, and I quote you, and if I misquote you, correct me. You said that "Credibility questions should be determined by the persons who heard the witnesses." You would not dispute the obvious, would you, Professor, that after five weeks of trial, [twelve] jurors who heard the credibility questions determined that Senator Williams was guilty of nine felonies. That is an obvious fact that is just not in dispute, is it?

**MR. BLAKEY:** That is true, but that fact is also irrelevant. The issue here is what Senator Williams did, not what the jurors did, and Senator Williams is entitled to . . . a fair trial before this body. . . .

**MR. BENNETT:** Let me go back to my question. You agreed with me that credibility questions should be determined by the persons who have heard the witnesses. My question is really a simple one; that is, in the first instance the jury heard this case. They heard all of the witnesses and convicted the senator on [nine] felony counts. That is a fact, isn't it?

**MR. BLAKEY:** Yes.

At this point I had elicited from Blakey key concessions that were helpful to the committee's case and it was time to point out the weaknesses in his testimony:

**MR. BENNETT:** You have told us there are certain things, Professor, that you have not done in preparation for your testimony today. What were the things you have not mastered or sufficiently analyzed in preparation for your testimony?

**MR. BLAKEY:** As I indicated to you, I have not had the opportunity to read the entire due process record.

**MR. BENNETT:** Anything else?

**MR. BLAKEY:** Let me say I said that I read the entire
transcripts. I have not mastered them. The trouble with reading
them through the first time is that the significance of various
passages will not come to you until you have seen them all. You
have to go back and read it again. Then you can read the
beginning in the light of the end, and read the end in light of
the beginning. When you go back through the third time, you
can put them in context and in place.

**MR. BENNETT:** Do you know how many tapes have been
introduced in evidence?

**MR. BLAKEY:** By number, no.

**MR. BENNETT:** Have you watched all the tapes?

**MR. BLAKEY:** I have not watched them all.

**MR. BENNETT:** Have you listened to all the audiotapes?

**MR. BLAKEY:** I have not listened to them all.

**MR. BENNETT:** Don't you think under this so-called doctrine
of completeness that you told us about that it would have been
appropriate for you to do that before testifying today?

**MR. BLAKEY:** No.

When he was finished, Blakey on balance had been more helpful
to me than Senator Williams. The key witness, however, would be the
senator. Senator Williams appeared before the committee and adamantly denied that he had committed any illegal or improper act.
When he began speaking before the committee there was silence in the
hearing room. Blakey was important, but this was the main event.
Williams spoke:

"But I tell this committee under oath that while I may have
been guilty of errors in judgment, while I may have crossed over
the line which divides appropriate service to constituents from
excessive boasting and posturing, I never engaged in any illegal
conduct, I never corrupted my office, and I never intended to do
anything that would bring dishonor to the Senate."

When he completed his opening presentation, I began cross-examination. This was a delicate and challenging responsibility. I certainly had an abundance of evidence to use on cross-examination, but I was concerned about several factors: Senator Williams was a pathetic and lonely figure who was fighting hard to keep his job. I knew that there were many senators, who while they disapproved of his conduct, felt sorry for him and were still angry at the Department of Justice for its aggressive investigative techniques. Moreover, the members of the jury—the committee members—were his friends and colleagues. If this were a regular civil or criminal trial, jurors with the same relationships would be recused from judging his case because of their friendship and relationship with him and their lack of independence. Under these circumstances, I knew that I had to be low key and respectful, but at the same time elicit from him testimony which would show that his claim of innocence was not supported by the evidence and that his acts were not simply errors in judgment because of misplaced friendship but were acts of personal greed.

Before I conducted any tough cross-examination, I wanted to elicit a number of admissions from him. Here is how I proceeded:

**MR. BENNETT:** It is a fact, isn't it, Senator, that this Piney River, if I can refer to it as a titanium mine, existed long before ABSCAM.

**SENATOR WILLIAMS:** Piney River is an area that has been mined by American Cyanamid. At Piney River, American Cyanamid did have a processing plant, as I understand it. They closed down that operation in the early seventies, I believe.

**MR. BENNETT:** So the titanium mine, if we can just refer to it as the mine, was not the creation . . . of any law enforcement authority. That was something already in existence. Isn't that fair to say?

**SENATOR WILLIAMS:** It is fair to say. It certainly was.

**MR. BENNETT:** It is also fair to say—I am not suggesting any impropriety at all about this—that you had a good friend, Sandy

Williams, who was interested in that mine and you to the extent that you legitimately could, prior to ABSCAM, wanted to assist Sandy. Is that fair to say?

**SENATOR WILLIAMS:** I did and I had. I knew his financial problems and as I believe I mentioned in my statement, had suggested an investment banking firm in New York to him. He went there and had fruitful discussions, though unsuccessful.

I was not with him. When it was all over, I called the person I had called at the firm and thanked him.

**MR. BENNETT:** You were such good friends with Sandy . . . that Sandy in 1976 gave to you what has been referred to as a gift letter and without regard to its legal status, he at least gave you something which indicated to you that he wanted you in the future to share in his success.

Is that a fair characterization of it? . . .

**SENATOR WILLIAMS:** It looked to me as though he was making a promise to me that sometime in the near future he would get me something. That is the way it looked to me.

**MR. BENNETT:** You took that, you gave it to somebody, and I believe it was put some place in your file.

**SENATOR WILLIAMS:** That is right.

I then wanted to show that his good friends who he trusted had testi-fied that the senator had a financial interest in the enterprise he was try-ing to help.

**MR. BENNETT:** Unfortunately, you had two friends: Sandy Williams and a friend, a lawyer by the name of Alexander Feinberg [a co-defendant in the criminal case], again to be distinguished from your present counsel. Is that right?

**SENATOR WILLIAMS:** Alex and Sandy, yes.

**MR. BENNETT:** At that point in time, Senator, is it fair for me to say that . . . you at least viewed them as good friends and at least up to that point in time you had no reason to question their integrity or their trustworthiness. Is that a fair statement?

**SENATOR WILLIAMS:** It is fair.

**MR. BENNETT:** My question to you is why would these friends, these loyal friends . . . whose truthfulness you said you had no reason to question . . . say . . . Senator Williams has an interest?

**SENATOR WILLIAMS:** The only one that I heard from what you just said was I was on the other line to hear Alex say, "Life will be beautiful." Is that right?

**MR. BENNETT:** Feinberg talks on Volume 6, page 88, Exhibit 13-A, he is talking to you about your meeting with the sheik and he says, "Life is going to be beautiful, Pete." The other reference is Volume 6, page 38, and in response to an inquiry, Sandy Williams says that Feinberg is there for the purpose of "keeping Pete Williams' interest."

**SENATOR WILLIAMS:** Are these in my [presence]—

**MR. BENNETT:** No, they are not in your presence, Senator. But where I am having some difficulty is why would your friends who you have admitted are good friends of yours and whose truthfulness you have just said you don't question, why should they be telling these people that you have an interest if you didn't have an interest?

Senator Williams could not answer the question and looked flustered.

I then confronted Senator Williams with the statements of Mel Weinberg, the FBI informant who had prepared him in a coaching session for his meeting with the sheik and who told the senator what to say. Unknown to the senator, Weinberg, a man with a sleazy reputation, was working as an FBI operative in this sting operation. The point I was trying to make was that an honest senator, only doing his job, would not be following a script prepared by the likes of Mel Weinberg. Much of what I was doing was suggesting to the senators on the committee that Williams acted differently than they would under similar circumstances.

**MR. BENNETT:** But let me read what Mel Weinberg says. He says on page 95, he says to you, a United States senator, he says,

"Without you there is no deal. You are the deal. You put this together. You worked on this and you can get, you have got the government contracts. Without me there is no government contracts. You know the names to mention. . . ."

Senator, my question to you is when he said that to you, when somebody like a Mel Weinberg said that to you, why didn't you get up and leave the room? . . .

Why didn't you walk out? Why didn't you tell him to go to hell? . . .

And you tried to impress the sheik with all of this even though, as you have just said a moment ago, you thought it was pie-in-the-sky?

SENATOR WILLIAMS: I thought the hundred-million-dollar Savannah job was pie-in-the-sky. I didn't think Piney River was pie-in-the-sky. That is why I, years before, a couple of years before, had introduced Henry Fowler, the investment banker, to these people, to Sandy Williams.

MR. BENNETT: Senator, you then made the conscious decision, which you have referred to as your major tragic mistake of puffing. Is that right, to the sheik?

SENATOR WILLIAMS: This was the first. This was, following the coaching session, which I interpreted as "try to impress the sheik." And I accepted that and I went up there and did, to a degree, and to an uncomfortable degree, talk about my importance, yes. . . .

MR. BENNETT: You say that you just knew you weren't going to get government contracts. Is that what you are saying?

SENATOR WILLIAMS: I was not going to deal with government contracts at all, no.

MR. BENNETT: Senator, let me direct your attention, if you will, to volume 6. This is the June 28, 1979, meeting, which was videotaped with you and others and most importantly the sheik. I am referring to page 108. Just prior to 108, you come in and you see the sheik and you meet him and you tell him that this fellow who owns the hotel the sheik is staying in owes you a lot of favors. You say at the bottom of the page, and I am going to quote. Now remember, you have just told us that you are not going to get contracts. You say the following:

"The Soviets are doing it; we're not. We are behind in this respect. They've got a fast submarine titanium sheathed. We don't. One of the reasons, I'm sure, is we are without supply of titanium available. There's only one manufacturer in the country of titanium metal. This is, this deposit presents an opportunity to come on [with] one of the most valuable metals that can be produced, titanium metal. And if this can be put together, in my position with, within our government here, which goes back decades, and knowing as I do the people that make the decisions, with, when we've got it together, we move. We move with our government and we catch up, we go ahead, we have what we need, which we don't have now. . . ."

Senator, my question to you is do you think a senator of the Senate of the United States of America, which has been described as the greatest deliberative body in the world, should be talking this way to some purported sheik? Does that hold this body in disrepute or doesn't it?

**SENATOR WILLIAMS:** I don't believe it does. For me to be bragging, made me, as I said, uncomfortable. To talk to a sheik about the people you know, who are in important positions, it would seem to me that this would be impressive to him. So if you are asking whether it is improper to do this to the sheik, I don't think it is improper. Whether it is wise or good judgment for a senator to do it, without regard to who he is talking to, I would say I don't think it is a very good practice. And I never do it. I did, in this context, do it.

Senator Williams was getting himself in deeper and deeper. He realized that he had to testify that he never promised government contracts, but in doing so he showed how duplicitous he was by implying that he would.

**MR. BENNETT:** You never wanted to get government contracts?

**SENATOR WILLIAMS:** Never, ever.

**MR. BENNETT:** Did you ever tell that sheik that?

**SENATOR WILLIAMS:** No. I never told the sheik "I will get government contracts," no.

**MR. BENNETT:** You certainly let him have that impression that you would though, didn't you, Senator?

**SENATOR WILLIAMS:** If he got it, he got it right from things other people said and it is true, I did not make a big speech against what was being said.

**MR. BENNETT:** You not only did not make a big speech, you didn't leave the room, you didn't contradict what was being said, and you let somebody like Angelo Errichetti [a New Jersey State Senator at the time of ABSCAM and a former mayor of Camden, New Jersey] say we move mountains and you said, well, you got two senators here. And you went on a litany of government officials, the president, the vice president, chairmen of departments.

That is what I don't understand, Senator Williams. Explain why you did that. Can you explain how that is in any way in keeping with the dignity of the United States Senate?

**SENATOR WILLIAMS:** I tell you, I did absolutely nothing wrong, improper. I boasted about people I knew. I don't like it, never do it, did it here, kick myself for doing it. It was part of something that was suggested in a meeting which, if you take out the obscenity of expression of Mel Weinberg, left me with the impression that this sheik can be impressed with a person in a high office. I still thought there was a shot at getting through to the sheik on the value of the little mine down in Piney River, not the big bonanza of Savannah, Georgia.

But this was the one shot and I tried to impress him according to the script. Unbecoming, but I told him about what I thought had a reasonable business possibility, my friend's mine. Whatever they got—well.

It was obvious to everyone in the hearing room that Senator Williams's denials of improper conduct were baseless. While I felt good about my examination, I also felt pity for a distinguished senator disintegrating in public. It was obvious to everyone. While I could have gone on, I decided that it would be overkill.

Following the July hearing, on August 13, 1981, I submitted the "Report of Special Counsel." My partner, Alan Kriegel, and I with the assistance of a young attorney named David Schlitz, worked night and day to analyze the record, reach our conclusions, and write a report within thirty days of the hearing. The committee specifically asked me to make a recommendation regarding the appropriate sanction, if we found a violation.

Following a careful analysis of the record, my recommendation was that Senator Williams's conduct was so egregious that he should be expelled. I did not take this recommendation lightly because no senator had been expelled since the Civil War. Nevertheless, I felt that the Senate as an institution would be seriously damaged if it imposed a lesser sanction. In my opinion, the public would be outraged if a convicted senator was allowed to remain in the Senate.

On August 24, 1981, the Senate Ethics Committee held an all-day closed-door session to consider its decision, and on September 3, 1981, the committee consisting of Malcolm Wallop, chairman; Howell Heflin, vice chairman; and members Jesse Helms, Mack Mattingly, David Pryor, and Thomas Eagleton recommended that the Senate agree to the following Resolution:

*Resolved,* That the conduct of Senator Harrison A. Williams Jr. of New Jersey in connection with his agreement to use his official position to further a business venture in which he and others had a financial interest was in violation of the laws of the United States and the Standing Rules of the Senate, was ethically repugnant, and tends to bring the Senate into dishonor and disrepute; and that therefore, pursuant to Article 1, Section 5, Clause 2 of the United States Constitution, Senator Harrison A.

Williams Jr. be, and hereby is, expelled from the United States Senate.

The matter now moved to the full Senate.

While it was indisputable that Senator Williams had committed crimes and had engaged in personal corruption by accepting a bribe in connection with his office, I was uncertain what would happen in the full Senate. One would think that expelling a senator who was a convicted felon was a no-brainer, but the bonds that tie members in one of the most exclusive clubs in the world are sometimes stronger than the demands of common sense or loyalty to the institution. Senator Daniel K. Inouye, a Democrat from Hawaii, agreed to act as Williams's lawyer on the Senate floor. Senator Inouye, a war hero, was one of the most respected members in the Senate, and I was concerned that his fellow senators did not want to say no to him. It was clear that Senator Williams was going to fight his expulsion aggressively. Senator Williams had tried to enjoin the Senate from acting on his expulsion by filing a suit in the United States District Court for the District of Columbia. This request was denied by District Judge Gerhard A. Gesell. Judge Gesell wisely concluded that this was a matter for the Senate and not the courts.

Williams had some success when at the request of Senator Inouye, the Senate agreed to a delay. Senator Inouye argued that he needed more time to prepare a defense. The leadership granted the request on the basis of senatorial courtesy. Following further delays for a variety of reasons, the Senate debate on the expulsion resolution was scheduled for March 3. The debate on the resolution lasted for five days. I was on the Senate floor with Vice Chairman Heflin, who I was honored to be sitting next to, when he presented the case against Williams. What was particularly memorable was that the chamber was full as the Senate leadership required all senators to be present. Senator Heflin made a powerful presentation and emphasized that in the face of such "sleazy characters" as were depicted on the tape, Williams should have walked away.

Senator Williams made a request to allow his personal lawyer, who was a private practitioner, to speak on his behalf, but this was denied. Under the rules of that chamber, only senators can speak on the floor. On March 4, Senator Williams presented his defense. Senator Williams's six-hour presentation was ineffective as he read his speech in a rambling fashion. As the floor debate went on, it became increasingly clear that if put to a vote, Senator Williams would lose and be expelled. As troubled as they were about the Justice Department's tactics, the senators could not ignore the fact that unless they took action against him, a convicted felon would remain in the Senate. If there was any doubt about the outcome, it ended when Senator Tom Eagleton of Missouri stood up to speak. As he rose, there was total silence in the chamber. Senator Eagleton was a respected liberal member of the Democratic party and a long-time friend of Williams, and if he did not support Williams, few others would. I will never forget that moment. Obviously upset with the situation in which he found himself, he then delivered the knock-out punch. He said, "Senator Williams has not had the good grace to withdraw from this body. We should not perpetuate our disgrace by asking him to stay."

Because of Eagleton's stature and relationship with Williams, he gave cover to others who would vote for expulsion. It was one of the most dramatic moments I have every observed. Senator Inouye knew that if he could not keep the support of fellow Democrats like Eagleton, there was no hope for Williams. During a short recess, he walked over to me and said, "Bob, it's over." Shortly thereafter, Williams gave his final speech in the Senate by announcing his decision to resign. It was a sad but dramatic ending as ninety-nine senators and then–Vice President George Bush, were in the chamber hearing his words. At the end of the day, Williams did not want to be the first senator to be expelled since the Civil War. Since 1789, the Senate had only expelled fifteen of its members. Fourteen of those were charged with supporting the Confederacy during the Civil War. Senator Williams would later go to prison because of his criminal conviction. Up to this time, in the entire history of the Senate, only four members have been convicted of a crime. It is always sad when a man who did so much good ends his public career in disgrace. This matter was a good example of how power corrupts and why those in power

must be careful because they are magnets for a whole variety of despica-
ble characters. Also, I learned from a trial lawyer's perspective, you cannot assume any fact finder—in this case a Senate body—will do the right
thing. You must make it impossible for the fact finder to do the wrong
thing.

# CHAPTER TEN

# DON'T BRING AIDES—THEIR FRIEND KEATING

I AM OFTEN ASKED which case in my career was the most professionally challenging and difficult. The answer is simple: The Keating Five. There isn't a close second. As Senator Warren Rudman wrote in his book *Combat: Twelve Years in the U.S. Senate,* "Bob Bennett, was in the fight of his life." There is a wonderful story of an Irishman who when walking down the street sees two strangers fighting outside a pub. "Excuse me," he says, "is this a private matter or can I join in?" Well, the Irish in me welcomed the challenge, but I must confess this was more than I bargained for.

The failure of Charles Keating's Lincoln Savings and Loan in California in 1989 was described at the time as the greatest financial scandal in the history of the United States. Lincoln was one of numerous S&Ls that went belly-up in the late eighties, in the wake of deregulation of the industry. The collapse of Lincoln, and the other savings and loans, wiped out the savings of many thousands of depositors and cost the taxpayers billions of dollars. A Special Commission created to study the causes of the crisis concluded that the total cost to the government of protecting insured depositories from loss as a result of the S&L collapse was estimated to be between $150 billion and $175 billion.

It was clear from the commission's report that the finger of blame could be pointed in many different directions, but what captured the press and the public was the report that five United States senators had accepted—in one form or another—in excess of $1 million in campaign contributions from Charles Keating or industries and employees related to him or his S&L. At the same time, they interceded on Keating's behalf with government officials who were trying to regulate his savings and loan's high-risk activities. While these senators did not cause the crisis, they became the highly visible poster boys for it. The public demanded action and the Senate Ethics Committee was virtually forced to open an investigation of what became known as the Keating Five.

Over the years, Charles Keating had been exceedingly generous with members of Congress and he was very aggressive in calling in his chits. Keating focused much of his lobbying activities against legislation that would limit the amount that federally insured S&Ls could invest in high-risk ventures. This legislation, known as the direct investment rule, struck at the heart of Lincoln's highly speculative ventures. Since the ceiling on federal deposit insurance had been increased in the Carter administration from $40,000 to $100,000, an entrepreneur like Keating could—without a direct investment rule—gamble with other people's money. It was like the United States government insuring your losses at a Las Vegas casino. When investigators began to question the activities of Lincoln, Keating lined up several senators who were beneficiaries of his generosity to take on the regulators.

The critical meeting that, when it became public, would turn the Washington scandal machine into high gear, occurred on April 2, 1987. The evening meeting took place in the office of Senator Dennis DeConcini of Arizona with Edwin Gray, the chairman of the Federal Home Loan Bank Board—also known as FHLBB, the regulator of Lincoln. Gray, who was appointed by Ronald Reagan, would testify that he was summoned to the meeting in Senator DeConcini's office and that he was told to come without aides. When Gray appeared at DeConcini's office, he found several powerful senators, also without aides present. Those in attendance were DeConcini, Senator Alan Cranston of California, Senator John McCain of Arizona, and Senator John Glenn of Ohio. A fifth senator, Donald Riegle of Michigan, was expected to attend, but did not. Gray testified that someone from Senator DeConcini's office had set up the meeting and that when he arrived, Senator DeConcini, who played the role of host, started the meeting by telling Gray that they were there to talk about "their friend" Charles Keating.

Understandably, Gray felt intimidated by this powerful show of influence exerted on behalf of Charles Keating. According to Gray, DeConcini offered a bargain. If Gray would not enforce the direct investment rule against Lincoln, "their friend," Charles Keating, would make more home loans. Gray later testified that while he felt intimidated, he stood his ground and said that he was just doing what Congress wanted him to do regarding S&Ls and that he would not make an exception for Lincoln. Gray suggested that the senators meet with his key staff people who were much more knowledgeable than he about Lincoln. On April 9, 1987, the second meeting took place. In attendance were the key FHLBB personnel, and Senators DeConcini, Glenn, McCain, Riegle, and Cranston made a brief appearance. While there was some disagreement as to what occurred at the first meeting, there was no dispute as to what occurred on April 9 in DeConcini's office because William Black, the general counsel of FHLBB, took twenty-eight pages of detailed notes, which read like a transcript. It was clear that Keating was getting special treatment. This was not normal constituent service. The regulators, to their credit, stood up to the senators. They told the senators that based on their investigation, they were sending a criminal referral to the Department of Justice. Upon hearing that there was a criminal referral, Senators McCain and Glenn pulled back on helping Keating with the regulators, but Cranston, Riegle, and DeConcini continued in their efforts.

Once the meetings became public and the financial links between Keating and the senators were widely reported, the scandal intensified. The public and the press demanded an investigation. On September 25, 1989, the ethics committee received a complaint regarding Senator Glenn filed by the Chairman of the Ohio Republican Party, Robert T. Bennett (no relation to me), and on October 13, 1989, Common Cause filed a complaint related to these allegations asking that the ethics committee conduct an investigation to determine whether the relationship between the senators and Keating violated the rules of conduct of the Senate or the federal election laws. Amid this escalating controversy, there was no way the Senate could avoid an investigation. I could not say no when Senators Heflin and Rudman asked me to take on the Keating matter. On November 17, 1989, I was appointed as special counsel.

While I have handled many matters involving politics, I have never allowed politics to interfere with my work. As a result, I have been asked to represent high-profile Republicans including former Secretary of Defense Caspar Weinberger and high-profile Democrats such as former President Bill Clinton and former Secretary of Defense Clark Clifford. While my representation of many of my political clients is publicly known, my representation of others is not. I have over the years developed trusting relationships and friendships on both sides of the aisle and with the leadership of both parties. These nonpartisan relationships would become invaluable to me in the Keating and other cases.

At the very beginning, I had to deal immediately with one problem that raised its ugly head. If I could not control it, my investigation was doomed to failure. That problem was ex parte contacts—that is, the backdoor contacts among the senators under investigation, either directly or through other senators with the members of the committee. For example, I learned that effort was made to limit my speaking role by making me only an advisor to the committee. Also, effort was made to prevent me from expressing my view as to the wrongdoing of any senator at the hearing. I was deeply troubled by such contacts. This inappropriate lobbying by the senators under investigation became so intense that I asked Chairman Heflin and Vice Chairman Rudman to send a letter to the senators under investigation admonishing them to stop contacting members of the committee, who after all, were the judges in the case. This letter was sent, but some ex parte contacts continued.

Even if there had been no partisanship, the Keating case would have been difficult for several reasons. First of all, in Keating we were dealing with two of the Senate's sacred cows—raising money and constituent service. Second, I very early on discovered that there were virtually no precedents to guide the committee in deciding what were the applicable standards to apply to the facts of the case. Most of the material in Senate archives related to Civil War cases where allegiance to the Confederacy was a basis for action. When I asked the committee to provide me with the applicable standards, they told me to make my own recommendations. Third, the senators under inquiry were some of the most powerful in the body, and a few, like DeConcini, attacked me personally as to my motives and my approach. For all those reasons and more, I was faced with a monumental challenge.

I asked my colleague Amy Sabrin to help me research the issues and precedents for resolving them. Amy and I read everything that would help us determine the applicable standards. We asked Senate Legal Counsel and the Congressional Research Service for help, but there were few modern precedents. Fortunately, Senator Paul Douglas of Illinois, a lion of the Senate, had written a report years before entitled "Ethical Standards in Government." Douglas was the chairman of the special sub-committee on the establishment of the Commission on Ethics. In addition, Douglas authored a short book entitled *Ethics in Government*, published by the Harvard University Press in 1952, which was the substance of three lectures he gave at Harvard that year. It is a brilliant work to which, unfortunately, the Senate has paid little attention. These materials were very helpful and guided us in our work.

Two other things were also of great help. I was familiar with the writings of Dennis Thompson, director of the Edmond J. Safra Foundation Center for Ethics at Harvard University and retained him as a consultant to help us wade through the issues. However, I recognized that notwithstanding my familiarity with the Senate, I was not a member. I did not have firsthand experience as a senator. Since I wanted to be sure I was being fair to the senators, I contacted a handful of former respected members of Congress—both House and Senate—who had unimpeachable reputations for the highest ethical standards. I told them that I would not disclose their identities to anyone but wanted their input. Also, I told them that I would not share with them any details I learned in my investigation. I simply wanted to discuss in general terms my approach to the investigation, the standards that I thought should apply, and get from them their views as to what kind of conduct crossed the line from legitimate fund-raising and constituent service into unethical conduct. These former members of Congress provided me with great insight and understanding and gave me the confidence of knowing that I was on the right track. It was my job to apply the standards of the Senate to the facts of the

case. It would not have been appropriate simply to apply what I thought
the standards should be. This is why I felt that as part of my preparation,
I must get the insight of former members of Congress who were known to
be honest and ethical. I wanted to know how they raised money and how
they handled constituent service. While I had a pretty good idea of how
Congress works, I wanted the insight of insiders.

I had put together an extraordinarily able team of lawyers from my
firm. Amy Sabrin served as my strong right arm, and we along with Bon-
nie Austin, Abby Raphael, Ben Klubes, and E. Vaughan Dunnigan conducted a thorough investigation of the matter to determine whether or
not any of the senators should face charges by the Senate Ethics Committee. Frankly, the Keating investigation should have been resolved in a few
months and not years, but because of the partisanship and fighting
among members and intrusion of the Democratic leadership, every issue
was endlessly debated, and I was often caught in the crossfire. Vice Chairman Warren Rudman, a Republican from New Hampshire, accurately described in *Combat* what occurred:

> For nearly two years, from late 1989 until late 1991, as we and
> the Democrats deadlocked along party lines, we were playing a
> dangerous game. The Democrats wanted the least possible pun-
> ishment for the Five and were stalling, hoping we would give in.
> We were stalling too. The difference, as I saw it, was our motiva-
> tions. The Democrats were trying to save their party. We were try-
> ing to save the Senate, which would be disgraced if the actions of
> three of the Five went unpunished.

During our investigation, we obtained documents from ninety individuals and organizations and interviewed approximately one hundred
and fifty individuals. Moreover, we took several depositions and obtained
fifty affidavits from people with relevant information.

Several witnesses who were subpoenaed to testify invoked their Fifth
Amendment constitutional privilege not to testify. As a result of the S&L
crisis, Mr. Keating and his companies were embroiled in multiple crimi-

nal and civil matters. By court order, I was given access to a document depository established by the federal court in Arizona. This gave my team and me access to thirteen thousand boxes of documents relevant to the activities under investigation.

Each of the senators was informed of the evidence concerning his conduct and was invited to make a response to the Common Cause complaint. In March or April, each of the senators was deposed behind closed doors in the presence of committee members, and each was given an opportunity to not only make written submissions, but to also appear before the committee in Executive Session.

At the completion of my investigation, I filed my report with the committee. I recommended that no further action be taken against Senators McCain and Glenn principally because once they learned that there was a criminal referral, they stopped aggressively doing Keating's bidding with the regulators. However, I also recommended that the committee proceed with ethics charges against Senators Cranston, DeConcini, and Riegle and hold a hearing to look into their conduct. I believed that the evidence showed clearly that these three had violated Senate Rules and should be held accountable. My recommendation that the only Republican in the group, John McCain, be exonerated caused a big political problem, but my recommendations were based on evidence and not politics.

After reviewing my report, the committee voted on October 23, 1990, to hold a public adjudicatory fact-finding hearing in the matter as to all five senators.

This was perhaps the first time the recommendation of a special counsel not to charge a senator was rejected. This was pure politics as the Democrats on the committee did not want to cut McCain loose so that only Democrats would remain in the proceedings. If Senator McCain was not going to be cut loose, in retaliation the Republicans were going to keep Senator Glenn in the proceedings. McCain was the victim of politics, and poor Glenn was held captive to the decision on McCain. So much for nonpartisanship. Also, the decision to hold a fact-finding hearing before any ethics charges could be brought was absurd and would cause a great deal of delay. I had been appointed special counsel on November 17, 1989. For almost one year, my staff and I investigated the case—we knew all of the facts that could be known. The senators on the committee were actively involved in the fact-finding process and the senators under investigation had been given full opportunity to present facts and arguments to the committee. Therefore, to suggest that the facts were not known and that it was necessary to schedule a public hearing for the purpose of finding the facts made little sense, but the senators under inquiry were successful in stopping the committee from making findings and filing charges against any of them, at least for the time being.

Despite their efforts, they were not successful in their efforts to derail a public hearing. While I was disappointed that the committee did not drop McCain and Glenn and did not immediately require Cranston, DeConcini, and Riegle to face ethics charges brought by the committee, I was pleased that I had won the most important battle, which was to hold a public hearing. I had forcefully argued behind closed doors that the integrity of the Senate required a public hearing and that the failure to hold one would cause great damage to the reputation of the Senate. Although the public airing of the factual details helped confirm why Senators McCain and Glenn should be exonerated of ethics charges, it hurt DeConcini, Cranston, and Riegle. They would have been better off if the proceedings were shortened and not lengthened and resolved in a manner without a public hearing. This is so because the facts were bad and the conduct of DeConcini, Cranston, and Riegle was far worse than that of McCain and Glenn. Also, because there was a public hearing that was televised for twenty-six days, the story of wrongdoing got maximum exposure and was the subject of daily press reports.

The hearings began on November 15, 1990; after twenty-six days of public sessions, which generated five thousand pages of hearing transcripts, they ended on January 16, 1991. The format clearly followed that of a criminal case in a federal court.

It became very clear from the beginning that the public was fascinated with the hearings and wanted an honest inquiry, to be done by special counsel. They did not like me being criticized or attacked by any senator. While there was often a great deal of tension between myself and Senator Heflin behind the scenes, this did not occur in public. Because of my position, the press and the public viewed me as an independent lawyer trying to do an honest job, and any public criticism of me, however mild, resulted in phone calls and letters to committee members telling them to leave me alone.

On one occasion, Vice Chairman Warren Rudman gently suggested that he did not particularly like a line of questioning I was engaged in. Here is what he said:

> "Now, Mr. Chairman, if I may take another minute, Mr. Chairman, I am just kind of concerned about the course of this morning.
>
> "I say this with great affection for our special counsel and in respect for this witness who I think is trying to be very truthful and very candid, and has been during our sessions for the last two days, but this morning sounds more to me like an oversight hearing of the FHLBB, and what Mr. Keating thinks about the world . . .
>
> "I am just going to speak for myself and say I do not care much about that."

At the break following this comment, Senator Rudman invited me into his office to meet recently appointed Supreme Court Justice David Souter. As I entered his office, Senator Rudman's phones were ringing off the hook. The callers were complaining that he should leave me alone and let me do my job. We all had a good laugh, and Rudman commented that I was all but untouchable from the public's perspective. I was thrilled to meet Justice Souter, and he bowled me over when he said his mother was watching the hearings and liked me and would be impressed that he had met me. Frankly, it was I who was impressed to meet Mrs. Souter's son.

Following my opening statement, which lasted more than four hours, the senators began their opening statements. If there was any doubt that this was going to be twenty-six days of warfare, that doubt was dispelled when Senator DeConcini gave his opening statement. He went on to attack me personally and accused me of trophy hunting. In response to DeConcini's "trophy" remark, I stated that the only trophy I wanted was a "big brown trout" from the Yellowstone River. Within days of that remark, I received a letter from Phil Wright, a fishing guide in Montana and a devoted follower of C-SPAN. He loved my remark and offered to guide me down the Yellowstone River in Montana. When I told him I had a home in Montana and was an avid fly-fisherman, our close friendship began. Phil, who was the best fly caster I ever met, and I spent many hours together on Montana rivers.

Behind the scenes, Senator Heflin admonished me to be as neutral as I could in my presentation of the evidence. The Republican senators, however, felt I should be more aggressive given the facts and the concern that if I was too neutral and understated in the face of five aggressive and top-flight defense lawyers, the hearings would be viewed as a whitewash. In response to one of his attacks, I responded, "Senator DeConcini and his counsel would like me to be a flower girl distributing the flowers at a wedding in equal shares to each senator without regard to the evidence. I will not do that." I would not do it for several reasons.

The culpability of DeConcini, Riegle, and Cranston far exceeded that of McCain and Glenn, and I did not think it fair to present the evidence in a way that made it look like all were equally culpable. Even those Democrats on the committee such as David Pryor and Terry Sanford, both fair-minded men, realized I had to defend myself. Accordingly, DeConcini and Cranston's adversarial approach made it easier for me to do the job the way I thought it should be done. DeConcini pulled out all the stops. Frankly, I did not take it personally, nor did I blame him, and at some level I respected his moxie. After all, he was fighting for his political life. As a former prosecutor, DeConcini knew how to lay traps hoping that I would fall into them. For example, he called as witnesses on his behalf two of the country's most respected public figures—

Senator Daniel Inouye and former federal judge and United States attorney general Griffin Bell. Both men testified that Senator DeConcini was a man of good reputation, that it was appropriate for a senator to intercede with regulators on a constituent's behalf, and that the fact that the constituent who received help contributed to the senator made no difference. Of course, Jim Hamilton, DeConcini's attorney, in his direct examination of them, wisely stayed away from the details of Senator DeConcini's actions. What was I to do? It was clear that the committee, particularly the Democratic members, were impressed with Senator Inouye and former attorney general Bell. Both were likeable witnesses.

Neither of them really hurt my case. Sometimes the best cross-examination is none at all because it communicates to the fact finder that the witness did not hurt your case. I decided not to take a chance because I was concerned that those committee members who wanted to exculpate the senators under inquiry would use unchallenged testimony to do just that. I decided that I would try to undercut their testimony without discrediting them personally. Had I attacked them as political friends trying to help out their buddies—which I might have done if we had a real jury of ordinary citizens—it could have backfired. In this situation, I had to proceed cautiously. In listening to their testimony, it was clear that they were not well versed in the details, and I concluded that being busy men, they did minimal preparation for their testimony. I therefore decided that I would take the approach that their conclusions were of little value since they didn't know the facts. Also, I knew that both Inouye and Bell were men of good reputation and personal integrity and that they would answer my questions truthfully. Based upon my knowledge of them, I thought that on a few critical issues I could turn Senator Inouye and Griffin Bell as favorable witnesses for us.

When I told the committee I wanted to cross-examine them, there were looks of surprise. Why would special counsel take on such prominent and highly regarded witnesses, particularly since the committee members were falling all over themselves to welcome them to the hearings? Sometimes a lawyer must go where angels fear to tread, and I did,

but was very careful. When I began my cross-examination of Senator Inouye, I reminded him of our earlier good relations in the Williams case.
It is sometimes important to make a witness feel comfortable; other
times, the opposite is true. In this case, the former was the way to go.
Here is how I dealt with him in cross-examination:

> **MR. BENNETT:** Senator, it is nice to see you again.
>
> **MR. INOUYE:** My pleasure, sir.
>
> **MR. BENNETT:** Senator, the last time we talked, you
> represented Senator Williams, and I had the good fortune of
> being special counsel in that case, and it is nice to see you again.

My approach with Senator Inouye was to get him to admit certain
principles that were at the heart of my case.

> **MR. BENNETT:** Senator, do you feel there are any limits to
> constituent service? Or do you feel that because one is a
> constituent, you as a United States senator can virtually do
> anything that they ask you to do?
>
> **MR. INOUYE:** Oh, there are limitations set by law, by Senate
> Regulations, Senate Rules.
>
> **MR. BENNETT:** Do you feel that, while a senator can
> intervene with a regulator, indeed put pressure on a regulator,
> do you feel there are any limits? Or do you feel a United States
> senator in the name of oversight, or in the name of constituent
> service, can put as much pressure on as he wants?
>
> **MR. INOUYE:** Within the law, and if he is wise, he would be
> politically conscious.
>
> **MR. BENNETT:** Do you believe, Senator, that a United States
> senator has a public trust, and that in the performance of his
> public trust he or she should at least be sensitive to the
> appearances of impropriety so that the American people have
> confidence in the integrity of government? You would agree
> with that?
>
> **MR. INOUYE:** As a major officer of the government, yes, sir.

A trial lawyer must appreciate that honey sometimes—and this was one of those times—catches more flies than vinegar, and so I proceeded as follows:

> **MR. BENNETT:** You do not remember, because you work with so many people, but one of the great pleasures in my life was working with you, albeit on slightly opposite sides, in the Williams case.
>
> You have always lived your senatorial life with great dignity, and with great concern that your actions appeared to your constituents to give them confidence that the government was working in the way it was supposed to be working.
>
> Is that not a fair statement?
>
> **MR. INOUYE:** I have tried my best, sir.
>
> **MR. BENNETT:** And from all reports, Senator, you have been enormously successful.
>
> So you would agree that it is important for senators to act in a way which appears to people to be honest and above-board? You agree with that, do you not?
>
> **MR. INOUYE:** Oh, yes. It would be politically wise to do that.

Assuming that Senator Inouye had not spent extensive time preparing, I wanted, in a gentle fashion, to suggest to the committee that his support of the senators under inquiry was not the result of an extensive review of the record.

> **MR. BENNETT:** What evidence, Senator, did you review in this case before testifying? And, if you can recall, when was it that you reviewed it?
>
> **MR. INOUYE:** I read this Arthur Young letter once, and I read the memo once, and that was some time ago.
>
> **MR. BENNETT:** But those are the only things that you have read?
>
> **MR. INOUYE:** Yes, sir. And I am not here as an expert witness on the facts, because they are rather complicated.

**MR. BENNETT:** Right. They are complicated.

That was my next point. It is fair to say, is it not, Senator, that you are not here testifying that you have reviewed all of the facts and the evidence in this case—

**MR. INOUYE:** Not at all.

**MR. BENNETT:** —and you have made a judgment or a determination that these senators, or any of them, did nothing wrong?

**MR. INOUYE:** I come here as a colleague of five senators to tell the committee that, like all of them, I have served with the five senators and throughout their service I have never found them to be wanting in honesty or integrity, that they are men of unimpeachable character.

**MR. BENNETT:** If I may, let me rephrase my questions.

You are not here testifying that you have reviewed all of the evidence in this case and you have come to a determination that what each and every one of them did on each event we have been talking about was ethical? You just do not know one way or the other.

**MR. INOUYE:** No, sir.

**MR. BENNETT:** Is that a fair statement?

**MR. INOUYE:** That is a fair statement, sir.

**MR. BENNETT:** Do you remember when it was, Senator, that you first read the evidence? We were notified that you would be a witness on November 9, 1990, by a letter from Mr. Hamilton.

When was it that you read the evidence, those two pieces of paper, or three pieces of paper?

**MR. INOUYE:** About a week before then.

**MR. BENNETT:** . . . [Y]ou did not read the depositions in the case, I take it?

**MR. INOUYE:** No, sir.

**MR. BENNETT:** Any of them?

**MR. INOUYE:** No, sir. . . .

Let me read four standards, and let me ask you if you agree or disagree with them. . . . One, "A Senator should not take contributions from an individual he knows or should know is attempting to procure his services to intervene in a specific matter pending before a federal agency."

As a general principle, do you agree with that?

**MR. INOUYE:** It is a quid pro quo, and that is wrong.

**MR. BENNETT:** The second standard: "A senator should not take unusual or aggressive action with regard to a specific matter before a federal agency on behalf of a contributor when he knows or has reason to know the contributor has sought to procure his services."

Do you agree with that?

**MR. INOUYE:** Do you mean that the contributor gave the money to the senator with the understanding that upon receipt he will provide the service?

**MR. BENNETT:** Yes.

**MR. INOUYE:** Well that is a quid pro quo. That would be wrong.

**MR. BENNETT:** All right. The third standard: "A senator should not conduct his fund-raising efforts or engage in office practices which lead contributors to conclude that they can buy access to him."

**MR. INOUYE:** That is a subjective decision made by the contributor. There are some who feel that all you have to do is contribute and the doors are open, and I think that is wrong.

**MR. BENNETT:** All right. But you would agree, would you not, that a senator can set up his office in such a way, hypothetically, that he is giving the appearance to contributors that [the contributor] has a key to his office? And I take it, if that were to occur, you would agree that that was wrong?

**MR. INOUYE:** It must be hypothetical, because I am not aware of any office that sets it up in that fashion.

**MR. BENNETT:** How does your office handle fund-raising?

**MR. INOUYE:** I do not. . . . Under the Rules of the Senate, I have designated one person in the past to be authorized to receive campaign contributions.

I have not had that in the last two years.

**MR. BENNETT:** Senator, do you ever have that fund-raising person write you memoranda asking you to ask a contributor for a hundred thousand dollars and bringing to your attention that that contributor might be in a good frame of mind because of some activity in the government?

Have you read the memorandum from Joy Jacobson to Senator Cranston?

**MR. INOUYE:** No, sir.

**MR. BENNETT:** Were you aware of the fact that Senator Cranston—Did you hear this opening statement?

**MR. INOUYE:** No, sir.

**MR. BENNETT:** Were you aware of the fact that Senator Cranston, in defense of what his practices were, said that everybody did it, and listed you as one of the senators on his charts as following similar practices as he—which I will tell you I know is not the case—but were you aware of that?

**MR. INOUYE:** No, sir.

**MR. BENNETT:** Now let me ask you this. You are aware of the Code of Government Ethics, which applies across the government?

**MR. INOUYE:** Vaguely, sir.

**MR. BENNETT:** You are aware that that provides an "appearance"-type standard?

**MR. INOUYE:** Yes, sir.

**MR. BENNETT:** Do you believe that other branches of government are subject to that, but United States senators are not?

**MR. INOUYE:** I think the political realities of life would dictate that whatever we do should please our constituents. Now oftentimes whatever pleases my constituents may not please their constituents.

We come from different parts of the United States, and our values may differ.

**MR. BENNETT:** Senator, did you know Senator Hart in whose building we sit?

**MR. INOUYE:** Yes, sir.

**MR. BENNETT:** Was he a friend of yours?

**MR. INOUYE:** I prided my friendship with him.

**MR. BENNETT:** Was he a man of honor and integrity?

**MR. INOUYE:** That is why we named this building after him.

**MR. BENNETT:** Let me read to you, Senator, [what you said] when you named the building after him.

"Philip Aloysius Hart, December 10, 1912 to December 26, 1976, United States Senator 1959 to 1976.

"This building is dedicated by his colleagues to the memory of Philip A. Hart with affection, respect, and esteem, a man of incorruptible integrity and personal courage, strengthened by inner grace and outer gentle manliness.

"He elevated politics to a level of purity that will forever be an example to every elected official. He advanced the cause of human justice, promoted the welfare of the common man, and improved the quality of life. His humility and ethics earned him his place as the conscience of the Senate."

You agree with all of that?

**MR. INOUYE:** Yes, sir.

**MR. BENNETT:** Would you also agree with me that, since senators are to be leaders and not followers, that a senator's conduct in performance of the public trust should not be limited to whether or not a specific rule or a specific standard is violated?

**MR. INOUYE:** I think your observation is correct.

**MR. BENNETT:** I have no further questions. Thank you.

**MR. INOUYE:** But I think it should be pointed out, sir, that there was only one Philip Aloysius Hart, and that is why we named this building after him.

All of us may strive to be another Philip Hart but, like intent and action, they oftentimes do not coincide.

We try our best, but we do fail every so often.

**MR. BENNETT:** Thank you, sir.

When you cross-examine a witness, you must in your preparation learn everything you can about them—what they have written or said before on the subject they are testifying about. This practice of mine was particularly helpful when I cross-examined Griffin Bell, a former judge and attorney general. In our research we found a book written by Judge Bell in which he wrote some things helpful to my position and so on cross-examination of Judge Bell I asked the following:

**MR. BENNETT:** Let me refer you to a statement that you made in a book. This was a tough book to find, Judge Bell.

**JUDGE BELL:** I have a few copies of it, if you want to get a few.

*(Laughter)*

**MR. BENNETT:** Well, I would be pleased to. We found this in the D.C. Public Library.

**VICE CHAIRMAN RUDMAN:** Would you like to give us the title and the year of publication, Mr. Bennett?

**MR. BENNETT:** It is 1982, I believe, and it is a wonderful book. I recommend it to you all. . . .

It is called *Taking Care of the Law* by Griffin Bell.

There is an interesting paragraph here on page 89, and I would just like to read it to you. You say:

"Hand in hand with the Barony principle," which I don't know what that is, I should add, "is the rampant self-dealing that I found to be operating on Capitol Hill. By self-dealing, I mean a member of Congress attempting to influence a government decision to reward himself indirectly by winning benefits for a valued constituent. Self-dealing is difficult to define or to outlaw because Congressmen properly and legitimately serve their constituents by seeking information about matters pending at the agencies.

"The propriety of such a contact comes into question if it is something more than a neutral request for information."

Do you remember writing that?

**JUDGE BELL:** Yes.

It was obvious to all in the hearing room that what troubled me about the kind of conduct engaged in by Senators DeConcini, Cranston, and Riegle also troubled Judge Bell in an earlier life. One thing that the evidence clearly showed was that their conduct was not neutral.

**MR. BENNETT:** What did you mean when you say "more than a neutral request for information," if you recall?

**JUDGE BELL:** That would be—I know what "neutral" means, because I always said we were operating a neutral Justice Department. It was a neutral zone in the government. It has to be neutral. Otherwise, people would not believe in the law. It is something like that that I had in mind, that you ought not to—you ought to be careful to avoid self-interests, not only not to be in a self-interest position, but to avoid the appearance of it. That was what I had in mind.

**MR. BENNETT:** Thank you, Judge Bell.

I do not have anything else.

As it turned out, these witnesses provided valuable testimony on the appearance standard—the standard that says senators must avoid the appearance of impropriety as well as the fact of it—which was important to the proceedings and which Senator DeConcini and the others opposed. If I could show his own witnesses supported such a standard, it would be enormously helpful. We had done much more preparation for our cross-examination of these witnesses than they did for their own testimony. By obtaining all of these relevant prior statements and writings, it gave me valuable information for cross-examination. When I was cross-examining Judge Bell on the helpful statement in his book, Senator Lott entered the room and asked if Judge Bell was my witness or a senator's. From this, I took comfort that my cross-examination was going well.

At the end of the session, Judge Bell thanked me for citing his book. He explained that it hadn't sold as many copies as he hoped and maybe this recent high-profile exposure might increase sales. We laughed and shook hands good-bye.

At the conclusion of the hearing, I presented a report that largely exonerated McCain and Glenn, but that recommended that DeConcini and Riegle be reprimanded and Cranston censured. The Democrats on the committee, notwithstanding the evidence, rejected those recommendations, and the committee was deadlocked for months. Finally, the committee reached a political compromise in which there would be no floor vote, but a decision to reprimand Cranston for improper conduct would be presented on the Senate floor. As to the others, no formal action would be taken but their conduct would be criticized in varying degrees.

As to Senator Cranston, the committee concluded that, "Senator Cranston's improper conduct deserves the fullest, strongest, and most severe sanction that the committee has the authority to impose. THEREFORE, the Senate Select Committee on Ethics, on behalf of and in the name of the United States Senate, does hereby strongly and severely reprimand Senator Alan Cranston."

In reaching its decision on Cranston, the committee noted that there were mitigating circumstances. Senator Cranston was in poor health and he announced his intention not to seek reelection to the Senate. All of this was carefully worked out and a script was agreed upon for presentation on the Senate floor.

While there is no doubt that the conduct of Senator Cranston was the most egregious, it was also obvious that by announcing his decision not to seek reelection, it made it easier for the committee to single him out for the most severe criticism, but also to find it not necessary to take harsher action. After all, he was leaving. I have no doubt that there were behind-the-scenes discussions encouraging his decision.

There were many times during the long and cumbersome process that I thought the committee would do far less, so I was generally satisfied.

Senator Helms, however, was furious and believed the committee had placed partisan politics above the interests of the institution. He was right. Helms was so angry that he took my private report to the committee, adopted it as his own, and publicly released it as his minority report. Throughout the case, Helms was a straight arrow, always placing the interests of the institution above that of any individual senator. Two of my staff were liberal Democrats who by the end of the case became admirers of Senator Helms for calling the shots as he saw them. One of them jokingly said she was losing her sanity. "I have to see a psychiatrist because I love him."

When the carefully scripted compromise regarding Cranston got to the Senate floor, Warren Rudman laid out the basis of the reprimand. Senator Cranston then shocked the chamber. Instead of following the script, he attacked the committee and argued that everybody did what he did. I was down on the floor sitting next to Senator Heflin. I looked at Rudman and he was shaking with anger. In an unforgettable moment, he rose and spoke to a silent chamber:

> "Mr. President, I must say regretfully that, after accepting this committee's recommendations, what I have heard is a statement I can only describe as arrogant, unrepentant, and a smear on this institution. Everybody does not do it.
>
> "Members of this body attempt, by word and deed, publicly and privately, to take great care with their personal conduct as it might be perceived by the American people. That is equally true for Democrats and Republicans, liberals and conservatives. I have found that to be the only unifying thread in this body.
>
> "For the senator from California to rise and give a speech on this floor, after accepting this admonition, this serious reprimand, a reprimand because of circumstances he knew full well, rather than a vote, which I would have preferred, and to blame it

on campaign finance and everybody does it, and you should all be in fear of your lives from the ethics committee, is poppycock. I repeat, regretfully, that the statement is arrogant, it is unrepentant; it is unworthy of the senior senator from California."

The committee was criticized for its leniency, and some claimed it was a whitewash.

While the final results were less than I had hoped for and less than what the evidence warranted, I do believe we accomplished something. While Cranston, Riegle, and DeConcini did not continue in the Senate, Senators McCain and Glenn did. What is more, I can tell you from personal experience, that since the Keating Five investigation, members of Congress are far more reluctant to interfere with executive department investigations on behalf of contributors. I knew that once the decision was made to hold a public hearing, good would come of it because my team and I knew the evidence and that at the end of the day, in the words of Senator Warren Rudman, "rough justice" was done. Also, as much as the committee members disliked the appearance of impropriety standard, the committee effectively adopted it. It was easier for them to say that a colleague appeared to do something wrong than to conclude publicly that he, in fact, did wrong. I was never so glad to have a matter completed as the Keating Five. Each of the committee members expressed their thanks to me. At the end of the hearing, an emotional Jesse Helms handed me a handwritten note that read, "God Bless You." I was deeply touched.

I DO NOT believe that the ethics committees of Congress do a good job. Their processes are cumbersome, structured to ensure delay, and weighted in favor of a member of Congress under investigation. Part of the problem is that ethics enforcement has taken a backseat to partisan politics. In the Williams case, Malcolm Wallop did not let politics enter the room, but by the time I was handling the Keating matter, we could not keep politics out.

Only recently, the House Republican leadership made attempts to weaken the power of the ethics committee after it rebuked leader Tom DeLay. And instead of being concerned that Mr. DeLay, who was under criminal investigation, might have violated House Rules, they worked to change the rules so that if indicted, he could continue to serve in a leadership position. Such an attitude is arrogant and contemptible and shows disrespect for the institution and the constituents it serves. Fortunately, when Congress returned in January of 2006, the leadership abandoned this effort as many rank-and-file Republicans opposed the change. Nevertheless, efforts continued by the leadership to remove Joel Hefley, a Republican from Colorado, who was chairman of the committee when it rebuked Mr. DeLay. I guess the leadership felt that Mr. Hefley was too independent and ethical to head the ethics committee. The sad fact is that many members of Congress, if totally left to their own devices, do not have the will to impose strong ethical standards and are reluctant to take appropriate action against their colleagues. They are frequently trying to devise all sorts of rules, practices, and procedures that are obstacles to a strong enforcement of an ethical culture. For example, the House engaged in a practice where only complaints filed by members could be considered. Can you imagine a big-city police department saying it would only consider complaints against cops filed by other cops and no one else? This, unfortunately, is one more example of Congress applying practices to itself that it would not condone if practiced by others.

Corruption in Congress will not be eliminated or controlled until it has a strong enforcement mechanism. The ethics process now in existence has been described by nonpartisan experts as an "empty" process. In their book *The Broken Branch: How Congress Is Failing America and How to Get It Back on Track*, Thomas E. Mann and Norman J. Ornstein observe that there must be "an independent, outside role in ethics adjudication consistent with Congress's constitutional requirements."

Based upon my experience, they are right. I also believe that the process should be shortened. There should not be a fact-finding investigation by special counsel only to be followed by another fact-finding investigation by the committee. In addition, there should be specified sanctions with fixed meanings that should be adhered to and the elimination of the practice of allowing a congressperson to negotiate a departure from the established sanctions and their common meaning.

During my representation of the Senate Ethics Committee, I found that endless hours were spent negotiating terms regarding sanctions. Senators and their creative lawyers always tried to use words that softened the political impact of a sanction. Terms such as *disapprove* or *admonish* or *denounce* were the subject of endless debate. This game-playing should be eliminated.

A shortened process would minimize delay and would change what is now a nearly endless opportunity for partisan dispute at each of the multiple steps that are part of the ethics procedures.

While I do not believe that Congress will ever agree to share any part of the process with a specially appointed independent body, I think that it would be in its interest to do so. There are many honorable men and women in Congress who adhere to appropriate ethical standards. Their ethical conduct should not be diminished by a cumbersome process that places politics above ethics and allows the unethical members of Congress to avoid being held accountable. A recent example of the refusal of Congress to hold its members accountable is the failure of the House Ethics Committee to find anyone accountable in the Mark Foley investigation regarding Mr. Foley's inappropriate conduct toward congressional pages. While the report of the committee acknowledges serious and troubling conduct and knowledge of that conduct by members of Congress and staff, it gives a free pass to all members and their staffs by not finding any violation on the part of any individual. This caused the *Washington Post* to ask in an editorial on December 9, 2006, "What, one has to wonder, would it take for the House Ethics Committee to hold a lawmaker or a staff member accountable?" And, on the same day, the *New York Times* in an editorial observed, "Watching our elected leaders in action, it's not surprising that Americans wonder if there is any limit to the crass misbehavior that members of Congress are willing to tolerate from their colleagues to protect their privileges and hold on to their own jobs. The House ethics committee answered that question yesterday with a resounding 'No.' "

If I were appearing before a congressional committee on behalf of a corporate client and had to defend a report where I found improper conduct but said no individual committed any violation, congressional members would crucify me.

There is no question that the insensitivity and arrogance of the Republicans on issues of ethics contributed to their defeat in the 2006 elections. Politicians of both parties got the message. As a result of a bipartisanship approach, meaningful reforms were passed in early 2007. These reforms focused on banning perks such as free entertainment and travel, and the Senate passed legislation that lobbyists will be required to disclose how they collect and bundle donations. Also, there will be more transparency on earmarks for special favorites of the legislators and a requirement that retiring members of Congress will have to wait two years before lobbying their colleagues. Perhaps I am too cynical, but having been in Washington for fifty years, I know that it will not take much time for members of Congress, staffers, and lobbyists to find loopholes so as to end-run many, if not all, of the objectives of these reforms. These are positive reforms. Unfortunately, efforts to include outsiders in the process by having some type of independent investigating body were rejected. I believe that until there is some independent enforcement, Congress will never get its ethical house in order.

The introduction of nonmembers into the ethics enforcement process would also give far more credibility to the decisions of an ethics committee and would make them more readily accepted by the public.

# CHAPTER ELEVEN

# THE SCANDAL MACHINE

As 1990 APPROACHED, I was getting restless at Dunnells, Duvall, Bennett and Porter. The personal relationships could not have been better, but professionally I was worried that very little white-collar business was generated from within the firm, and I felt a heavy burden to introduce it. I also felt a great sense of obligation to the many young lawyers I had recruited and was concerned that too much depended on me to keep them busy. Plus, a few of my partners outside of my practice area were spending a significant amount of time pursuing private business interests, which were natural outgrowths of their practice areas; given my practice of criminal law, those opportunities were not available to me.

I realized that it would be gut-wrenching to leave some of my partners. However, at the time, I wanted more long-term security for my family and me. I also came to the realization that in order to accomplish my professional goals, it required that I move on.

Carl Rauh and Alan Kriegel also shared many of my concerns. We decided to form a boutique firm specializing in a white-collar practice. As we were making plans, I received a call from a headhunter in New York who told me that he was representing a major New York law firm looking for a high-profile white-collar lawyer for their Washington, D.C., office and asked if I would be interested. My initial reaction was negative, and before I had any further discussions, I would have to know the firm and what they had in mind.

When he mentioned Skadden, I did not react one way or the other.

Frankly, at the time I did not know that Skadden even had a Washington office. To me it was a big New York firm that specialized in corporate law, and while I could not really understand why they were interested in me, I agreed to meet with them. Skadden partner Tom Schwarz took the initial lead in discussing the firm with us. Peter Mullen was the managing partner at the time and was incredibly impressive and persuasive in a low-key way.

After several meetings with Peter Mullen, Tom Schwarz, and others at the firm, Carl, Alan, and I decided to give it a shot. It was agreed that Carl and Alan would join me as partners. If we did not like it, we could always leave.

I also made it clear to Skadden that I would consider joining them only if all of my group at Dunnells could join me in the move. Neal McCoy, the manager of the Washington office, agreed that Skadden would hire any of our associates who met Skadden's standards. I sized up Neal as a guy who you could trust and agreed. At the end of the day, fifteen of us joined Skadden. Carl, Alan, and I had assembled a fantastic group of young lawyers who easily met Skadden's high standards. It made a lot of sense for the firm to take our entire group because we brought with us a considerable amount of business that had to be staffed. Several significant clients, such as Boeing, agreed to continue with us at Skadden, and several high-profile matters, like the Keating Five case, would become Skadden matters. When we made the move, Richard Brusca, Ed Meehan, Andy Sandler, and Ken Gross, first-class lawyers who had been at Skadden before we arrived, helped the Washington litigation group expand in areas outside the criminal area. Shortly after we arrived, Al Turkus, a former assistant U.S. attorney in Washington joined us. Al is probably the best tax litigator of the century.

My decision to join Skadden was a good one. It is a fabulous firm consisting of world-class lawyers who are the gold standard in terms of talent and client service. While we have offices all over the country and the world, the firm operates as a single unit and is exceptionally well run by Bob Sheehan, our executive partner in New York. Mike Rogan, who is also a top corporate lawyer, runs the Washington office with great skill, and Bill Frank, a fellow Georgetown graduate, heads the firm's world-wide litigation practice.

Our practice has grown by leaps and bounds at Skadden; currently our group has more than a hundred lawyers who focus on white-collar criminal matters, SEC enforcement, congressional representation, and civil litigation. A few years ago, Colleen Mahoney, a former official at the SEC, joined us, and she, Chuck Walker, and Erich Schwartz, both of whom were also at the SEC, have developed a first-class SEC practice. The Securities and Exchange Commission regulates corporate America and has as its goal the protection of the investing public.

As I said, at Skadden our practice continued to boom and the high-profile cases kept coming—many from the outside, but to my great satisfaction, many were generated from within. Skadden has the greatest client base in the world and a great deal of work came to my group from other practice groups in the firm.

In the July/August 2006 issue of *Corporate Board Member* magazine, Skadden was selected for the sixth year in a row as the best corporate law firm in the United States. This kind of recognition helps guarantee a steady flow of work, but an important part of Skadden's culture is that we do not rest on our laurels, we feel that every day is a new day requiring us to give our all for our clients. This is the culture created by one of the firm's founders, Joe Flom, probably the best corporate lawyer of the twentieth century. With all of the resources of a 1,700-plus lawyer firm in twenty-two offices all over the world, our group has been able to climb mountains higher than ever before.

In addition to representing many of America's leading companies and business entities in major cases, our group in Washington represented several high-profile individuals. In a relatively short period of time, we represented Clark Clifford, former secretary of defense under Lyndon Johnson; Caspar Weinberger, former secretary of defense under Ronald Reagan; and William J. Clinton, president of the United States, all of whom got caught up in the Washington scandal machine. Each of these cases was different and presented its own special challenges, but there are a number of general observations that apply to all.

Media coverage in high-profile cases, such as these, is almost always negative. I have found it ironic that the media, which is usually cynical of government action regarding most issues, becomes unquestioningly supportive of the government when it charges a high-profile person or company with criminal wrongdoing. It doesn't seem to matter if the defendant has a reputation for honesty and integrity built up over many years. There is something about seeing the mighty fall that whets the appetite of the media, and with a pack mentality, they pile on much like wolves chasing a wounded deer. Also, Washington loves conspiracies. The operating premise, it seems, is that whenever something goes wrong, there must be a conspiracy behind it. Sigmund Freud has been credited with the comment that "sometimes a cigar is just a cigar," but Washington has never learned that lesson. Accordingly, dealing with the press has become an integral part of representing a client in our current climate of scandal mongering.

When I am retained in one of these high-profile cases, I am often asked to be the spokesperson for the client and to deal both on and off the record with the reporters. Over the years I have developed excellent relations with the reporters who cover these stories and usually, but not always, am able to help my client in the court of public opinion. Most investigative reporters and journalists I have dealt with are honest, strive to be fair, and have a passion for accuracy, but even the best of them can get caught up in a media frenzy.

I have found that most high-profile clients are more concerned about their reputations than the prospect of jail. Let me make it absolutely clear that it is always best if your client is not written about and there is no need to deal with the press. You deal with the press because you have to. Attempts to initiate coverage to generate sympathy in a potential jury pool or to convince the public of your client's innocence is almost always a bad idea. But when your client is written about on a daily basis, it is important to fight back and do your best to get coverage that is fair and balanced. High-profile companies, business persons, and public figures want to assure their many friends and constituencies that they are innocent and will vigorously fight the charges. Unfortunately and unfairly, silence in the face of negative allegations is often taken as an acknowledgment that what is being said about your client is true.

Because things move so fast in our 24/7 world and with the phenom-
enon of bloggers, a great deal of bad or at least distorted information
makes its way into the media. It is often critical that damaging errors be
promptly corrected and false allegations responded to. There is an old
saying that "a lie travels halfway round the world before the truth gets its
boots on." In today's fast-moving world, this is particularly true, and a
good defense lawyer must be prepared to respond quickly. Unfortunately, some reporters would rather be wrong then be scooped. As a result, these reporters do not take the extra time to be sure of the accuracy
of their stories; I have found that standards have been lowered. Things
get into print or on the air today that would not have years ago.

The early nineties would put our team to the test with clients Clark
Clifford and Caspar Weinberger. The period of 1991–1993 would be incredibly challenging and stressful. These cases were public relations
nightmares.

Weinberger was indicted on June 16, 1992, at the age of seventy-four.
Clifford was indicted one month later, on July 29, 1992, at the age of
eighty-five, together with his law partner, Bob Altman. While the underlying facts were different, the two cases had a lot in common.

These were overly zealous prosecutions, which never should have
been brought because of the paucity of credible evidence and because a
fair reading of all the evidence showed innocence and not guilt. I believe
prosecutors Lawrence Walsh and Robert Morgenthau lost their sense of
balance and judgment and allowed their desire for a big kill to interfere
with sound prosecutorial decision-making.

Both cases were driven by a press frenzy. Bringing down a big name is
a blood sport in Washington. This is why I call it a mean town. Both Clifford and Weinberger got quite ill during their prosecutions, and Clifford
would suffer from a serious and life-threatening heart condition.

Unfortunately, in both cases the prosecutors did not give any consideration to Clifford's and Weinberger's outstanding reputations for honesty and integrity and their outstanding contributions as public servants.

Both cases were interwoven with politics as elected officials called for
prosecutions, and high-profile congressional hearings were scheduled so

congresspersons could show their constituents they were chasing wrong-doers. As usual, the facts took a backseat to the political rhetoric. Of course, Republicans were generally outraged by what was being done to Wein-berger, and many Democrats took the same position regarding Clifford.

## CLARK CLIFFORD — MR. DEMOCRAT

I first met Clark Clifford in the early 1970s when I was an associate at Hogan and Hartson, which at the time was located at 815 Connecticut Avenue in a building where Clifford also had his offices. Clifford had been a friend and advisor to four presidents. He was Harry S. Truman's White House counsel, served as secretary of defense under Lyndon Johnson, was John Kennedy's personal lawyer, and was an international emissary and advisor to Jimmy Carter. He was an advisor to presidents and a counselor to the powerful. Clifford, who was in his sixties at the time, had movie-star good looks and incredible presence. He was tall, elegant, courtly, and always impeccably dressed. He would tip his hat to the ladies and would never enter the elevator in the lobby of our build-ing until all members of the opposite sex had gone before him. If you asked any lawyer in the country who was the icon of lawyers, the over-whelming response would be Clark Clifford. He was considered the savviest and most intuitive lawyer in Washington, one who could navi-gate his clients safely through the legal minefields that lay hidden within the Beltway.

While I would occasionally say hello to him in the lobby, I never en-gaged him in conversation—at least not until the right opportunity pre-sented itself. That opportunity occurred when I headed the luncheon committee of the Young Lawyers Section of the D.C. Bar. It was my re-sponsibility to invite prominent speakers to our monthly luncheons. One day I called Clifford, introduced myself, and asked him to speak to our group. His manner of talking was unforgettable. He spoke in absolutely perfect phrases with beautiful rhythm and soft tones. You felt you were listening to a great actor. Clifford told me that his mother was involved with the theater and had encouraged him to take acting and drama lessons; this, he explained, was why he spoke as he did.

When I first asked him to speak to our group, he graciously declined. He explained that he had been ill and as a result he had to delay the handling of business abroad, but promised that when things cleared up, he would call me. I knew a brush-off when I heard one but I had to admit this was as gracious and impressive a rejection as I had ever experienced. Well, I was wrong. A year had gone by when my secretary buzzed me and, to my surprise, said that Mr. Clifford was calling. "Mr. Bennett, this is Clark Clifford; I don't know if you remember, but you asked me about a year ago if I would speak to your group. I have since dealt with my medical problems, finished my business obligations abroad, and if the opportunity is still available, I would be delighted to speak to your group." I was both dumbfounded and starstruck. I told him I was pleased that he was better and assured him that we would love to have him speak. He asked me to make an appointment with his devoted secretary, Eileen, so that we could discuss his talk. I showed up at his office at the agreed-upon time. His office was only a few floors above mine. However, instead of a windowless cubbyhole—like mine—his overlooked the White House, and the indicia of power emanated from every inch. This was a power office if I ever saw one. We talked at length about what would be a suitable topic, and I believe that we settled on the Vietnam war and his opposition to it. I thought to myself, "This man prepares." It was a valuable lesson for me, which I have followed my whole professional life in private practice: Always prepare. If the task is worth doing, do it well.

On the day of the speech, I met him in the lobby of our building and we walked to the location where the presentation was to take place. It was like walking with Gary Cooper or Jimmy Stewart. Everyone seemed to know Clifford or to recognize him. I am convinced that some of the onlookers neither knew him nor recognized him, but due to his presence, knew that he was important. As we walked, we chatted about his incredible career. I asked him several questions that only an insider like him could answer. For example, I had always wondered about the longevity of J. Edgar Hoover as the director of the FBI and decided to ask Clifford about it. Specifically, I asked him why Lyndon Johnson, to whom Clifford was an advisor, kept Hoover as head of the FBI given the controversy surrounding him in his later years. Clifford said that he had asked President Johnson the same question. According to Clifford, Johnson replied, "Clark, I keep him on because I would rather have him inside the tent pissing out than have him outside the tent pissing in."

This was a great insider story and I asked Clifford if he would please tell the story to the luncheon audience. I remember him asking me, "Bob, will there be women present at the lunch?" When I told him there would be several, he said that he simply could not repeat such a story in mixed company. Times have certainly changed, but Clifford's speech was great and I thanked him for his effort.

In the hours we were together, I was sure to tell him that I was working hard at developing a white-collar practice and of course told him about my days as a federal prosecutor. I was hopeful that he might keep me in mind if someday one of his clients needed a criminal lawyer. A lawyer, especially a young one, must always plant seeds in the hope that some will take hold and bloom into future business. I always carry a big bag of seeds with me wherever I go and drop them along the way. Many seeds never take hold, but a surprising number bloom. As we headed back to our offices, I thanked him and secretly wished he would someday refer a client to me. Little did I know that some twenty years later, he would call and ask me to represent him in the most high-profile case in the country at the time.

In May of 1991, Ellen and I went to the Mayo Clinic in Rochester, Minnesota, to undergo complete physicals. My uncle Dr. William B. Walsh, the founder of Project Hope, regularly went there and recommended we do so. On our last day at the clinic, I was preparing for a final test and was in a somewhat embarrassing position to conduct business. The phone rang in our room at the Kahler Grand Hotel. Ellen said, "Clark Clifford is on the phone—should I tell him you will call him back?" I said no and she handed me the phone. I knew at the time that he was under investigation in New York by District Attorney Robert Morgenthau and that he had retained the prominent attorney Robert Fiske to represent him. I also knew the Department of Justice and Congress were beginning investigations and that he was looking for Washington counsel. Flat on my stomach on the floor, I said, "Hello, Mr. Clifford, it's been a long time." After some brief small talk, he asked if I could meet with him immediately as he would like to discuss retaining me in connection with the BCCI–First American investigation.

We agreed to meet the following day at his office. Clifford and I met alone. He explained that he and Robert Altman were under investigation in both Washington and New York in connection with First American Bank's relationship with the Bank of Credit and Commerce International (BCCI). There were both federal and state criminal investigations as well as congressional hearings. Clifford was the chairman of First American Bank, and his protégé and law partner, Bob Altman, was the president. BCCI was the investment adviser and communications link to the wealthy Arab royalty who owned First American. Clifford said he would like to retain our firm to represent Bob and him. He was very impressed with my lawyering in the Keating Five investigation and our firm's work in a number of other tough cases. He also commented that in addition to my white-collar experience, he wanted my skills in handling the press and the public-relations aspects of this high-profile matter. Needless to say, I was flattered.

BCCI was imploding and the bank and those even marginally connected with it were being pursued by investigators, prosecutors, and regulators all over the world. Clifford explained that there were allegations that he and Bob were in violation of federal banking laws and, contrary to representations made to regulators, that BCCI secretly owned First American and illegally influenced its operations. If this were the case, it would be a violation of federal and state banking law and would be contrary to representations made earlier by both Clifford and Altman to the banking regulators. His presentation was a mixture of sorrow, distress, and anger. He explained that he had accepted the position at First American because the last thing he wanted to do was retire "and wheel a grocery cart down the aisles of a supermarket" with his wife. He wanted a new challenge and thought his background prepared him well for the position of the bank's chairman. He went into detail about how Bob Altman and he ran the bank with honesty and complete integrity. He explained how First American had grown and prospered under his and Altman's leadership, and unlike many other bank cases, was proud that no depositor at First American ever lost a cent. He was particularly adamant that both Bob and he were unaware of any secret ownership of First American by BCCI. When he finished, I absolutely believed him, and years later, after many investigations, I still do.

At the end of the meeting, I told him how honored I would be to represent him and Bob.

I was aware that any client in his position would be concerned for his reputation of honesty and integrity as much as the threat of criminal liability.

We agreed to meet again the next day and begin preparing his defense. As I left his office, I felt sad and was absolutely determined that I was not going to let this eighty-five-year-old giant of the profession, and his respected partner Bob, be destroyed.

Carl and I assembled our team and began the Herculean task of mastering the facts and hundreds of thousands of documents.

While the state and federal investigations of Clifford and Altman were taking place, Clifford was completing his memoir, *Counsel to the President*. Clifford had spent a great deal of time and energy on this project. The publication of the book was to be a happy and gratifying time, but with the Washington scandal machine in full gear, it became a sad one. Clifford gave me a copy of the book with the inscription "To my friend, Bob Bennett with respect, admiration and appreciation, May 25, 1991." It was not as if I needed any more encouragement to fight the war for him, but this simply added to my motivation.

Realizing that the book could not ignore the scandal, Clifford in a lengthy footnote explained the situation as follows:

> In 1991 an unfortunate controversy arose concerning the relationship between First American and an international bank, the Bank of Credit and Commerce International (BCCI). First

American had been acquired in 1982 by a group of Middle Eastern investors, some of whom also were shareholders of BCCI. After determining through careful checking with the State and Treasury departments that our government had no objection to the acquisition of First American (or, as it was then called, Financial General) by foreign investors, our law firm acted as legal advisers to the investors in meetings with the banking authorities in Washington, and later, in New York. During those meetings, I stated, based on representations made to me and to the regulators by the investors, that First American would be operated completely separately from BCCI, and that BCCI would not own or otherwise control the operations of First American. When the Federal (and later New York State) authorities completed their review, they approved the acquisition. The investors, headed by Sheikh Kamal Adham, a wealthy Saudi Arabian related by marriage to the king, asked me to serve as First American's chairman. On the assurance that the investors would not interfere with First American operations or give us instructions, I ac-cepted, selected a group of distinguished Americans to serve on the First American Board, and hired experienced bankers to build a strong banking institution out of the debris of Financial General.

I accepted this offer at the age of seventy-five because I wanted a new challenge in my life, and felt that my prior experience as a lawyer with many corporate clients would be a firm base from which to fulfill these new obligations. In this aspect of my work I was not mistaken; over the next nine years First American grew into the largest bank-holding company headquartered in the Washington area, and served its customers well.

The investors and BCCI never interfered with our operations. However, as First American prospered under our leadership, BCCI, which was operating in over seventy countries around the world, ran into serious difficulties. In 1988 investigators in Florida discovered that BCCI was involved in a drug-money laundering scheme, and several employees went to jail. As the investigations proceeded, BCCI began to implode, and in 1990 its founders were replaced and the bank taken over by the ruler of the immensely wealthy Gulf state of Abu Dhabi, Sheikh Zayed al-Nahyan, who was also an important investor in First American. When his new team began the process of rescuing BCCI, they examined its files. What they found was still, as of the time of publication of this book, not yet entirely clear, but I am informed that documents were found suggesting that some of First American's investors had, at some point, bought stock with secret loans from BCCI, had used the First American stock as collateral for the loans, and had failed to repay the loans. The investigators thus began examining the possibility that these secret financial dealings overseas resulted in an illegal transfer of control of certain shares of First American stock to BCCI.

When I was first informed that United States law might have been violated, I was both appalled and embarrassed. Never, in my nine years as the bank's chairman, had I received any instructions from any BCCI representative. Furthermore, my repeated assurances to both Washington and New York authorities that First American and BCCI were two separate entities had been made in good faith. Finally, I knew nothing of any secret loans or other financial arrangements that may have existed overseas between First American investors and BCCI, and that may have resulted in BCCI's control of some First American stock. If the Federal Reserve Board and other authorities had been deceived, so had I. It was possible that I had been used, I realized with a combination of outrage and deep concern, by a group of foreign investors. The operations of First American, for which I had been responsible, had been honest, ethical, and successful, as I stressed to reporters; no depositors had ever lost a penny. Nor had there been any misappropriation of funds from First American, no "bailout" by the government, as in the colossal savings-and-loan scandals. But I realized that even while successfully running a large group of banks, it was possible that I had been deliberately misled. No event in my entire career caused me greater anger and outrage.

This footnote outlined our defense. Clifford in a sense had become the victim of his own success and iconic reputation. His acknowledgment that he may have been deceived and misled by the Arabs and BCCI and was therefore an unknowing victim certainly undermined his reputation. How could the great Clark Clifford be fooled? How could he not know what had occurred? These were the questions repeatedly asked of me by the press, and while I had no doubt that he had been misled and deceived, the press rejected the notion that this could be the case. The fall of Clark Clifford was too good a story to let the facts get in the way.

The more we learned about the facts, the more we realized that there was simply no case. The Federal Reserve and other regulators conducted the most comprehensive audits of the bank, and concluded First American had been run honestly and that there was no evidence of any improper dealings with BCCI. There was no evidence of BCCI influence over First American. While there were suspicious circumstances, once you carefully looked at them, they dissipated. Like cotton candy, it looked good, but after one bite, you realized there was nothing of substance. The facts did not sway the runaway train the prosecutors were on. The evidence clearly showed that neither Clifford nor Altman was aware of any secret ownership and that none of the decisions at the bank were made by secret owners. Clifford and Altman ran the bank honestly; no foreigners interfered. All such evidence was ignored by the prosecutors.

Our team made every effort to convince the government that there was no case. We prepared a lengthy submission, which took apart the government's theory and factual assumptions, and along with Bob Fiske submitted a nearly three-hundred-page memorandum with a separate volume of exhibits to New York District Attorney Robert Morgenthau. The submission proved beyond doubt that there was no case against either Clifford or Altman. Waiving their constitutional protections, both agreed to testify before the federal and state grand juries. During the same time, we had to deal with simultaneous investigations and public hearings in the House and Senate, accompanied by much political grandstanding and hype. Though warned of the legal risks, both Clifford and Altman proceeded to testify under oath before each committee. Both gave a full factual account, disregarding the legal jeopardy of such appearances.

Meanwhile, the allegations were the subject of unrelenting, highly sensationalized news stories, complete with regular leaks about the investigation. Unfortunately, the media frenzy had a tremendous impact on the prosecutors. The New York prosecutors received continual hype and praise in the media, including a fawning article (with photos) on them in *Vanity Fair*, and similar treatment by the *Wall Street Journal*. They were portrayed as fearless public servants unafraid to take on powerful interests, ignoring their leaks, abuses of power, and the baseless allegations at the heart of the case. The United States Department of Justice was criticized regularly for dragging its feet and Morgenthau's aggressive tactics were putting additional pressure on the feds. There was outright hostility between the federal and state prosecutors and there seemed to be a competition to see who would first get the scalps of Clifford and Altman. Investigative reporter Jim McGee observed on July 25, 1991, in the *Washington Post:*

> The chief of the Justice Department's criminal division, stung by news reports that the investigation of the Bank of Credit and Commerce International (BCCI) has been stifled because of alleged CIA links, said he has taken personal charge of the probe and that 10 federal prosecutors are working on various parts of the international banking scandal.
>
> "We are left with the appearance of, one, foot dragging, two, perhaps a coverup . . . or at perhaps best a lack of enthusiasm for aggressiveness," said Assistant Attorney General Robert S. Mueller. "Nobody has ever accused me of . . . lacking aggression. . . . There are allegations out there and we are pursuing them," Mueller said, responding to charges of delays made by

Manhattan District Attorney Robert Morgenthau as well as recent published reports.

Mueller defended the work of federal prosecutors, noting that they may have moved with less fanfare than prosecutors with the Manhattan District Attorney's Office, who first obtained evidence that BCCI had gained control of First American Bankshares' holding company.

This was a bad situation for us. Hopefully prosecutors resist outside pressures and look at the evidence dispassionately, but unfortunately this did not happen. Even though the case was nothing more than prosecution theories in search of evidence, the train had left the station and was moving fast down the track. Even within Morgenthau's office, there was quiet opposition to indicting the case. As a result of our several meetings with the prosecutors and other intelligence we received, it was clear that a few experienced prosecutors in Morgenthau's office were opposed to indicting Clifford and Altman. However, we felt that Morgenthau would go forward because he wanted a big win in a major case for ego reasons, loved all the press attention, and wanted to show up the feds. It was clear that the attorney general was under a great deal of political pressure to indict because of Morgenthau's public statements. If Morgenthau indicted, which was clearly in the cards, the Department of Justice, it was feared, would look bad if they did not follow suit.

Shortly before Clifford's indictment, Bob Fiske and Carl Rauh met with Morgenthau and argued that Clifford's advanced age and poor health were grounds not to indict. Morgenthau paid little attention to this plea. All of our efforts and those of Bob Fiske failed, and in a carefully coordinated effort, the Department of Justice and the district attorney of New York returned federal and state indictments on July 29, 1992. While this was expected by our clients, it was devastating. Clifford and Altman, to their credit, and with my everlasting respect, stood tall and didn't whine or whimper. Adding insult to injury, Morgenthau, without any prior notice to us, had secretly secured an order from a New York judge freezing millions of dollars in Clifford's accounts in New York as well as the assets of Altman—bank accounts, credit cards, and all. The seizure was revealed to us for the first time at the arraignment. This extraordinary tactic, normally used in the most extreme racketeering prosecutions, was intended to put the greatest possible pressure on Clifford and Altman to plead. They refused.

On July 30, 1992, the *Washington Post* reported:

> Legendary Washington lawyer and presidential adviser Clark M. Clifford and his law partner, Robert A. Altman, were charged in criminal indictments yesterday with lying to banking regulators, accepting bribes and falsifying records to help the Bank of Credit and Commerce International illegally acquire U.S. banks, including Washington's First American Bankshares Inc.
>
> Indictments against the two men by separate state and federal grand juries were announced by New York District Attorney Robert M. Morgenthau in Manhattan and U.S. Assistant Attorney General Robert S. Mueller III in Washington. The Federal Reserve Board also brought civil charges against Clifford and Altman for lying to the Fed when they said BCCI would have nothing to do with First American.
>
> Shortly after the indictments were announced, the 85-year-old Clifford, tall but stooped, walked slowly down the aisle into the courtroom in New York's criminal justice building, holding his trademark fedora, and said: "I plead not guilty" in a clear, strong voice. A somber Altman, 45, preceded Clifford into the state Supreme Court courtroom of Justice John A. K. Bradley and also pleaded not guilty.
>
> "The bringing of these indictments is a cruel and unjust abuse of the prosecutorial function," Clifford and Altman said in a joint statement. "We totally and categorically deny all charges. . . . They are the result of mean-spirited suspicion and unfounded speculation. . . . We shall fight to establish our innocence."
>
> "We are confident that our clients will be vindicated in the end," Robert S. Bennett and Carl S. Rauh, attorneys for Clifford

and Altman, said in a statement. "On the level playing field of a courtroom . . . the outrageousness of the government's action today will be abundantly clear."

Normally, in a case of this kind, the defense does not want a speedy trial. Since Clifford and Altman were free pending trial and since it would take many months of investigation and preparation, an early trial would be disadvantageous. After all, the government had been preparing for years and presumably did not bring an indictment until it was prepared to go forward. Yet, time was not a luxury we could afford because of Clifford's declining health. Clifford had a serious heart condition and was convinced that if the trial was delayed, he would not have his day in court. Being acquitted at trial was critically important to Clifford, so we appeared before United States District Court Judge Joyce Hens Green in Washington and asked for an early trial date. On July 31, 1992, two days after the indictment, Judge Green set a trial date for October 26, 1992, less then four months away. Carl and I had some concern about our ability to get ready, but we had already done a lot of work and our three-hundred-page submission to the government was our road map for trying the case.

To be candid, we wanted to try the federal case first. We felt that an acquittal in federal court would give us a better chance at obtaining a dismissal of the state indictment on grounds of double jeopardy. However, the principal motivation for an early trial in federal court was Clifford's health. Clifford's doctors all felt that any trial was risky, but that if Clifford had to live in New York, sleep in a strange bed, and be without ready access to his doctors for many months, it would be especially risky. We had estimated the New York trial would take at least six months, and his doctors believed that Clifford would not survive it. In short, just going to trial in New York could be a death sentence.

Like a junkyard dog fighting over a bone, Assistant District Attorney John Moscow requested Judge John A. K. Bradley, the judge assigned to the New York case, to set the trial in New York four days before the already scheduled federal trial. We vigorously opposed and advised Judge

Bradley that Clifford's doctors were of the view that to require Clifford to stand trial in New York would be his death sentence. Perhaps, for the first time in the case, a few reporters were starting to question the prosecutor's tactics, and Clifford and Altman were getting at least some sympathy. Here is what the *Washington Post* reported:

> In the scramble to bring attorneys Clark M. Clifford and Robert A. Altman to trial in the First American–BCCI case, state prosecutors from New York yesterday jumped ahead of their federal counterparts, securing an Oct. 22 court date here—just four days before a federal trial was scheduled to begin in Washington.
>
> The jousting over court dates arose after New York District Attorney Robert M. Morgenthau and the U.S. Justice Department announced related but separate indictments last week against Clifford and Altman, the former top executives of Washington's First American Bankshares Inc. . . . They have denied the charges.
>
> Over sharp opposition from Clifford and Altman's attorneys, New York Supreme Court Justice John A. K. Bradley set the Oct. 22 date for the beginning of a trial on the New York charges.
>
> Robert S. Bennett, the lead defense attorney in the federal case, quoted Clifford's doctors as saying the trial will be "a death sentence" for the former secretary of defense. "I am sorry to say that Mr. Moscow is trying to manipulate the system," Bennett told the judge with a chilled politeness.

Having been federal prosecutors ourselves, and given the Department of Justice's commitment to Judge Green to give Clifford a speedy trial, Carl and I were quite confident that the Department of Justice would fight for the October 26, 1992, Washington trial date set by Judge Green, especially since it was set first. Also, the Department of Justice usually takes the position that a federal court action on the same matter would have priority over a state case. Well, we were wrong. The DOJ shamelessly capitulated and agreed that the New York trial could go first.

I believe that the federal prosecutors knew that they had an extremely weak case and were more than happy to have Morgenthau end up with egg on his face.

As Clifford's health was deteriorating steadily, we submitted medical reports to Judge Bradley in an effort to get him to allow the Washington case to go first. Bradley denied this request and, after further pretrial proceedings, set the New York state trial for March 30, 1993. According to Clifford's doctors, he had to have open heart surgery in March and opined that Clifford would not survive if he did not have it. The doctors also believed that there was a significant risk that Clifford would die on the operating table.

Clifford was vehemently opposed to our using his illness as a basis for dismissing or delaying the trial. With the support of strong medical reports, we finally convinced him that he should allow us to raise the point. In callous fashion, Morgenthau's office opposed our position. Despite all evidence to the contrary, they argued that Clifford was able to proceed in New York. Charles Stillman, a well-known criminal lawyer in New York, represented Clifford in regard to the health issue before Judge Bradley. Obviously troubled by the medical evidence presented to him, Judge Bradley decided that he would appoint medical experts to examine Clifford. Finally, when court-appointed doctors concurred with Clifford's doctors regarding the seriousness of his condition and the likely fatal impact of requiring him to stand trial in New York, Judge Bradley severed Clifford's case from Altman's.

On March 22, only eight days before the scheduled trial, Clifford underwent open-heart surgery for several hours. While he survived, his health would never be the same and, ultimately, both the federal and state prosecutions would be dismissed against Clifford. Altman would have to go it alone, and vindication for Clifford would have to come through Altman's trial.

Having isolated him, the prosecutors made repeated attempts to get Altman to plead guilty to one felony count in exchange for a guarantee of no jail. Despite facing a lengthy term of imprisonment if convicted, Altman refused all offers. Later during the trial, the prosecution agreed to accept a plea to a misdemeanor in exchange for dropping all other charges, but Altman insisted he would never falsely say he had committed any crime.

The trial of Altman began in New York before Judge Bradley on March 30, 1993. The defense team consisted of Gus Newman, an experienced criminal trial lawyer in New York; my partner Mitchell Ettinger; and William Shields, also an experienced criminal lawyer in New York. District Attorney John Moscow and his team, which included a representative from the Department of Justice, Tony Leffert, presented the prosecution's case over a period of five months and called forty-five witnesses in their case. It became very clear early on that the prosecutors had no case. The pumped-up prosecution's theories simply had no evidence to support them. On cross-examination, the prosecution witnesses were cut to shreds, or provided evidence that actually supported the defense.

Although the government called forty-five witnesses, its case against Mr. Altman was built principally upon the testimony of two former BCCI senior officials. Dildar Rizvi and Imran Imam gave incredible testimony about Messrs. Clifford and Altman's knowledge of a secret plan to take over First American Bank.

Both Mr. Rizvi and Mr. Imam were viewed by federal authorities as central participants in the multibillion-dollar fraud at BCCI. Mr. Rizvi, who had been charged with numerous felonies in the United States, including money laundering, was a fugitive from justice. In order to obtain his presence at Mr. Altman's trial, the New York district attorney disregarded the fact that he was wanted by American authorities and guaranteed him immunity from prosecution in the United States in return for his testimony. Gus Newman's cross-examination of Mr. Rizvi underscored the great lengths to which the prosecution went to secure Mr. Rizvi's testimony; the jury fully grasped Mr. Rizvi's motive to fabricate a story and rejected his claim that there was a conspiracy with the Arab owners of BCCI to hide information from the Federal Reserve.

Mr. Imam was cross-examined at trial by Mitch Ettinger. Imam had been interviewed by federal and state authorities no less than fifteen times and appeared before two grand juries. He, too, had been immunized from prosecution in the United States. The New York District Attorney's Office even intervened on Mr. Imam's behalf with the British authorities, requesting that they drop its criminal charges against him. Mr. Morgenthau's office went so far as to pay Mr. Imam more than $12,500 for personal expenses, including reimbursement for heating costs for his home in England. The twenty-one sets of interview notes and grand jury transcripts, which were seriously inconsistent, laid Mr. Imam bare for a grueling two-day cross-examination. Mitch relentlessly went after the gross conflicts between Mr. Imam's trial testimony and his previous statements, as well as the compensation Mr. Imam received from U.S. authorities and his pending request to be paid $100,000 by the Federal Reserve for his testimony in the Altman trial. When Imam ultimately disavowed his own sworn grand jury testimony, claiming that the stenographer failed to record his verbatim testimony accurately, members of the jury laughed aloud and made clear with their body language that his testimony was worthless to the prosecution.

At the end of the prosecution's case, Judge Bradley dismissed a number of the charges, including the central count of bribery. The court stated that after five months of trial, there had been "no evidence" presented to support the main charge in the case. As to the remaining charges, it was so clear that the prosecutors failed to prove anything, the defense decided to rest without putting on any witnesses. On August 14, 1993, the jury returned a verdict of not guilty on the remaining charges. The jurors eagerly met with the press to criticize the prosecution and proclaimed that Altman was unquestionably innocent.

For the very first time after years of uniformly negative coverage, the press was forced to confront the truth about the case. On August 18, 1993, *Washington Post* investigative reporter Sharon Walsh reported that

> [t]he prosecution's biggest mistake appears to have been its failure to deliver what it promised, according to neutral observers and jurors . . . "Somebody made a really bad decision" in indicting Clifford and Altman, said Stephen A. Saltzberg, a professor of

criminal procedure at George Washington Law Center and former special counsel to the Justice Department.

According to the *Washington Post* repeat interviews with jurors following the acquittal showed that they were contemptuous of the prosecution's case, believed that Altman was "unquestionably innocent" and that the prosecution was not a "search for truth but was a game."

It was over, and neither the Department of Justice nor Morgenthau's office would ever try Clifford. Clifford's health would continue to deteriorate. In the final years of his life, he felt vindicated by Altman's acquittal, but he was smart enough to know that his reputation would never be the same. Clifford died on October 10, 1998. Altman has done well in the years following the acquittal. Nevertheless, this baseless prosecution caused untold damage to him, his family, and many others, and, ironically, even Robert Morgenthau could not avoid the fallout. As the *Washington Post* reported:

The swift not-guilty verdict was a serious blow to Morgenthau . . . a storied prosecutor who over 40 years has built a reputation as a scourge of white-collar crime. In a strange turn of events, the case that many thought would stain the venerable reputation of Clifford, a former U.S. Defense Secretary and top Washington banker, may instead besmirch Morgenthau.

Finally, at long last, the press recognized the validity of what we had been telling them all along. After our successful representation of Clifford and Altman, I was asked by members of the press how they could have been so wrong. I told them that the story line—an icon's fall from grace—was too good and caused them to get carried away and accept at face value all that was told to them by out-of-control prosecutors. While the press now knew that they had been misled, this was of little consolation to Clifford and Altman. The situation reminded me of former Secretary of Labor Ray Donovan, who after his acquittal in a criminal case asked the press to which office he could go to get his reputation back. This was true in spades for Clifford. Altman, much younger and healthy, at least had time, but this would not be true of Clifford, a great American, who was wrongly prosecuted.

## CASPAR WEINBERGER — MR. REPUBLICAN

Cap Weinberger, a great statesman with a reputation for honesty and integrity, became the target of an overly zealous and unfair prosecution by Independent Counsel Lawrence Walsh.

Walsh, a former prosecutor, Wall Street lawyer, and federal judge, was appointed to be the independent counsel in what became known as the Iran-Contra affair—the secret arms-for-hostages deal of the Reagan administration. Let me give you a little background. American hostages had been taken in Iran. At the time, the United States had an arms embargo against Iran. On June 17, 1985, Robert McFarlane, the National Security advisor to President Reagan, transmitted a draft National Security Directive to Secretary of State George Shultz and to Weinberger. He suggested in the directive that an effort be made to open a dialogue and establish a "good working" relationship with moderate leaders in Iran. To Cap's shock, McFarlane, in the belief that dealing with Iranian moderates might bring about the release of the hostages, went so far as to suggest giving Iran arms. Cap thought this suggestion was absurd, and in his official response said the following:

> "Under no circumstances should we now ease our restrictions on arms sales to Iran. Such a policy reversal would be seen as inexplicably inconsistent by those nations whom we have urged to refrain from such sales, and would likely lead to increased arms sales by them and a possible alteration of the strategic balance in favor of Iran while Khomeini is still the controlling influence."

Because of his strong opposition, as well as that of Secretary Shultz, Cap thought the matter was dead. He later learned that at McFarlane's instigation, the plan went forward and that, because his strong opposition was well known, he was kept out of the loop.

In a December 22, 1986, memorandum to Al Kheel, the acting assistant to the president for National Security Affairs, Cap, deeply troubled about being kept out of the loop, wrote:

> When the President announced in late November or early December that all further arms shipments to Iran had ceased, and after it became apparent that the channels we were using to discuss hostage release, and other matters with the Iranians were, at the very least, ineffective, and, as it was easily apparent now, totally counterproductive, I had assumed that we were finished with that entire Iranian episode and so testified to Congressional Committees during last week. I was astounded, therefore, to learn, on Friday, December 19, 1986, *after* my testimony, that United States "negotiators" were still meeting with the same Iranians. . . .
>
> I must point out as strongly as I can that any attempt to conduct major activities in the security field with the deliberate exclusion of those who have some responsibility for security cannot succeed in anything but adding to the troubles we already have. I would very much have appreciated an opportunity to present to the President arguments as to why we should *not* continue dealing with these channels in Iran. . . .
>
> I think the President was entitled to have the advice of all of his security advisers, and I must strongly object that the continuation of this practice of secrecy and attempts to exclude various advisers whose advice it is apparently feared may not support the agenda of [certain administration officials], can only get us in more and more difficulty, and serves the President very badly.

Knowing that Weinberger was vehemently opposed to the secret arms deal, Lawrence Walsh, in the early phase of his investigation, reached out to Cap. For approximately five years, Cap thought he was a cooperating witness with the Walsh investigation. When he was first contacted by

Walsh, Cap sought the advice of his law partner Bill Rogers, who had previously served in the roles of attorney general of the United States and secretary of state. While Rogers attended one or two meetings with Cap and Walsh, Cap met with the authorities on several occasions without Rogers being present. Both Cap and Rogers assumed that since Cap was vehemently opposed to the arms deal and because he did nothing wrong, there was no need for him to retain a criminal lawyer.

Cap, a law-and-order guy, trusted Walsh, a former federal judge and federal prosecutor, and he certainly never thought that Walsh, a prominent Republican, was out to get anyone in the Reagan administration. Also, it was no big deal for Cap to speak with the FBI or other government agents because he had innumerable conversations over the years with them on a wide range of security matters.

What Cap did not know was that Walsh was spinning a web in which he would soon be caught. That realization hit home when a letter from Craig Gillen, the deputy independent counsel, was hand-delivered to Cap at his law offices.

On the morning of April 2, 1992, my secretary buzzed me and said that Judge William P. Clark was on the phone and would like to talk to me. While I did not know Judge Clark, I certainly knew of him. Clark had held numerous high-level government positions. He had been chief of staff to Governor Ronald Reagan and later served as advisor to President Reagan for National Security Affairs. He had been deputy secretary of state and a justice on the California Court of Appeals. He was on innumerable boards and commissions. At the time of his call, he was a prominent businessman.

Clark explained that he was calling on behalf of former secretary Caspar Weinberger, a close friend, and that he and Cap would like to come to my office as soon as possible. He said that Cap had just gotten a target letter from the independent counsel and would like to discuss my representing Cap in the matter. I insisted on going to Cap's office and said I would be over in a matter of minutes. When clients are in trouble, they want a lawyer who is responsive. This is why I dropped what I was doing to take Judge Clark's call. An immediate response communicates to a client in trouble that you really care about them, and that their problem is a high priority for you. Also, I have learned over the years that even the slightest delay in responding to a potential client in a crisis can cause you to lose that client. Someone like Cap would know many lawyers; after all, he was one himself, and this was the kind of case every criminal lawyer in the country would want.

I went to Cap's firm, where he served as a senior counsel, and was quickly escorted into his office. As soon as I entered the room, it was obvious that he and Clark were in a state of disbelief. Clark handed me the letter dated March 30, 1992:

*Dear Mr. Weinberger:*

[T]his Office is continuing its investigation of possible violations of federal laws relating to the Iran/Contra matter. The federal grand jury is conducting an investigation of possible violations of federal criminal law involving, inter alia, conspiracy to commit offense against the United States, 18 U.S.C. § 371; knowing and willful false or fraudulent statements, 18 U.S.C. § 1001; obstruction of proceedings, 18 U.S.C. § 1505, perjury generally, 18 U.S.C. § 1623; and concealment, removal or mutilation of records, 18 U.S.C. § 2071.

An aspect of the grand jury's investigation has focused on portions of your 1987 testimony to the Select Committees investigating Iran/Contra and your statements to this Office in the fall of 1990.

Your status is that of a "target" of the grand jury's investigation.

The purpose of this letter is to extend to you an opportunity to testify before the grand jury if you so desire. We have arranged for your testimony to begin at 10:00 a.m. April 8, 1992 in the event you choose to give testimony.

The word *target* is a term of art with a well-established meaning to criminal defense lawyers. In Department of Justice parlance, people are either witnesses, subjects, or targets. Being a target in an investigation means you are likely to be indicted. Cap Weinberger, who had served with an unblemished record in the cabinet under two presidents, had just been told he was probably going to be indicted for conspiracy, obstruction of justice, and perjury.

After listening to Cap and Judge Clark, and considering what I had heard and read about the case, it did not make sense that Cap would be given a target letter. Cap retained me on the spot and I explained to him the process. About the initial question as to whether he should accept the invitation to appear before the grand jury, I explained that it was probably not a good idea but that before we made any final decisions, I wanted to meet with Judge Walsh. Target letters are not Hallmark greeting cards, and much care must be exercised before responding to them.

A great deal had been written about the investigation over the years, so this was one of those instances where extensive news coverage enabled us to learn a lot about the case very quickly, and what Walsh was up to.

Immediately after being retained, I scheduled a visit with Judge Walsh. On April 9, Carl Rauh and I met with him and his deputy, Craig Gillen.

The meeting did not go well. It seemed obvious that he had all but made up his mind as to Cap's guilt and had little interest in anything we had to say. Walsh did not dispute that Cap was opposed to any arms transfer to Iran, but expressed his view that Cap had knowledge of the transfer of arms that took place, that he lied about his knowledge to Congress, and that he intentionally withheld relevant notes from the independent counsel. Walsh believed there was a massive conspiracy at the highest levels of the Reagan administration and, while Cap was opposed to what they did, that he was a knowing conspirator. We were dumbfounded. We asked Walsh not to take any action against Cap until we had the opportunity to show him that he was wrong. As to Cap's appearance before the grand jury, we told Walsh we would get back to him shortly. There was no doubt in our minds that Cap should not testify before the grand jury. Walsh simply wanted to lock Cap into testimony and lay a foundation for a perjury charge. Cap's cooperation over several years got him no benefit.

When we met with Cap and reported the results of our meeting, he was both upset and outraged. We told him that we thought Walsh was setting a perjury trap for him and he should not go to the grand jury. We reminded him of the famous remark that a prosecutor can get a grand jury to indict "a ham sandwich." Cap was troubled with our advice not to testify before the grand jury. While he reluctantly accepted our advice, he felt strongly that he should meet with Walsh outside the grand jury.

On April 13, we wrote Craig Gillen advising him that Cap would not appear before the grand jury but requested a meeting with Walsh.

While we knew it was a long shot, we felt an informal meeting with Walsh was far better than a grand jury appearance. Since Weinberger had already met with Walsh's team and the FBI on multiple occasions, one more meeting, especially one where Cap would be fully prepared by us, was a risk worth taking. Also, at such a meeting, Carl and I could be present, whereas we could not be at the grand jury.

In theory, the grand jury is supposed to be a buffer between the individual and the government. In practice, the grand jury almost always does what the prosecution asks. Moreover, it is a powerful tool of the prosecutor because the grand jury can subpoena witnesses to testify and can demand the production of not only official documents but private papers as well. In practice, a prosecutor using the tool of the grand jury can conduct a fishing expedition into your private life and business affairs. On occasion you will read about a grand jury refusing to indict. I am confident that in most of these cases, you would find that the prosecutor steered the grand jury in that direction. This is a convenient way for a prosecutor to avoid taking the heat in a controversial case. "It was the grand jury that refused to indict, not our office" is a claim commonly heard.

Over the next several weeks our team worked night and day and assembled powerful evidence undermining the independent counsel's case.

Walsh contended that Cap lied to the Senate committee investigating the Iran-Contra matter. He believed that Cap had given materially false testimony before the Senate committee when he said he did not have contemporaneous knowledge of the 1985 arms shipment to Iran. In order to prove the charge, Walsh would have to show that the information Cap allegedly failed to testify about would have been important or "material" to the Congressional committee before which he testified. I called Senator Warren Rudman and asked if I could meet with him. Rudman was the vice chairman of the Senate Iran Contra Committee, the committee before whom Cap allegedly lied. I had worked closely with Senator Rudman in connection with the Keating Five case in the Senate. He is a decent, intelligent, and honorable man, a great lawyer, and has the courage to stick his neck out when it is the right thing to do. I explained what Walsh was up to and asked for his help. Warren was surprised that Cap's testimony before his committee might be the basis for a criminal charge against Cap. He told me that he thought that the chairman of the committee, Senator Daniel Inouye, would feel the same way.

Rudman's view was that if Cap was wrong as to his recollection of certain events, it was not material to the committee. Since materiality is a crucial element of the offense Walsh was considering, I felt that if we could get a statement from the chair and vice chair of the committee, even Lawrence Walsh would relent.

Senators Inouye and Rudman sent me the following letter dated April 29, 1992:

*Dear Mr. Bennett:*

You have asked us, as Chairman and Vice Chairman of the Senate Iran-Contra Committee, whether if Secretary of Defense Weinberger learned of arms shipments to Iran in the fall of 1985 as opposed to a later time that would have been material for the Committee's purposes. As Chairman and Vice Chairman of the Committee, we directed and supervised the investigation and defined the issues that had to be addressed.

While Secretary Weinberger testified that he did not have contemporaneous knowledge of the 1985 arms shipment to Iran through Israel, he indicated that his recollection of dates was not as good as it once was and that he had difficulty sorting out what he knew at any particular time from what he had learned later.

We were aware that his recollection as to the state of his knowledge in the fall of 1985 might have been imperfect as he had a poor recollection as to certain documents. We were also aware that Secretary Weinberger received intelligence reports concerning the Iranian initiative which contained suggestions that shipments might be taking place in the Fall of 1985. What was important to us, however, was not the date on which the Secretary knew or could have inferred from other information that arms shipments might have taken place, on which the testimony and evidence was murky, but the adamant position that the Secretary consistently took with the President in opposing sales to Iran on which the testimony was incontrovertible. The fact that his advice, like that of Secretary Shultz, was overridden by the President and rejected by the National Security Advisor was a key finding of our investigation and was described in our report.

We confirmed that Secretary Weinberger was opposed to the sales, not only by the testimony of other witnesses such as Admiral Poindexter, Mr. McFarlane, Secretary Shultz and Donald Regan, but from contemporaneous documents, including a PROF note written by [Oliver] North in which William Casey was described as believing that Secretary Weinberger would continue to create "road blocks" to arms sales to Iran. We even elicited testimony from Secretary Shultz that Secretary Weinberger warned the President that the sales to Iran might be criminal violations. In short, we focused on Weinberger's staunch opposition to the sales, which was material to our investigation, not on the communications that might have alerted him to the fact that transfers might have been taking place earlier than he recalled.

While this was all I could have asked for, the senators gave more. The final paragraph stated:

Finally, we shall end on a personal note. Our relationship with Secretary Weinberger is professional and not personal.

Based upon our dealings with him over the years, we know Secretary Weinberger to be a man of the highest integrity and honor. It is inconceivable to us that he would intentionally mislead or lie to Congress.

> Sincerely yours,
>
> Daniel K. Inouye        Warren B. Rudman
> United States Senator    United States Senator

When we provided this letter to Walsh, instead of reconsidering his position, he went ballistic. How dare I communicate with a senator and ask for such a letter! How dare they give it to me! Walsh and his team knew that with such a letter, any charge against Cap based on his testimony before Congress was destined to fail.

When we met with Walsh and Gillen, they also emphasized that certain notes taken by Secretary Weinberger had not been turned over to the Select Committee on Ethics and they believed this was done by Cap willingly and with corrupt intent. Of course, they had no evidence of any such corrupt intent, but this did not seem to matter to Walsh.

Beginning in law school, Weinberger would, on a daily basis, write notes on 5-by-7-inch pads memorializing his daily activities. He continued this practice throughout his professional life, including his tenure as secretary of defense. These were not official documents or records and were in the nature of a private diary. The diary notes, while they included relevant information being sought by the investigators, also included entries about his personal activities, family events, doctors' appointments, social activities, appointments for his dog, etc. Cap never viewed these as materials being sought in the government investigation. More important, the Pentagon lawyers whose responsibility it was to gather the materials sought from the secretary never asked him about the existence of such notes notwithstanding the fact that Weinberger instructed that all materials sought by the investigators be provided. There is absolutely no doubt in my mind that Cap would have willingly produced these notes had they been focused upon. As far as he knew, his instructions were followed by his subordinates and all subpoenaed material had been provided to Congress and the independent counsel. Frankly, had we been representing

Cap at the time of the subpoena, I am sure we would have identified these notes and would have turned over the relevant portions. I am sure that what happened was that Pentagon lawyers, who likely were not experienced in responding to document subpoenas or requests in a criminal investigation, were reluctant to press the secretary on what he had and didn't have and simply relied on others in the secretary's office to give them the requested materials, which were on file in the Office of the Secretary.

When we asked Cap about these notes, he said he sent them to the Library of Congress during his final days in office. We questioned Cap about his final days at the Pentagon and took him through each hour of every day. He told us that on the final days, a photojournalist for a national publication, whose name he could not recall, took pictures of him packing up his office.

We asked Cap if there was any chance the photojournalist took a picture of him packing these notes. The answer was maybe. If we could show that Cap allowed someone for a national publication to photograph him packing these notes for delivery to the Library of Congress, this would undermine any suggestion that Cap was concealing or secreting them. I assigned one of our team to find the photojournalist, and fortunately, after tedious inquiry, we found him.

The photojournalist confirmed that he took pictures of Cap in his final days in office. I asked him to please check his archives, and that's when we caught a break. One of the photographs he took during Cap's final days shows him packing these 5-by-7-inch notepads. No one could seriously think that Cap would allow a picture to be taken of him packing these notes if he were concealing them from investigators, and Walsh and his team could not contend that Cap destroyed or otherwise disposed of the notes since they were at the Library of Congress. Incredibly, however, when Walsh was told that these notes were at the Library of Congress, he claimed that Cap hid them at the library.

At this point we had all but decided that Walsh would go forward against Cap no matter what the evidence unless he was convinced he would lose the case, but we still tried. My team went to the Library of Congress to learn everything there was to know about the notes. Where were they filed? How were they filed? Who had access to them? Were logs kept? Who had been given access? Again, as I have said before, you leave no stone unturned.

What we learned as a result of answering these questions was nothing short of amazing. First, we discovered that Cap had given Walsh permission to have access to these notes by a formal letter to the Library of Congress. Moreover, we examined the access logs of the Library of Congress, and to our utter amazement, we learned that Walsh's investigators had been given access to the boxes in the Library of Congress containing these notes.

During our many interviews with Cap, it became clear that General Colin Powell was a vital witness. I knew that if we ever had to try this case, Powell would be our star witness. He had knowledge of the critical issues in the case, because he was Cap's senior military assistant during the relevant time period. I placed a call to his office. Powell, at the time, was the chairman of the Joint Chiefs of Staff. I was a little concerned about my ability to get an interview with him not only because of his position, but at the time, he was deeply involved with several international crises. I was wrong. I will never forget his response. He immediately returned my call and said he would be available to help me any way he could. On April 16, 1992, Carl and I went to the Pentagon and were promptly escorted to Powell's office. Different from most high-level officials in Washington, he was not surrounded by a group of aides. He met with us alone. Powell shared with us his high regard for Cap and how outrageous it was to think he would be involved in wrongdoing. I could not help but think that this guy was a class act. He was always available to us. He had no pretense and no bloated ego. On April 29, 1992, he provided us with the following affidavit:

I, Colin L. Powell, depose and say that
1. I am currently the Chairman of the Joint Chiefs of Staff. I was appointed to this position by President Bush. My term began on October 1, 1989 and I was reappointed for a second term beginning October 1, 1991. Prior to being named to my pres-

ent position, I served as Commander in Chief, Forces Command, headquartered in Atlanta, Georgia. I also served as Assistant to the President for National Security Affairs from December 11, 1987 to January 1989. . . .

2. From July 1983 to March 1986, I served as Senior Military Assistant to Secretary of Defense Caspar W. Weinberger. I was his chief executive assistant. I saw virtually all the papers that went in and out of his office, and consulted with him on a daily basis. I was the person who largely determined who would or would not have access to him and it was my responsibility to see to it that he was fully and properly briefed on all relevant matters.

3. During the period I worked with Secretary Weinberger at the Department of Defense, I observed on his desk a small pad of white paper, approximately 5 by 7 inches. He would jot down on this pad in abbreviated form various calls and events during the day. I viewed it as his personal diary which reflected a record of his life. Knowing Secretary Weinberger as I did and knowing the routine way he would jot down notes on these pads, it is entirely possible that it would not have occurred to him to associate or link these private notes on the 5-by-7-inch pads with a governmental request for "notes" in the context of the Iran-Contra matter. I do not believe that he would have viewed these as official documents. While I had open access to his office and papers, I never read the notes on the 5-by-7-inch pads because I considered them a private diary.

4. Secretary Weinberger's diary notes were never dealt with in a secretive way. The pad with his notations would sit on his desk with the completed pages turned over. When he completed a pad, it would go into his desk drawer and he would begin to write on a new pad.

5. Secretary Weinberger was extremely astute regarding the matters at hand which we were working on. Once we moved on to other things, his memory for past events was not particularly

good. He would forget facts, dates and details. One of my responsibilities was to see to it that his memory was refreshed
and that he had all the details and information necessary when
he was required to deal with past meetings, conversations and
events. In this regard, I often helped prepare him for his Congressional testimony.

6. I believe that Secretary Weinberger was one of the true heroes
of the Iran-Contra matter. He was adamantly opposed to the
sale of arms to Iran and spoke up forcefully inside the government in an effort to prevent it from occurring. In the last several weeks, I have been asked to review a number of Secretary
Weinberger's diary notes by both Independent Counsel and
Mr. Weinberger's attorneys. While I have not reviewed them
all, the notes I have seen show a person committed to trying to
stop the Administration from transferring arms to Iran but
who was frustrated in his efforts. I would have discussed the
events referred to in the notes with Secretary Weinberger
when they were happening. I shared his views and worked
closely with him in the effort to defeat a proposal which we
both thought was misguided. When his position was rejected
and the President approved the sale of arms to Iran, Secretary
Weinberger asked me to handle the matter for the Department of Defense ("DoD") and in doing so to minimize DoD's
involvement in the sale of arms to Iran. I did so until my transfer in March 1986. At all times he insisted that everything
would be done by the book.

7. Some of the notes I reviewed covered the fall of 1985. These
notes do not suggest to me that Secretary Weinberger knew, at
the time that they were prepared, that Israel had sent missiles
to Iran. I do not believe that I knew in the fall of 1985 that Israel had sent missiles to Iran. While I believe we may have
heard about discussions or proposals or suggestions involving
such activities, to the best of my recollection we did not know
that any such activities had actually been carried out until long

after. I also wish to emphasize that while the Iran-Contra matter has been given a great deal of attention, it was only a "blip" on the screen in the Secretary's office during 1985. In the fall of 1985, neither of us spent a great deal of time on this issue. It became important much later.

8. During all of the years I have known Secretary Weinberger, I have never known him to lie about anything. He is a "straight arrow" and one of the most honest men I have ever known. It is inconceivable to me that he would lie to Congress or to the Office of Independent Counsel. Moreover, it is impossible for me to believe that he would have lied about the existence of his diary notes had he understood that they were relevant to what was being asked of him.

This affidavit was a devastating blow to Walsh's case alleging the corrupt concealment of notes, but again to Walsh, so hell-bent on going forward, it made little difference to him.

There was at least one more thing we could do to help convince Walsh not to go forward—give Cap a polygraph examination.

I wasn't sure how Cap would respond to this suggestion. I assured him that I didn't need a test to convince me of his innocence, but I thought a clean test might help us with Walsh. Without hesitation, he told me to go forward. I was confident that Cap would pass. While the results of lie-detector examinations are not generally admissible in court, they serve a few useful purposes. Sometimes a prosecutor will be influenced by a passing test in a close case. Also, such a test provides a prosecutor with something to point to if he chooses to decline prosecution. I had another reason for such a test. I knew that in the court of public opinion a favorable result could be very helpful. I selected Paul Minor to conduct the test. Paul has a reputation for being tough. He was the chief polygraph examiner for the FBI for approximately twenty-five years. His credentials could not be challenged. I have used Paul over the years and I knew there was no guarantee as to what he would conclude. On May 5, 1992, Cap was given the test and he passed with flying colors.

With all of this exculpatory material in hand, Carl and I met again with Walsh and Gillen. How could any prosecutor go forward, given the exculpatory evidence we presented them? Within moments we realized we would not be successful. The prosecutors we met with that day were frustrated and angry. Walsh was upset that he didn't know about his investigators having access to the notes at the Library of Congress. He was mad that Senators Rudman and Inouye had given us an exculpatory letter and that we obtained a strong affidavit from General Powell. Also, he obviously was concerned that the public might learn that Cap passed a lie detector test on all of the critical issues.

Walsh and Gillen told us that they had decided to go forward with an indictment of Cap. They then offered us a deal. If Cap would cooperate by providing evidence against President Reagan and other high-level officials of his administration, they would accept a misdemeanor plea and would support a recommendation of no jail. If Cap rejected this offer, he would be indicted on multiple felony counts. Carl and I were furious and could not believe what we were hearing. We were stunned by Walsh's threat and bullying tactics.

As we left their office I commented to Carl, "This guy is gunning for the president of the United States [Reagan] and is pressuring Cap to turn on him." We shook our heads in disbelief.

We now heard with our own ears what we suspected—but found hard to believe: Walsh was after President Ronald Reagan, and the decent, honorable, and innocent Cap was but a pawn in a conspiracy that existed in Walsh's mind but nowhere else. After discussing Walsh's offer with Cap, he told us, "I will not lie to get out of this. Tell him to go to hell."

When we reported back to Walsh that their offer was rejected, I never felt prouder of a client in my whole life. There was nothing more we could do but prepare Cap, his family, and friends for the indictment. While all of the exculpatory evidence we gathered was not successful to prevent an indictment, we believed it would be helpful in getting an acquittal at trial or with a lot of luck a presidential pardon before trial.

On June 16, 1992, six weeks before the indictment of Clifford and

Altman, the grand jury returned a multicount indictment against Weinberger. The case was assigned to United States District Court Judge Thomas Hogan.

At the time the indictment was released, Cap was out of town appearing on a TV program regarding global business and world economic conditions. I immediately called him and, when he returned the call, I had to deliver the bad news. I told Cap he should return to Washington so we could schedule a press conference in order to respond to both the indictment and Walsh's press conference. I told Cap that since this matter was now in court, this would be the one and only time he should speak publicly until the case was over.

We scheduled a press conference in our offices at Skadden, Arps in Washington. Cap delivered the following statement before a packed conference room:

> "I am deeply troubled and angry at this unfair and unjust indictment. A terrible injustice has been done to my family and to me.
>
> "I vigorously opposed the transfer and sale of arms to Iran and fought it at every turn inside the Administration. As everyone knows, I strongly disagreed with President Reagan on this issue.
>
> "I fully cooperated with every aspect of the investigations conducted by Congress and the Office of Independent Counsel. I even gave the Office of Independent Counsel access to all the papers they requested which have been at the Library of Congress for many years. At no time did I ever knowingly misrepresent the facts or deceive Congress or anyone else.
>
> "In order to avoid this indictment, I was not willing to accept an offer by the Office of Independent Counsel to plea to a misdemeanor offense of which I was not guilty, nor was I willing to give them statements which were not true about myself or others. I would not give false testimony nor would I enter a false plea. Because of this refusal, which to me is a matter of conscience, I have now been charged with multiple felonies.

"The decision to indict me is a grotesque distortion of the prosecutorial power and a moral and legal outrage.

"I am innocent and will fight this injustice to the end with the assistance of my counsel, Robert Bennett and Carl Rauh.

"Because this matter is now in the Courts, I am told by my attorneys that I should have no further public comment until the matter is finally resolved.

"For that reason, I am sorry to say I will not be able to follow my usual practice and answer your questions. Thank you for your attention."

Not only was the indictment of Weinberger outrageous, but so, too, was the manner in which Walsh and his team handled the case after indictment. Walsh would engage in many actions which enabled us to show that he was an unfair and overly zealous prosecutor who was abusing his office. This would help our efforts to secure a pardon.

Walsh, not content with trying his case in court, went to the airwaves. Only days after the indictment, Walsh appeared on *Good Morning America* and *Nightline*. Walsh explained that "as long as [his office] continue[d] to work up toward the center of responsibility, it [was] very difficult to give a good reason for stopping the investigation of Iran-Contra." In addition, Walsh commented upon his internal discussions regarding Cap's prosecution. I was outraged. After this appearance I wrote to Walsh as follows:

*Dear Judge Walsh:*

Now that you have indicted Mr. Weinberger, we do not think it appropriate for you to appear on national television to discuss this matter and defend your actions regarding it. When invited to appear on *Nightline* and *Good Morning America,* I declined to accept because I felt it was improper to do so.

As a former federal judge, you should appreciate that public statements by the prosecutor may impact on a fair trial.

And on June 25, 1992, Walsh abused the reporting function of the independent counsel statute by issuing a public report to Congress that went into matters not intended by the statute. While he acknowledged that this investigation has continued for five and a half years at a cost of $31.4 million, he baldly suggested wrongdoing at the highest levels of the administration. On June 26, 1992, I again wrote Walsh as follows:

> It is highly improper for you to issue interim reports or any other reports regarding Mr. Weinberger or the facts alleged in the indictment against him until the case is resolved in court. As you know, I have previously complained about your television appearances.
>
> By issuing such reports, you are prejudicing the right of my client to a fair trial. For example, in your report of June 25, 1992, you categorically state that there was a "cover-up" by which high administration officials deceived the American public, and strongly suggest an actual crime was committed.
>
> Given the allegations in the indictment, these public comments are grossly improper. Moreover, it is terribly unfair to announce to the world that you have developed "new and disturbing evidence."
>
> If you have any intention of issuing any future reports or making any more public appearances or statements which in any way relate to my client or issues covered by the indictment, please advise me so that I can seek appropriate relief from Judge Hogan.
>
> While I fully realize that you are an Independent Counsel, you are not so independent that you can disregard fair play.

We were getting ready for war. While my trial lawyer juices were flowing, I was deeply troubled that Cap, an innocent man, and his family would be put through the ordeal of a trial. While we had a strong defense, I, of course, was concerned about the end result. Juries do not always reach the right result. Frequently we see felons released from jail on the basis of DNA evidence, after being found guilty by juries. Any honest trial lawyer will tell you that trying a case before a jury is a crapshoot. Frankly, I prefer the odds in Las Vegas. My principal concern in Cap's case was that the Reagan and Bush administrations were disliked by a great many people in the District of Columbia and I was worried about Cap getting a fair shot before a D.C. jury. I am all but certain that Walsh also perceived this and that is why he opposed our request that the case be tried before Judge Hogan without a jury. Walsh knew that Hogan would be a fair judge, but he obviously was so obsessed with winning a conviction that he wanted a jury that he knew from the start might be hostile to Weinberger.

Upon careful examination of the indictment, we discovered that Walsh had made multiple blunders. The first count, which charged obstruction of Congress, failed to state an offense under the law. Also, the fifth count charged Mr. Weinberger with lying to the attorneys from the Office of Independent Counsel and specifically named Mr. Gillen in the charge. Because Mr. Gillen was going to be the lead prosecutor, this was a bush-league error.

We filed a motion to dismiss the first count for failure to state an offense, which was granted by Judge Hogan. Count one was actually knocked out of the indictment twice. This reduced the government's case to nonsense. It now consisted of three alleged false statements to Congress and an alleged false statement to Walsh's office. We also filed a motion to disqualify Mr. Gillen on the grounds that Count 5 made him a witness in the case, and, as every first-year law student knows, a prosecutor can't be both prosecutor and witness in the same case because to allow this would give a prosecutor an unfair advantage and would inject his own credibility into the trial.

Unlike every other motion in this case, Walsh personally argued for the Office of Independence Counsel against disqualification of Mr. Gillen. The court did not buy Walsh's argument and warned Walsh about what was to come:

> [T]he Court is concerned about how opening statements, closing arguments, and related matters would be handled. The Court is mindful that even an inadvertent error in any of these

areas could be prejudicial to the defendant and lead to a mistrial at the least. Accordingly, the Court will not rule on this motion until after further discussion with Mr. Gillen at a future pretrial conference. Unless the Court is satisfied that Mr. Weinberger will not be unduly prejudiced by Mr. Gillen's involvement in the case, Mr. Gillen will be disqualified. If the Court determines the proposed prophylactic measures will not protect Mr. Weinberger from undue prejudice, the OIC will be given the option of removing Mr. Gillen or dismissing this count of the indictment. Accordingly, to avoid any delays in trial should problems arise, the OIC is advised to have other counsel available to proceed if necessary.

At a subsequent status hearing, Gillen advised the court that Walsh would get other counsel to try the case.

As Gillen's replacement, Walsh appointed a well-known liberal Democrat from San Francisco, James Brosnahan, as lead trial counsel. Brosnahan, a first-rate trial lawyer, was not liked by the Republican administration because of his political activities, including his public testimony against William Rehnquist to be chief justice of the United States.

My initial reaction on hearing of Brosnahan's appointment was favorable. I hoped that this would offer me the opportunity to meet with Brosnahan and convince him not to go forward. I was hopeful that Brosnahan would display better judgment than Walsh. At our first meeting at the federal courthouse, I introduced myself to him and asked if we could meet to discuss the merits of the case. Brosnahan cut me off and bluntly stated that he was hired to prosecute the case and would not engage in any discussions about Walsh's decision to indict. I was extremely disappointed and angry. Brosnahan was acting like a hired gun coming into town with two guns strapped to his side. So be it. We would be ready for him.

Following Judge Hogan's dismissal of the lead count of the indictment, Walsh and his team then committed a monumental error of judgment, which showed to the world that their prosecution was simply out of control. The first count of the initial indictment in 1992 charged Weinberger with obstruction of Congress for his alleged failure to turn over his notes to the Select Committee in response to their document requests. This count was dismissed on September 29, 1992. Instead of trying to cure the defect in the charge, Walsh on October 30, 1992, filed a new indictment charging Weinberger with a different lead offense—an omnibus charge of making false statements to Congress.

This new indictment was issued only days before the 1992 presidential election when George Bush, who had been Ronald Reagan's vice president during Iran-Contra, was seeking reelection. This new indictment gratuitously included specific references to then Vice President Bush, which appeared in Cap's notes. The notes that were quoted suggested that when he was vice president, Bush had knowledge of wrongdoing in the Iran-Contra matter. Why were these references made now when they did not appear in the first indictment? Why was the new indictment filed only days before the election? Whatever his intent, this new indictment was viewed as an effort by Walsh to do political damage to President Bush. There was an explosion in Washington, and Walsh was blasted for injecting himself into the presidential election. This put both Walsh and Brosnahan on the defensive. Walsh's Republican credentials would no longer give him the benefit of any doubt.

Four days after the new indictment was filed, President Bush was defeated by Bill Clinton in a very close election.

In early December, the new charge was dismissed because this time it was brought beyond the statute of limitations, further suggesting to some that it was included in the new indictment only for political purposes. Nonetheless, the damage had been done.

From the very beginning of our representation, the possibility of a pardon was on my radar screen. Whenever I had the opportunity to mention it to a member of Congress, I did, but early on there were no takers. Usually, a pardon is granted only after conviction and after the individual serves a significant portion of the sentence. However, the pardon power is extremely broad and could be used in this situation. Over time, Walsh's arrogance, blunders, and imperious attitude were taking hold; now people were listening to me when I raised the possibility of a pardon.

Obtaining a pardon was a long shot, so we had to assume that the trial would begin on January 5, 1993. I was working on two tracks—a trial track and a pardon track. On a typical day, I would work on my opening statement and trial strategy in the morning and pursue pardon possibilities in the afternoon. I reached out to members of Congress to push along the idea of a pardon. Several members of Congress who liked Cap and thought Walsh was out of control helped me in the pardon effort.

White House Counsel Boyden Gray was the point person for the White House. Boyden, an accomplished lawyer with great political insight, was of critical importance in our efforts. In addition, Senators Dole and Hatch and Congressman Les Aspin and others were gathering support for a presidential pardon. I spent a great deal of time building support for a pardon in the White House, Congress, and the press. In order to be successful, I had to convince those close to the president that if a pardon was granted, it would be a one- or two-day story and no more, and that the president would not be lambasted. To accomplish this, I had to get assurances that the Democrats would not raise a holy stink. Tom Foley, the Democratic Speaker of the House, assured us that if Cap were given a pardon, the Democrats would not make a big deal about it. This was of critical importance. Everything was coming together and support was building. I often joke that if a plumber went to the Oval Office to fix a toilet, he would, before he left, suggest to the president that Cap get a pardon. The goodwill and reputation for integrity that Cap built up over the years was working in our favor. At the same time, Walsh kept helping us with one blunder after another.

Throughout December, only weeks before the trial, we were working feverishly to get the pardon. On December 18, I submitted the formal request for a pardon. This is usually the first step, but this case was different since we were trying to get a pardon before trial. A few days before Christmas, my colleague Saul Pilchen and I were in court before Judge Hogan. Saul was arguing a motion in connection with CIPA—the Classified Information Procedures Act. Because much of the evidence in the case dealt with highly classified documents, we had to have extremely high-level security clearances in order to gain access to the materials. As Saul was arguing a procedural point, a U.S. marshall entered the closed courtroom and handed the courtroom deputy a note for Mr. Weinberger. The deputy gave me the note, which read, "Urgent, call Senator Bob Dole, immediately." Knowing that pardons are usually granted around Christmas,

we thought this could be it. Cap and I excused ourselves from the courtroom and ran down the hall to a bank of phones. Cap and I together
squeezed into a narrow booth, and Cap called Dole's office. I saw the
blood leave Cap's face and heard him say, "And Merry Christmas to you,
Senator."

All Senator Dole wanted was to wish Cap a Merry Christmas. We had
a major letdown, and it was all so absurd that we broke out into uncon-
trollable laughter. Whenever we got together over the following years,
Cap and I relived the story.

On Christmas Eve morning, Boyden Gray called me from Camp
David and said that the president had granted Cap a pardon. He asked if
Cap would have any objection if the president granted pardons to others.
I said of course not. The president, in addition to Cap, granted pardons
to others who had either pled or who had been convicted in Iran-Contra
cases brought by Walsh. They were Robert McFarlane, Elliot Abrams, and
CIA officials Clair George, Duane Clarridge, and Alan Fiers.

Walsh's reaction was predictable. He called a press conference and
denounced the president. He ranted and raved about corruption at the
highest levels of government.

I believe that President Bush granted the pardons because he
thought it was the right thing to do. As he recognized in his pardon statement, "Caspar W. Weinberger is a true American patriot." Cap was innocent of all the charges made against him, and I believe he would have
been fully vindicated at trial. His indictment was a gross miscarriage of
justice perpetrated by an irresponsible prosecutor.

As we stated in our response to Walsh's final report, Walsh's obsession
with Iran-Contra enjoyed some literary parallels. As Herman Melville
recounted over 150 years ago in his masterpiece *Moby-Dick:* "All evil, to
crazy Ahab, were visibly personified, and made practically assailable in
Moby-Dick."

FORTUNATELY, THE INDEPENDENT counsel law has expired and
I hope it is never renewed. While it sounds good on paper, in practice it
was a disaster. It is very dangerous to take the entire law enforcement
power of the United States government and place it in the hands of one

person. As a defense lawyer, I usually have the opportunity of arguing my client's cause at different levels of the Department of Justice and appeal to the good sense and judgment of several professionals. With an independent counsel, you are stuck with one all-powerful person who has only one case and unlimited resources to pursue it. I am well aware of the argument that an attorney general cannot be expected to investigate allegedly criminal activities of his political colleagues. While this argument has some merit, it has never been persuasive to me because if an attorney general abuses his or her power by not going forward in a case for political reasons, a huge political price will be paid. The appointment of a nonpartisan career prosecutor as a special counsel in an appropriate case is far better than the independent counsel regime. These prosecutors will not likely be affected by the political aspects of a case. In my experience, the cure of an independent counsel has been far worse than the illness it was supposed to treat. Beware of the lawyer with only one case. An independent counsel with one case has no other matters competing for his or her time. From my experience, Justice Scalia got it right when, in his dissenting opinion in *Morrison v. Olson* in which the Supreme Court upheld the constitutionality of the independent counsel statute, he observed:

How frightening it must be to have your own independent counsel and staff appointed, with nothing else to do but to investigate you until investigation is no longer worthwhile—with whether it is worthwhile not depending upon what such judgments usually hinge on, competing responsibilities. And to have that counsel and staff decide, with no basis for comparison, whether what you have done is bad enough, willful enough, and provable enough, to warrant an indictment. How admirable the constitutional system that provides the means to avoid such a distortion. And how unfortunate the judicial decision that has permitted it.

The best reason why the independent counsel law should never be brought back to life is Lawrence Walsh. Walsh's prosecution of Weinberger was one of the greatest abuses of prosecutorial power I have ever encountered.

When you represent someone who is the target of a criminal investigation or one who is indicted, you usually develop very intense personal relationships. You find, understandably so, that your client and their families are on an emotional roller coaster. To be effective, you must be not only a good lawyer in the traditional sense, but you must also be a friend and confidante. Clients find themselves in totally unfamiliar surroundings and don't know what to do. Often, especially with very successful people, their natural instincts fail them. Successful people have great confidence in their ability to convince others of all sorts of things. Unfortunately, this doesn't usually work with prosecutors and grand juries. The idea of clamming up by asserting one's Fifth Amendment right not to talk to the authorities or appear before the grand jury is foreign to them. Some days your clients are hopeful and other days they see their world ending. I have over the years developed wonderful relationships with most of my clients. Some, like Cap, wanted to keep the relationship going after the case was successfully completed. Others, say, "Bob, I love you, but you remind me of the worst time in my life. If I get in trouble I'll call you, but until that happens, good-bye and good luck."

Cap and I remained good friends until he died in 2006. He was a great American, and our success in his case was one of my proudest achievements as a lawyer.

AROUND THIS TIME I also represented Tex Moncrief Jr. of Fort Worth, Texas, who was being investigated for tax issues involving his oil and gas business. After a long and contentious fight with the United States Attorney's Office, we prevailed and no charges were brought. Tex was innocent. He and I spent many long hours together talking about the case. There is no client I am closer to. Tex never forgets a birthday or holiday and because of Tex's generosity, a student suite at Georgetown Law School is named after my father. I will never forget him.

IF YOU WANT to drive someone out of office because you disagree with their policies or management style, or if you want to beat a political opponent, don't waste your time taking the issues head-on. While that may be an honest and straightforward approach, it often doesn't work and when it does, it usually takes a very long time. While the Tony Soprano approach is much too crude and violent for most folks in Washington, the scandal machine—however unfair and vicious—is perfect for "whacking" the target. It gets the job done quickly.

The scandal approach is simple: Attack your target's integrity and suggest that he is corrupt. And if you can, toss in a sex angle that will insure extensive media coverage. It almost always works. So it was with the effort to drive Paul Wolfowitz, the president of the World Bank, out of office. As I have said before, "a lie travels halfway around the world before the truth gets its boots on." In this case, the lie got all the way around the world before we were able to show that the allegations against Paul were false.

On June 1, 2005, Paul Wolfowitz became the tenth president of the World Bank, which consists of 185 member countries. The bank's primary mission is to help the poor by providing financial and technical assistance to developing countries around the world. It is run by its president and executive board of directors.

By custom, the United States, which is the largest contributor of funds to the World Bank, always picks the president. In recent years, this has become a source of irritation to other countries, particularly to the Europeans. Moreover, Paul's views on corruption added to this frustration. When he came to the bank he had a strong anti-corruption focus, which he believed was key to getting financial aid to the poor, particularly to those in Africa. He also tried to push bank personnel to leave their cushy Washington offices and move to the countries receiving aid. Instead of being in the field where they were closer to those they were supposed to serve—the world's poor—most of the bank officials lived comfortably in Washington with their large tax-free salaries, extensive perks, and bloated budgets.

When Paul attempted to reduce aid to countries whose governments were doing nothing to curb corruption, this raised a furor at the bank. Apparently Paul was expected to go along with the comfortable relationships built up over time, which worked well for everyone except the impoverished—added to this was the desire of the European nations to flex their muscles and diminish the strong influence of the United States. There was also a lot of hostility toward Paul because of his advocacy for the Iraq war in his former role as deputy secretary of defense. In short, they were out to get him and formed a well-organized cabal to do the job. Day in and day out, selected leaks by anonymous sources created the picture that Paul used his power as president to award his "girlfriend" a sweetheart financial arrangement. This phony scandal erupted in early April 2007 and quickly gathered steam with daily calls for his resignation.

On April 18, Paul left me a voice message, which I promptly returned. He said that he would like to retain me and I readily agreed.

Paul and I met several times at my home over the next several days, during which he filled me in on the facts. I was outraged by what they were doing to him. I had never met him before, but I instantly liked him. He was obviously brilliant, extremely analytical, articulate, and soft-spoken. He had an academic's demeanor. He was also from Brooklyn, so we had an instant rapport. For the bulk of his professional life, Paul was a dedicated and accomplished public servant. He had spent almost twenty-five years in government service under seven different administrations. He served in high-level positions within the Defense Department, the State Department, and the U.S. Arms Control and Disarmament Agency. He was also an ambassador to Indonesia and, in between his roles in government, he served as dean of the School of Advanced International Studies at Johns Hopkins University.

It did not take me long to conclude that bank officials were railroading him. Their approach was simple—make it so uncomfortable for him by publicly humiliating him that he would put his tail between his legs and resign. But they seriously misjudged Paul. He is tough and principled.

At our first meeting, he made it clear that he would not resign in the face of phony charges and that the bank's board would have to vote him out on those bogus charges before he quit. He wanted to fight aggressively, and asked me to lead the charge for him before the bank and in the public forum.

The allegations against Paul were that he arranged a sweetheart deal for his companion Shaha Riza, a World Bank employee, and that this violated personnel rules and practices. Shaha, who had been employed there for eight years before Paul was appointed president, was told that she had to physically leave the bank to avoid a conflict of interest, but she would be assigned to the State Department and remain on the bank's payroll.

This was an unnecessary and harsh result and, in practical terms, it was a disaster to her career since she would be away from the bank for the length of Paul's tenure, which could be as long as five to ten years. She was justifiably furious and fought for her rights with the assistance of a friend who was also a lawyer. She prepared a submission to the bank to mitigate the damage to her career. With the assistance of Paul and with the knowledge of others at the bank, her salary went from approximately $150,000 per year to $180,000 a year with a commensurate increase in pension entitlements. Given her expertise and the fact that she would have to be assigned outside the bank for a period well in excess of the norm, this seemed reasonable. It was also a good deal for the bank because it avoided litigation and a reputational nightmare resulting from Shaha's unfair treatment.

Paul did not want to be involved in this personnel matter and tried to recuse himself. However, the ethics committee did not accept his request for recusal. It was obvious that because of his relationship with her they thought he was in the best position to resolve this potentially explosive situation. Against his better judgment, Paul followed the guidance of the ethics committee who wanted him to get this resolved in a practical and prompt way.

Our case on behalf of Paul was powerful. In our submission to the ad hoc group, which was a special committee appointed by the board to investigate the facts, we pointed out that Paul acted at all times in good faith in accordance with the guidance of the bank's ethics committee. We presented overwhelming evidence largely based on the bank's own documents that:

- Before Mr. Wolfowitz came to the World Bank, he disclosed his personal relationship with Shaha Riza, a senior communications officer at the bank.

- He proposed that he would recuse himself from all personnel matters concerning her.
- The issue was submitted to the ethics committee.
- The committee decided that recusal was insufficient.
- The committee decided that Ms. Riza should be relocated outside the bank, despite her objections.
- The committee also said she should receive a promotion that she was due before she was out-placed, and also that the terms of her forced departure should recognize the damage this would do to her career.
- The committee members did not want to implement this plan themselves, however, because they said they could not interact directly with staff member situations. Instead they told Mr. Wolfowitz, over his strong and repeated objections, that he would have to work with the vice president of human resources to implement their advice.
- At the time, Mr. Wolfowitz understood that the committee was the final arbiter of ethics questions, so he followed its advice.
- The agreement reached with Ms. Riza was in line with other World Bank settlement agreements and was consistent with the goals that the ethics committee set out for treating her fairly.
- The committee reviewed the resolution of this matter on two occasions and determined that it had been dealt with in a manner consistent with the committee's findings and advice.

Because the World Bank and its officials are immune from suit, litigation initiated by Paul was not an option. One option we did have was to create public and political pressure to force the bank to give him a fair process, so as to enable him to make his case. The board members, however, objected to Paul retaining lawyers and fighting back publicly. While Paul's companion for several years, Ms. Riza certainly was not "the girlfriend" with the negative implications described in the press. She is an accomplished Muslim woman and Middle East expert. A British citizen, she was born in Saudi Arabia and holds degrees from Oxford University and the London School of Economics. Despite being the subject of a steady stream of leaks from inside the bank, including details of her personnel files that under bank rules were supposed to be confidential, when she followed the rules and sought leave of the bank to tell her side of the story in an op ed piece, she was denied permission.

While we knew that many of the executive directors, particularly the Europeans would not give Paul a fair hearing, we nevertheless believed that there were a few members of the board who would look at the evidence and judge him fairly. Most important, we knew that those who wanted him out would be reluctant to vote against him as this would cause a serious rupture with the United States. Because President Bush and his top aides were solidly behind Paul, we made it absolutely clear to the board that he would force them to a vote rather than capitulate in the face of phony ethics charges.

It was not easy to make our case to the bank. The ad hoc group was headed by the Dutchman Herman Wijffels. Under his leadership, the committee reminded me of Lewis Carroll's Red Queen who agreed that while the thief who stole her tarts was entitled to a trial, she wanted to sentence him first. While they allowed Paul to appear before the committee, it was clear that this was only to give the appearance of being fair. They, in fact, had no intention of being fair, and they were not. The fact is that they did not care about the evidence as they knew exactly what they wanted to do—and that was to run him out. They believed that if they found that he violated bank ethics rules—even if there were no basis for such a finding—he would be shamed out of office. During this period, several leaks came out of the ad hoc group suggesting they had reached adverse conclusions even before they saw our evidence or heard from us. On Sunday evening, May 6, 2007, the ad hoc group delivered to us its draft report with transcribed witness statements and exhibits that totaled more than six hundred pages. As expected, the draft report was harshly critical and found a variety of violations. Amazingly, they even criticized Paul for defending himself in public against the steady barrage of inaccurate leaks coming from the ad hoc group and others within the bank. It was clear that the committee all but disregarded any evidence we had provided them. Incredibly, they gave us only forty-eight hours to respond. So much for fair process. On the following day, Paul wrote the committee chair, Wijffels, requesting one week to respond. This request was arrogantly denied and we were given only one additional day. World Bank rules, that govern disciplinary proceedings, give staffers at least five business days to respond to preliminary findings, but surprisingly the president was denied this right. When an institution is immune from suit, there is no need to be fair or to follow the rules. By bringing the committee's outrageous denial to public attention, however, we embarrassed them into giving us a few more days to submit a written response.

Our response to the committee was a real team effort with contributions from Paul, Robin Cleveland, a senior aide to Paul, my colleague Amy Sabrin, myself, and several associates on my staff. Amy took the lead in putting pen to paper and on May 11, only five days after receiving the draft report, we made our response. We did in five days what normally would have taken thirty. Three days after receiving our response, the ad hoc group made its decision and submitted its report to the full board of the World Bank. Again it was obvious that they ignored the evidence we presented. Of course, the negative findings were leaked before they were even delivered to the board, and we had no choice but to respond publicly.

Since the committee had no authority to take any action against Paul, but could only make recommendations to the full board, the fight moved to the board.

On May 15, 2007, at 5:00 P.M., Paul Wolfowitz appeared before the board. Amy and I attended the meeting but were not allowed to speak. Paul delivered a powerful statement which consisted of our essential themes throughout this ordeal. Here is part of what he said:

> Mr. Chairman and Members of the Board. Thank you for allowing me and my counsel Bob Bennett and Amy Sabrin to appear before you today.
>
> This has been a difficult time for all of us. It has been difficult for the World Bank family, and it has been difficult for me and my family.

I have spent nearly all my professional life in public service. Some people have disagreed with my policies and positions. But never before have they questioned my honesty or integrity.

In the last month, Shaha Riza and I have been held up to public ridicule. I have been caricatured as a "boyfriend" who used his position of power to help his "girlfriend." She, a talented and productive professional staff member, has been demeaned. I have had to explain to my children, my friends, and my professional colleagues that this was not the case.

I tell you that so that you can understand why I have been fighting so hard to defend myself. I know that you would do the same if you were in my position.

But this is not only, or even principally, about me personally. My children and those who I care about deeply know I have integrity. This is about the World Bank. For the sake of the bank, and for your sake, this process has to be fair.

If you want to have a discussion about my leadership, my management style, and the policies I support, let's do it. That's fair. That's legitimate. But let's get past this conflict-of-interest matter that was resolved over a year ago.

Relying in large part on the bank's own documents, Paul then presented in detail the reasons why the ad hoc group report was wrong. It was obvious that, given his relationship with Ms. Riza, they wanted him to solve the problem and avoid a grievance procedure available to her, and therefore refused his request to recuse himself.

Finally, in a soft but firm voice, he said:

In closing, let me say that I know some people may get some short-term satisfaction out of finding that I engaged in wrongdoing. I hope that none of you feel that way. But if you do, I ask you to stop and think about the long-term interests of the bank.

I implore each of you to be fair in making your decision, because your decision will not only affect my life, it will affect how

this institution is viewed in the United States and the world. I fear
that the way this recent inquiry is handled has the potential to do
greater long-term damage to the institution than the alleged underlying ethics issue that was, in point of fact, put to rest over a
year ago.

You still have the opportunity to avoid long-term damage by
resolving this matter in a fair and equitable way that recognizes
that we all tried to do the right thing, however imperfectly we
went about it.

We, of course, were quite concerned about whether the full board
would be fair. I believed that Paul's presentation and the evidence we
submitted made a real impact on some of the members. Since almost
everything was now in the public record, I am sure they realized that they
could not vote him out on the evidence before them without losing whatever little credibility they had left.

A few of the members, who wanted to avoid a vote and a serious rupture with the administration, tried to convince other board members that
they should abandon the findings of the ad hoc group. During the negotiations, Paul, Amy, and I were in Skadden's conference room planning
and executing strategy, which involved the White House, U.S. Treasury
officials, and foreign finance ministers. Since the board members would
not meet directly with the lawyers, Robin Cleveland spoke directly with
board negotiators and reported back to us frequently. The point we repeatedly made was that Paul would not resign in the face of phony ethics
charges. If they wanted him out they would have to vote him out and this
would result in serious ramifications for the bank. After much internal
debate, the board accepted Paul's claim that he acted ethically and in
good faith.

On May 17, 2007, the executive directors of the bank issued the following statement:

Over the last three days we have considered carefully the
report of the ad hoc group, the associated documents, and the

submissions and presentations of Mr. Wolfowitz. Our deliberations were greatly assisted by our discussion with Mr. Wolfowitz.
He assured us that he acted ethically and in good faith in what
he believed were the best interests of the institution, and we
accept that.

With his integrity and reputation intact and a matter of public
record, he resigned effective June 30, 2007.

In its May 18, 2007, editorial the *Wall Street Journal* said it all when it
observed:

> So after weeks of nasty leaks and media smears, the World
> Bank's board of executive directors yesterday cleared President
> Paul Wolfowitz of ethical misconduct for following the board's
> own advice on how to handle a conflict of interest involving his
> girlfriend. And Mr. Wolfowitz in turn will resign from the bank at
> the end of June. . . .
>
> We've said from the beginning that the charges against Mr.
> Wolfowitz were bogus, and that the effort to unseat him
> amounted to a political grudge by those who opposed his role in
> the Bush Administration and a bureaucratic vendetta by those
> who opposed his anti-corruption agenda at the bank. That view
> was vindicated by yesterday's statement, which showed how little
> the merits of the case against Mr. Wolfowitz had to do with the
> final result.
>
> Mr. Wolfowitz "assured us that he acted ethically and in good
> faith in what he believed were the best interests of the institu-
> tion, and we accept that," the directors said, thus rejecting the
> findings of a rigged investigating committee that had ignored
> key evidence. . . .
>
> This all may pass as World Bank justice. For the rest of us, it
> has served as a window into an institution that seems to observe
> no rule other than the interests of the unaccountable mandarins
> who consider themselves its rightful owners. There have been

plenty of outrages in the bank's treatment of Mr. Wolfowitz, but
for sheer chutzpah nothing exceeds the argument of last week's
report by the investigating committee of the board that he had
put the institution "in a bad and unfair light" by daring to defend
himself publicly against selective and false media leaks designed
to smear him. Had Mr. Wolfowitz taken that advice, he would
have been out on his ear without so much as the benefit of the
formal acquittal he has now received.

By making it clear that he would force them to a vote, Paul showed
his strength and principle.

In a short period of time this crisis brought us together. I totally immersed myself in this matter and was determined to clear Paul's name.
During this relatively brief but intense period, my defensive juices were
flowing and my need to protect him all but overwhelmed me. At the matter's conclusion, Paul was very gracious in his thanks to me and I felt that,
under all circumstances, we had done well. I know that we bonded as
only two guys from Brooklyn could, and I look forward to spending hap-
pier and calmer times with him.

# MARGE THE SCAPEGOAT

.

O N  D E C E M B E R  1, 1992, Bud Selig, the president and chief executive officer of the Milwaukee Brewers, wrote Marge Schott, the general partner of the Cincinnati Reds, on behalf of the executive council of Major League Baseball advising her that a committee was appointed to investigate "the alleged racial and ethnic remarks and conduct attributed to you." The committee included Bill White, president of the National League, and Dr. Bobby Brown, president of the American League. The letter advised Marge that the investigation would be thorough and fair.

On December 22, 1992, a mere three weeks after sending the letter, the executive council issued its report. It was neither thorough nor fair. It was based largely on hearsay provided by individuals who had an axe to grind with Marge, such as former disgruntled employees and a litigant who had sued her. The report made no effort to present Marge's side of the issues. The report lacked context and specifics. Moreover, the conclusions in the report were based on superficial interviews over the phone, and no effort appeared to have been made to determine the credibility of witnesses. In short, the report was a hatchet job and even included highly irrelevant and mean-spirited material, such as an allegation that a male relation of Marge frequented a house of prostitution. Also, it suggested that Marge was a Nazi supporter and it cited evidence that a visitor to her home saw a swastika armband in a drawer.

A lawyer friend recommended me to Marge, who promptly called me. Right off the bat she said, "Honey, I need your help, they are out to get me. Will you represent me?" I arranged to travel to Cincinnati and meet with her. It was a cold, rainy, miserable day when an associate, Stephen Vaughan, and I arrived at her forty-room mansion on a seventy-acre estate. I was not prepared for what I observed. Marge had a reputation for being a chain-smoking, tough-talking elderly woman raised in a rough, all-male culture. While much of this was true, I found a sad and lonely woman who was afraid that her fellow owners would take her team away from her and deprive her of the only joy in her life—going to the Reds' stadium with her dog, Schottzie 02 (Schottzie 01 had died), and signing autographs for the hundreds of children who surrounded her in the owner's box.

The massive house was dark and depressing. It reminded me of an old mens' club in a Victorian movie that had seen better days, with portraits of stern dead ancestors looking down from dark, wood-paneled walls. We quickly learned that the house's only occupants were Marge and her dog. There was no sign of a housekeeper or staff of any kind.

We spent several hours with Marge learning her background, the operation of the team, and the facts that might relate to the allegations in the report. Marge readily acknowledged that on occasion she used politically incorrect language, but urged me to speak to her many African-American and Jewish friends who would confirm that she was neither a bigot nor a racist. As to the swastika, she told us that a friend, Jay Carrigan, a war hero, had given it to her as a memento of the war to celebrate the defeat of Hitler and his regime.

By the end of the day, I agreed to take her case and to call Bob Kheel, the attorney handling the matter for the executive council. When I spoke to Bob, I learned that the executive council wanted to resolve the matter with "dispatch." To my dismay, the hearing was scheduled only four weeks after the release of the report. I concluded that the executive council didn't intend to give Marge the fair hearing she had been promised, but was more interested in getting the matter over with fast.

Initially, I was puzzled. The game of baseball is not known for its political correctness. Does anyone seriously doubt that ethnic, racial, and gender slurs are common in the locker rooms, dugouts, and even the private clubs and boxes of the owners? Why would they want to get involved in this issue, particularly since it involved private conduct and utterances by one of their owners? I wasn't puzzled for long, however. It became clear to us that Marge was the designated scapegoat. The major league owners were under tremendous public criticism by civil rights organizations for their hiring policies regarding minorities. Marge gave them an opportunity to show that they were tough and really cared about racial and ethnic issues. I was concerned that the sentence had already been decided and all that remained was the trial. Nevertheless, I was hopeful that by submitting credible evidence—not the garbage relied upon in baseball's report—and by showing that the council was on the verge of violating Marge's free-speech rights and that we were prepared to take it to court, just maybe we could convince the council to back off or at least to impose a sentence Marge could accept. We had to convince the owners that they should not curry favor in the short term with the civil rights activists by making Marge a scapegoat, but should focus on the longer term impact of what they were about to do not only to Marge but to themselves as well. Also, we wanted the owners to understand that by taking the action planned, they would be enhancing the power of the commissioner. Since at the time there was no commissioner, the council was acting in that capacity in this matter. If they punished one owner's private speech, it could be a precedent used against all of them in the future.

Over the next several weeks, we conducted our own investigation. We obtained affidavits given under oath from many people who directly rebutted the allegations in the report.

We developed overwhelming evidence of Marge's kindness and fair treatment of minorities and everyone else Marge was supposed to be prejudiced against. We never disputed that Marge on occasion used bad language and occasionally made politically incorrect remarks, but suggested, that while not appropriate, this was part of the baseball culture and was not deserving of harsh treatments.

While I knew that we could never get civil rights organizations on our side, I felt that we should meet with them and try to make peace on

Marge's behalf, impressing upon them that it would be grossly unfair to make Marge the scapegoat for all of baseball. Carl Rauh and I met with Jesse Jackson and local civil rights leaders in Cincinnati. These meetings went very well and lowered the heat and anger toward Marge.

We made our submission to Major League Baseball and, frankly, ripped apart their report. We emphasized that they could not fairly decide the facts unless we had an opportunity to cross-examine the witnesses cited in their report. We made it clear that to punish Marge for private speech raised serious issues under Ohio law and clearly communicated, without throwing down the gauntlet, that we would go to court if this matter was not resolved in some acceptable fashion. I also let it be known that if we were to get into litigation, I looked forward to deposing other owners regarding their use of offensive language and minority hiring practices.

The hearing before the executive council took place on January 22, 1993, at the Hyatt Regency Hotel in Dallas. While we would not be given the opportunity to cross-examine witnesses, we were allowed to respond to the report. Also, it was agreed that following my presentation, Marge Schott would appear and would respond to questions from the council's attorneys.

While the press was not allowed in the hearing room, they were all over the hotel. Notwithstanding the council's repeated statements that Marge would be treated fairly, I knew this was not the case. How could the council reach conclusions based on uncorroborated hearsay of biased witnesses who the council members never met, spoke to, or questioned? We also knew that the council wanted to make a decision immediately after the hearing, and that they wanted to make this a big media event. Marge would be crucified.

I could not let this happen. During my presentation, I made it clear that what they were about to do was unlawful, that it would establish a precedent—punishment for private speech—that could be turned against them. Also, I made it clear that I had met with representatives of the civil rights organizations. As a result of these meetings, I said, "Let me tell you point blank: Marge Schott is the appetizer and you all here are the main course." I then methodically went through the allegations and picked them apart. I introduced sworn statements based on firsthand knowledge of the critical points in the case. For example, I presented the affidavit of Mr. Carrigan, who gave Marge the swastika and explained that this was a memento of war in celebration of the defeat of Hitler and not a symbol of Nazi sympathizing. Finally, I tried to appeal to their human side and emphasized that harsh action would deprive her of the only things in her life that brought her joy. And, in case this didn't work, I made it clear that they would be causing problems for themselves if they took aggressive action against Marge. By the close of my presentation, the report on which their actions would be based was in shreds and everyone knew that if the case was not dismissed or resolved to our satisfaction, we would go to court. The members of the council had to know they were on thin ice and that an amicable resolution would be best for everyone.

Finally, we submitted the following statement of Marge's to the council:

I appreciate the opportunity to come here today to address the allegations against me. The past months have been very difficult. Many things have been said about me that simply are not true. However, as I already have acknowledged, I have occasionally made insensitive remarks in private conversation that I now realize have hurt others. I sincerely apologize for those remarks.

I want to emphasize that I never intended to offend anyone. Like many people my age, I was raised at a time when racial and ethnic remarks were commonplace. Growing up, I heard those words and phrases at home and at school. As an adult, I heard them at work—in the brickyards and in the car dealerships. In Major League Baseball, I heard similar language. Perhaps subconsciously, I may even have thought that these words made me sound "tough," "aggressive," or masculine" to my male competitors in the business world.

But my purpose is not to offer excuses for why I made these comments. My purpose is to acknowledge my mistakes and to apologize for my insensitivity. Although I did not intend to offend anyone, it is now quite obvious that I have done so. I sincerely apologize for having used offensive language and for the hurt that I have caused. I am firmly committed not to use such language in the future.

I want to be part of the solution, not part of the problem. In that spirit, I have instituted an Equal Employment Opportunity Program at the Reds. This program addresses minority hiring problems. Furthermore, I have established a Human Resources Advisory Group, comprised of local African-American community leaders, to advise the Reds on community relations and human resources issues. I also have established a scholarship to assist financially needy students at the Cincinnati Academy for Physical Education—a school whose students are predominantly African-American. I have scheduled meetings with the NAACP, the National Urban League and several prominent Jewish organizations to determine what else can be done.

When I purchased the controlling interest shares of the Cincinnati Reds in 1984, it was a decision made with my heart and not my head. I did it because I did not want the oldest franchise in baseball to leave the hometown that I love. I soon realized that, from a financial standpoint, it was not one of my better decisions. The organization was in serious financial distress. The Reds were losing vast sums of money and attendance was dropping dramatically. I acted quickly to bring in new personnel who would be willing to do things my way. I acknowledge that I was both demanding and impatient. My tough style of management improved the Reds' financial condition, but it also sowed the seeds of this current controversy.

Many of my accusers are disgruntled, former employees. For example, I fired Timothy Sabo because of his performance. While I was still providing him with paychecks, he was keeping a secret diary of things he hoped to use in a vengeful lawsuit against me. After bitter litigation, the court dismissed two of his claims and he voluntarily withdrew the others. His allegations are entirely untrue. As for Sharon Jones, I want to stress that I did not make the comments that she has alleged. I have never and would never say anything like that.

In addition to Mr. Sabo and Ms. Jones, some others have made unsubstantiated allegations against me and the media and others have been quick to judge me based on these allegations. For example, Senator Howard Metzenbaum declared me to be "un-American" for keeping a swastika armband in a drawer in my home. Unfortunately, Senator Metzenbaum did not bother to discover that this was memorabilia from World War II that I received as a gift from an employee named Jay Carrigan, a veteran who earned two Purple Hearts and was left disabled as a result of his fight against Nazism. I was proud to accept this gift from a man who risked his life for his country. I resent the suggestion that my acceptance of this gift means that I support Nazism. This is outrageous.

As a woman in this male-dominated "fraternity," I have never been fully accepted as an equal. Now, once again I feel as though I am being discriminated against. My attorneys advise me that the Commissioner's Office has never disciplined any owner, player, or manager for the type of speech alleged here. Moreover, in those few instances where the Commissioner has punished some-one for any kind of speech, the maximum penalty was a $5,000 fine. Thus, the suggestion of some critics that I be suspended, that my management authority be removed, or that I not be permitted full access to Riverfront Stadium is grossly disproportion-ate and unjust.

Calvin Griffith, the former owner of the Minnesota Twins, made terribly ugly racist remarks, far in excess of anything I said, in a public speech in 1978. In fact, he indicated that a cru-cial baseball decision—his decision to move his team from Washington to Minnesota—was racially motivated. However, nobody in baseball suspended Mr. Griffith or restricted his man-agement authority. Indeed, he was not even reprimanded.

When I read in the papers that a few are suggesting that I be suspended or barred from Riverfront Stadium, I cannot help but think that I am again being singled out because I am not "one of the boys."

I believe that I am good for the Reds, good for Cincinnati, and good for baseball. Many people agree with me. I have received hundreds and hundreds of letters written by people from all across the country who like what I have done with the Reds. They like the fact that we have the lowest ticket prices in the game. They like the fact that I am one of the few owners in Major League Baseball who really spends time talking to fans at the ballpark.

Those fans, particularly the children, are my greatest joy as an owner. I try to make every decision with them in mind. Going to the stadium and visiting with the fans is like visiting with my family. I love the Reds, I love the fans, and I love Cincinnati. I would never deliberately hurt them, and I will work to make them as proud of me as I am of them.

Marge was then called as a witness. She acknowledged using inappropriate language but denied she was a racist or bigot. On cross-examination she denied some things and could not recall others. She was a fish out of water in contrast to the powerful and mostly elegant members of the council.

We knew that Selig and his aides were talking to the press and we did not want the next day's press coverage to be shaped only by the council. So, I asked my colleague, Mike Levy, to go to the press area and hand out our packet of information, which included our response to the report and Marge's statement. The press gobbled up our material and Marge did well in the next day's press coverage.

Following the hearing, I was standing in the hallway outside the hearing room when Dr. Bobby Brown approached me and complimented me on my advocacy on behalf of Marge. As I spoke with him for a moment, I was no longer an advocate, but a twelve-year-old kid back at Ebbets Field in Brooklyn, New York. I said, "Dr. Brown, this is not very professional of me, but can I have your autograph?" I explained to him that while I hated

Me, Dad, Mom, and my new little brother, Bill, in 1943.

Bill and me with Mom on the steps of our house on Saint Marks Avenue in Brooklyn.

With my dad in Prospect Park, Brooklyn, New York.

My grandmother
Irene Szalay and my
stepgrandfather
Dr. Stephen Charles
Szalay. He was the
only grandfather
I knew.

My mother Nancy and my
grandmother.

Bill and me
in front of the
family car.

The Brooklyn Prep debate team with Owen Daley, S. J., our devoted moderator. We won first place in the St. Peter's College Debate Tournament circa 1957.

My mentor and friend Thomas G. Corcoran. The smartest man I ever met.

To Bob Bennett
who left this nest
to fly to fame

The United States Attorney's Office for the District of Columbia, circa 1970. In the front row, second from left, is our leader Thomas A. Flannery.

Cap Weinberger and me leaving the federal courthouse in Washington, D.C.

BELOW: Cap Weinberger packing his notes for transmittal to the Library of Congress. This photo would have been key evidence in proving Weinberger's innocence had we gone to trial.

*(Photograph by Roger Sandler)*

Clark Clifford facing the press after his indictment. *(Courtesy of AP)*

Ellen and me with President Clinton at a Christmas party.

In 2006, Jonice, Saul, and I received the President's Award from the International Union of Police Associations for our work on the Kenny Conley case (Kenny is standing next to me).

Justice Anne Burke, Bill Burleigh, and me when we visited the Vatican to speak with several cardinals in connection with the sexual abuse crisis.

With Cardinal Theodore McCarrick on *Meet the Press.*
*(Courtesy of NBC)*

Following my 2001 keynote address at the Ninth Circuit Judicial Conference, Justice Sandra Day O'Connor, Chief Judge Jack Shanstrom of Montana, and I went fly-fishing.

With Judith Miller.
(*Courtesy of the
New York Times*)

Carl Rauh, Mitch
Ettinger, and I
strategizing.
(*Photograph by John
Whyman*)

Nancy Buckner, Colleen Mahoney, Saul Pilchen, Amy Sabrin, Carl Rauh,
me, and Mitch Ettinger. (*Photograph by John Whyman*)

My little angels
(Catherine, Sarah,
and Peggy), who
have grown up to
be mature, inde-
pendent, and
accomplished
women.

From left to right:
Sarah, Catherine,
and Peggy.
*(Photograph by Matt
Mendelsohn)*

The love of my life
and best friend,
Ellen Gilbert
Bennett.

the Yankees, for whom he played, I admired him and that my parents singled him out as a role model because at the same time he was playing Major League Baseball he was also attending medical school. He responded, "Bob, I can do better than an autograph, I'll send you something." Within a few days of my return to Washington, an autographed baseball appeared and it now sits on my bookcase.

Following the hearing, several members of Jesse Jackson's entourage spontaneously surrounded Marge in the hotel lobby and asked for her autograph. So much for Marge being viewed as a racist.

In the days following the hearing, I reached out to Bob Kheel to see if they were willing to negotiate a reasonable resolution. We had to decide whether or not to file our lawsuit and wanted to do so before the council acted. Bob got back to me and indicated that they were willing to negotiate. The art of settlement is simply this: to know what your client needs and what the other side needs and to try to fashion a resolution that satisfies both sides. What was essential to Marge was to keep her team and preserve her status as general partner and finally to protect her right to attend the games with her beloved dog.

On February 2 and 3, my colleagues, Tom Schwarz and Mike Levy, and I met with the representatives of baseball in Chicago to see if we could negotiate a resolution. Negotiations took place over a two-day period. Bob Kheel represented the executive council, and Robert DuPuy, Bud Selig's lawyer, joined him. After initial disagreements with much posturing, we started to make slow but steady progress. We were successful in getting agreement that Marge would remain as general partner and, with some modification, would have access to the stadium. We agreed that for a short period of time she would not sit in the owner's box, but could sit nearby or in an executive suite. The sticky point for baseball was they wanted a one-year suspension. This we objected to. This point was so important to baseball that at the end of the second day of negotiating, Bud Selig personally got involved. We agreed to a one-year suspension, but only after the council guaranteed that she would be reinstated in eight months if she complied with the other conditions of the agreement.

The suspension of Marge from day-to-day control of the operations was not a big deal to her since she was not really running the club anyway. However, we insisted, and baseball agreed, that Marge could select her current staffer, Jim Bowden, to be the official day-to-day manager. Also not important to Marge was the twenty-five-thousand-dollar fine, which was only a fraction of what could have been imposed.

When the deal was made, I suggested that we give a joint statement for the press. I was prepared, on behalf of Marge, to express our mutual satisfaction that an amicable resolution was reached. As we were discussing these details in the presence of Selig, I noticed that he was very anxious and impatient. He seemed to be in a real hurry to leave our meeting. As Selig hurried out the door, I followed him out since I suspected something was going on but wasn't sure what. I learned that he was headed toward a previously planned press conference, which no one had bothered to tell us about. Tom, Mike, and I followed him to the press conference, which was a mob scene. I believe some TV stations were carrying it live. It was obvious that Selig was in a hurry because he wanted to make a statement in time for the evening news. We were not invited and it was obvious that baseball did not want us there. I was angry at this game-playing. I pushed past security and stood in front of the press only a few feet from Selig. I let it be known I would speak after Selig. I hoped that my presence would restrain him in his remarks about Marge. When Selig spoke, our jaws dropped. He said that the council "imposed" a "sanction" and told the media that this was not a negotiated agreement. We were flabbergasted since we had just spent the better part of two days negotiating the final resolution. There is an old adage well known to trial lawyers, "If you open the door for your adversary, he'll walk through it." While I had been prepared to give baseball its due and express satisfaction with the agreement, I was frankly outraged by Selig's remarks. The moment he finished, I grabbed the microphone and commented that my colleagues and I had just spent two tiring days negotiating this "nonnegotiated agreement." I then explained point by point that Marge had gotten everything she wanted out of the agreement. I explained that she had to sit in a different sky box, not the owner's box on the field, only during April, and that after April she would have to sit one section over from the owner's box. Selig was not happy, but he brought it on himself. As a result of what occurred, the coverage the next day and following days were as favorable to Marge as they could be under the circumstances.

I flew back to Washington thinking the affair was over. While I believed that baseball was focusing on the wrong issues—private speech rather than real change—I was surprised by what happened next. I received a letter from their lawyer Bob Kheel on February 26, 1993, advising me that baseball, in addition to what had been agreed to, thought that "it would be inappropriate" to allow Mrs. Schott's dog, Schottzie 02, on the field during the 1993 season. In a subsequent phone call, Bob explained that this should have been included in the agreement but was overlooked. I said something like, "Bob, you are kidding, aren't you?" Mike Levy and I could not believe it. We decided that in response we would try to communicate the message, "C'mon guys: it's only a dog! Stop taking yourselves so seriously. Baseball is supposed to be fun." So on March 1, 1993, I sent the following letter to Kheel with copies to Bud Selig, Bill White, and Bobby Brown:

Re: <u>Schottzie 02</u>

*Dear Bob:*

I am in receipt of your letter of February 26, 1993, in which you indicate that "it would be inappropriate" to allow Mrs. Schott's dog and the Cincinnati Reds' Club Mascot, Schottzie 02, on the field during the 1993 season. As a dog lover, I am dismayed and disappointed at baseball's inhumane and insensitive treatment of this fine animal, who is a totally indiscriminate lover of mankind.

Your letter identified no provision of the Major League Agreement or Rules that gives the Executive Council the power to exclude a Mascot from the field of play on the basis of alleged insensitive remarks by his owner and trainer. Certainly nothing in the Agreement and Impending Resolution signed earlier this month by Mr. Selig and Mrs. Schott, which governs the terms of Mrs. Schott's suspension, purports to affect Schottzie 02 in any way.

Moreover, to the best of my knowledge, Schottzie 02 himself has never used racially or ethnically offensive language. If you are aware of any accusers, please bring them to my attention as soon as possible. I would, however, caution the Council to be wary of any claims made by cats. They are notorious prevaricators, and many of them have exhibited deep envy of Schottzie 02's stature. If the Council's concern is offensive conduct rather than offensive speech, rest assured that at all times Schottzie 02 will be restrained by a leash in the hands of a responsible dogmeister and he will not be given free run of the field.

On a more serious note, Schottzie 02 is the Reds' Official Team Mascot. His predecessor, Schottzie, was officially honored with a photograph and caption in the Reds' 1992 Yearbook and similar treatment of Schottzie 02 likely will occur in the 1993 Yearbook. Banishing Schottzie 02 from the field of play does not punish Mrs. Schott, who has been punished quite enough already; it punishes the fans of Cincinnati—and especially the children—who look forward to seeing Schottzie 02 at the games. If the fans in Montreal can have their Youppi, the fans in Philadelphia can have their Phanatic, and the fans in Miami can have their as-yet-unnamed fuzzy fish, then the fans in Cincinnati should not be deprived of their loveable Schottzie 02.

Moreover, any restraint on Schottzie 02's presence at Riverfront Stadium as the Official Team Mascot of the Reds would constitute an unconscionable restraint of trade. By what right should other baseball owners—the Reds' competitors—be allowed to interfere in one of the Reds' most important and successful marketing tools? Surely the Council does not seek to eliminate from Riverfront Stadium anything that might remind the fans that Mrs. Schott—who is still the General Partner and can attend all the games—owns the Club. Will you next try to prohibit the Club from wearing the new uniforms she helped design?

Plainly, there is nothing inherently offensive about Schottzie 02, who carries with him none of the negative aspects of Chief Noc-a-Homa or the tomahawk chop. Nor is he even remotely as troublesome as the old Oakland Athletics' mule, Charlie O., who rumor has it repeatedly made quite an ass of himself.

Schottzie 02 is not a symbol. He is a dog. To turn him into a pariah for matters that occurred outside of both his ken and his kennel would be grossly unfair. Is the Council trying to take all the fun out of baseball in Cincinnati? I am sure that Seattle's Moose, St. Louis's Fred Bird, and Pittsburgh's Parrot would agree with me that team mascots are an important part of baseball's success. For the fans' sake, let Schottzie 02 on the field and let's play ball.

Sincerely,

Robert S. Bennett

Mike and I never had more fun drafting a letter than this one.

After this last letter, I had little contact with Marge over the years. When I read of her death, I recalled our investigation that revealed her many acts of personal kindness to people in all walks of life and diverse ethnic groups. Some were her real friends. My guess is that she had many more real friends among those she allegedly demeaned than did the other owners, but since we never went to trial, I never got the opportunity to prove it. Had we litigated the case, the world would have known what I knew, but on balance, I feel we did the right thing in resolving the matter as we did. I know Marge and Schottzie 02 thought so.

I recently thought about Marge's case when the baseball steroid scandal exploded on the front pages of the national press. It seems that many of our baseball heroes and role models for our kids are really frauds and cheats. A few stars such as José Canseco and Ken Caminiti—who died at forty-one—confirmed using steroids, and others, including Barry Bonds and Mark McGwire, continue to duck and weave in the face of allegations against them.

Dave Kindred, the sports columnist for *Sporting News,* wrote the following in his January 28, 2005, column:

Two and a half years ago, Caminiti confirmed to using steroids over the last six years of his major league baseball career. He told his story to *Sports Illustrated*'s Tom Verducci. He said that maybe half of all major league players were on the juice. Though Caminiti backed off that percentage, he retracted only the number and not the truth as he saw it. He saw baseball as dirty with 'roid boys.

Every day the sports pages reveal new information about the illegal use of steroids in baseball.

What was the reaction of Major League Baseball, who had landed so hard on Marge, for her political incorrectness? Frankly, it was shameful. Where were those leaders who were so aggressive against Marge Schott? Where was the executive council? Are they imposing stiff fines and banishment from the field for steroid users? As noted by Kindred, "In the world of athletics, baseball's new steroid rules are laughably lenient." Why haven't the leaders of baseball been as outraged about steroid users as they were about Marge? Only when publicly castigated and threatened that if they didn't address the issue, Congress would, did the owners at long last exercise some leadership on the steroid issue. And what will baseball do now that Senator Mitchell's report has confirmed widespread steroid use? It remains to be seen if they are really serious.

While Marge was not a warm and gregarious person who one immediately liked, she brought out in me the need to protect her. I always find the good in my clients and try to explain to the world those good qualities. Representing the underdog always satisfies some unexplained need that I have.

# CHAPTER THIRTEEN

# REPRESENTING A PRESIDENT

**B**ROOKLYN, NEW YORK—where I am from—is a tough town, but it does not compare with the nation's capital. Washington, D.C., is not only tough but also mean, a town where the practice of personal destruction has been elevated to an art form. Vince Foster, the Clintons' family friend and a White House lawyer, wrote in a note discovered after his suicide that in Washington "ruining people is considered sport." Many years before, President Harry Truman made the famous observation that if you want a friend in Washington, you should "buy a dog." I have two, Rumpus and Rocco. My friend Plato Cacheris, a prominent Washington lawyer, and I have often commented that a friend in Washington is someone who stabs you in the chest rather than in your back. During my fifty years in Washington, I have often felt that being born in Brooklyn and having had a few hundred street fights under my belt was better preparation for practicing law here than receiving law degrees from both Georgetown and Harvard. The meanness of Washington was on full display in the Clifford and Weinberger cases, but it reached a new level during my representation of President William Jefferson Clinton over a five-year-plus period of time.

I was retained by President Clinton on May 3, 1994. Here is how it happened: I had never met or spoken to the president or the first lady, but had the good fortune of successfully representing both Harry Thomason, a close childhood friend of the president, and Harold Ickes, the president's deputy chief of staff. It seemed that anyone close to the president would get ensnared in the Washington scandal machine, which was in full gear from the very beginning of his tenure. In fact, President Clinton had long been the target of the scandal-mongers when he was the governor of Arkansas and before. Extreme right-wing haters, with the help of partisan politicians, kept pouring fuel on the fire by demanding investigation after investigation of the president and those around him. This was all part of a long-range plan to defeat the president for reelection in 1996. Everything from allegations about an Arkansas real estate transaction, known as Whitewater, to allegations of sexual indiscretions by the president filled the daily newspapers and television stations. Although it was 1994, all of political Washington was gearing up for the 1996 presidential election, and it was believed by those close to the president that his reelection could be in jeopardy if the various allegations were not handled properly.

My first discussions about the possibility of representing the president arose out of conversations with Harry Thomason. Harry believed that the president's lawyers had to take off the gloves and respond to the daily allegations against him. Harry said that he and others close to the president were troubled that the Whitewater and related matters under investigation were being treated only as legal problems without adequate regard to their political impact. It would be a Pyrrhic victory to win the legal victories down the road but lose the political ones, resulting in a defeat in the 1996 elections. Handling the strictly legal aspects of these matters was very important, but so, too, was the political and public relations aspects of them. Harry, who was playing an active behind-the-scenes role in advising the president, told me that he and others wanted me to join the team. I told him that if I could help, I would be delighted to. I was excited about the possibility of being part of a legal team representing the president of the United States. Toward the end of April, I received a call from Harold Ickes asking me if I would meet with First Lady Hillary Clinton. I readily agreed.

I met Harold at the White House and he escorted me to an elegant sitting room near the first lady's office. I had never met Mrs. Clinton and was more than a little curious as to why I would be meeting with her. However, I was pleased to have the opportunity. I liked her from the moment she entered the room. We spoke for about one hour. It was obvious that she was very knowledgeable about the several matters under investigation and she asked me several questions as to how I thought they should be handled. I found her to be very bright, charming, and attractive, with a winning smile. I felt we hit it off. Ickes later called me and said the meeting went very well and I would probably hear from someone at the White House very soon.

A few days later I was in my office when my assistant, Judy Sachs, said that White House Counsel, Lloyd Cutler, was on the phone. Lloyd was a friend and one of the country's great lawyers and public servants. He was a Washington wise man and one of the founders of one of Washington's great law firms, Wilmer Cutler and Pickering. In addition to a successful private law practice, he also found time to serve the public interest in a variety of roles. Unfortunately, Lloyd passed away in 2005 and I feel I've lost a good friend.

Lloyd asked me to have breakfast with him at the Four Seasons hotel on the edge of Georgetown. When we met, Lloyd began the conversation by telling me that the president and Mrs. Clinton wanted me to join the legal team representing the president. "Bob, I want you to have a seat at the table." Obviously, I was incredibly flattered. Lloyd went on to explain his many frustrations and how he thought I could be of help to the Clintons. Lloyd made it clear to me that one of my chief responsibilities would be to take an active role speaking publicly on behalf of the president and to deal with the media in responding to the daily attacks. Lloyd explained that as White House counsel, he could speak for the president in his institutional capacity, but he felt that it was more appropriate for the president's personal lawyer to respond to personal attacks on the president, particularly those of a sexual nature. He went on to explain that the White House did not want the public affairs and communications personnel of the White House to take on this role.

Lloyd further explained that David Kendall, the president's personal lawyer in the Whitewater investigation, did not like dealing with the press and media and that it was felt that his strengths were in more traditional legal roles. The plan was for all of us, Lloyd, David, and myself, to work together when that was appropriate.

Shortly after meeting with Lloyd, I was called to the White House and met personally with the president. Without any fanfare, he made reference to my lengthy meeting with Mrs. Clinton and asked me to represent him. I gladly accepted. As I walked back to my office, which was one block from the White House, I had a smile on my face and a bounce in my step. I could not believe my good fortune.

While Lloyd's initial plan was for me to work on a wide variety of matters, there was one case that was brewing immediately prior to my retention.

Paula Jones, a former low-level employee of the Arkansas state government, claimed that she had been sexually harassed by Bill Clinton when he was the governor. Harry Thomason told me a story that was later confirmed by Bruce Lindsey, the president's close advisor and one of his White House lawyers: that Paula Jones's initial lawyer, Daniel Traylor, had contacted an Arkansas friend of Bruce Lindsey and told him that he had a client—Paula Jones—who had been harassed by Bill Clinton and that she would go away if given $25,000 or a job with one of the president's Hollywood friends. Harry assumed he was the Hollywood friend. This offer was refused.

On May 6, 1994, only a few days after I was retained, Paula Jones filed her lawsuit in the United States District Court for the Eastern District of Arkansas. This was not your typical complaint. Prior to the filing, I made every effort to convince Paula's lawyer, Gil Davis, to hold off the filing, but I was unsuccessful. It was a scurrilous and mean-spirited document intended to embarrass the president and titillate the media. I immediately scheduled a press conference and said that the complaint was nothing more than "tabloid trash with a legal caption on it." The press picked up on this line and it reverberated around the world. From that day forward, I would be deluged with press calls. My representation became national and international news. When this happens, there are lots of unexpected results. One funny incident I recall involved Don Imus, the famous radio personality.

One day a colleague of mine came to my office with a big grin on his face. Apparently, the radio-talk-show bigwig Don Imus was complimenting me on his show and apparently threatened a limousine company that was dunning him for money by announcing that he had retained me to sue them. Apparently the company backed off and Imus gave me credit. Of course, I am sure his comments about them on the air did more to scare them off than my alleged representation of him. I knew nothing about this beforehand as I had never spoken to Imus about my representing him. Frankly, I thought it was pretty funny, and when Imus offered to pay for my services—which he never really retained—I said no, particularly since the free publicity was worth far more than anything I could have billed.

With respect to the Paula Jones case, I felt strongly that a sitting president should not be distracted with a baseless lawsuit while in office. Also, it was clear to Lloyd and me that the lawsuit would be used as a vehicle to defeat President Clinton in the upcoming 1996 election. Therefore, my immediate goal in the Jones case was to delay it. In one meeting with Lloyd Cutler, he said, "Bob, if you can delay this case until after the election, we will have won." The case presented a threat to the president's re-election effort because as long as it was at center stage, the president could not get his message across, and, as everyone knows, negative attacks on a political figure almost always work.

Given the nature of the case, I was given a wide latitude by the president in dealing with the press. As previously explained to me by Lloyd, the White House wanted to put distance between itself and allegations of sexual impropriety by the president, so it was decided that it would be better for the president's personal counsel, who would also have a better understanding of the facts, to deal with the media. While the focus of my attention was what the press called the bimbo eruption, I was frequently asked to address publicly issues totally unrelated to it. On a pretty regular basis, the White House and occasionally David Kendall would ask me to deal with a press issue even though it was unrelated to the Jones case, my primary mission. For example, when the famous billing records were found and the first lady was attacked, I was asked to go on ABC and defend her, which I was happy to do. On another occasion, the White House Public Affairs Office, which at the time was headed by Mike Mc-Curry, asked me to help. McCurry had turned down *60 Minutes,* which was preparing what the White House believed was a "hit story" on the president. I was asked to attend a meeting in the White House counsel's office. When I arrived, a dozen or so presidential advisors were there. The decision was made that they should reverse their course and that someone should appear on behalf of the president, as it would look bad if it was reported that the president refused to participate.

The group decided that I should appear and speak on behalf of the president. Considering that I had spoken to *60 Minutes* in the past and Lesley Stahl had done a very favorable profile of me previously, it was thought that I would at least have a shot at minimizing the damage. Mc-Curry and I then spoke directly to Don Hewitt, the majordomo at *60 Minutes,* to set some general rules. Before agreeing to appear, I said to the assembled group of advisors, "If this doesn't go well and I read any criticisms by anyone in this group about what I said or didn't say, you will hear from me." The reason I said this was that from time to time some "unnamed sources" in McCurry's office would criticize something I said, suggesting that I was either wrong or unauthorized to speak. Usually, the source would be identified as "a senior White House official." Since I never said anything without the approval of those who were involved, this would infuriate me. Everyone in the room understood what I was saying and why and thanked me for being the "sacrificial lamb" since we knew it would be a bad story. I did the show and while, as expected, it was a hit job, we did far better than if no one had appeared. Incidentally, I am always amused that you never read a story where the press identifies a source as "a junior official" at the White House.

Because of the nature of the Paula Jones case, I dealt directly with the president and did not go through any chain of command, nor was I expected to follow the normal protocol for meeting with the president. When I called the White House switchboard, I almost always was put right through to the president or received a return call within an hour. When I met with him, it was usually alone or occasionally with my partner, Mitch Ettinger. On a few occasions, when certain issues were discussed, Bruce Lindsey attended a meeting; when an issue bearing upon the institution of the presidency was to be discussed, White House counsel would be present. However, most of the time it was the president and me. Had I been younger and less experienced, I might have been intimidated meeting one on one with the president, but I had been around a long time. I spoke candidly with the president and was not shy in giving him advice in a straightforward and direct way.

This is perhaps a good time to make something absolutely clear. I have never divulged any conversation I had with the president unless he authorized me to do so, and I will not do so here. I know this is a disappointment to some readers, but there is a bond of confidentiality between a lawyer and a client. On some issues, the president would authorize me, as his spokesperson, to tell the press or a particular reporter certain things, which I dutifully did, but beyond this, I would not and will not go.

When I wanted to see the president, I would usually call his administrative assistant, Nancy Hernreich, or his secretary, Betty Currie, and would promptly get on his schedule. When he wanted to talk to me, the White House switchboard would find me. The White House switchboard is legendary for its ability to reach anyone to whom the president wants to speak. I can attest firsthand that they are excellent, though on one occasion they were stumped, but more about that later.

Most of the meetings with the president took place in the evenings or late afternoons in his office at the residence. Its large windows overlooked the magnificent lawn behind the White House. At night it had a spectacular view. The room itself was elegant and you felt history pouring out of every wall. In the mornings or early afternoons, we would meet in the Oval Office. Always, an aide would offer me a drink—and I would have a soft drink—and shortly after, the president would enter. He never kept me waiting, and, frankly, each time he entered the room, for at least a moment, I was taken aback that this was the president of the United States and I was meeting with him privately. One night, just before midnight, I arrived at a heavily guarded side entrance, was waved through, and parked directly behind the residence. I was driving my car with D.C. plates. The steward who would escort me upstairs said, "Good evening, Mr. Bennett; by the way, are you from New York?" Somewhat surprised and thinking maybe I knew him from the old days, I said, "Yes, how do you know?" His response floored me: "Mr. Bennett, I've noticed since working here that the only people who park where you parked but still lock their car are from New York." I am at least glad that I didn't put a safety bar on the steering wheel.

Paula Jones wanted money and enjoyed the celebrity the lawsuit brought her; the right-wing haters and their supporters who backed her saw the case as a vehicle to engage in vicious partisan politics. Their goal was to interfere with the president's agenda and to generate so much negative publicity that it would result in the defeat of the president in his reelection effort a few years away.

While I am not sympathetic to Paula Jones, because she brought a frivolous case, I do believe that she became a pawn of the right-wing Clinton-haters who shamelessly used her.

The president, a lawyer by training and a former attorney general of Arkansas, was clearly in charge of all his cases. He was always accessible, knowledgeable, and interested in all aspects of the representation. As president, he was always getting input from lots of people—including lawyers and nonlawyers—even though most of them knew little about the facts of the case. A president has many friends, advisors, lawyers, and others who want to be part of the action, and it seemed all of them were giving the president advice as to what to do and what not to do. Unencumbered by the facts, some of the advice was awful. I was usually able to deal with it, but I was always worried about advice that never came to my attention.

The case itself was not complicated. Jones's lawsuit was based on conduct alleged to have occurred three years earlier, in 1991, before President Clinton took office. The claims were filed under a federal civil rights statute and state tort law. She alleged that when she went to a room at a hotel at which Governor Clinton was giving a speech, she was sexually harassed and improperly detained, and as a result she suffered emotional distress. She also claimed that because she would not submit to the president, she suffered consequences at her job.

The president adamantly denied the allegations of the complaint and

I was instructed to defend him vigorously. It did not take us long to discover just how incredibly weak the case was. It was absolutely clear that Ms. Jones suffered none of the consequences at work she claimed. One of Paula Jones's responsibilities was to deliver mail to the governor's office. Following the alleged incident, she continued to do so and, according to several witnesses, she showed considerable interest in the whereabouts of the governor. Moreover, she never took the actions you would expect a harassed employee to take. She never complained to her superiors about what allegedly occurred, she never asked to be relieved of the duty of going to the governor's office, and instead of trying to avoid the governor, she made every effort to see him.

Unfortunately, in our legal system, even the most frivolous cases take time to resolve. While we were convinced that no jury would decide for Paula Jones, we knew delaying the case beyond the election, if we could accomplish that, would be the best strategy. Our team, Carl Rauh, Mitch Ettinger, Amy Sabrin, Katie Sexton, and several others, got down to work. On June 27, 1994, we filed a motion asking the District Court to delay any action on the Jones case until the issue of presidential immunity was resolved. On July 21, the judge granted this request and on August 10, 1994, we filed a motion to dismiss the case on grounds of presidential immunity.

Our theory was quite simple. A sitting president of the United States, given all the demands and responsibilities of the office, should not be required to engage in the burdensome demands of litigation, particularly where there were no circumstances compelling the case to go forward immediately. We did not assert that Paula Jones could never bring suit, only that it should be delayed until the president left office. We felt, as did a number of constitutional scholars, that this was a constitutionally strong position. We also felt that since Paula Jones did not sue Mr. Clinton when he was governor, even though she had almost two years to do so, but waited until he became president, she could not really complain about an additional delay, which served the national interest.

On August 5, 1994, only days before we filed our motion to dismiss on immunity grounds, Kenneth Starr, the former solicitor general and prior to that judge on the United States Court of Appeals for the District of Columbia Circuit, was appointed the independent counsel for the Whitewater investigation. This decision would have far-reaching consequences for the nation, for President Clinton, and for Ken Starr. At the time of his appointment, I was fishing with Chief Judge Jack Shanstrom in the Yellowtail Reservoir in Montana. When we returned to his home in Billings, Montana, late in the evening, Audrey, his charming wife, met us at the door in near panic. "The president has been trying to reach you." Even the legendary White House telephone staff could not locate us in the canyons of Yellowtail. The White House operator had left a message to call the president at Camp David. I called and was put right through. While I will not go into detail, we discussed my wonderful day of fishing, the beauty of Montana, and the appointment of Starr.

The appointment of Starr was not a good one because he had significant political baggage. Starr would replace Robert Fiske, who had served as special counsel—not independent counsel—since January of 1994. Fiske, a solid Republican, was a highly experienced former United States attorney with a sterling reputation for being tough, thorough, and fair. Rather than simply appointing Fiske as independent counsel and capitalize on his firsthand knowledge of many aspects of the cases, the special three-judge court in Washington replaced him because they said that Fiske was inappropriate since he had been appointed by the Clinton administration as special counsel; they said they wanted to be sure that the counsel's independence and impartiality could not be questioned. Based on this reasoning, Starr's appointment was strange. He was an outspoken critic of the president, was considering a run for the United States Senate as a Republican from Virginia, and had publicly questioned the president's claim of immunity in the Paula Jones case. As a result of the appointment, there was a public uproar. It was obvious that any findings by Starr against the president would not be accepted by a large segment of American society. Also, what aggravated the situation was that Fiske had made a few preliminary findings favorable to the Clinton administration that outraged some Republican critics. Fiske had determined that Deputy White House Counsel Foster had committed suicide and that his death was not the result of some conspiracy. He also had cleared White House aides in connection with certain issues involving Whitewater. This did not go down well with many powerful Republicans, who wanted Starr to take a fresh look at Fiske's earlier decisions. Since it was well known in Washington that Starr wanted to be on the Supreme Court, but to date had been passed over, there was justifiable concern by the Clinton administration that the president would not get a fair shake and that Starr would have a general disposition against him and might well be affected by a desire to please those who could help him be selected for the Supreme Court should a Republican gain the presidency. While Starr had probably lost his opportunity to be on the high court by this point in time, "Hope springs Eternal."

While I never questioned Starr's personal integrity, I thought this was an ill-advised appointment not only because of the appearance that he had a conflict of interest, but also because Starr had virtually no experience in investigating matters of this kind. His qualifications for this type of assignment paled in comparison to those of Bob Fiske.

While Starr was not a close personal friend, our children had attended the same school and I knew him and both liked and respected him. I knew him to be a very book-smart lawyer and a man of integrity. While I did not think his was a good appointment, I was troubled by many of the personal attacks by some partisan Democrats who tried to paint him as a political hack. Many called for his removal. I believed that Starr, under all the circumstances, should step down voluntarily.

On August 8, 1994, the *Washington Post* reported:

> President Clinton's lawyer in a sexual harassment lawsuit yesterday called on Kenneth W. Starr, the newly appointed independent counsel to investigate Whitewater, to step down from the case because of an appearance of "partisanship" against Clinton.
>
> The attorney, Robert S. Bennett, said he had no personal doubts about Starr's "intellect and integrity." But he pointed to Starr's recent comments opposing Clinton's argument that he is immune as president from being sued by former Arkansas state

employee Paula Corbin Jones and to news reports that Starr had planned to file a friend-of-the-court brief opposing Clinton's position.

"I think Starr should decline it," Bennett said of Starr's appointment Friday as independent counsel. "I think there is a real appearance of unfairness. If Starr found anything wrong, I don't think anybody could have any confidence in that."

I was not happy about the situation I was in because while I respected Starr, I had a client to represent who came first. It was part of my job to comment publicly on his appointment. Of course I was not the only critic of the appointment. Speaker of the House Foley and many others were quite vocal, and justifiably so, in their criticisms of the appointment.

Back in Arkansas, on December 28, 1994, District Judge Susan Webber Wright issued her opinion on our immunity motion. She "split the baby." She ruled that President Clinton would not have to stand trial until after he left office, but that the fact-finding process, including deposition testimony from the president, would proceed. Both sides were unhappy. Anyone who knows anything about civil litigation knows that the trial is often the least time consuming part of the process. Discovery, which is now the mainstay of our Rambo-like world of litigation, is usually more oppressive, distracting, and burdensome than the trial; we felt that it was wrong for the nation and the president to be put through this while he was sitting as president. Also, we believed that any morsel harmful to the president which came to light in discovery and was leaked to the press could be politically harmful. Both sides appealed. While we were pleased with one part of the decision and not pleased with the other, one real silver lining was that with both sides appealing, there would be further delays. We simply had to delay the case beyond the election. In addition to this political motivation, I felt very strongly that a sitting president should not be burdened by Paula Jones's allegations at a time when the president was dealing with national security issues and a looming international crisis involving Iraq. If we had to go forward, we wanted the trial to take place after the president's reelection.

On April 5, 1995, we filed our brief in the Eighth Circuit Court of Appeals, which covers Arkansas. On that same day, Iraq had denied claims that it was trying to make biological weapons. The day before, the president had publicly stated that Iraq could be regaining a capacity to produce such weapons.

On September 13, 1995, I traveled to St. Paul, Minnesota, for the oral argument before the Eighth Circuit Court of Appeals on the issue of presidential immunity. A very funny incident occurred on my way to Minnesota. Greta Van Susteren, the outstanding television journalist on legal matters, traveled on the same plane as did I to cover the argument. I always liked Greta and believe her success at CNN and later at Fox was due to the fact that she was an excellent criminal defense lawyer in Washington, D.C., so she knows what she is talking about.

When we landed, I offered her a ride to the hotel where we were both staying. The car we rented was a lot smaller than I expected. With our legal team and bags largely filling it up, the only place for Greta to sit was on my lap on the passenger side in front. As we approached the hotel, there was a mob scene in front. Press from all over the world—flashbulbs, television crews. When we got out of the car, the press closed in. I decided to make the most of it and in a loud voice said to Greta, "Honey, do you have the toothpaste?" Several of her press colleagues gave her a look as if to say, "Now I see why you have an inside track," which of course wasn't the case. On my return the next day, Greta was also on my return flight. As we were waiting to board, a middle-aged woman approached me and said, "Mr. Bennett, I love you, I think you are a great American, but tell me, how can your brother represent President Clinton?" She had obviously confused me with my brother, Bill. I wasn't in the mood for a fight and simply said, "Ma'am, you really have to get to know Bob. He's really a great guy!" Greta and I often laugh about the trip. What I did not know at the time, but learned from her years later, was that she had arranged to sit near me on the plane in the hope of getting an interview before the others. So when I offered her a ride and she wound up on my lap, it was even more than she had planned for.

The Court of Appeals would take almost one year from the filing of

our notice of appeal to render its decision. On January 9, 1996, in a divided opinion, a majority of the panel affirmed Judge Wright's decision
that discovery could go forward, but reversed the decision to stay the
trial. Frankly, the decision was not unexpected. But one very bright note
was that we were getting much closer to our goal of delaying the matter
until after the election. Circuit Judge Donald Ross wrote a powerful dissenting opinion. Of all of the judges in all the courts that wrote opinions
on the Clinton matter, I strongly believe that Judge Ross was the only one
who got it right. In his opinion, suits such as the one filed by Paula Jones

> . . . could be pursued merely for the purpose of gaining parti-
> san political disruption, public notoriety, unwarranted financial
> gain, or potential extortion. Indeed, any number of potential pri-
> vate claims could be contrived to entangle a sitting President in
> embarrassing or protracted litigation, alleging unwitnessed one-
> on-one encounters that are extremely difficult to dispose of by
> way of a pretrial motion.
>
> The well-known travail of litigation and its effect on the abil-
> ity of the President to perform his duties, as well as the subjection
> of the President to the ongoing jurisdiction of the courts and the
> attendant impact on the separation of powers, dictate the post-
> ponement of non-exigent, private civil damages litigation until
> the President leaves office.
>
> In my opinion, the stay should include pretrial discovery, as
> well as the trial proceedings, because discovery is likely to pose
> even more intrusive and burdensome demands on the Presi-
> dent's time and attention than the eventual trial itself.
>
> Out of respect for the separation of powers and the unique
> constitutional position of the President, I conclude the President
> ordinarily should not be required to defend himself against civil
> actions until after the completion of his service in office; the
> plaintiff should have to demonstrate convincingly both that delay
> will seriously prejudice the plaintiff's interests and that immedi-
> ate adjudication of the suit will not significantly impair the Presi-

dent's ability to attend to the duties of his office. Absent such a
showing, the litigation should be deferred.

The Supreme Court accepts very few cases that are appealed from the
nation's circuit courts. The chances of the Supreme Court taking the
case on appeal from a federal appellate court are increased, however,
when there is a strong and well-reasoned dissenting opinion by a respected judge. I believed that even though the Supreme Court accepts
only a small percentage of cases for review, that since this case raised an
important issue involving a sitting president, the chances were good that
it would be accepted for review, particularly given the strong and well-
reasoned dissenting opinion of Judge Ross.

On the same day we lost in the Court of Appeals, the president's time
was taken up by other matters. Talks between Congress and the president
over a balanced budget were suspended, and the White House announced that the president would fly to Bosnia to visit the American
troops.

As we appealed the case through the court system, we were always
successful in obtaining what is called a stay. This means that even though
District Court Judge Wright ruled that discovery in the case, including
discovery from the president, could go forward, it would not go forward
until the president's appellate rights were exhausted.

On May 15, 1996, we asked the Supreme Court to hear the case, and
on June 24, 1996, our request was granted. As a result, the lawsuit was
once again put on hold. As reported in the *New York Times,* Iraq signed an
agreement that same day with the United Nations to speed up the elimination of weapons of mass destruction so economic sanctions could be
lifted.

When we received word that the Supreme Court would take the case,
we celebrated. We knew that because the Supreme Court had agreed to
hear the case, the litigation would not move forward until after the election. I spoke to Lloyd Cutler, who was ecstatic. "Bob, we won." Of course,
what he meant was that we had achieved our goal of keeping the case on
hold until after the election. The president was very generous in his

praise of our victory, and a great burden was lifted off the shoulders of those who were working around the clock to reelect him.

We now turned our attention to writing our brief for the Supreme Court. Our position before the court as explained in our summary was as follows:


### SUMMARY OF ARGUMENT

I. A. The President, unlike any other federal official, has the sole responsibility for an entire branch of the federal government. For that reason, litigation against the individual who is serving as President unavoidably impinges on the constitutional responsibilities of the Executive Branch. The Framers explicitly recognized this point, as has this Court, on several occasions.

A personal damages action is bound to be burdensome and disruptive. This is especially so in a lawsuit that seeks to impugn a defendant's reputation and threatens him with enormous financial liability. It is inconceivable that anyone, including the President, could remain disengaged from such proceedings. Even if a President ultimately prevails, protracted personal damages litigation would make it impossible for him to devote his undivided energies to one of the most demanding jobs in the world. Judge Learned Hand once commented that, as a potential litigant, he would "dread a lawsuit beyond anything else short of sickness and death." In this respect the President is like any other litigant. The President's litigation, however, like the President's illness, becomes the nation's problem.

There is also no reason to believe that, if it is established that private damages actions against sitting Presidents may go forward, such suits would be rare. To the contrary, parties seeking publicity, partisan advantage or a quick settlement will not forbear from using such litigation to advance their objectives. The usual means of discouraging or disposing of unfounded civil complaints would be especially ineffective in these cases.

B. Even the panel majority did not dispute the basic point that personal damages litigation against an incumbent President threatens the functioning of the Executive Branch. Deferral of litigation against an incumbent President would wholly eliminate this problem, while still enabling courts to provide effective relief for wrongdoing. The panel, however, rejected deferral of the litigation as a remedy, and instead concluded that "case management" by the trial court could adequately protect the interests at stake. But "case management" only exacerbates separation of powers problems, by entangling the Executive and Judicial branches in an ongoing and mutually damaging relationship.

In concrete terms, trial court "case management" means that whenever a President believes that his responsibilities require a change in the schedule of litigation against him, he will have to seek the approval of the trial judge, state or federal. That judge will be authorized to insist on an explanation of the President's reasons for seeking a schedule change, a problematic state of affairs in itself. The trial judge will then review the President's explanation and decide whether to accept it, or whether the President should instead rearrange his official priorities to devote more time and attention to the litigation.

The President's priorities, however, are inseparable from the priorities of the Executive Branch of the federal government. Judges should not be in the position of reviewing those priorities. If they are, the effect will be to enmesh the President and the judiciary, to the great detriment of both branches, in a series of controversies over highly sensitive and, in an important sense, deeply political issues about the President's official priorities.

Moreover, state courts are likely to become the natural venue for private civil damages actions against an incumbent President, because such suits often will not involve federal claims. The Framers were well aware of the potential for conflict between the states and the federal government, particularly the Executive Branch of the federal government. They could not possibly have contemplated that state trial judges would have the power to control a President that is inherent in "case management"—much less that they would have the power to compel an incumbent President to stand trial in a state court. This further demonstrates that deferral, not "case management," is more consistent with our constitutional scheme.

C. The temporary deferral that the President seeks here is not, contrary to the court of appeals, an extraordinary remedy, and it does not place the President "above the law." In a variety of circumstances—ranging from the automatic stay in bankruptcy to the doctrine of primary jurisdiction to the suspension of civil actions while criminal proceedings are pending—litigation is delayed in our system in order to protect significant public or institutional interests. The public interest in protecting the Presidency from disruption is at least as strong as, if not stronger than, the interests underlying these well-established doctrines.

Deferral also does not place unreasonable burdens on respondent. In many cases—for example, where absolute, qualified, or diplomatic immunities apply—settled doctrines deny recovery outright to innocent individuals who may have been grievously injured. Deferral of this litigation, by contrast, will not preclude respondent from ultimately seeking a remedy and, if warranted, recovering damages. Deferral leaves the President no less accountable for his conduct. Only the timing of the litigation is affected.

II. Respondent's suit, in particular, should be deferred under separation of powers principles. The suit is based on conduct that occurred before the President took office, and therefore presents no risk of abuse of Presidential power. Respondent seeks only damages, and can be made whole even if personally and directly, not peripherally, so it is especially likely to impinge on his ability to perform his official duties. And respondent could have sought relief long before the President assumed office, or sought other avenues of relief, but chose not to do so.

For these and all of the reasons set forth more fully below, the decision of the court of appeals should be reversed, and this litigation should be deferred in its entirety until the President leaves office.

It was decided that I would argue the case before the Supreme Court on behalf of the president. Since the institution of the presidency was involved, the United States of America would also appear before the court, and Walter Dellinger, the acting solicitor general, would argue for the United States. I was delighted to work with such a distinguished Supreme Court advocate.

On August 8, 1996, the day we filed our brief with the Supreme Court, other things were happening that demanded the president's time. Tensions between Iran and the United States worsened after Iran claimed that U.S. war planes had entered its airspace earlier in the month and used that as a pretext to engage in provocative acts. Also, Russian troops battled to regain control of Grozny. Again, I doubt that the president had time to read our brief on his behalf that day. Fortunately, in the months before the election, little was happening in the Paula Jones case and the president was able to escape for a while from the daily torrent of stories about it. On November 5, 1996, President Clinton was reelected to his second term as president of the United States. Of course, the credit for his reelection had to go to the president and all of those who worked for him. However, in some small way, my team and I felt we had made a contribution. By putting this nasty litigation on a shelf until after the election, we played a part and we felt good about it not because of politics but because we served our client. Paula Jones, a vehicle to defeat the president's reelection, was unsuccessful.

I looked forward to arguing on behalf of the president before the Supreme Court. This was a dream assignment. With the election won, some of the pressure was off, but still I knew everyone would be watching and I certainly wanted to do a first-rate job. I have never spent more time and effort in preparing for an oral argument than I did for this one. Anand Raman, a bright young lawyer in my group, suggested that his friend Akhil Amar, a well-known constitutional law expert and professor at Yale Law School, might be willing to help us in preparing for the oral argument. We called him and he signed on. His insights were very helpful. Amy Sabrin and Alan Kriegel, who have practiced with me for many years, are two of the best writers I have ever met, and along with Carl, Mitch, and me, we prepared a powerful brief. Also, we were fortunate to have the excellent assistance of professors David Strauss and Geoffrey Stone, both of the University of Chicago.

While I had substantial appellate experience in my many years at the bar, I had never before argued a case before the Supreme Court. I wanted very much to do it. Think about it—arguing on behalf of the president of the United States before the highest court in the land would be an experience very few lawyers have ever had. I was very confident in my ability and was immensely flattered that the president had confidence in me, but I had one concern. Given the stakes, would the president be better served by an advocate who regularly appeared before the high court? Could that make a difference? Since I have always put my client's interest before my own, I decided to raise the issue. Walter Dellinger and I met in his office to discuss this case. "Walter," I said, "I want to ask you a question and I want your honest opinion. Should I get an experienced Supreme Court advocate to make the argument?" I certainly knew it would not be difficult to find someone to argue this case. Every appellate advocate in the counrty would jump at the chance. As I recall his words, Walter said something like: "Bob, the most important point to be made in this appeal is to convince the Court that the time and energy of the president will be severely interfered with if he is required to engage in modern-day litigation—there is no one I can think of, based on your litigation experience, who would have more credibility on that issue than you." He then comforted me by adding, "I will be there to handle any of the esoteric constitutional issues." Had my talk with Walter gone differently, I would have bowed out or at least would have told the president of the solicitor general's view.

While I had been a member of the Supreme Court Bar for many years, I went to the court several days before the argument to watch other arguments. I felt that it was important to soak up the atmosphere shortly before I was on deck.

On the night before the argument, I had difficulty sleeping and got up around 4:00 A.M. to do a few more hours of final preparation before leaving for court.

When we arrived at the court on the morning of January 13, 1997, I escorted Ellen and my daughters to their seats and then waited with the other attorneys for the case to be called. The courtroom was packed. It was the hardest ticket to get in town. It was like waiting for the bell to ring in a prize fight. Then it rang.

As I said at the beginning of this book, I was filled with pride. While this was as high as a practicing lawyer can go, it simply would not have meant as much to me if Ellen, Catherine, Peggy, and Sarah were not present!

I had carefully prepared an initial opening that covered all of the essential points I wanted to make, and this included issues I thought would be of concern to the individual justices. It would take less than three minutes, so I knew that I would have very little time before being interrupted but I was surprised that the first of many interruptions occurred in less than one minute. What many lawyers do not appreciate is that this is not the lawyer's time; it is the time for the justices, who have read the briefs and know the case, to ask the questions on their minds.

Justice Souter was skeptical of my argument that if the case went forward, it would consume much of the president's time. He suggested that while it would keep me busy, it would not significantly interfere with the president's schedule. I felt my efforts to convince Justice Souter and the rest of the court that, in the real world of litigation, the president would be required to spend significant amounts of time defending himself failed. However, all and all, I felt I did as good a job as I could and felt that we had the better of the oral argument. Gil Davis, who argued for Paula Jones, was given a much tougher time than I was, and if one were to predict the outcome based on the argument, we should have prevailed. After the argument, several observers commented that, based on the argument, the Court was going our way. This was not to be. Anyone who

follows the Court will tell you that you should never predict the outcome
of a case based on the oral argument.

I exited the Court from the front door and walked down the magnificent steps. The Court deserves its nickname, "The Marble Palace." I felt
on top of the world. As I walked down the steps to meet Ellen and my
daughters, who were waiting for me at the bottom, I observed several
men dressed as chickens—yes, chickens. As I approached the last step,
one of them flashed me. Only in America. This was my day and even this
sicko couldn't spoil it for me.

Four and a half months later, on May 27, 1997, the United States
Supreme Court decided 9–0 to affirm the majority opinion of the Eighth
Circuit Court of Appeals. On that same day, President Clinton signed an
accord with leaders of other NATO countries and President Boris Yeltsin
of Russia on security and mutual cooperation. Also, the *New York Times* reported that the president-elect of Iran blamed the United States for two
decades of animosity and suggested that future relations would depend
on changes in America's attitude toward Iran.

The opinion delivered by Justice John Paul Stevens decided that President Clinton did not have temporary immunity, that the separation of
powers doctrine did not require the federal courts to stay a private action
against him until he left office, and, finally, that the District Court abused
its discretion in deferring the trial until President Clinton left office.
Based on the argument and the strength of our case, I had expected a 9–0
vote, but I thought it would be the other way. Let me tell you a little secret:
A trial lawyer gets depressed if he loses anything, but to lose 9–0 in this
case really hurt. I guess if it had been 5–4, I might have felt worse thinking that if I had only done a little better, I would have gotten the fifth vote.
With a 9–0 vote against you, I honestly think that no one could have won,
and there was nothing else I could have done to change the outcome.

Some cases can't be won, although trial lawyers believe they all can
be. Something else about trial lawyers: they take it personally. The
Supreme Court's decision was my loss—I lost the case and I was down
and it took me several weeks to get over it. If you ever hire a lawyer who
doesn't think or feel this way, go to someone else. It is the personalization

of the process, the total identification with the client—a client's loss is your loss—that makes the best trial lawyers what they are. I don't care if Ted Williams or Ty Cobb hit only 400. I want and expect—although I really know I can't—to bat 1,000.

Over the years I have known a number of the justices on the Supreme Court, and I consider a few of them my friends. I have the greatest respect for the Court as an institution. Whatever we think of its decisions, we must learn to live with them. However, we are allowed to disagree with the justices, and I strongly disagreed with their decision in the Clinton case. I firmly believe in the rule of law and part of that includes respecting the Supreme Court's decisions no matter how deeply we feel otherwise.

For the past forty years I have observed our three branches of government—Congress, the executive, and the judiciary up close. My legal practice has enabled me to work with all three branches. As a result, I believe that the federal judiciary is the jewel of our system of government. Our federal judicial system is the envy of the world. One major reason our capitalist system thrives and attracts foreign investment is because of the stability, integrity, and independence of our federal judiciary. The world knows that you will get a fair shake in our federal courts. Moreover, respect for the independence of the federal judiciary guarantees that issues will be resolved by law and not violence. When the Supreme Court decided *Bush v. Gore*, which handed the presidency to Mr. Bush, a diplomat friend from the former Soviet Bloc said to me, "You Americans are remarkable. Had our court decided a presidential election, the tanks would have been in the streets within hours." The reason that this did not occur in the United States was because of the respect most Americans have for our federal judiciary, which is based on their belief that it is truly independent.

The Founding Fathers emphasized in the Federalist papers the importance of an independent judiciary. Alexander Hamilton, in the "Federalist No. 78," observed that "the complete independence of the courts of justice is peculiarly essential in a limited Constitution"; and James Madison, often called the Father of the Constitution, described an independent judiciary as "an impenetrable bulwark against every assumption of power in the Legislative or Executive." Unfortunately, in recent years, that independence has come under attack by members of Congress. The attacks take several forms. Some congresspersons condemn the judiciary in vicious terms for specific decisions. This usually is nothing more than congressional pandering to a political base. Frequently, in order to pass legislation, members of Congress avoid dealing with the tough issues and leave them for the courts to decide, then bash judges when they do not like the results. Other attacks include proposals to limit jurisdiction of the federal courts or legislation to create an inspector general for them. These are foolish and destructive attacks on judicial independence. A more indirect attack is the refusal of Congress to raise judicial pay. For example, all of the Supreme Court judges combined make less money than a single senior partner at many of our major law firms, and Supreme Court law clerks usually start at salaries higher than the chief justice of the United States. Something is wrong.

While judges should not be above criticism, they should not become whipping posts for congresspersons who are unable to resolve issues in the political process. If legislators did their jobs, many of the most emotional issues of the day would not be dumped on the courts. In the Terri Schiavo case, which dealt with an effort to interfere with a decision to terminate treatment of a hopelessly brain-damaged young woman, Eleventh Circuit Judge Stanley F. Birch Jr., in rejecting the claims of Terri's parents, wrote: "In resolving the Schiavo controversy it is my judgment that, despite sincere and altruistic motivation, the legislative and executive branches of our government have acted in a manner demonstrably at odds with our Founding Fathers' blueprint for the governance of a free people—our Constitution." Following the court's decision, then–House Majority Leader Tom DeLay made the outrageous and inflammatory statement "Mrs. Schiavo's death is a moral poverty and a legal tragedy. This loss happened because our legal system did not protect the people who need protection most, and that will change. The time will come for the men responsible for this to answer for their behavior, but not today." Such attacks only encourage disrespect for the courts and increase the risk of threatening conduct and even physical threats toward judges and their families. Common sense and fairness dictate that we protect our federal judiciary, which is truly a national treasure.

After the Supreme Court's decision in the Jones case, it would become clear in the many months ahead that the nasty and aggressive tactics of modern-day litigation would consume a great deal of the president's time and attention, not, as suggested by Justice Souter, only my time. The Paula Jones suit was not simply a case of a private litigant against the president for pre-presidential conduct. Rather, it was a weapon used by the Clinton-haters to disrupt his agenda, malign him on a daily basis in the press, and to require him to divert his attention from his presidential duties. While we thwarted the effort to use the case to undermine his reelection, the Supreme Court's decision enabled these other efforts to continue.

I often wonder if the Court would decide the case the same way today if President Bush were the target of a civil lawsuit. Since 9/11, haven't we learned that it is critically important to have a president who is not distracted from his or her presidential duties? I remember one day when I met with President Clinton alone in the Oval Office. Adjacent to the office was an elegant conference room, and to my surprise members of the cabinet were assembling to meet. My discussion with the president lasted longer than expected, and on two separate occasions George Stephanopoulos, who at the time was one of the president's principal advisors, came into the Oval Office imploring the president to join the cabinet meeting because one or more of the cabinet secretaries had to leave. The notion that our nation's business was delayed because of my meeting with the president regarding Paula Jones is upsetting. Do we want a president spending long hours with his lawyers rather than with his National Security advisors? I think not.

Following the Supreme Court's decision, we became fully engaged with subpoenas and the incredibly burdensome discovery process. I recall one day that I spoke to the president four separate times about the case when he was dealing with issues involving Iraq. I often think about the craziness of the situation. Why should we be taking the time of the president for the Paula Jones matter, given the circumstances in the

world? Are we nuts? I spent a lot of time with the president in private
meetings and engaged in innumerable phone conversations and I can
categorically tell you that the president spent a great deal of time with his
lawyers in the Paula Jones and other investigations involving him. However, his ability to focus is truly remarkable and I never saw any evidence
that he allowed these problems to distract him from fully performing his
duties.

The country was very fortunate that President Clinton could com-
partmentalize matters as well as he did and that he did not allow the vicious personal attacks to paralyze him as they would most people.

Now that the Supreme Court had decided that the case could go forward, there was an added incentive for both sides to consider a resolution
short of a trial. Unfortunately, "outsiders" had gotten to Paula Jones.
Paula had become friends with political activist Susan Carpenter McMillan, who became her media spokesperson and general advisor. It was reported that McMillan was quietly helping Paula and her husband, Steve,
in negotiations for a book contract, and it was believed that if the case
was resolved, the book would have less value. Moreover, the Clinton-
haters did not want the case resolved, since the Jones suit, a valuable
fund-raising tool for right-wing organizations, would be gone and so
would the money. Moreover, once the case was settled, the press would
move on to other things, and this was not what the Clinton-haters
wanted.

One day, somewhat surprisingly, Paula Jones's lawyers, Gil Davis and
Joseph Cammarata, scheduled a conference call with Judge Wright and
explained to her that they would have to withdraw from the case. They
explained that they could not ethically continue. They did not detail
their ethical concerns, but to me they were obvious. This was no longer
about a legal dispute, but was solely about doing damage to the president
of the United States, and they no longer wanted to be players in this
game, especially with a client they could no longer control and who was
looking for other counsel with the help of McMillan.

The departure of Davis and Cammarata was troubling to us. While
both disliked Clinton and did not mind causing him grief, I never felt

they were representing a cause, only a client in a case. I have no doubt that they had Jones's interest foremost in mind. When they departed from the scene, there could no longer be any doubt that Jones was a pawn—a knowing one perhaps—in a much larger political game. What was about to occur was the very best evidence of why a sitting president should not be subject to litigation of this kind.

The Paula Jones civil litigation had been hijacked by the Clinton-haters. Most of them did not care about Paula Jones. They simply saw her case as a means to humiliate President Clinton and interfere with his running of the country. It became clear to us that there was a whole network of lawyers and advisors who were behind the scenes, anonymously furthering this essentially political effort.

McMillan had begun the search for new counsel while Davis and Cammarata were still onboard. In a press conference in the front of her home on October 1, 1997, it was announced that the Dallas, Texas, law firm Radar, Campbell, Fisher and Pyke would represent Paula Jones, with John Whitehead of the Rutherford Institute serving as cocounsel. The case would now be run by lawyers who in my opinion wanted to hurt Bill Clinton as much as they could.

Judge Wright scheduled the president's deposition for January 17, 1998, and set the trial for May 27, 1998.

One of our discovery goals was to show that the Jones case was less about a good-faith piece of litigation and more about mean-spirited efforts to humiliate and destroy a sitting president.

On January 11, 1998, we sent a subpoena to an organization named Citizens for an Honest Government, run by Patrick Matrisciana. Matrisciana was close to political activists and religious elements of the extreme religious right. He produced films that alleged that Bill Clinton participated in a host of ridiculous conspiracies. It was reported that Matrisciana and Jerry Falwell collaborated in one called *The Clinton Chronicles,* a vicious and scurrilous video designed to harm the president. Paula Jones had appeared in the video and we subpoenaed all tapes of her. In response to our subpoena, we received a package containing several videotapes. I assigned an associate to review them all. One of the tapes was what I would call a smoking gun. When I watched it, I could not believe my eyes. The tape was of Paula Jones and her husband, Steve, at the beach. The tape shows her giggling and laughing and seeking guidance from her husband as to what she should say about her encounter with President Clinton. She would ask if she got the story right and, like a scriptwriter, those helping her make the film would make suggestions off-camera. Following Paula, Steve took his turn in front of the camera and practiced looking and speaking angry and offended.

Selected portions of the tape were released by those wanting to hurt President Clinton, but in my opinion no jury in the world would decide for Paula Jones if they saw the entire tape.

Prior to the taking of the president's deposition, District Court Judge Wright required the parties to file witness lists with the court. Judge Wright would not permit the president to be questioned about anyone not on the list, and so it was important for us to see the list prior to the president's deposition.

The list was provided to us on December 5, 1997. With our team, Mitch Ettinger and I did a thorough due diligence on all of the persons identified in the list. One such person was witness #80 "Monica Lewisky [sic]" whose address was given as The Pentagon.

Even though the relationship with the Radar firm was not as cordial as it was with Davis and Cammarata, we still maintained a professional relationship and never let it get personal because that could interfere with the best interests of the client. As a result of discussions with them, Mitch Ettinger learned that Monica Lewinsky was on the list because Jones's lawyers wanted to question the president about what they believed was an improper relationship with her. Armed with that information, we conducted a careful due diligence as to this assertion before the president's deposition.

One of the people we spoke to was Monica's former attorney, Francis Carter. Frank was an experienced criminal lawyer who had headed the Public Defender Service in Washington, D.C., and was highly regarded. After Monica had received a subpoena to testify in a deposition in the

Paula Jones lawsuit, Carter, in an effort to get her out of testifying, prepared an affidavit based on Monica's discussions with him. The affidavit,
which was executed under oath by Ms. Lewinsky on January 7, 1998, said,
"I have never had a sexual relationship with the president. . . ." Carter
presented this to the court in Arkansas.

Carter sent me a copy of the affidavit prior to the president's deposition. When I spoke to him about it, he told me that he was confident of
its accuracy and that he had gone over it carefully with Monica more than
once. I remember saying to him, "Frank, I am always interested in what is
not put in an affidavit; was there a kiss or anything else I should know
about?" Frank said no. It is clear that Frank was lied to by Monica, and his
representations to the court and me were made in the utmost good faith.

Mitch and I had prepared the president for his deposition over a
several-day period. The news at the time reported that Saddam Hussein
had threatened to expel arms inspectors from Iraq and that Syria had issued a warning to the United States.

The day of the deposition, the president invited me to ride with him
to our offices at 1440 New York Avenue, which is only one block from the
White House. In another era we probably would have walked. The deposition took place in Skadden's eleventh-floor conference room, which
overlooks the White House. In the conference room is a large, oval-
shaped conference table with a black-gray marble top. Surrounding the
table are high-backed black-leather chairs.

We had asked Judge Wright to attend the deposition. Normally, a
judge does not attend a deposition, but I felt that with the judge in attendance, Paula Jones's lawyers would be more restrained than they otherwise might be. Also, with the judge present, she could immediately rule
on any objections and this would minimize the time the president would
be away from work. We anticipated many objectionable questions and felt
that her presence would expedite the process. If she were not there, we
would have to interrupt the deposition, get the judge on the phone, and
let the president cool his heels.

The president sat at the head of the table. Judge Wright was several
chairs down to his left. Across from Judge Wright, to the president's right,

were the lawyers for Paula Jones, and next to them was Paula herself. Frankly, it was a surreal moment as I looked around the room. Next to the president sat the stenographer who transcribed the testimony. At the end of the table were the videographers taping the deposition. Jones kept trying to make eye contact with the president, unsuccessfully, and he did not engage her. In addition to Mitch Ettinger and the lawyers on my staff, Charles Ruff, the White House counsel, was present, as was the Secret Service. Ruff had succeeded Lloyd Cutler as White House counsel. The deposition started on time and there were only a few short breaks. There were no fireworks, probably because of the presence of Judge Wright, and the deposition appeared to go smoothly.

We knew that Jones's lawyers would try to embarrass the president by asking questions about several women. Where we knew that there was no factual or legal basis for doing so, we asked the judge not to allow such questioning. During the deposition I introduced the affidavit of Monica Lewinsky, in which she denied under oath that she had had any sexual relationship with the president. I quite emphatically stated that this was a fishing expedition by Jones's counsel and that there was, plain and simple, no sexual relationship of any kind. When I said it, I believed it with all my heart.

The judge decided to permit some questioning about Monica and others, but agreed with us as to other women. When the deposition was over, both Chuck Ruff and I complimented the president on doing an excellent job. We all felt that the deposition was uneventful and that the questioning of the president was so imprecise that the Jones lawyers failed in their efforts.

The presidential limousine had been parked in the secured parking garage in the basement of the building. The president asked me to ride back to the White House with him. As we exited the garage, the flashbulbs were blinding as literally hundreds of photographers and reporters watched us head for the White House. For a brief moment, I wished the White House was miles away rather than one block, as it wasn't every day a kid from Brooklyn rides in the presidential limo sitting next to the president of the United States.

I looked forward to taking a few days off as we had all been working incredibly long hours in a stressful situation. Unfortunately, this was not to be.

In the days before the president's deposition, an ominous series of events took place. Linda Tripp, who was a friend of Monica Lewinsky, had met with Ken Starr and allowed herself to be wired while FBI agents and Starr's deputies listened to conversations between Tripp and Lewinsky.

Starr and his deputies wanted to expand their mandate to include the Jones case. They asserted to Attorney General Janet Reno that efforts to suborn perjury in the Jones case fell within the jurisdiction of their investigation or, alternatively, that their jurisdiction be expanded to include the Lewinsky matter because they were already familiar with the issues. She agreed. On January 16, 1998, one day before the president's deposition, the Special Division of the Court that first appointed Starr now gave him authority to investigate allegations of perjury and obstruction of justice in the Jones case. Ken Starr, the independent counsel investigating Whitewater, was given the authority to investigate sex allegations involving the president in addition to the Whitewater land transactions.

I was enormously troubled by this turn of events. Ken, a very strait-laced guy, has a Boy Scout persona about him. I was very concerned that Ken would be so incensed about the sexual allegations against the president that he would lose any objectivity he might have and that sex would dominate his investigation. This, of course, is exactly what happened. Attorney General Reno made a horrendously bad decision in approving this expansion of authority for Starr. If such matters had to be investigated, they should have been investigated by someone other than Starr.

As I said earlier, Starr had political baggage because he had become involved with the Jones team and in the Jones litigation before his appointment as independent counsel. He consulted on several occasions, before his appointment, with Jones's attorneys, who billed for their time in conferring with Starr. Moreover, he had publicly commented on the Jones litigation. For him now to get directly involved in the Jones matter created something far more than just bad appearances. Moreover, as a result of our investigation and that of others, it would also become clear that several people affiliated with Starr, including a lawyer at his law firm, had become active participants, behind the scenes, in assisting Paula Jones. I was outraged that the independent counsel, his deputies, and his professional colleagues were working hand-in-glove with Paula Jones's lawyers to get Bill Clinton. On January 23, 1998, I was quoted in the *Washington Post* as follows: "We should think long and hard before we have a sting operation involving a sitting President." I couldn't help but think that the president had been set up by the Clinton-haters. Once Starr was emboldened by his new authority, this largely became a sex investigation of a sitting president. While Starr and his deputies would argue it was not sex but rather a perjury and obstruction investigation, all one need do to understand the hollowness of this assertion is review the salacious materials handed over by Starr to the House of Representatives in support of the impeachment process. If ever there was a time, for the good of the nation, for reasonable people to bring about a sensible resolution, it was now. Instead, the volatile combination of sex, partisanship, and political activism would make our country look like a laughingstock to the rest of the world. I am sorry to say that the shortsighted, and I believe wrong, decision of the Supreme Court allowed "the hunting of this President" to take place.

On January 29, 1998, twelve days after the president's deposition, Judge Wright issued a ruling excluding all evidence relating to Lewinsky from the Jones lawsuit. It wasn't relevant after all. We now had an opportunity to ask Judge Wright to again throw out the case, and we filed what is called a motion for summary judgment on February 17, 1998. When you file such a motion, you are saying to the court that now that all the facts are on the table, there is still no case.

Our team worked long and hard on our motion. We argued that there was no case here and judgment should be entered on behalf of the president. On March 13, 1998, Jones's lawyers filed their opposition to our motion. In their response, which did not really respond effectively to our legal arguments, they included nonsensical material that Jones was, seven years after the incident, still suffering from a stress disorder, that she suffered from sexual difficulty, and that things were so bad that she could not even watch President Clinton on television. Nevertheless, shortly after filing that response, Paula Jones, all gussied up, attended the White House Correspondents dinner in Washington with her guru, Susan Carpenter McMillan. It was held in honor of the president, so I guess she must have closed her eyes when he spoke. I attended the same dinner and avoided her, but it was clear to all who saw her that she loved the attention. She did not seem under any stress, and was eating up the exposure. According to Jeffrey Toobin, the writer and legal analyst, she and McMillan were the guests of Sun Myung Moon's *Insight Magazine.*

On the day of the dinner, my friends, Tammy Haddad, one of the best producers of political shows in the country; her husband Ted Greenberg, a former Department of Justice official; and others hosted a garden party at Tammy and Ted's home. All of Washington was there, and a main topic of conversation was Paula Jones. Fortunately, Paula was not in attendance.

On April 1, 1998, Judge Wright granted our motion for summary judgment, throwing out the lawsuit. After full access to the discovery process, Paula Jones could not even get to a jury because of the fundamental weaknesses in her case. When I deposed Paula Jones, it was clear that she had suffered no consequences as a result of her alleged claims. She had received every raise available to her, and no adverse action had been taken against her in her employment situation. Her case was baseless from beginning to end, but nevertheless it was shamefully used to humiliate the president. This should never have been allowed.

Before the decision to throw out the case was made public, the lawyers for the parties were given an advance courtesy call by the judge's chambers. I recall sitting in my office and being told by my assistant, Judy, that the judge's law clerk was on the phone. When I was connected, he told me that the judge had granted our motion for summary judgment, meaning Jones's case was determined to be without merit. I was ecstatic—I was even higher than I was low when the Supreme Court decided that the case could go forward. I told Judy to order lots of champagne and gather the troops who worked on the case for a celebration, but first I had to tell the president. I knew that he was in Africa but that he could be reached through the White House secure communications network. "Just a minute, Mr. Bennett, I will reach the president," said the communications officer. As I was waiting, my eyes focused on my calendar on the top of my desk. To my horror I saw it was the first—April Fool's Day. Was that really the judge's clerk? Was the case really tossed? I thought for a moment that the voice from the judge's chambers sounded very much like my partner Richard Brusca, a world-class prankster. I was in near panic—what if the president got on and I told him of our victory and it was all an April Fool's Day joke? I called out for Judy and said, "Get Judge Wright's chambers immediately on another line." When she put the judge's clerk through on the phone, I was holding the phone to my left ear with the other phone to my right ear waiting for the president. I confirmed from the clerk that his call was legitimate. My heart had nearly stopped, but I breathed a sigh of relief. I am sure the judge's law clerk thought I was crazy. Within seconds of his confirmation, the president got on the line and I told him the good news. Shortly thereafter there was worldwide film of the president, who was on a state visit in Senegal, beating on an African drum.

Both Walter Dellinger and I had warned the Supreme Court about the realities of modern-day litigation. But unfortunately they did not appreciate what would occur by allowing the case to go forward. Their belief that a district court judge, through "effective case management," could protect a sitting president was shown to be misguided.

One unpleasant but ethically required task I had to attend to was correcting the record regarding the Lewinsky affidavit I had submitted at the president's deposition. On September 30, 1998, I wrote the following letter to Judge Wright:

> As you are aware, Ms. Monica Lewinsky submitted an affidavit dated January 7, 1998, in the above-captioned case in support of her motion to quash the subpoena for her testimony. This affidavit was made part of the record of President Clinton's deposition on January 17, 1998.
>
> It has recently been made public in the Starr Report that Ms. Lewinsky testified before a federal grand jury in August 1998 that portions of her affidavit were misleading and not true. Therefore,

pursuant to our professional responsibility, we wanted to advise you that the Court should not rely on Ms. Lewinsky's affidavit or remarks of counsel characterizing that affidavit.

Paula Jones appealed the termination of her lawsuit to the Eighth Circuit Court of Appeals. While it was on appeal, the impeachment proceedings of President Clinton were underway. The word from those congresspersons sympathetic to President Clinton suggested that it would be wise to get rid of the Jones case. This would avoid any possibility of a reversal of Judge Wright's decision by what was viewed as a hostile Court of Appeals, and it was thought that a settlement might help in the impeachment proceedings. On November 13, 1998, we settled the Jones case for $850,000. There was no admission or apology by the president, which had previously been demanded in all settlement discussions.

The Senate acquitted the president of the impeachment charges on February 12, 1999. During the impeachment proceedings, the president was brilliantly represented by Charles Ruff and Cheryl Mills of the White House Counsel's office along with David Kendall, the president's private attorney in the Whitewater and Lewinsky matters. In addition, Gregory Craig, Nicole Seligman, and former Senator Dale Bumpers played important roles on behalf of the president.

The Paula Jones case was over after four and a half years. I hope that the courts, if ever faced with this issue again, will consider what occurred here: namely, that a sexual harassment case, ultimately thrown out by the court because it could not even reach a minimum threshold of proof, was allowed to inflict the damage it did. The Clinton-haters and partisan bomb throwers got away with using the courts and our legal system to distract our nation, harm our president, and undermine what was in the national interest.

BECAUSE WASHINGTON IS in some sense the capital of the world, all Washington scandals become national and international scandals. The DNA of any scandal—the valid ones and the ridiculous ones—is that they need, like Count Dracula, fresh blood every day to survive. Also, the scandal machine has only one speed—high speed. There is simply no sense of proportionality. A recent example of this is "Quail-Gate" involving Vice President Dick Cheney. First, a little background.

Judy Richards Hope, a good friend of Ellen's and mine, wrote a wonderful book entitled, *Pinstripes and Pearls*. A great lawyer, Judy was a real trailblazer for women in the legal profession. As the parents of three accomplished daughters, Ellen and I are grateful to Judy, and the colleagues she wrote about, for leading the way. Boyden Gray, Ellen and I, and others hosted a book party for Judy at Boyden's magnificent Georgetown home. It was quite a party with Washington's A+ list in attendance. One of the guests was Vice President Cheney. I had met him before and we engaged in small talk.

At that point in time, the Bush White House was pretty much scandal-free. When the vice president asked me how things were going, I told him in a kidding fashion that the Bush administration was bad for my business because there were no scandals. With a smile on his face, he reminded me that this was Washington and said, "It's just a matter of time." How right he was.

Quail-Gate is the name given by the press to the unfortunate incident in which the vice president accidentally shot his friend, a prominent lawyer named Harry Whittington, when they were quail hunting. Fortunately, it was not fatal. The scandal machine geared up and was out of control—it dominated the news and pushed aside more serious news that deserved far more attention.

Now let me make it clear, it is a legitimate story when the vice president shoots someone. Also, it is fair for reporters to report it and for talk-show hosts like Leno, Letterman, Stewart, and Maher to make wisecracks. But what happened here was insanity. It is a good example of my point that the scandal machine has no sense of proportionality. The press and media undercut their own credibility when they make such a big deal about an unfortunate accident and let it dominate the news.

It should be noted that the vice president and his advisors did not handle the situation well. I tell my clients that whenever you are facing a crisis, whether justified or not, you get out all the facts, both good and bad, immediately, say you're sorry, promise to take steps to be sure it will never happen again, take those steps, and move on. Obviously, this would not be my advice if the client's candor could lead to a criminal prosecution. Admittedly, by being forthcoming, the story will not completely go away, but it will be limited to a few days, not perpetuated as in Quail-Gate. Cheney and his advisors, by not getting it all out quickly and by appearing secretive, gave Count Dracula a little blood every day, which is what keeps him alive.

As a result of this ridiculously inflated scandal, the administration had difficulty in conveying messages on a variety of issues of far greater importance to the nation. One day after reading maybe a dozen stories about the incident, I read in the middle section of a paper that the avian flu had moved from China to Europe. This real bird threat got far less attention than did the quail-shooting incident.

On a personal level, the representation of President Clinton had both ups and downs. Because any good trial lawyer completely identifies with his client, the vicious personal attacks on the president hurt and angered me. The daily pressure and anxiety of being a spokesperson for the president was incredibly stressful. While I handle stress well, I must confess that the lows in the case really tested me personally, but regular exercise with my trainer, Kim Kruse, kept me sane and reasonably fit. This also helped me offset the first-rate dinners at Tosca, The Prime Rib, The Palm, and The Bombay Club, my favorite Washington restaurants.

During the entire period I represented the president, while we had some robust discussions, never a harsh word passed between us. President Clinton is someone you enjoy being with. He is very curious about everything and has a razor-sharp intellect. He is one of the most well-read individuals you will ever meet, especially in the areas of politics and history. One night at the end of a meeting at the residence, he handed me a five-hundred-plus–page book on world history and recommended that I read it. He had just finished it the night before. I recall asking the president how he could find time to read such a book. I couldn't find any time to read for pleasure given his case and my other clients, and here he— the leader of the free world, and heavily involved in quarterbacking all of the investigations against him—still found time. One answer is that he needs little sleep. I recall receiving a call from him late in the evening when it was after 3:00 A.M. in Italy, where he was. He told me how beautiful it was where he was staying, and then discussed recent developments in our case. A testament to his intellectual qualities was his ability to master the facts no matter how small. One evening at a dinner party at the home of Ellen's and my dear friends Marylouise Oates, a former journalist and now mystery writer, and Bob Shrum, a leading political journalist in Washington, the dinner conversation turned to Bill Clinton. Present at the party were several very high-level government officials who shared Bill Clinton stories. The common denominator was that President Clinton not only knew the big picture of the most complex issues coming before them but he also mastered the details. The head of a critical agency said, "Bob, he knew more of the details than did my staff who were working on the issues for months."

Whether you were a prince or pauper, Bill Clinton was interested in talking to you. I have never in all my years in Washington known any political figure or, for that matter, anyone else who could relate to people better than he could. He made everyone feel that what they had to say was important, and when he heard things, he filed them in the internal computer in his brain for later use. Let me tell you a few incidents that support these observations.

On March 22, 1996, Ellen and I held a reception in the Federal Suite at the Hay-Adams Hotel on Lafayette Square in honor of our friend Chief Judge Jack Shanstrom of Montana and his wife, Audrey. Jack, a long-time federal judge, had been recently appointed chief judge of his court. The Federal Suite faces the White House and is one of the most beautiful rooms in all of Washington. Because it was in honor of Jack and Audrey, I asked for their guest list. We invited a total of about sixty people and, except for a few good friends, partners of mine, and immediate family, all the invitees were friends of Jack's or those he wanted to meet.

Jack, a good Republican, asked us to invite his favorite icons, including members of the Supreme Court and members of Congress. He also wanted to meet my brother, Bill. Except for Ellen and myself and a few others, the guest list was overwhelmingly conservative and Republican.

About a month before, I was with the president and told him that

Ellen and I were having this reception. I warned him that there would be very few supporters of his invited to the reception but that I would appreciate his coming. "You're right across the street, so drop over for a drink," I said. Of course, it is not that simple for a president to simply cross the street. He said he would try to make it. I didn't give further thought to the president's coming, and I certainly never told Jack because if I got his hopes up and the president didn't come, he and everyone else would be disappointed no matter how great the party. A few days before the reception, I was with the president and he asked me if the party was still on. When I said yes, he said he would try to make it. I was amazed that he remembered.

On the night of the party, I did not know if the president was coming. Shortly after the party began, a security person for the hotel approached me and said that a Secret Service agent would like to speak with me. The president was about to arrive. Now that I was sure of his presence, I approached Jack and told him that I had invited the president of the United States. Jack thought I was kidding until the president entered the room. When a president walks into a room, time stops. Whether you are a waiter serving drinks or a Supreme Court justice talking to a colleague, you notice. (At the time of the party, the Clinton case was not before the Supreme Court. Had it been, I would not have invited the president to a party where Supreme Court justices were guests. Even though it was a social occasion, that would have been awkward.)

The president was at his best. He spent time with everyone and knew a lot about each of the guests and what they were doing. At a time like this, no one is a partisan and everyone enjoyed the party. The president stayed at the reception for a long time and did not focus his attention only on the justices or the members of Congress. He spent time with everyone. He spoke to my brother and his wife, Elayne, and complimented Elayne on her Best Friends Foundation. He had taken the time to learn about what the guests were doing and bowled them over. Think about it, the president of the United States knows about you and what is important to you.

The following December, Ellen and I had a Christmas party. Again, I invited the president. He came and stayed for a long time. He talked with everyone and made each person he talked to feel like they were the only person in the room. He did not engage in the common Washington practice of shaking someone's hand while looking over their shoulder to see if someone more important is in attendance.

One evening I rushed home from the office because my daughter Sarah was home celebrating her birthday. I told her that I was expecting a call from the president, so please be sure to answer the phone and get me no matter what I was doing. I showered and dressed and came downstairs. Sarah was on the phone and I asked if the White House called. She nodded yes and whispered, "I'm talking to the president now." The president and Sarah had a long talk. Sarah told him she knew his daughter, Chelsea, as both had attended the Sidwell Friends School in Washington. When Sarah told him she attended Vassar College, he asked about one of his favorite professors who taught there. Sarah's friends standing in the kitchen could not believe that she was talking to the president of the United States. This was a very special birthday present.

Before I was retained by President Clinton, it is fair to say that because of high-profile clients like Cap Weinberger, Clark Clifford, and the United States Senate Select Committee on Ethics, I was well known throughout the country, at least by lawyers. But none of these past cases would prepare me for the higher profile I would have as the president's lawyer. This was both good and bad. Certainly, I no longer enjoyed the same degree of privacy I had before President Clinton. Reporters would wait for me at the front door of my home as I left for work and reams of correspondence would be sent to me, some of which was very nice but some of which was vile and threatening. There are a lot of sick people out there and many of them wrote to me. Most of the letters were directed at the president, but some were directed at me. On balance, however, it was a very positive experience. Trial lawyers, myself included, have big egos, and frankly you like being recognized in airports and restaurants, as long as it doesn't occur too often. On the night that Judge Wright threw out the Paula Jones case, Ellen and I went to the Palm Restaurant, one of Washington's favorite places to celebrate. Tommy Jacamo, who runs the Palm, told me dinner was on the house. In the middle of the meal, a well-dressed gentleman approached our table and asked if I was Clinton's lawyer. When I said yes, he began yelling and screaming at me at the top of his lungs. He was quickly escorted from the restaurant. This unfortunate incident did not spoil our evening because shortly before, when we were taken to our table, many of the diners stood up and gave me a standing ovation; others came to our table offering congratulations. I would be a liar if I said I didn't like it.

Many other good things happened as well. Please understand it really wasn't about me; it was the love and attachment many Americans had for Bill Clinton. It has often been said that Bill Clinton was the first "black president," meaning that minorities throughout the country trusted and loved him and felt that he was on their side. Several times cab drivers offered me free rides with kind words like "Thanks for helping the president." I never accepted their offers but it made me feel good inside. I recall one late afternoon when I was returning to the St. Regis Hotel in New York, where I was preparing for an upcoming trial. I heard a voice say, "Mr. Bennett." When I turned, there was a young man selling watches from his makeshift stand. He said, "Thanks for what you are doing," and offered me a free watch. I thanked him but declined his offer.

One of my favorite stories occurred when I was in California representing a major insurance company. Following a successful meeting at the insurance commissioner's office, the general counsel of the company and his senior legal staff and I went out for a few drinks. During the discussion of several pending cases, the general counsel asked me if I thought that it would be helpful if the company hired an African-American lawyer in a trial that was upcoming in a major city with a large African-American population. I gave him my honest view that he should not hire a lawyer just because he or she was African-American because African-American jurors would see through that and might be offended. I did, however, tell him that I knew first-rate trial lawyers who happened to be African-American and that they would be good choices for his case. In the hope of getting the business for myself, I did tell him that I had a lot of credibility with minorities given my representation of President Clinton and emphasized my experience as a federal prosecutor in Washington, where I had a 95 percent–plus conviction rate before primarily African-American jurors. As we left the hotel and were saying our good-byes, a bus pulled up to the front. It was filled with a group of African-American congregants who were attending a church convention of some kind at the hotel. One of them spotted me and within a moment I was surrounded and asked to sign autographs. The general counsel looked at me and said, "You couldn't have planned this—or did you?" Of course I hadn't.

Representing the president was an exciting roller-coaster ride. While there were some lows, there were many more highs, and I am grateful for the experience.

# CHAPTER FOURTEEN

## FROM BROOKLYN TO TBLISI

LATE IN THE evening of January 3, 1997, Gueorgui Makharadze, the second highest ranking diplomat at the Georgian embassy in Washington, was involved in a fatal car collision. A sixteen-year-old girl, named Joviane Waltrick, suffered massive trauma to her head and torso that resulted in her death. In addition, other individuals were seriously hurt. According to the police report, Makharadze, while intoxicated, drove in excess of eighty miles an hour in a twenty-five-mile-per-hour zone in the Dupont Circle area of Washington, D.C., lost control of his vehicle, and collided with several cars.

As a diplomat, Makharadze had diplomatic immunity, which meant he could be recalled by his country and avoid the consequences of his actions. That diplomatic immunity might be asserted caused a furor on Capitol Hill and in the press. As a result, tremendous pressure was put on the government of Georgia to waive immunity. At home, political pressure was put on President Eduard Shevardnadze to recall Makharadze and free him from the clutches of the American authorities. Shevardnadze was in an impossible position.

A colleague of mine at Skadden, Marty Hoffman, and I met with Tedo Japaridze, who at the time was the Georgian ambassador to the United States. The Makharadze case was becoming a big Washington scandal with international overtones and consequences. Tedo retained us to represent the government of Georgia.

Had Makharadze been a diplomat from a powerful nation, this occurrence would have caused a furor but would not have threatened the stability of his home country. In 1991, Georgia declared independence and seceded from the Soviet Union. It was weak both politically and economically. Politicians took to the floor of Congress demanding that U.S. aid to Georgia be cut off unless the government of Georgia waived immunity. This was a real threat to the survival of Georgia, because Georgia was very dependent on U.S. economic aid and political support. The Russian government was always creating incidents on its border with Georgia, and without the U.S. behind them, they were in deep trouble. This was all incredible to me. A fatal accident by a drunk driver was a serious matter, but was it so serious as to threaten the stability and future survivability of a country? Well, in short-order, I learned that it was.

While often frustrating to Americans, diplomatic immunity serves an important purpose. If foreign diplomats are subject to the law enforcement authorities of our country for their wrongdoings, then our American diplomats all over the world are in a similar position. This is of particular concern to our State Department because while our judicial system is a fair one, this is not always the case in other parts of the world and we do not want our diplomats to be railroaded abroad.

One of my first stops was to our State Department. I met with several State Department officials and sought their assistance. Surely, I thought, they would see the wisdom in supporting a claim of diplomatic immunity for Mr. Makharadze.

Wouldn't the State Department understand that it would be a dangerous precedent to force Georgia to waive immunity? How could we require Georgia to waive immunity, but then assert it for ourselves when the shoe was on the other foot? Frankly, I was naive. Our State Department said that they wanted Georgia to waive immunity and pressured it to do so. I was troubled because I felt our government's position was totally hypocritical.

I asked my colleague Ed Ross to research all the cases where American diplomats or their families found themselves in similar situations abroad. The results were shocking. In one case, the spouse of a female diplomat in the United Kingdom committed an act of "gross indecency" against a minor child. The offense involved a young girl under the age of thirteen. The British government considered the incident a serious matter and requested the United States to waive diplomatic immunity.

We refused. Surely we could not argue that the judicial system in England was inadequate or unfair, particularly since so much of our own system derives from theirs.

Nevertheless, the U.S. Embassy issued a statement acknowledging Britain's request for a waiver, then stated, "After due consideration of the case and consistent longstanding U.S. government policy in such issues, the Embassy declines to waive immunity." It claimed that it regretted the incident, but declined to even identify the perpetrator or his diplomat wife. Our embassy, after declining to waive immunity, whisked him out of the country the day after the incident.

In another incident, which occurred near in time and close in facts to Makharadze's, a car driven by a U.S. diplomat struck and killed an eleven-year-old girl and injured her mother and sister in the Soviet Union. The Moscow police claimed that the diplomat was "driving in a nonsober condition." What did our government do? To avoid prosecution of our diplomat in the Soviet Union, we recalled the diplomat within thirty-six hours of the incident.

Notwithstanding our own practice of not waiving immunity, the State Department on February 11, 1997, issued the following statement through formal diplomatic channels:

> The Department of State refers the Embassy of the Republic of Georgia to its diplomatic note of January 9, 1997, in which the Department requested a waiver of Minister Gueorgui Makharadze's immunity to enable the U.S. Attorney for the District of Columbia to pursue criminal charges in connection with the January 3 accident that resulted in the death of a young woman and personal injury to others. . . .

And after describing the charges and the punishment if convicted, the State Department went on to say:

> At this time, the Department of State renews its request that, pursuant to Article 32 of the Vienna Convention on Diplomatic Relations, the Government of the Republic of Georgia waive

immunity so that Mr. Makharadze may face trial for the above-mentioned charges, and if convicted, be sentenced pursuant to U.S. law. This waiver would include possible detention of Mr. Makharadze pending trial if requested by the U.S. Attorney and ordered by the court. . . .

The Department of State wishes to thank the Government of Georgia and in particular the Embassy for its complete coopera-tion in this difficult and tragic matter. The Department offers its assurances that Mr. Makharadze will receive a fair trial that com-ports with all of the protections provided criminal defendants under U.S. law.

Department of State,
Washington, February 11, 1997.


Stunned by the hypocrisy of the State Department's position and frus-trated that there seemed to be nothing that could be done about it, I placed a call to former Secretary of State Jim Baker, who was a supporter of Georgia and a friend of Eduard Shevardnadze, and asked him if there was any recourse I had not thought of. He confirmed that there was noth-ing more that I could do. It was clear that this was simply a question of power. The United States doesn't waive because we have the power not to and no one can impose consequences on us that would make us waive. But poor Georgia was in a different situation. Had they recalled Makharadze and asserted immunity, which was clearly their right to do, they would lose U.S. money and support, which would be disastrous to them. Frankly, I was ashamed about the double standard I was seeing firsthand from our own government. While I am not an advocate for the assertion of diplomatic immunity in all cases because it defeats justice in individual ones, I am an advocate for equal justice and I do not think it should matter whether a country is weak or strong. The decision to waive should be a principled one, not one based solely on power.

Without the strong support of the State Department, it would have been suicidal for Georgia to assert immunity and so the decision was made to waive. As I often say, sometimes a client must rise above principle.

During this critical time, I was in constant contact with Ambassador Japaridze and had several conversations with various leaders of the Georgian government. My job had become crisis management. In addition, I was asked to be the public spokesperson in the United States for the Georgian government in this matter.

The United States Attorney's Office in Washington, D.C., my former office, took an aggressive stance in the case. They wanted to prosecute Makharadze to the full extent of the law. Under our system of law, every individual has a right to vigorous representation. This included Makharadze. We decided that it was in the best interest of both the government of Georgia and Makharadze for him to have separate counsel. We could never lower the temperature of the crisis for Georgia if its lawyer was also vigorously challenging the government's case against Makharadze.

Larry Barcella, a prominent white-collar lawyer, was retained to represent Makharadze. Bob Mueller, now the director of the FBI, was the principal prosecutor.

Larry worked out a plea agreement with the United States Attorney's Office. On October 8, 1997, Makharadze pleaded guilty to involuntary manslaughter and several counts of aggravated assault before the Honorable Harold L. Cushenberry, associate judge of the Superior Court of the District of Columbia. He received a sentence of seven to twenty-one years. After serving three and a half years, on June 30, 2000, Makharadze was transferred to his native Georgia to serve the remainder of his sentence pursuant to an international agreement that allows for such transfers. The sentence was unusually harsh, and upon his return was reduced to satisfy the requirements of Georgian law. After serving additional time in a Georgian prison, he was released in 2002 and is now a businessman in Georgia.

President Shevardnadze was praised as a statesman and earned immense goodwill in the United States for his decision to waive immunity. The congressional attack dogs backed off and Georgia continued to benefit from United States aid. A crisis had been resolved. While I continued to be troubled by the hypocrisy I saw firsthand, I was pleased that I was able to help Georgia in her crisis.

Ambassador Tedo Japaridze and his lovely wife, Tamar, became good friends of Ellen's and mine. They are both charming and wonderful people. One day after the matter had been resolved, Tedo called and said that President Shevardnadze was very grateful for the help I had given Georgia and for running interference with the Department of Justice and State Department authorities—and that the president would like Ellen and me to visit Georgia as his guests.

Ellen and I arrived in Tblisi, the capitol of Georgia, on the morning of August 9, 1997. It is a beautiful, historic city on the Mtkvari River. A country of more than five million people, Georgia shares borders with Turkey, Armenia, Azerbaijan, and its problem neighbor Russia.

Within a few hours of our arrival, we would be feted at our first of many lunches and dinners. Irakli Menagarishvili, the minister of Foreign Affairs, with whom I spoke during the crisis, hosted us at a wonderful lunch at the Nikala restaurant. This was followed by a tour of Tbilsi. That evening Tedo hosted us at dinner. That dinner, as all Georgian dinners, was a sumptuous multicourse affair. The Georgian wine was flowing, and there was much joy and laughter and innumerable toasts. The Georgians love to toast. A good toastmaster in Georgia, called a "Tamada," holds a position of honor and respect. We toasted everything and when we ran out of toasts, we toasted the best toasts.

That evening we stayed at Krtsanisi, the official government residence. On the following day we visited Gori, the birthplace of Stalin. While he was a Georgian, most of the Georgians we met hated him. I recall visiting a museum in Gori and observing a prominent Georgian in our group standing before a portrait of Stalin and crying hysterically and screaming, "You destroyed our country!" I was deeply moved and taken back by the visceral reaction this Georgian had to a lifeless portrait.

The highlight of our trip was a private meeting with President Shevardnadze. At around noon on August 11, Ellen and I were escorted into his office. Because of the frequent attacks on his life, one of which was only two weeks before our arrival, there were several bodyguards outside his office. President Shevardnadze entered moments after our arrival. He had a warm and open face and striking white hair. You knew immediately that you were in the presence of a very special person. The president does not speak much English, so generous use was made of his interpreter. We spoke about the case and his prior visits to Washington.

Following our private visit, we were invited by the president to a reception in honor of a visiting American delegation of members of Congress, including Senators Kay Bailey Hutchison, John McCain, Mitch McConnell, and Congresspersons Sonny Callahan, Nina Laurey, and others.

At some point during the reception, I was standing alone with the president and we were discussing his incredible career. During the conversation, he volunteered to me that Ronald Reagan and Mikhail Gorbachev never hit it off and did not trust each other. He said that this caused him much concern at the time because he felt there was a real opportunity for peace between the superpowers. Shevardnadze, at the time, was the foreign minister of the Soviet Union. He said that he developed a special and trusting relationship with George Shultz, the secretary of state under Ronald Reagan, and then with Jim Baker, the secretary of state under George Bush. He gave much credit to the end of the cold war to the warm and trusting relationship that developed between him and Shultz, and later with Baker. Of course, Presidents Ronald Reagan, George Bush, and Mikhail Gorbachev were vital players ending the cold war, and because of their wisdom a confrontation between the world's superpowers was avoided.

I can't explain to you how I felt. A kid from Brooklyn drinking Georgian cognac with the president of Georgia, a world leader, who was telling me an inside story about one of the most significant events in history. He also told me which of the cognacs I should drink.

I recall making a smart-ass remark during the reception to a leader of the Georgian parliament. He was talking to me about how the Georgians were modeling themselves after the United States in all respects. I jokingly told him I thought that was great but warned that they should not let their press model themselves after our vigorous and sometimes overly aggressive press. While I was somewhat kidding, he was not in his comment to me. In a deadly serious tone, he said, "Bob, we will gladly put up with the American-style press because with all its faults, it is better than what we have had in the past, which is tomorrow's news being written today in a government office." I will never forget that remark and of course I agree with it.

During the late afternoon of the eleventh, Ellen, Tedo, and I had a memorable meeting with Ilya the II, the patriarch of all Georgia. It was extremely hot and humid and all of us were dripping with perspiration. As we entered the patriarch's meeting room, we were concerned about our appearances. When the impressive patriarch entered the room, I noticed that there was not a bead of sweat on him even though he was fully dressed in what appeared to be heavy black clerical garb. I later asked Tedo if he was wearing ice packs under his outer garments. If not, it had to be a miracle.

As a lawyer, I am always interested in the legal system of the countries that I visit. This was particularly true of Georgia since it just recently separated from the Soviet Union. Tedo asked me if I would be willing to address the Supreme Court of Georgia. I said, "Are you kidding, why would they want to hear from me?" In any event, on August 12, I visited the Supreme Court. Before speaking to the full court, I met Justice Mindia Ugrekhelidze, the supreme justice of the Supreme Court, in his private chambers. He was an impressive figure and took great pride in telling me how the Georgian legal system was modeling itself after the United States. After our visit, I was escorted by him into the court. All of the judges were sitting at a massive U-shaped table in their judicial robes. I told them how flattered I was to be asked to speak to them and promised to be brief.

Ellen, Tedo, and I sat with the supreme justice on an elevated bench in the beautiful courtroom. After I spoke, Ellen was given the center seat between the justice and myself for picture taking. It is a wonderful memory. The Georgian people, notwithstanding their poor economic condition and daily troubles, are open, generous, and fun loving. If food, wine, and good cheer made for a wealthy country, it would be the richest of all.

Several months after our visit, I received the following letter:

*3 December, 1998*

*Dear Mr. Bennett,*

On behalf of the Government of Georgia I would like to personally extend my deep appreciation for the assistance you have provided to our embassy in Washington concerning the Makharadze case. Your advice and counsel has always been timely and well received. This was an extremely difficult experience for many Georgians. You helped us through this experience with sound advice. But most importantly you provided a commodity which we need most, the moral support which comes from commitment and friendship.

Wishing all the best to you and your family.

Sincerely yours,

Eduard Shevardnadze

Sometime later, in a personal note referring to our working together, Ambassador Japaridze wrote:

We all have gone through traumatic times, my friend, and you navigated me and Georgia safely through these troubled, turbulent, and unfriendly waters.

This personal note meant a great deal to me.

# CHAPTER FIFTEEN

# A DEATH ON FILM

O N   N O V E M B E R   22, 1963, Abraham Zapruder, a Dallas businessman, left his office on Dealey Plaza to watch President John F. Kennedy's motorcade. Initially, Mr. Zapruder, an amateur photographer, wasn't going to film the motorcade. But he changed his mind and drove home to retrieve his 8mm movie camera so that he could record the president's visit for his family. Shortly before the arrival of the president's motorcade, Mr. Zapruder climbed onto a rectangular concrete block at the end of a row of steps. From this vantage point, with the exception of a break in his line of sight caused by a road sign, Mr. Zapruder had a virtually unobstructed view of Dealey Plaza, from the corner of Houston and Elm Streets, downhill to a triple underpass on his right. Mr. Zapruder set the lens of his camera to the extreme telephoto position. Initially, he made a brief test shot of the assembled crowd and then a seven-second film of three motorcycle-mounted police officers swinging around the corner from Houston Street onto Elm Street.

Realizing that this was not the sequence he wanted to capture, Zapruder stopped filming and waited for the presidential limousine to arrive. Several seconds later, as President Kennedy's blue Lincoln Continental convertible moved into view on Elm Street, he again began filming. Holding his handheld camera steady, he kept the president's car and its occupants within continuous view for approximately nineteen seconds, the time it took for the motorcade to reach the triple underpass. Although several others were filming the president's motorcade as it proceeded through Dealey Plaza, Mr. Zapruder captured the only uninterrupted film of President Kennedy's car before, during, and immediately after the assassination.

On that very day, Henry G. Zapruder, Abraham's son, was working as an attorney at the United States Department of Justice in Washington, D.C. Shortly after returning from lunch, he heard a report that there had been an attempt on the life of President Kennedy. Within minutes of hearing this report, he received a call from his father, Abraham. According to the son, "He was crying. He said that the president was dead. I protested that this was not true, that the radio had reported that he had been taken to Parkland, the emergency hospital in Dallas. There was no way, my father said, that the president could have survived. He told me that he had seen the president's head 'explode.' He kept saying how horrible it was that Mrs. Kennedy had been there when this happened to her husband and expressing his own horror at having seen the president 'shot down in the streets.' "

Mr. Zapruder returned to his office after filming the president's assassination and placed his still-loaded camera in his office safe. He then immediately notified the Secret Service. Later that day, Mr. Zapruder, accompanied by a Secret Service agent, had the film developed.

In the days following the assassination, Abraham, given the media reaction, was concerned about the uses to which the film would be put. He did not want it to be exploited or used in bad taste because of concerns for the Kennedy family and Mrs. Kennedy in particular. For these reasons, he refused to entertain bids to buy his film but eventually agreed to sell it to Time/Life, believing that they would handle the film with dignity and good taste. The agreement provided that Time would pay Mr. Zapruder $150,000 in six $25,000 installments. Zapruder never saw this as an opportunity to make a financial killing, so he never tried to sell it to the highest bidder. Partly out of charitable instincts and partly in order to avoid the appearance of selfishly profiting from the film, he decided that the first payment of $25,000 be given to the widow of Officer J. D. Tippit, the Dallas police officer who was gunned down by Lee Harvey Oswald.

Abraham Zapruder died in 1970 and, according to his son, he was so troubled by what he filmed that he would never again look through a motion picture camera lens. In 1975, Time/Life decided to sell the film back to Abraham Zapruder's wife, Lillian, and children, Myrna and Henry, for $1.00. They formed a company, LMH—based on their first names— and in 1978 they deposited the original film with the National Archives and Records Administration for storage and safekeeping. Digital copies were made available to viewers over the years. The family rejected all requests for use of the film in advertising and, at their own expense, made it available to those who had a worthy cause. Where they felt it appropriate, moderate charges were made for the leasing of the film.

On April 4, 1997, acting pursuant to the John F. Kennedy Records Collection Act of 1992, the John F. Kennedy Assassination Records Review Board (ARRB) conducted hearings on whether to take the Zapruder film from the family for inclusion in the John F. Kennedy Assassination Records Collection. At the hearing, several experts, called by the government in order to justify the taking, testified repeatedly about the unique importance and value of the film. This testimony would later prove to be very helpful to me in the subsequent litigation handled for the Zapruder family. On April 24, 1997, the ARRB directed that, effective August 1, 1998, the Zapruder film be transferred to the Records Collection within the National Archives and Records Administration. It was no longer there for safekeeping. It was there because the government seized it by law and now owned it. Following the film's seizure, the Zapruder family, their corporate attorneys, and the government could not agree on fair compensation.

Throughout, the Zapruder family was reasonable, but the government was not. On December 31, 1997, the Zapruder family retained Skadden, Arps to represent them in the dispute. When Henry Zapruder met with me, he made it clear that the family wanted the government to have the film and that their preference was not to challenge the seizure by the government. Most important to them was that any litigation with the government over the amount that would be fair compensation had to be handled in a dignified and professional matter. Henry, like his father, had great concern for the Kennedy family and, therefore, he did not want this part of the president's legacy to become the subject of a litigation war. While I am very comfortable in a brass-knuckled affair, I respected the family's feelings and hoped the government would feel the same.

I asked Richard Brusca, one of Skadden's very able litigation partners, to join me along with Harold Reeves, a brilliant young associate. Also joining us was Dana Freyer, a litigation lawyer in our New York office specializing in alternative dispute resolution. Dana is a cousin of Henry Zapruder's wife. While Dana and Rich are still with the firm, Harold has since decided to become a priest; after studying at the North American College in Rome, he was ordained in the spring of 2006. I am sorry he left us, but it's tough to compete with a higher calling.

One of the first steps I took on behalf of the Zapruders was to contact Frank W. Hunger, who was at the time the assistant attorney general in charge of the Civil Division of the United States Department of Justice. Frank was an experienced lawyer who also was Vice President Al Gore's brother-in-law. I explained to Frank that our firm had been retained by the Zapruder family to represent their interests. I explained that while we were prepared to litigate the matter if we had to, we preferred reaching an amicable resolution. Also, I made clear that if we had to litigate, we wanted to do so in a nonacrimonious manner given that the dispute centered on a national tragedy. Frank was a gentleman and a real professional. He readily agreed that we might have to disagree, but that we would do so in a civilized and appropriate way.

For several years, the government was adamant that they would not pay much at all. Their best offer was $750,000, which was far below the film's fair market value. Experts we had retained concluded that if sold at auction, which they believed was the best way to determine the film's value, it would command a price of no less than $25,000,000. During my several conversations with Assistant Attorney General Hunger, the message was delivered that the government might be willing to go as high as $2,000,000, still far below a fair price.

Under the circumstances, we had little choice but to litigate. While the Zapruder family wanted the government to have the film, if we had to litigate, I could not disregard the fact that there was a serious issue as to whether the Assassination Records Review Board had the authority to confiscate the film, given the ambiguous language of the Records Collection Act. If we won on this point, the film could then be sold to the highest bidder. We were all convinced that in an open market, the film could be sold for sums well in excess of what the Zapruders were willing to take for it. Because the family did not want to sell it to the highest bidder and believed the film should be owned by the United States, I made one more attempt to resolve the matter.

After settlement discussions failed, we agreed that rather than litigate in court, we would arbitrate the matter. After several conversations, we reached an agreement on the terms and conditions of the arbitration. However, because of technical, procedural concerns, we decided that it was necessary to preserve the family's rights by filing in the United States District Court for the District of Columbia a civil complaint against the government seeking a judgment from the court that the United States government lacked the authority to take the out-of-camera original Zapruder film; we also asked the court to rule that LMH was the legal owner of the film and had a right to its release from the archivist of the United States. At the very same time, we filed with the court, with the government's agreement, a motion to stay the judicial proceedings pending arbitration.

Under the arbitration agreement, we agreed to a trial-like proceeding before three arbitrators. The arbitrators were Judge Arlin M. Adams, a retired federal judge of great stature, and two prominent attorneys—Kenneth Feinberg, who would later serve as the master in the 9/11 cases involving compensation to families of the victims, and Walter Dellinger, who had served as the solicitor general of the United States. You will recall I had worked with Walter on the Clinton case when it was before the Supreme Court. Under the terms of the arbitration agreement, the only issue to be decided was, "What is the amount that the government must pay to LMH in order to provide just compensation as required by the Fifth Amendment to the United States Constitution for the taking of the out-of-camera original film?" It was agreed that the decision of the arbitrators was binding and therefore there would be no appeal of their award.

The hearing was set for May 25, 1999. We had a big job ahead of us to present credible evidence as to the value of the film. It is not enough in a court or arbitration proceeding to prove something is valuable; you must also present specific evidence so that the trier of fact can reach a number supported by concrete evidence. The more commonplace an item, the easier it is to determine its value because of the ready availability of comparables. When, for example, you want to value a house or a car, there are usually many other similar houses or cars that have been sold from which you can determine value. However, the more unique something is, the more difficult it is to find comparables from which a logical conclusion as to value can be reached. There simply were no comparable films of the assassination of presidents. It was clear to all of us that this would be a battle of experts, and so we set about the task of identifying those individuals who would assist us in the case.

Dana, Rich, Harold, and I immersed ourselves in the worlds of fine art, collectibles, historical artifacts, presidential memorabilia, and finally the auction process. We initially spoke to a wide variety of experts in these areas.

At the end of our search, we selected several experts who we would retain. The most significant ones were Stephen Johnson, an expert in the field of film and the audiovisual medium; Dr. Jerry Patterson, a world-renowned independent appraiser who had been a senior vice-president at Sotheby's, the world-famous auction house and head of the division of books, manuscripts, autographs, stamps, and coins; Sylvia Leonard Wolf, a private appraiser who had been the president of the Appraisers Association of America; and Beth Gates Warren, an independent appraiser who had been the director of the photograph department at Sotheby's in New York. In addition to these experts, who focused on the value of the film and the methodology of reaching that value, we retained Joseph Barabe, the director of Scientific Imaging for McCrane Associates, Inc., who would provide evidence as to the very good condition of the film. Finally, we retained William Landes, a professor of law and economics at the University of Chicago Law School, whose expertise was economic analysis.

With the benefit of these experts, we decided that the best way to determine the value of the Zapruder film was to determine what it would bring at an auction. Using this approach, our experts valued the film in the range of $25 million to $40 million. These experts opined that the film, in the words of Mr. Patterson, was a "rare, unique and historically significant relic and icon" and was not simply a strip of stock film footage—like an old newsreel—as suggested by the government.

Since we had to give the arbitrators something specific to compare the Zapruder film with, our experts spent considerable time focusing on what was the best comparable. We finally decided that one of the best comparables was the *Codex Leicester* by da Vinci. This is how our expert Johnson described it:

> The *Codex* is the only manuscript by da Vinci in America, a lively record of the thoughts of the great Renaissance artist and scientist about moving water as a natural phenomenon. The *Codex* is in Leonardo's own hand. He wrote it in such a way that it may only be read by holding it up to a mirror making it difficult for most people to read and understand. It was compiled between 1506 and 1508. It is composed of 72 pages on 18 double sheets of handwritten notes and diagrams in 36 folios. The *Codex Leicester* represents only a small portion, about one percent, of the total pages of extant scientific writing by da Vinci. The vast majority of the remaining body of da Vinci's work, however, estimated at about 5,000 pages, has long been owned by public institutions.

The *Codex* was sold in 1994 at an auction at Christie's in New York for $30,800,500. In detailing why this manuscript was a valid comparable for determining the value of the Zapruder film, Johnson explained as follows:

> The *Codex* and the Film, therefore, are comparable in that they both derive considerable portions of their value from their place in history and culture: the *Codex* is representative (although, not *the* single premiere representative) of the flourishing of the human mind in the Renaissance and is associated (although it is

not the item most closely associated) with da Vinci, one of the greatest minds of that period; the Zapruder Film is the premiere icon of a dramatic turning point in American history. Our history and culture have been influenced both by the Zapruder Film and by the works of da Vinci. The Film is universally recognized in its own right; the same can be said of Leonardo (although, certainly more for the *Mona Lisa* and *The Last Supper,* than for the *Codex*). As discussed earlier, however, the Zapruder Film has had more of an impact upon contemporary political, social and cultural history—and would be immediately recognized amongst a much larger pool of potential auction bidders—than the *Codex Leicester.*

Our other experts made references to other great works of art and collectibles but agreed that the da Vinci *Codex* was a particularly apt comparison.

At the hearing, in addition to submitting the affidavits of all of our experts, we called Beth Gates Warren and Jerry Patterson as witnesses. Rich Brusca and Dana Freyer skillfully took them through their qualifications and their analysis as to the value of the film. On cross-examination the government lawyers were unable to lay a glove on them. The same was not true of the government witnesses. Where our experts were consistent in their approach and conclusions, the government experts were inconsistent in their approaches. This was something we could exploit. Also being lucky is sometimes better than being good. We were lucky. And here's how. . . .

Just prior to the hearing, Stephen Johnson called me and told me that one of the government's experts, Dr. Cameron Macauley, had asked him to appraise some films in his personal collection. He didn't know if this was important but wanted me to know. I jumped out of my chair because I knew this could be dynamite. Just to be extra careful, I got an affidavit from Johnson that I knew I could effectively use at the hearing.

Armed with the knowledge that Macauley had sought to hire our expert Johnson, who valued the film far in excess of Macauley, I cross-examined Macauley following his direct testimony in the government's case.

> **MR. BENNETT:** What about Mr. Johnson? You have read his report? Steve Johnson.
>
> **MR. MACAULEY:** Yes, I have.
>
> **MR. BENNETT:** He is a film man, is he not?
>
> **MR. MACAULEY:** With limitations he is. I know him very well.
>
> **MR. BENNETT:** You know him very well. He is an expert in film; is he not?
>
> **MR. MACAULEY:** He's not an expert from a technological point of view at all nor from a production point of view. He has been in the audiovisual—he was in the audiovisual department at Indiana University when I first met him, and he got an education degree in audiovisual education, an ADD, but he hasn't had the depth of experience of hands-on knowledge of motion pictures.
>
> **MR. BENNETT:** You agree that he is an expert appraiser of films?
>
> **MR. MACAULEY:** He's highly qualified.
>
> **MR. BENNETT:** And you are aware that he valued this film at $33 million?
>
> **MR. MACAULEY:** Yes, I am aware of that.
>
> **MR. BENNETT:** In fact, Dr. Johnson is such a good expert you hired him last week to appraise a film of yours. Is that not correct?
>
> **MR. MACAULEY:** I did?
>
> **MR. BENNETT:** Did you not?
>
> **MR. MACAULEY:** This is news to me.
>
> **MR. BENNETT:** I have an affidavit here, Mr. Macauley. Let me read it to you.
>
> **MR. MACAULEY:** Please do.
>
> **MR. BENNETT:** Because if this affidavit is wrong, Dr. Johnson is going to have some difficulty. "Steve Johnson, being duly sworn, deposes and says "In late 1998 or early January 1999,

C. Cameron Macauley telephoned me and asked me if I would appraise for donation purposes some films that he owned."

Is that correct?

**MR. MACAULEY:** Films. We've discussed off and on the possibility of exchanging work, but I'm not sure what this film refers to.

**MR. BENNETT:** . . . You deny that in late 1998 or early 1999 you asked him if he would appraise for donation purposes some films?

**MR. MACAULEY:** I have generally talked to him about that. I don't recall the time or the details of it.

**MR. BENNETT:** So you do not dispute then it was 1998 or early January 1999?

**MR. MACAULEY:** I'm not sure.

**MR. BENNETT:** Let me go to the second paragraph.

**MR. MACAULEY:** All right.

**MR. BENNETT:** "On Sunday, May 16,"—that is ten days ago—"Mr. Macauley again telephoned me . . ." Did you talk to him ten days ago?

**MR. MACAULEY:** Yes.

**MR. BENNETT:** ". . . to ask me if I would appraise for donation purposes a vintage film that he owns about a rare bird."

**MR. MACAULEY:** Oh, yes. Uh-huh. I don't own it. I co-own it.

**MR. BENNETT:** I did not ask you about owning it. I asked you is that a true affidavit?

**MR. MACAULEY:** Yes, that is correct.

**MR. BENNETT:** So you thought he was pretty good to appraise this film for you?

**MR. MACAULEY:** Oh, yes. Yes. I think he would do a good job.

The devastating impact of this testimony was obvious to everyone. He not only enhanced the credibility of our expert Johnson by hiring him for his own purposes, but hurt his own credibility by not readily admitting that he had done so.

The government's next witness was John Adam Staszyn, who was identified as an expert in appraising nonprint media such as motion pictures. He came up with a value of about $1 million.

During his examination by the government, Staszyn took an entirely different—and inconsistent—approach than Dr. Macauley. In trying cases, you never want there to be an inconsistency in your own case or between your experts. Based on his testimony, I saw an opportunity to exploit the internal inconsistency in the government's case and to use one of their experts to impeach the other. Also, during his examination, Staszyn made an embarrassing mistake. During his testimony, he testified that Margaret Bourke-White had photographed the *Hindenburg*. I felt that if I could show he had made a fundamental error, he would lose credibility as an expert in the eyes of the arbitrators.

Remember: A good cross-examiner is like a guerrilla fighter. You go in quickly, make your hits, and get out. I decided that with this witness I wanted to establish on cross-examination that he was not really well qualified, that he made a fundamental error an expert should not make, that our evaluation approach was the correct one, and that he disagreed with the approach of the other government witnesses. Here is how I established these points.

> **MR. BENNETT:** Now, you testified in your field of expertise, and if I heard you correctly, you were describing a photograph of the *Hindenburg* by Margaret Bourke-White.
> **MR. STASZYN:** Yes.
> **MR. BENNETT:** Are you sure she did a photograph of the *Hindenburg*?
> **MR. STASZYN:** The *Hindenburg*.
> **MR. BENNETT:** She never did the *Hindenburg*, did she? I thought you testified about Bourke-White.
>     Look, I do not want to play games with you. Let me show you the Sotheby's photograph book in New York. There is a Margaret Bourke-White [photograph] of a dirigible, but—

**MR. STASZYN:** Yes.

**MR. BENNETT:** This is what you were talking about?

**MR. STASZYN:** This is what I'm referring to. Correct.

**MR. BENNETT:** And that is not the *Hindenburg*?

**MR. STASZYN:** No.

**MR. BENNETT:** You were mistaken?

**MR. STASZYN:** Yes.

**MR. BENNETT:** That is the *Akron*?

**WITNESS:** Correct.

That the government's expert made such a fundamental mistake was not lost on the judges and certainly did not help the government's case.

I then decided to show that our approach to valuation was the right one and that Staszyn really wasn't well qualified to opine on the value of the Zapruder film:

**MR. BENNETT:** Now, you testified on direct that you do matting.

**MR. STASZYN:** Yes. I do archival matting and framing of photographs, animation cells, paper—usually paper material.

**MR. BENNETT:** Is that a significant part of your business?

**MR. STASZYN:** At some points of the year it's significant, yes.

**MR. BENNETT:** And you heard our witness, our expert witness, Ms. Warren, yesterday say that she had actually hired you to do some matting for Sotheby's?

**MR. STASZYN:** Correct.

**MR. BENNETT:** Okay. Have you ever headed a department at Sotheby's?

**MR. STASZYN:** No.

**MR. BENNETT:** Have you ever been employed by any of the major auction houses as an employee of the auction house, not as an independent contractor?

**MR. STASZYN:** No.

**MR. BENNETT:** Have you ever had responsibility for taking a

valuable collectible and seeing that it was marketed and
auctioned off properly?

**MR. STASZYN:** I've taken material for clients to auction, yes.

**MR. BENNETT:** No, no. I mean for an auction house.

**MR. STASZYN:** No.

**MR. BENNETT:** Would you agree with me that it is a fair
statement to say that Mr. Patterson and Ms. Warren have far
more expertise than you in the auction business? Is that a fair
statement?

**MR. STASZYN:** As working for an auction house, yes.

**MR. BENNETT:** Knowledge of the auction process?

**MR. STASZYN:** Correct.

**MR. BENNETT:** Okay. Now, you have examined the film—

**MR. STASZYN:** Yes.

**MR. BENNETT:** —as you just testified to. By the way, during
direct examination, counsel for the government asked you your
methodology, and the sum and substance of it was that you
made a number of comparisons. You took a market comparison
approach. Is that correct?

**MR. STASZYN:** Yes.

**MR. BENNETT:** And you compared the film to things other
than film?

**MR. STASZYN:** Yes.

**MR. BENNETT:** Do you really feel that is a legitimate way
to do it?

**MR. STASZYN:** Yes.

**MR. BENNETT:** And that is the way Ms. Warren did it and
Mr. Patterson did it? Is that not correct?

**MR. STASZYN:** I don't think it was a thorough job.

**MR. BENNETT:** You think you did a more thorough job than
they did?

**MR. STASZYN:** Yes, because I considered more—

**MR. BENNETT:** Okay.

**MR. STASZYN:** You know, I considered more markets.

**MR. BENNETT:** Do you know—

**MR. STASZYN:** Would the *Codex* fall in the photograph market? No.

**MR. BENNETT:** This may be unfair, but for the moment I am asking the questions.

You agree that a comparative approach is the right approach?

**MR. STASZYN:** Correct.

**MR. BENNETT:** And you agree that you looked at things outside the film?

**MR. STASZYN:** Yes. I was forced to.

**MR. BENNETT:** And you agree that Ms. Warren and Mr. Patterson likewise followed a comparative approach? Is that correct?

**MR. STASZYN:** Yes.

**MR. BENNETT:** So when Mr. Macauley testified earlier today that you do not go to the comparative approach, but you go by taking $150,000 and adding to it a rate of return . . . you do not agree with his approach, do you?

**MR. STASZYN:** I don't use that approach.

**MR. BENNETT:** I did not ask you if you used it. I read your report. You did not use it. Do you agree with that approach? Yes or no?

**MR. STASZYN:** I am not sure whether that is the proper approach.

**MR. BENNETT:** You do not think—

**MR. STASZYN:** I am not sure.

**MR. BENNETT:** You do not think it is, do you?

**MR. STASZYN:** I'm not sure.

It was our position that at the time the government seized the film, there were many wealthy people who would be willing to pay top dollar for a one-of-a-kind item. Whether it be a $10 baseball hit by Mark McGwire for a home-run record—resulting in a $3 million purchase—or a serious work of art or the da Vinci *Codex,* a substantial amount of money would be paid for the one-of-a-kind Zapruder film and that the best way to determine how much would be paid was by selling it at auction. The government virtually ignored the auction process, and its experts did not compare with ours in the areas that the arbitrators found to be important.

When the case was submitted to the arbitrators for decision, we were very confident. Henry Zapruder thanked me for the job we did and said that no matter what the outcome, he felt we could not have done better.

The decision of the arbitrators was delivered on July 19, 1999. We prevailed by a 2–1 decision. Arbitrators Feinberg and Adams awarded us $16 million plus interest, which amounted to a total of $17 million. While less than the value testified to by our experts, it was far in excess of what the government offered and was much more than the Zapruders would have accepted in settlement. We considered it a substantial victory.

In reaching their decision, Feinberg and Adams accepted our auction approach and were obviously impressed with the quality of our experts. The dissenter, Walter Dellinger, would have awarded us far less, but even in his view, it would have been a sum substantially more than that offered by the government.

Several months after the decision, I was invited to address an annual meeting of leading auctioneers in New York. The Zapruder case was of great interest to those in the field of auctions. This is one of the great things about what I do for a living—my cases take me to places seemingly far removed from the law. In this case, I met very interesting people in the world of auctions and fine art. Such experiences enrich my life and enhance my knowledge.

On February 8, 2000, I delivered the annual Brennan Lecture at the Cardozo School of Law in New York. This is an important lecture series named after former Supreme Court Justice William J. Brennan Jr. My speech was about legal ethics. To my amazement, Jerry Patterson, my expert in the Zapruder case, was in attendance. When I asked him what on earth he was doing there, he explained that as a result of the Zapruder case and his involvement with me, he found the law to be of real interest, so he decided to come to the lecture. I guess it works both ways.

# CHAPTER SIXTEEN

# AN HONEST COP

I N SEPTEMBER 2001, Congressman Bill Delahunt of Massachusetts called me and asked if I would be willing to assist a Boston police officer, Kenneth M. Conley, who had been convicted of perjury and was facing a three-year jail sentence. Bill believed strongly in Kenny's innocence. He explained that Kenny's case was of special interest to the late congressman Joe Moakley, and that he had promised to carry on the battle for Kenny. Ironically, Kenny had been convicted in the courthouse named after Moakley. I told Bill I would look at the record and let him know if I could be of help. I asked my partner Saul Pilchen, a former federal prosecutor, and associate Jonice Gray Tucker to help me. We devoured the record and spoke with Kenny. Two things were absolutely clear. First, we believed Kenny had been wrongfully convicted, and second, it would be a real uphill fight to get his conviction overturned. Kenny's conviction had been affirmed on appeal by the First Circuit Court of Appeals, and the Supreme Court declined to review the case. Moreover, an earlier challenge to set aside the conviction that had been successful at the trial level was reversed on appeal.

I told both Bill Delahunt and Kenny that we would take the case pro bono, but given the case's history, a successful result was unlikely. There was, however, a glimmer of hope. On September 28, 2001, District Judge Robert Keeton, who presided at the trial, granted for the second time Kenny's request to set aside his conviction based on the failure of the prosecutor to turn over evidence favorable to Kenny. Judge Keeton found that the prosecutor withheld certain key evidence. Since the first such ruling setting aside Kenny's conviction on similar grounds was reversed on appeal, we could expect the United States Attorney's Office to appeal the second ruling. We would have to convince the Court of Appeals that Judge Keeton got it right and that Kenny was entitled to a new trial. But first, we decided to appeal informally to United States Attorney Michael Sullivan. Sullivan had the authority to abide by Judge Keeton's ruling and give Kenny a new trial or dismiss the case.

How did Kenny get in this awful situation? Let me give you some background.

In the early morning hours of January 25, 1995, following a homicide at a restaurant in Boston, numerous police cruisers responded to an erroneous call that an officer had been shot. Both uniformed and plainclothes officers responded and engaged in a chase of four African-American male suspects who fled the scene of the homicide in a gold Lexus. The suspects fled to a cul-de-sac in a housing project known as Woodruff Way. One suspect, Robert Brown, emerged from the car and ran toward a fence. A police cruiser, occupied by Michael Cox, an undercover African-American police officer from an antigang unit, began to chase Brown. Cox was not in uniform and was wearing a black hooded sweatshirt and a black jacket. At Kenny's trial Cox testified that he grabbed Brown's jacket in an attempt to pull him back from the fence, but Brown made it to the top and dropped down on the other side.

As Cox prepared to climb the fence and pursue Brown, he was struck from behind with a blunt object by other police officers who mistook him for one of the suspects. Cox was beaten unmercifully until someone recognized him as a police officer. The officers who were beating him fled. Cox was left bleeding and unconscious in the street. He was seriously injured and later taken to the hospital for treatment.

Officer Kenneth Conley arrived on the scene after Cox. He testified that he saw one of the suspects scaling a fence and pursued him. Kenny scaled the fence, chased the suspect Brown, and apprehended him. He said that he never saw the beating of Cox, nor did he see anyone directly in front of him as he chased Brown over the fence.

After an unsuccessful investigation by a Suffolk County grand jury in

April of 1997 to determine who beat Officer Cox, a federal grand jury in
Boston began an investigation of the beating. Kenny was called before
the grand jury and testified. According to a later court opinion, Kenny's
testimony was described as follows:

> When he arrived at the dead end on Woodruff Way, [Con-
> ley's] vehicle was about the fourth or fifth police car in line be-
> hind the suspects' gold Lexus, approximately forty feet away. . . .
> Also consistent with Cox's account, Conley testified that once the
> Lexus skidded to a stop, a black male wearing a brown leather
> jacket exited from the passenger side of the Lexus and ran to the
> right, toward a fence. Conley exited his vehicle in pursuit. While
> in pursuit, Conley observed the suspect scale the fence, drop
> down on the other side, and start to run. . . .
>
> Conley testified that he made all of these observations as he
> pursued the suspect, beginning from the time the suspect first ex-
> ited the gold Lexus up to the time when the suspect landed on
> the other side of the fence and started to run. According to Cox's
> testimony, Conley made these observations at precisely the same
> time that Cox was chasing "right behind" the suspect. . . . How-
> ever, before the grand jury, Conley testified that during that time
> he did not observe anyone—either in plainclothes or in uni-
> form—between him and the suspect. In direct conflict with Cox's
> account, Conley testified before the grand jury, in response to the
> prosecutor's questions, as follows:

**MR. MERRITT:** Did you see anyone else in plainclothes
behind him as he went toward the fence?
**OFFICER CONLEY:** No, I didn't.
**MR. MERRITT:** Did you see, as he went on top of the fence or
climbed the fence, another individual in plainclothes standing
there, trying to grab him?
**OFFICER CONLEY:** No, I did not.
**MR. MERRITT:** So that didn't happen; is that correct? Because
you saw the individual go over the fence?

**OFFICER CONLEY:** Yes, I seen [*sic*] the individual go over the fence.

**MR. MERRITT:** And if these other things that I've been describing, a second—another plainclothes officer chasing him, and actually grabbing him as he went to the top of the fence, you would have seen that if it happened, is that your testimony?

**OFFICER CONLEY:** I think I would have seen that. . . .

Conley further testified that when he got to the fence, he climbed over it in "approximately the same location" that he had observed the suspect go over the fence, and continued in pursuit. . . . Eventually, after chasing the suspect for approximately one mile, Conley apprehended him and effected an arrest.

The assistant United States attorney investigating the case believed Kenny was lying and that he saw what happened. Based upon his grand jury testimony, Kenny was indicted for perjury and prosecuted. At trial the prosecutor presented the testimony of Brown, who placed Kenny at the location of the beating. He also presented the testimony of Officer Richard Walker, who also placed Kenny at the location of the beating at the time it occurred. The jury convicted Kenny of perjury with respect to his testimony that he had not seen anyone behind Brown at the fence, but acquitted him with regard to his testimony that he had not witnessed the beating. The jury also convicted Kenny on obstructing justice charges. Kenny was subsequently sentenced to thirty-four months in jail. Kenny's trial counsel appealed his conviction.

The First Circuit Court of Appeals affirmed the conviction and in so doing stated that the testimony of Officer Michael Cox, Officer Richard Walker, and Robert Brown constituted sufficient circumstantial evidence of Kenny's guilt. It was clear from the court's opinion that Walker was a key witness. What the Court of Appeals did not know at the time was that the prosecution withheld critical evidence about Walker that would have undermined his credibility.

Following Kenny's conviction and appeal, his trial counsel, Willy Davis, discovered that important exculpatory evidence had been withheld from him. Theodore Merritt, the federal prosecutor, had not given trial counsel a statement of the prosecution's key witness, Walker, in which Walker stated that if the FBI would "hypnotize" him, he might have a better recollection of what occurred. This and other material not provided to the defense, casting doubt on Walker's recollection of the events, formed the basis of Judge Keeton's rulings that Kenny had been denied a fair trial.

When we read the transcripts of the trial, we were outraged by prosecutor Merritt's tactics. We believed that he had improperly suggested to the jury that Kenny was part of a "blue wall of silence" and that Kenny had purposely failed to file a report so as to conceal his presence at the scene of the beating. The prosecutor further suggested that Brown was acquitted of the murder that occurred on the night of the Cox incident in part because of Kenny's failure to file a report. The suggestion was that had Kenny filed the report, his existence would be known to the homicide investigators, who would have called him as a witness at Brown's trial, and Brown would have been convicted.

As a defense lawyer for many years and a former federal prosecutor, I knew the devastating impact such arguments would have on a jury. Moreover, the detailed and repetitive testimony regarding the vicious beating of Cox, even though all agreed that Kenny was not part of it, so inflamed the jury that in our opinion, Kenny didn't have a chance.

Kenny advised us that under existing police procedures, he was not required to file the report suggested by Merritt and that what he had filed was all that was required. This was consistent with his grand jury testimony, but was disregarded by the prosecutor.

We easily confirmed that Kenny was right about the reporting requirements. We also learned that the acquittal of Brown had nothing to do with Kenny. I personally called the district attorney with supervisory responsibility for the homicide case against Brown; he confirmed that Merritt's argument was unfounded and that the acquittal was due to factors totally unrelated to Kenny. We then secured affidavits from retired senior officials of the police department who stated that Kenny was not required to file the report suggested by Merritt and that Kenny followed all applicable police procedures on the night in question. Based on this evidence, I believed that the prosecutor's case was built on false assumptions. Most troubling was Merritt's failure to provide Kenny's defense team with the FBI interview of Walker in which this important corroborating witness expressed his desire to be hypnotized, so he could better remember what occurred. It was clear to us that Kenny had been wrongfully convicted and that there could be no confidence in the verdict. I hoped that United States Attorney Sullivan, in the face of the evidence we gathered, would drop the case or at least agree with Judge Keeton and give Kenny a new trial.

Sullivan met with us on October 19, 2001. The meeting was attended by Assistant U.S. Attorney Merritt and his supervisors. While professional and cordial, it was clear that the career prosecutors did not agree with our position that the trial verdict was unreliable and that Kenny's conviction was a miscarriage of justice. Although it was difficult to read Sullivan, I thought we had a shot. Usually, the biggest hurdle to overcome in these situations is the desire of the U.S. attorney to support his troops, and we knew that after we left the meeting, Merritt and his supervisors would vigorously oppose our request. At the meeting, we told Sullivan that we would be making a detailed written submission in support of our position. On October 30, 2001, I wrote Sullivan and attached our submission, which dissected the trial record and provided powerful factual and legal arguments as to why the case should be dropped. In the letter, we emphasized our view that no important law enforcement purpose would be served by pursuing the matter any further and that what had occurred to date had already done severe damage to Kenny's personal and professional lives.

Following our meeting with Sullivan, we were advised that the U.S. attorney was prepared to consider making a deal under which Kenny would not have to serve his sentence, but his conviction would stand. Under the circumstances, this was a victory because it was not likely that Judge Keeton's latest new trial ruling would be upheld on appeal. The idea of Kenny going to jail was frightening, especially since he was a police officer. When we told Kenny about the offer, he rejected it. He was adamant. "I'm not guilty of anything and if I accept this deal just to stay out of jail, my mother would turn over in her grave." Saul and I explained to him the risks of not accepting the deal and pointed out that the Court of Appeals that twice ruled against him might do the same a third time. Kenny said, "No! I'm not guilty! I can't do it!" And so we discontinued any further discussion with the government of a deal, and they promptly appealed Judge Keeton's ruling. Our team prepared a powerful brief and Saul gave a strong argument in the Court of Appeals. However, a divided panel of the First Circuit again reversed the lower court and ruled that the thirty-four-months sentence should be executed right away. We were running out of options. There was, however, one small glimmer of hope. Chief Judge Michael Boudin wrote a strong dissenting opinion saying that Kenny deserved a hearing on his claim that exculpatory evidence was withheld. We decided to ask the entire court to hear the case. These requests are not usually granted because usually only a panel of three judges hears a case.

Fortunately, the full court granted our petition for a rehearing and withdrew the panel decision. Once again, Ken Conley had dodged a bullet—at least for a little while. Saul gave a great argument before the entire court, and in a 5–2 decision with Chief Judge Boudin writing for the majority, the full court threw out the panel decision and sent the case back to the District Court. Because they had reversed District Judge Keeton twice in this case, the First Circuit decided that, for appearances sake, the matter should be heard by a different judge. The matter was assigned to Chief Judge William G. Young with instructions to "master the trial record" and to "take a fresh look" at Kenny's claims.

On July 23, 2003, with Kenny and his devoted wife, Jennifer, in the courtroom, accompanied by other family members and friends, we appeared before Judge Young. I argued on behalf of Kenny, and Merritt argued the case for the government. I was surprised that Merritt argued it because with his conduct at issue, it would have been a better decision to let someone else from the U.S. Attorney's Office argue the case. However, this presented me with a good opportunity to focus at least some of my argument directly on Merritt. Also, while I almost never make personal attacks on an opposing counsel, I decided that it was called for in this case and that, if done carefully, it would help Kenny's cause and not hurt it. Frankly, I wanted to put Merritt in a position where he had to defend himself in front of Chief Judge Young.

I decided to take Merritt head on.

**MR. BENNETT:** . . . Mr. Merritt did a terrible thing at trial. I don't mean to be offensive, your Honor, but he did a terrible thing at trial. He knew his case wasn't strong and he knew the climate in which it was being tried. There was this blue wall of silence. And he was suggesting to that jury in no uncertain terms . . . that Officer Conley failed to file a report because he did not want people to know he was there, and he further went on to say and suggest to the jury that one reason Mr. Brown was acquitted of murder was that the so-called arresting officer was not known to the homicide investigators or the district attorneys.

That, sir, was unconscionable. Mr. Merritt knew, or he should have known, that that was not true. Your Honor, when a federal prosecutor stands in front of a jury, that jury looks very specially at that person. They say, "Here is a law enforcement officer." They know what the reporting responsibilities are of a policeman. . . . A jury is sitting there and they're looking at a federal enforcement officer, who says this man Conley, he was supposed to file something and he didn't file it and a murderer got off. . . .

Well, your Honor, that was the most powerful thing in that whole case if you ask me. And what did we find out, because we had the luxury of time. We presented to you two affidavits—one from the highest ranking police officer in the Boston Police Department before his retirement, who said he read the arguments [and he says that] Mr. Merritt's argument was wrong. . . .

And I myself, your Honor, have submitted an affidavit which I don't usually do in a case. . . . I personally called the district attorney and I said, Mr. Martin, I'm pro bono counsel. Mr.

Merritt claims that my client contributed to the acquittal of Mr.
Brown in the murder case. And Mr. Martin said to me, he said
that doesn't make sense to me, or words to that effect, call me
tomorrow, I'll check it out. He checked it out. He said that's not
the case.

We have an affidavit of the defense lawyer, [who said] that
was not the case. . . .

. . . I don't know if you read Sherlock Holmes. And this will
be my final point. You know, there's that great old Sherlock
Holmes story about the dog that didn't bark. . . .

Well, it's kind of like that here. We have submitted
affidavits that have categorically said that Mr. Merritt did
something terribly wrong. I think he should have been
ashamed of himself. And we put in these affidavits, your
Honor, and what do we get back? We don't get anything back.
We don't—oh, no, you're wrong, Mr. Bennett. Oh, no, here's
an affidavit from someone else. I think in the real world things
like that are quite telling.

Thank you, your Honor.

Since some of these points I had argued had not been preserved for
appeal, I knew that they could not be a basis for overturning the conviction. I felt, however, that they provided important context for the court
in determining the reliability of the trial verdict. I hoped that by making
these arguments, the district judge would, if he could, decide in favor of
Kenny. If a judge believes that someone is wrongfully convicted, there is a
much greater chance that he or she will rule in his favor. Accordingly, I
crafted my argument to appeal not only to the intellect but to the heart
as well. I then turned my attention to the critical point we were relying
upon, which was the failure of the prosecution to turn over the critical
piece of evidence that the key witness Walker suggested he be hypnotized
to help him remember what occurred.

Had trial counsel known of the evidence, he would have undermined
the credibility of Mr. Walker. I could tell that I was scoring points with the
judge. In doing our homework before the argument, I was aware that

there was tension among the judges of the District Court and the United States Attorney's Office. Some judges felt that the office was not providing the broad discovery to the defense that the court required. Judge Young noted:

> **THE COURT:** . . . Lots of these problems would be ameliorated if there was broader discovery prior to trial. And this district, and I take no credit for it but I'm intensely proud of it, has as broad discovery obligations on the government as any district in the nation.
>
> All right. Now, we're five years after the trial . . .
>
> **MR. BENNETT:** And I'm doing the best I can five years after the trial.
>
> **THE COURT:** And you go ahead.

When I finished the argument, I felt good. I believe that I had convinced the judge that Kenny was denied a fair trial because Merritt withheld a critical statement of an important witness that the prosecutor relied on and that he had taken several other cheap shots, which put the fairness of the conviction in doubt. I knew no matter what happened, I had given Kenny the best I had.

We expected a decision in a few months, but it would be more than a year before we would hear from Judge Young. Finally, on August 18, 2004, I received a call from my Boston partner Tom Dougherty, who told me the good news. Judge Young, in an exhaustive opinion, granted the relief we sought. In words that were music to our ears and Kenny's, the judge concluded his fifty-page opinion as follows:

> For all the reasons set forth above, this Court grants the Great Writ of habeas corpus. Unless the government, within sixty days of the date of this Order, moves for a retrial, the now pending charges shall be dismissed. Because the government has withheld crucial information, Kenneth M. Conley did not receive a fair trial. Insofar as it is in my power, he shall have one.
>
> SO ORDERED.

The judge explained that Officer Walker's FBI statement was critical evidence and the failure to provide it undermined the court's confidence in the verdict; because of that, Kenny was entitled to a new trial.

Immediately after receiving word from Dougherty that we had won, I called Kenny. He was overwhelmed. He got emotional at the good news and said, "Thanks, you saved my life." Any trial lawyer will tell you, this is what we live for. However, I did have to explain to Kenny that while the odds were now for the first time in our favor, it was not over. It would be up to U.S. Attorney Sullivan to decide whether to go forward with the case at a new trial or to drop it.

I was at our summer home on Damariscotta Lake in Maine in early September doing a little fishing and relaxing. Ellen, my daughter Catherine, and I had just sat down for lunch when I received a call from a reporter at the *Boston Herald*. He asked me if I had heard that U.S. Attorney Sullivan had decided to drop Kenny's case. This was not the first time I heard important news about one of my cases from a reporter. I immediately called Sullivan, who, when he got on the line, said, "Bob, I was about to call you. At three P.M. today I am going to announce that we are dropping the Conley case." I thanked him.

I called Kenny right away. I wanted him to hear it from me and not a reporter. When I called, his answering machine came on and I said, "Kenny, it's over." At that moment, an emotional wave came over me, my voice cracked, and tears welled up in my eyes. Ellen and Catherine asked if I was okay. I said, "I feel great. Today I really feel like a lawyer. This makes it all worth it." It is because of moments like this that I have not retired, and as long as clients want me, I never will. No one in the whole world except maybe Kenny and Jennifer felt better than I did that day. One more thing: I am sure that Mrs. Conley, Kenny's mother, smiled down on us and can finally rest in peace.

Ellen and I had dinner in Maine with Ellen's brother, Dr. James Gilbert, and his wife, Mary Ann. Jim is a world-class neurologist at Brockton Hospital in Brockton, Massachusetts. He had been following the Conley case, and so with great pleasure I gave Jim and Mary Ann a blow-by-blow description of the matter with a grin on my face which went from ear to ear.

Unfortunately, the failure of prosecutors to turn over exculpatory evidence occurs far too often. Some prosecutors, convinced that a defendant is guilty, are reluctant to turn over information that may be used to
acquit.

I do not question that Merritt believed he was prosecuting a guilty defendant, but he rationalized his conduct and, I believe, got caught up in
the game-playing aspects of litigation. Litigation is not supposed to be a
sporting event. What Merritt did was terribly wrong. Fortunately, we were
able to expose his improper conduct and win for Kenny. What bothers
me is the thought of defendants who have been victimized by prosecutorial misconduct but who do not have the ability to retain a vigorous defense lawyer who can expose it.

BASED ON MORE than forty years of experience, I truly believe that
the overwhelming number of prosecutors play it straight. I have never
met a prosecutor who knowingly prosecuted someone he or she knew to
be innocent. State Prosecutor Michael Nifong, the district attorney in the
Duke lacrosse case, has caused me to question this statement. My involvement in the case was as follows: I represented one of the players on
the lacrosse team who was not charged but who attended the party where
the allegations of rape, now discredited, supposedly occurred. Also, a few
of the parents of the players asked me to assist in dealing with the media.
I was eventually successful in getting at least a few reporters to question
the earlier stories and start giving the accused young men a fair shake.
Also, the North Carolina lawyers representing the defendants did an excellent job in bringing to national attention the terrible wrong that was
being done to their clients. This case was another example of where the
story line was simply too good to get fair reporting in the beginning.
Black v. White, Rich v. Poor, Town v. Gown themes were so compelling
that reporters abandoned their usual cynicism and convicted the
charged young men before the trial. Even many university officials and
faculty members assumed guilt and disregarded the presumption of innocence. The world now knows that it was a bogus case and that Nifong
was a runaway prosecutor obviously disregarding the demands of justice

in pursuit of his political goals. Even the attorney general of North Carolina, Roy Cooper, who took over the case on January 13, 2007, castigated District Attorney Nifong in his public statements and dropped all charges on April 11, 2007, against Reade Seligmann, Collin Finnerty, and David Evans. Justice was long in coming but at least it finally came. Fortunately, these young men who were falsely charged could afford to hire good lawyers who had the time and resources to expose this travesty of justice.

All lawyers are instructed by the codes of professional responsibility that they are the guardians of the law and that they have an obligation to adhere to the highest standards of ethical and moral conduct. As lawyers, we are taught to promote respect for the law and our profession. And, finally, we are taught that we must be zealous advocates.

While these goals are easy to articulate, they are often difficult to apply because in the real-world practice of law, they often conflict. The zealous advocate, particularly the defense lawyer, often acts in ways that to the public may seem morally questionable and less than candid; this in turn, at least in the eyes of the public, does not promote respect for the law.

I am a firm believer in zealous advocacy but do believe that there are limits. A defense attorney's obligation is to represent a client zealously even if it means that the absolute truth is not achieved in a particular case. Defense attorneys are entitled to put the prosecution case to the test, and a defendant has a constitutional right to have his lawyer do so.

Our society has decided that a defendant must be free to be fully candid with his or her lawyer without suffering any consequences and that legal guilt is to be decided in the courtroom, not in the lawyer's office. Often the public unfairly criticizes lawyers for seeking the acquittal of a defendant irrespective of the client's guilt. This is particularly true when the crime is heinous. I cannot tell you how many times over my career I have been asked, "How can you represent someone you know is guilty?"

Unfortunately, the public believes that as officers of the court, our only goal should be the truth. This is unfair to us because it must be remembered that the criminal justice system does not treat truth as its sole goal. There are other goals in our system. This is why truthful confessions and relevant evidence are often suppressed and excluded in trials, because laws, procedures, and policies are not followed. It is obvious that the Bill of Rights, particularly the Fourth Amendment's prohibition against unreasonable searches and seizures, are often obstacles in reaching the truth. Sometimes, in our legal system, the truth must be sacrificed for more important principles.

Also, let us not forget that we sometimes allow the police to engage in untruthful practices, such as lying to suspects about the evidence against them, in the hope that they will confess their guilt. It is not uncommon for the police to tell a suspect that their fellow suspects incriminated them, or that they were identified in a lineup, or that their fingerprints were obtained at the scene of the crime, or that they flunked a polygraph even though these assertions are false. Such ruses—indeed lies—have been condoned by some courts.

But how far should lawyers—as officers of the court—be allowed to go? Is it appropriate for one who is an officer of the court to present a false defense or to present evidence that supports such falsity? Is it appropriate for a lawyer to make any argument in an effort to lead the jury to reach a conclusion that the attorney knows is not the truth? How much maneuvering, or to put it more harshly, chicanery or trickery, can a lawyer engage in without crossing ethical and moral boundaries? Can one be an ethical lawyer and still engage in morally questionable behavior?

I have often felt that, rather than dealing with the issues head-on, we lawyers often duck the hard questions by engaging in facile distinctions and faulty logic. Some lawyers offer the glib notion that the only "truth" in a criminal trial is what a jury tells us the verdict is, or that the attorney cannot know what is true or false until the jury speaks. Sometimes lawyers hide behind the assertion that it is the job of the jury, not the lawyer, to decide the case, thereby evading the tough moral questions.

Some years ago I participated on a panel with some of the country's best-known defense lawyers at the Hastings College of the Law in San Francisco. To my astonishment, several of them said that they never tried to mislead or deceive jurors. Not surprisingly, there were snickers in the auditorium, including my own. These distinguished lawyers were not lying to the audience but they gave very narrow, and I believe, unsupportable definitions to the terms *misleading* and *deception.*

First-rate trial lawyers, even though their personal credibility should not be part of any case, work very hard at inserting their own credibility into a trial for the benefit of their clients and, when necessary, use that credibility to argue to the jury propositions that they know are not true. Oftentimes, hoping to make them appear as fools or liars, we use our training and skills to discredit truth-telling witnesses.

The prestigious American College of Trial Lawyers (of which I am a proud member), whose membership consists of the elite of the trial bar, tells us in their Code of Trial Conduct that in our representation of our clients we should not engage in chicanery.

Does such an admonition bear scrutiny? Doesn't a good lawyer regularly try to induce beliefs in juries that the lawyer believes to be false, and in doing so deceive the jurors? Is this not chicanery? And in picking jurors, don't lawyers, even where there is a strong case of guilt, seek out jurors who they believe, or at least hope, will disregard the evidence and return a verdict based on prejudice or passion? Is this not chicanery? When lawyers do these things, are they promoting respect for the law? Are they upholding the high ideals stated in our canons and codes of professional responsibility? In thinking about these issues, a few real-world examples help focus on the issues I am raising.

Assume that my client confesses to me that he mugged an elderly victim and that before she got a good look at him, he knocked off her glasses. My client wants to testify and deny that he was the mugger. I believe that I cannot ethically allow him to take the stand and commit perjury. To do so would be a violation of the code of ethics. As an officer of the court, such conduct cannot be condoned.

On the other hand, when playing the role of the zealous advocate, am I not permitted to rip the elderly victim to shreds on cross-examination and raise serious questions about what I know to be the ultimate truth by suggesting that the victim didn't get a good look at the mugger, or that her sight was bad or her recollection faulty because of age? Under our adversary system, such advocacy is considered ethically appropriate. Moreover, can't I argue to the jury at the close of the case that the truth-telling victim was not believable or credible?

While the general public has great trouble with such tactics by a defense attorney, there is solid support for such activity. Our justification for such conduct is found in the unique role played by the zealous advocate in a criminal case who is defending a client who has been given a very special status in constitutional law.

One of the very best explanations of that role is found in a dissenting opinion by former Supreme Court Justice Byron White—no liberal jurist to be sure—in *United States v. Wade,* 388 U.S. 218 at 256–258 (1967). This was the case that established the principle that a suspect has the right to counsel at a lineup. After pointing out that law enforcement has an obligation not to convict the innocent and must always be dedicated to reaching the truth, he makes clear that this is not the obligation of the defense lawyer.

In the words of Justice White:

> "Law enforcement officers have the obligation to convict the guilty and to make sure they do not convict the innocent. They must be dedicated to making the criminal trial a procedure for the ascertainment of the true facts surrounding the commission of the crime. To this extent, our so-called adversary system is not adversary at all; nor should it be. But defense counsel has no comparable obligation to ascertain or present the truth. Our system assigns him a different mission. He must be and is interested in preventing the conviction of the innocent, but, absent a voluntary plea of guilty, we also insist that he defend his client whether he is innocent or guilty. The State has the obligation to present the evidence. Defense counsel need present nothing, even if he knows what the truth is. He need not furnish any witnesses to the police, or reveal any confidences of his client, or furnish any other information to help the prosecution's case. If he can confuse a witness, even a truthful one, or make him appear at a disadvantage, unsure

or indecisive, that will be his normal course. Our interest in not convicting the innocent permits counsel to put the State to its proof, to put the State's case in the worst possible light, regardless of what he thinks or knows to be the truth. Undoubtedly there are some limits which defense counsel must observe but more often than not, defense counsel will cross-examine a prosecution witness, and impeach him if he can, even if he thinks the witness is telling the truth, just as he will attempt to destroy a witness who he thinks is lying. In this respect, as part of our modified adversary system and as part of the duty imposed on the most honorable defense counsel, we countenance or require conduct which in many instances has little, if any, relation to the search for truth."

Justice White went on to describe the role of the prosecutor, who must try to ascertain the truth. A prosecutor may strike "hard blows" but "not foul ones." The blows struck by Assistant U.S. Attorney Merritt in Kenny Conley's case were foul.

After the case was dropped, Kenny was reinstated and received his back pay. On January 27, 2007, twelve years and two days after the incident, Kenny and Jennifer Conley held a magnificent dinner and party in the Boston area. Kenny's and Jennifer's families were at the party along with approximately four hundred, present and former, officers; police officials; Ray Flynn, the former mayor of Boston; Congressman Bill Delahunt; and many friends. Saul, Junice, and I, with our families present, received awards. But the greatest gifts were the comments of Kenny and Jennifer and their families who thanked us for saving their lives. There were many hugs and kisses that evening, and I shed many tears of joy. It was an emotional evening that I will never forget.

## CHAPTER SEVENTEEN

# SCANDAL IN THE CHURCH

UCH OF THIS BOOK is about scandal, and, having dealt with it in its many forms over the years, there is, to be frank, very little that surprises me. However, when I was asked to play a central role in investigating the sex abuse scandal in the Catholic Church and advising the bishops regarding it, I was in for a real shock.

Theodore Cardinal McCarrick, the former archbishop of Washington, is a great and humble man of the church. He never allowed the high office he held and the perks that go with it to cause him to forget that he is a priest and a pastor to his flock. When the sex abuse scandal in the church exploded in 2002, the cardinal and I had conversations about the church's handling of the crisis. We both were concerned and troubled for the church. One such conversation occurred on June 4, 2002, at Tosca, one of the finest restaurants in Washington. When I made the reservation, I told my friend Paolo Sacco, one of the owners, that the cardinal loved French fries and asked if he could arrange for some for our lunch. I remember them being presented to the cardinal with great fanfare. At lunch we talked about the severe problem facing the church and I gave him a number of suggestions of what should be done. The church was facing a serious crisis and needed to treat it as such, but, in my opinion, was violating the most fundamental rules of crisis management.

As we left the restaurant, the cardinal commented to Paolo that the French fries were so good that they should be added to the menu, and, while we all had a good laugh, the cardinal and I weren't in a very happy mood. We both realized the seriousness of the problem and what it was doing to the church, the faithful, and the moral authority of the bishops.

On June 11, one week after my lunch with the cardinal, I was returning home from Skadden's New York office on the train. My assistant, Judy, reached me on my cell phone and told me that Bishop Wilton Gregory, the president of the United States Conference of Catholic Bishops, called and wanted to speak with me.

When I returned the call, Bishop Gregory explained that at a conference in Dallas, the bishops of the Catholic Church of the United States created a National Review Board of lay Catholics to assist the church in this time of crisis. Because the bishops themselves had lost a great deal of credibility, they decided that a lay board would be helpful in restoring credibility to the church. The bishop asked me to be a member of the core committee of the board and I readily accepted. Without a moment's hesitation, I told Bishop Gregory that I was honored to be asked and that I would help in whatever way I could. The church, and Jesuits in particular, had guided me as a young man. They were great teachers and instilled in me a strong sense of right and wrong, which has served me well in my personal as well as professional lives. I now had an opportunity to pay them back in at least some small way. Little did I know at the time, but this would become an enormous undertaking requiring a major commitment of time and energy. One reason I admire and respect Skadden, Arps is that the partners of the firm were pleased that I took on this major assignment on a pro bono basis. This is particularly generous for a firm that is secular in nature and consists of a large number of non-Catholics. This is just one example of why Skadden is a jewel in the legal profession and has a reach and impact far beyond the law.

Before I tell you about our work and our findings, let me tell you about our wonderful board. I have never before worked with such a dedicated group of decent, intelligent, and honorable men and women. The board was diverse in all respects. Some were conservative Catholics, others liberal, but each in his or her own way was committed to helping the church, and every one of us cared deeply about her. The first chairperson was the Honorable Frank Keating, the governor of Oklahoma. By appointing Frank, who had a reputation as a plain-talking law-and-order leader, the message of the bishops was clear. This was not going to be a whitewash. Frank brought passion and commitment to the board's work. At times, however, Frank's over-the-top public statements angered the board and made our job more difficult. Following his tenure as governor, Frank relocated to Washington, D.C., where he became an executive in the insurance industry and left the board. Frank was replaced as chair by the Honorable Anne Burke, a judge in Chicago who now serves on the Illinois Supreme Court. The other members of the board, all distinguished in their respective areas of expertise, included Dr. Michael Bland, who has a doctorate in clinical psychology and a doctorate in ministry. He was formerly a seminarian and is a thriving survivor of clerical sexual abuse as a minor. Another member, William Burleigh, was the chairman of the board and a former chief executive officer of the E. W. Scripps Company. Nicholas P. Cafardi was the dean of Duquesne University Law School and held degrees in civil and canon law. Also, for many years he represented the Diocese of Pittsburgh. Jane Chiles was the former executive director of the Catholic Conference of Kentucky. Alice Burke Hayes, Ph.D., was the former president of the University of San Diego and a member of numerous corporate boards. Other board members included Pamela Hayes, a high-profile trial attorney in New York City; the Honorable Petra Jimenez Maes, the chief justice of the New Mexico Supreme Court; Paul McHugh, M.D., the former psychiatrist-in-chief at the Johns Hopkins Hospital for more than twenty-five years and a Distinguished Service Professor at the Johns Hopkins School of Medicine and professor at the Bloomberg School of Public Health at The Johns Hopkins University; the Honorable Leon Panetta, a former United States congressman and chief of staff to President William Jefferson Clinton, and director of the Panetta Institute for Public Policy at California State University and a member of the faculty; and Ray Siegfried II, the chairman of the board of the Nordam Group, an aviation company in Tulsa, Oklahoma. As one of the first members chosen, I am proud to say that I helped select this incredible board.

I have never before experienced such collegiality as existed on this board. Much of this was due to the wise leadership of our chair, Anne Burke. Several members commented that the Holy Spirit had been watching over us given the strong-willed and independent-minded nature of the board members. There were many vigorous discussions. However, we treated one another with respect and over time I believe true affection, indeed love, developed among us. I consider my fellow members to be dear friends and, while the original board's work is over, we have remained close.

While each of us had our own personal reasons for agreeing to such a major commitment of time, there were some common reasons. Each of us in our own way felt obligated to the church, each of us felt that we had derived much benefit from the church, and each of us saw this as an opportunity to give something back.

In my own case, I do not think I would be where I am today had it not been for the guidance and tough love I received from the Jesuits at Brooklyn Prep. My wife, Ellen, has for several years been committed to an organization called SOAR (Support Our Aging Religious), which raises money for elderly religious, especially nuns whose basic living needs are not being provided for. Also, Ellen is on the board of directors and served as a volunteer teacher in a nonprofit organization, Language ETC. The mission of the organization is to teach English to thousands of immigrants in the Washington, D.C., area so as to enable them to get better jobs and improve their lives and the lives of their families. While not a church-sponsored organization, the activities are conducted at Our Lady Queen of the Americas Church. I once asked Cardinal McCarrick to attend a fund-raiser for Language ETC. He addressed the attendees in six different languages. I am not sure that even Bill Clinton could have done that.

The generosity of the church is repeated thousands upon thousands of times each day all over the world. The church and its diocesan priests, nuns, and brothers care for those no one else will care for. They run hospitals and schools and they care for the needy, sick, and dying. And yet, in the first few years of the twenty-first century, the church was not being praised for its great works, but rather denounced because some priests committed horrible acts of child abuse and the church found itself, largely through its own fault, in a full-blown crisis. And so when I was asked to help in this crisis, there was only one answer.

The Charter for the Protection of Children and Young People (the "Charter"), which the United States Conference of Catholic Bishops adopted in June of 2002, directed the National Review Board to "commission a comprehensive study of the causes and context of the current crisis." Also, the charter created an Office of Child and Youth Protection within the structure of the bishops conference. Our board was asked to assist the bishops in identifying candidates to fill the important position of director of that office. We interviewed several outstanding candidates, but one stood out. Kathleen McChesney was the third highest ranking official of the FBI and the highest ranking woman. When I checked her out with my law enforcement friends, she got rave reviews. I promptly set up an interview and she bowled us over. This bright and capable woman came in a petite package, but she was large in talent and presence. Kathleen had a number of years left before retirement from the Bureau, but told us that as a devout Catholic she wanted to help the church at this time of crisis.

We communicated with Monsignor Fahy, the secretary of the bishops conference, and scheduled an interview with him. While Kathleen, if hired, would have a reporting responsibility to the board, she would be an employee of the conference. During the meeting, Kathleen did a fabulous job answering the monsignor's questions. One question and answer was particularly memorable. "Kathleen, how will you deal with these old bishops?" Without missing a beat, she said, "One at a time." She also pointed out that she had successfully handled the good ol' boy network at the FBI and "they had guns. I think I can handle the bishops."

The board was unanimous in recommending Kathleen, but we had two concerns as to whether she would be accepted. One was that she was a law-enforcement official and the bishops were somewhat wary given some of the aggressive comments made by Governor Keating when he was chairman. Also, I knew that the hierarchy of the church are not as comfortable with women as they are with men. Fortunately, merit won out, Kathleen was selected, and she did a fabulous job in getting that office on its feet.

In addition to Kathleen, the board was blessed with the help of two very remarkable clergy: Sister Andree Fries (a treasure who passed away on July 14, 2007) and Reverend Cletus Kiley. Both of them ran interference for the board with the bishops conference and were valuable advisors on many of the issues. We always felt better after being with these two devoted, wise, and caring people. Throughout my service on the board, and especially in the beginning, there was a tension between the board and some of the church hierarchy. They simply were not used to lay outsiders snooping, as they would describe it, into their business and bristled at the notion that any group of laypeople would be in a position to tell them what they should do.

On occasion, Kathleen would get caught in the middle. While an employee of the bishops conference, Kathleen also reported to and got direction from us. The board wanted Kathleen to reach out to the dioceses and educate them about the board's work. The board felt that it was important to the church that its faithful members know that something was being done about the crisis. Kathleen had agreed to speak at a church in New York to enlist their support in our effort. This was clearly an appropriate part of her job and consistent with the board's wishes, but it provoked the displeasure of Edward Cardinal Egan of New York. How dare she speak to members of a church in his jurisdiction without his express permission? The board insisted that she honor her commitment to speak and we made clear to her that we wanted her to do more of it. With great diplomatic skill, Kathleen communicated the position of the board and worked it out with the cardinal's office to our satisfaction.

It was important for the board that we be independent and not do whatever some bishop or cardinal demanded. There are some members of the hierarchy who feel that the only positions appropriate for the laity are kneeling and standing, but the board was not about to sign on to that approach. We felt a tremendous obligation to the church, the laity, and the children of the church to do our job honestly, vigorously, and independently. Cardinal Egan would again be furious when board member Bill Burleigh, a senior member of the Knights of Malta, invited the board to the Annual Knights of Malta dinner without first checking with him. He objected to our coming. The Knights of Malta is a lay religious organization that does great service to the church. Usually there are hundreds of people invited to the dinner; a few members of the board were already members. Also, many outsiders attend. Bill was so angry, he refused to attend the dinner. I did not go, but was later told that the cardinal was rude and unfriendly to those members of the board who did attend.

Frankly, I wish the cardinal, with his knowledge, skills, and experience with the very issues we were investigating, had been more supportive of the board's work. Fortunately, despite some notable exceptions, there were many bishops and cardinals who got it and were of great assistance to us.

When the board began its work, it was important to learn the facts. No one really knew the extent of the abuse, and most of what we knew was anecdotal or based on surveys conducted by the press. One of the board's earliest decisions was to recommend to the bishops conference that we retain the necessary expertise to help us determine as best we could the nature and extent of the problem. As a result, the bishops conference, through the board, commissioned a research group at the John Jay College of Criminal Justice of the City University of New York to conduct a comprehensive survey involving all dioceses and religious orders in the United States. These surveys requested detailed information about the number of allegations of sexual abuse of minors by priests, the nature of the abuse, the responses of the church leaders to that abuse, and related matters. The time period covered by the survey was 1950–2002. Also, each diocese and religious order was directed to report the total amount of money it paid to victims, including money paid for counseling services and attorney fees.

Only by getting this information could the board understand the scope of what we were dealing with. By agreeing to participate in this exercise and by directing the dioceses to cooperate, the bishops showed real leadership and should be complimented. The sexual abuse of minors by all segments of society is one of America's dirty secrets and it is not unique to the church. It occurs in many other institutions. I only wish that other institutions in our society would follow the lead of the Catholic bishops in examining the issue.

Because of the cooperation of the bishops, the response rate to John Jay's inquiries was very high. Ninety-seven percent of all dioceses representing approximately ninety-nine percent of the Catholics in the United States completed the surveys.

As a result of the responses, the John Jay College researchers determined, as of the date of their report, that during the period of 1950–2002, church records revealed that 4,392 priests were accused of engaging in sexual abuse of minors. This number represented about 4 percent of the 109,694 priests active in the ministry during this time. The records revealed that there were approximately 10,667 minor victims of clergy sexual abuse during this period and the church spent more than $500 million in dealing with the problem. I have no doubt that these numbers, as shocking as they are, are low. Given the secrecy of the church and the fear of scandal, I have no doubt that records were not kept of many incidents and that victims and their families were discouraged from coming forward and reporting what occurred. I believe the cost was probably well in excess of $1 billion. But even these lower numbers were a shock to everyone, as they were larger than anyone expected. On July 15, 2007, it was reported that the Archdiocese of Los Angeles agreed to a staggering $660-million settlement, which was the largest payout in the child sex abuse scandal.

The board asked me to head a research committee consisting of several other board members to dig into the causes of the crisis. We conducted lengthy interviews with approximately one hundred witnesses, including cardinals, archbishops, and bishops in the United States and at the Vatican. We interviewed diocesan officials; priests; former priests; seminarians; victims of abuse; experts in psychiatry, psychology and sexual abuse; civil lawyers; canon lawyers; and law enforcement authorities. We interviewed concerned lay Catholics including leading Catholic thinkers and authorities. In addition to these interviews, we reviewed and analyzed a variety of writings, grand jury reports, books and studies on the problem, and news accounts. Because of the breadth of our inquiry, we not only learned about the sexual abuse crisis in all of its aspects, but also reviewed a broad perspective on church history and culture. Because of our promise of confidentiality, most of the people we talked to were very candid. Indeed, one bishop told us that he had been more open and honest with our board than he ever could be with his fellow bishops.

While the focus of our work was the sexual abuse of children, many other problems came to our attention as a result of our inquiry—including active homosexual conduct in our seminaries, alcoholism, and the crossing of boundaries by heterosexually oriented priests with women parishioners. Why this conduct occurs to the extent it does in the church should be the subject of further inquiry. I cannot help but think that the requirement of celibacy contributes to these problems. Is there a connection between mandatory celibacy and the sexual abuse crisis? By requiring mandatory celibacy, is the church attracting a disproportionate number of sexually dysfunctional men who are more likely to engage in improper sexual behavior? To answer this requires further scientific study, which hopefully the church will do.

Some priests believe that to have sex with another man is somehow not a breach of the promise of celibacy. How is that for rationalization? God, in order to perpetuate our species, made man a sexual being. It is a critical part of us. To require a priest to give up sex is a lot to ask. While celibacy may be a gift to some, I have little doubt that it is a terrible burden to others, leading to loneliness, alcoholism, the crossing of boundaries, and other harmful conduct. In my personal opinion, if the church allowed celibacy to be voluntary, it would attract many more dedicated Catholic men to the ministry and there would not be the shortage of priests that is undermining many aspects of church life. Converts to the Catholic priesthood who were married before becoming Catholic priests and who have remained married have, as far as I know, functioned well. I do not suggest that the elimination of mandatory celibacy would solve all the church's problems, and undoubtedly it would introduce some new problems, but it should at least be examined and discussed. Perhaps, at the end of the study and discussion, the decision would be made to retain mandatory celibacy, but shouldn't it at least be a matter of study and discussion?

One aspect of mandatory celibacy that became very clear to the board was that very little effort was made to help young seminarians and priests comply with the requirements of celibacy. Without help and guidance, failure was inevitable. Many priests told me that no one discusses it, and that you are on your own in this area.

The board scheduled February 27, 2004, as the date we would issue our report. Neither the bishops nor anyone other than board members were given drafts of the report and no one other than board members, except for the researchers at John Jay College, contributed to the report. The final report was adopted unanimously.

Because we knew that the bishops would be questioned about the report, we gave them a copy approximately twenty-four hours before its release so they would not be blind-sided by our conclusions and so that they would have an opportunity to be prepared for the inevitable press onslaught.

We decided to release our report at a press conference at the National Press Club in Washington, D.C. When I arrived, the place was packed. Several board members were in attendance. Our chair, Anne Burke, gave some introductory remarks and I presented our findings.

Our report, as disturbing as it was, was well received. I recall speaking in the following days at the Catholic University of America and running into Father John Neuhaus, the influential publisher of the conservative Catholic journal *First Things*. Father Neuhaus introduced himself to me and said, "Mr. Bennett, I want you to know that I was opposed to the idea of a National Review Board and in particular to you being on it, but I was wrong; you and the board have given a great gift to the church." This, of course, was very satisfying to me because Father Neuhaus is an important voice in the church and his words were a sign to others that they could approve of our report.

The board gave the church a first-rate play book and I only hope they use it. Now that the immediacy of the crisis is over, I hope that the bishops will not clip the wings of the board and interfere with its independence, but to be honest, I am worried. Old habits are hard to change. Also, a bad sign is that not a single bishop has been punished for his failures. Indeed, even Cardinal Law, after being forced out of Boston by the laity and his priests, was given a position of honor in Rome by the Vatican. He heads an important basilica. Was this too much forgiveness? I think so.

What we found after our inquiry, which lasted well over one year, was very disturbing. Due to the fear of bringing scandal to the church, many bishops did all in their power to conceal sexual abuse by priests. In many cases, records were not kept, or, if they were, they were secreted.

Rather than dealing harshly with predator priests, they went out of their way to protect them. I came to the conclusion that they saw the victim rather than the predator priest as the threat to the church. What was most disturbing was that there was no sense of outrage by the bishops as to what had been done to the young.

Naively or worse, many bishops believed that if they transferred abusive priests to other locations, the scandalous conduct could be contained. Of course, all this accomplished was the continued abuse of minors but in new locations.

The board looked for the reasons why this conduct occurred within the church. While it was not possible to pinpoint any single cause, several came to our attention. One of the major factors was that dioceses and religious orders did not do adequate, if they did it at all, psychological screening of its candidates. As a result, many sexually dysfunctional and psychologically immature men were admitted to the priesthood.

Also, we found that seminaries, where young men study for the priesthood, failed miserably to prepare the seminarians for the challenges of the priesthood, particularly the challenge of living a chaste and celibate life.

One of the most difficult issues faced by the board was the issue of homosexuality and the role, if any, it played in the sexual abuse crisis. It is undeniable that there is a very large percentage of homosexually oriented priests in the church. The board concluded that homosexuality did not cause the crisis but found that more than 80 percent of the abuse we examined was of a homosexual nature. The board was satisfied that while many homosexually oriented priests would never abuse a minor and were good and sensitive priests, the large number of homosexual acts underscored the need for the church to screen candidates carefully and determine if the candidate for priesthood is capable of living a chaste and celibate life. Given the fact that a candidate for priesthood is entering a predominately male culture and will probably be exposed to many more young men than women, extra care must be taken to be sure that the homosexually oriented seminarian will be able to honor his commitment. Of course, heterosexually oriented men must also be carefully screened to be sure they, too, are able to live a chaste and celibate life. The true pedophile focuses on very young children. We were advised by the experts that most pedophiles are not homosexually oriented priests. One thing that was very clear to the board was that further study must be done on the causes of abuse and the nature of the predator because much is unknown and anecdotal in nature.

As I have said, the response of the bishops was woefully inadequate. Bishops and other church leaders did not understand the broad epidemic of sexual abuse that was present in the church. This was due in part to the fact that dioceses are independent of one another and that bishops, as a general rule, are quite isolated and operate in a culture of secrecy, lacking transparency not only with the laity but also with one another.

As a lawyer, I was particularly troubled by the fact that lawyers for the dioceses had an unfortunate impact on the bishops. Many bishops, in their desire to preserve the assets of their dioceses, went along with hardball litigation tactics. Often bishops, would not talk to victims because lawyers told them not to. One bishop, who did not follow his lawyer's advice, told the board that "anyone should have seen the horror of it. But unless you listen to victims, you don't really have that sense of horror." This, perhaps, explains why there was no sense of outrage.

During our study, we also found that many bishops and other church leaders were too ready to rely on mental health experts who sometimes would advise a bishop that a predator had recovered. This, of course, was what many bishops wanted to hear. They often did not use their good judgment in transferring a priest and did not carefully monitor him once transferred. We found instances where a bishop concealed relevant information from the health professional, and in others, did not follow the advice of such professionals. In any event, as one bishop told us, "I don't think any bishop has the right to blame the treatment centers for anything because the ultimate decision is the bishop's, not theirs."

In investigating the facts and preparing our report, we decided early on that there was no issue off the table as long as it was relevant to our mission. We also agreed that we would not use our positions to advance our own personal views about church doctrine or practice. For example, I believe the ordination of women should be allowed. I believe the church's position on this subject is indefensible, narrow-minded, plain wrong, and certainly not required by doctrine. Moreover, it is counterproductive to the goals of the church. Nevertheless, I, and others who agreed with me, put aside such issues.

While I did not believe this issue was particularly relevant to our mission, I did wonder if women priests and bishops would have reacted differently to what was occurring. Would the nurturing instincts of a woman be more sympathetic to the young victims of abuse? I think so, but we certainly had no hard data to support my feelings. The all-male clergy often showed unbelievable insensitivity to the victims and much greater concern for the priests against whom allegations were made. What bothered me most was, as I have said, the absence of outrage. I wish the hierarchy had shown similar outrage regarding the abuse of the young as they showed toward the book *The Da Vinci Code.* In the later case, all they accomplished was increasing the sales of the book and movie. Cardinal Law seemed particularly insensitive and unconcerned about the sexual abuse of minors in his diocese. I do not think he was motivated by evil but rather was not paying attention. Nothing should have been more important to him than protecting the young, but unfortunately this was not true in his case. It seemed that there was more concern about liability issues by the bishops than what was being done to the young. The bishops were not acting as leaders of the church. They acted more like risk-assessment officers for insurance companies than pastors protecting the young in their flock. This surprised and depressed me.

Also what came as a great surprise to me was the mind-set of the priest abuser. Before conducting our investigation, I assumed (as a lawyer I have learned you should assume nothing) that a priest abuser was probably a tormented and conflicted individual. How could a man of God abuse a child? Wouldn't such a person be racked with guilt and self-loathing? Apparently not. I would learn from the experts that most abusers, but not all, were arrogant and narcissistic individuals who rationalized their conduct and had difficulty understanding the impact that their evil conduct had on their young victims. Rationalization is often a soothing balm for the guilty conscience; these abusers took rationalization beyond all limits. Some abusers actually convinced themselves that they were simply teaching the young about sex—a part of life's experiences. How ironic, that men of God who gave up sex in their own lives for a greater good, now saw themselves as teachers of sex to the young, notwithstanding the immorality and illegality of their actions.

One major fault line that contributed to the crisis is the structure of the church. Each bishop is virtually unaccountable. While accountable to the Pope, it must be remembered that Rome is far away and the Pope is a very busy man. A bishop, in practice, can do what he wants with no interference. One bishop does not dare to confront another and fraternal correction is nonexistent. One example of this is Bishop Fabian Bruskewitz, of Lincoln, Nebraska. Even though our board was created by the bishops conference and each bishop was mandated by the conference to cooperate with us, Bishop Bruskewitz refused to do so. Apparently he felt that he took his orders from God, and perhaps the Pope, but no one else. Bishop Bruskewitz made it clear that no one was going to tell him how to run his diocese. The board noted in its report the following:

> In this regard, the Board notes that although the bishops in general demonstrated support for the work of the Board and the John Jay College survey, the vicar general for the Diocese of Lincoln (Nebraska) wrote a letter indicating that the Most Reverend Fabian Bruskewitz, Bishop of Lincoln, would not cooperate with the efforts of either the Board or John Jay College. Specifically, the letter stated that Bishop Bruskewitz "does not recognize any

jurisdiction claimed over him or his pastoral activity by the 'National Review Board' " and that he "is prepared to take any appropriate and suitable measures necessary, including legal action, were that Board, your institution, or the United States Conference of Catholic Bishops to attempt to coerce him by adverse publicity, the threat of such, or other similar actions."

One of the suggestions I made in an informal setting with a small group of responsive and concerned bishops was that they should have a "swat team" of influential bishops who could enforce fraternal correction on their errant peers.

Another example of insensitivity was that of the Apostolic Nuncio in Washington, Archbishop Gabriel Montalvo. The board repeatedly tried to meet with Archbishop Montalvo to tell him about our work and to seek his assistance in arranging for appropriate meetings with cardinals in Rome. He refused to meet with us. Some clerical subordinate responded to us suggesting that the Apostolic Nuncio lacked jurisdiction over the matter. The matter was the sexual abuse of children and he lacked jurisdiction to help? Please, give me a break. I believe he and others underestimated the commitment of the board to get answers. Through the good offices of a few American bishops and Cardinals McCarrick and James Francis Stafford, however, Anne Burke, Bill Burleigh, and I arranged to meet with a few cardinals at the Vatican who were willing to meet with us. Cardinal Stafford, the former bishop of Denver, was particularly helpful to us and was interested in our work. Through his efforts we were able to meet other cardinals, one of whom was the very impressive Francis Cardinal Arinze from Nigeria. He made us feel very welcome and wanted to learn everything we knew about the issue. He understood the seriousness of the problem.

What struck me on our very productive visits to the Vatican was that the officials there had been told very little by the American bishops about the scandal. I felt that they were hearing the full extent of the horrors for the first time from us. We certainly disabused them of the notion that this was a scandal wholly created by the American press.

On our return to the United States, Anne Burke, Bill Burleigh, and I decided that we needed additional information and answers, and we felt it was important to reach out to more cardinals. Given the structure of the church, we knew that informing the cardinals at the center of power—at the Vatican—and gaining their understanding of our work was important for the long-term solution to the crisis. On our return to the United States, Anne sent faxes to several important cardinals asking them to meet with us. One of those who responded favorably was Joseph Cardinal Ratzinger, the head of the Congregation for the Doctrine of the Faith. He was at the time the second-most powerful official in the church, second only to the Pope.

On January 22, 2004, Anne, Bill, and I made our second trip to the Vatican and met with Cardinal Ratzinger. When he entered the conference room, you knew you were in the presence of a very special person. His most striking physical features were his gentle appearance and his beautiful white hair. He was small in stature with penetrating eyes, and you could tell behind them there was a powerful mind at work. He showed great interest in what we had to say. This was no courtesy visit. The cardinal spent more than two hours with us and took copious notes. When he read them back to us, it was clear that he understood exactly what we were saying. We pulled no punches and we all believed that he appreciated our candor. Not long after our meeting, following the death of Pope John Paul II, Cardinal Ratzinger would be elected by his fellow cardinals as Supreme Pontiff of the Church and adopt the name Pope Benedict XVI. We were all very impressed with him. How ironic, Bruskewitz and Montalvo would not deign to meet with us but Cardinal Ratzinger—now Pope Benedict—did. When it was later learned that we communicated with Cardinal Ratzinger by fax, we were told by a representative of the bishops conference that we violated appropriate procedure. Well, we did what we had to do—we got our meeting and Cardinal Ratzinger did not seem concerned about our method of communication; in fact, his office responded to our fax by sending their own fax. I guess the lesson is, who needs the apostolic delegate when you have a fax machine?

I have little doubt that children and young people in our church are safer today. Because of the board's work and the commitment of many bishops to protect them, children in the future will attend Catholic schools and, like myself, enjoy a fabulous education in a safe surrounding.

One influential clergyman who came to Washington for his interview with the board told us the following story: "As I was walking toward an airport restroom, I saw a mother with her two young sons, and daughter several feet in front of me. The mother told the boys to go into the men's bathroom while she took the daughter to the ladies' room. At that moment, she observed me and my Roman collar and saw that I was headed to the restroom. She quickly called the boys to come to her. Bob, at that moment the crisis became personal to me. I felt like a stake had been driven in my heart." Hopefully, incidents like this will never happen again and the bishops will regain their moral stature and voice and the clergy will again wear their collars with pride.

The crime of sexual abuse is not a problem unique to the Catholic Church. According to data gathered by the U.S. Department of Human Services, there were 903,000 victims of child maltreatment in 2001, of whom 90,000 were sexually abused. The actual numbers are, I am sure, much higher because sexual abuse of the young is underreported. This is our nation's big dirty secret. While the Catholic Church is justifiably criticized for what occurred, it should at least be given credit for doing something about it. Other segments of our society must do the same.

On October 6, 2005, one of our members, Ray Siegfried, passed away. Throughout our investigation and preparation of the report, Ray worked as hard as anyone even though he was suffering from the advanced stage of amyotrophic lateral sclerosis, commonly called Lou Gehrig's disease. In our report, we wrote:

> The other members of the Review Board feel compelled to note the exemplary dedication to this task that Ray Siegfried, who is in an advanced stage of Amyotrophic Lateral Sclerosis, has exhibited during his tenure on the Board. Ray's service to the Church in what he has called the "twilight of my life" stands as a testament to him and to the Church, which brings forth so much

good from so many. We are all grateful to him for his strength, integrity, and commitment.

Ray showed all of us what dying with dignity means and how, with a strong faith, one can turn the most challenging circumstances into an act of dedication to and love for one's church and fellow man. None of us will ever forget him.

# CHAPTER EIGHTEEN

# RING AROUND THE WHITE COLLAR

W HEN I WAS a federal prosecutor in the late sixties and early seventies in Washington, D.C., "white-collar prosecutions," to the extent there were any, consisted of the prosecution of bookies and those who sold alcohol illegally. Only occasionally would there be an investigation of a major company or its executives. For the most part, regulators such as the SEC handled corporate wrongdoing with civil fines, injunctions, and regulatory sanctions. Rarely did a corporate executive see the inside of a courtroom, much less a jail cell. Yet, when I left the U.S. Attorney's Office, there was something in the air. Things were changing and I wanted to be there at the beginning. I knew in my gut that the defense of corporate crime would become a growth industry. In the late seventies and throughout the eighties, I saw the steady increase of white-collar prosecutions, but even I was shocked by the explosion that occurred in the 1990s and the first part of the twenty-first century. In the past, prosecutors were often criticized in the press for putting a young ghetto kid in jail for robbing a store but looking the other way when a white corporate executive cooked the books or cheated investors. Throughout the seventies and eighties, most law firms shunned criminal work as being beneath them and, therefore, most of the criminal defense was done by boutique firms, like my old firm Dunnells, Duvall, Bennett and Porter. Since corporations usually paid for the representation of their employees who were in trouble, the money was good. Of course, as the defense of corporate crime grew and became profitable, the big corporate firms got into the action. In addition to the fees, they wanted to be able to tell their corporate clients that they were full-service firms and could handle their criminal problems as well as their other work. Now, most major firms have former federal prosecutors in their ranks, so they do not have to farm out this lucrative business. Fortunately, I had gotten in early, so the increased competition had no effect on my practice.

Just as big law firms were expanding their expertise in the white-collar area, so, too, were the Department of Justice and United States attorney offices around the country. Special white-collar units and task forces were created; the FBI, Postal Service, and other law enforcement agencies were doing the same. Politicians and journalists, who feed off each other, of course, joined the action. The average citizen called for the prosecution of the big shots, not just the little guys. When Willie Sutton, the world's most famous bank robber, was asked why he robbed banks, he made his famous statement "Because that is where the money is." However, the sentiment behind the old adage that you can "steal more with a pen than with a gun" helped fuel the public demand that prosecutors focus on white collar fraud as much as street crime. If you want to know the government's law-enforcement priorities, you should simply follow the money. In building my practice, I have always kept an eye on where the money was being spent. Also, which political party is in power can make a difference. I have always felt that there was more business for criminal lawyers representing companies when the Republicans were in power rather than the Democrats. I am not sure why this is the case. Perhaps it is because the Republicans are sensitive to the accusation that they are too friendly with business and so the prosecution of a company and its officers can be good politics.

One of the big differences in the prosecution of corporate crime as compared to street crime is the vast amount of discretion a prosecutor has in deciding whether a case should be pursued. Can you imagine a group of homicide detectives and prosecutors hovering over a bullet-ridden body and asking, "Do we go civil or criminal on this one?" The whole area of white-collar prosecution is filled with such questions, and the answers are often arbitrary.

In the 1980s and 1990s, if an individual officer or employee committed a crime that was generally within the scope of his employment—say paying kickbacks or bribes to get business for his company—the typical prosecutorial response was to charge both the individual and the company. If I made the argument on behalf of a corporate client that the actions of the employee were against company policy or that the company was a good corporate citizen that had never been in trouble before, the usual response was that those factors go to the issue of sentencing and not whether the company should be charged. Though not always, there was usually a knee-jerk reaction to charge the company if an employee committed a crime related to the company's business. Obviously, if an employee went on a "frolic of his own," a favorite phrase in the law, and robbed a bank on his lunch hour, the company would not be charged, but few other arguments worked.

The prosecution of a company for an employee's criminal conduct was the rule rather than the exception. The government believed that if the CEO of a company knew that his company would be found criminally liable for its employees' activities, the CEO would see to it that no employee violated the law. Since by entering a plea of guilty or being convicted at trial, a company could lose its license to do business or could be suspended or debarred from government contracts, there was a tremendous incentive to see to it that employees followed the law. A corporate conviction could affect thousands of employees who had absolutely nothing to do with the wrongdoing. This wasn't fair, but that's the way it was. Incidentally, most countries in the world do not charge companies for the acts of its employees. In my view, this is the better practice. I do not believe that a company should be charged unless it is corrupt to the core because the collateral consequences to innocent people—including employees and shareholders and others—can be devastating.

As a result of the government's approach in the past, a defense lawyer representing a company had to take all legal and ethical steps to avoid an indictment of an employee so as to prevent a corporate charge. This forged a unity of interest between an individual and his or her employer. Accordingly, company counsel and counsel for the individuals under investigation often entered joint-defense agreements, enabling them to share privileged material and work together on the defense. Also, it was almost always to the company's interest to pay the legal fees of its employees. The first line of defense was to help the individual avoid indictment so that there would be no vicarious liability for the company. Furthermore, because of the identity of interests, companies would often enter a deal with the government whereby it would enter a corporate plea, pay a fine, and work out a global settlement with the prosecutors and regulators on the condition that no individuals be charged. This approach enabled the company to get the entire matter behind it so it could move on and concentrate on what it did best, make money for its shareholders. This was the pattern for many years. Then things changed.

In the late nineties, the Department of Justice adopted a series of guidelines regarding the prosecution of companies. A recent version of the guidelines became known as the Thompson Guidelines, named after Larry D. Thompson, the deputy attorney general under President George W. Bush who also chaired the Corporate Fraud Task Force of the Department of Justice. Those guidelines were issued on January 20, 2003. No longer was a charge against a corporation automatic. If the corporation cooperated with the government's investigation, it could avoid being charged. The arguments that in the past were only relevant to sentencing now became relevant to the charging decision. Most important, the government said that if a company fully cooperated with its investigation, it could avoid indictment and the resulting collateral consequences. This gave the prosecution tremendous power over companies.

*Cooperation* usually meant that the company acknowledge its responsibility and assist the government in the investigation of wrongdoing. What is required to satisfy the requirement of cooperation has expanded over time. The government has gotten greedy. In practice, this sometimes means that the company now is expected to waive the attorney-client and work-product privileges and produce the results of the attorney's internal investigation, including memoranda of witness interviews. It has gotten to the point that to get the benefit of cooperation, the government often requires the company to conduct an investigation of itself—which can be tremendously expensive—and turn the results over to the government. The effect of these changes was to drive a wedge between the company and its employees, when previously they were allies—albeit, sometimes uncomfortable ones—in the defense of a criminal case. Some of these extreme demands have caused outrage in the corporate community and in 2007 were modified in what we now call the McNulty Guidelines, named after the Deputy Attorney General Paul McNulty. Under these revisions, prosecutors will no longer, absent special circumstances, ask companies to waive the attorney-client privilege as a sign of cooperation.

While prosecutors claim that they do not pressure companies to do what the government wants, every defense lawyer knows that in the real world companies are under tremendous pressure to do what the government wants so that they will not be charged. I have always thought of myself as an aggressive defender, but I must confess that on some days I see myself more as a great cooperator. Any lawyer defending a corporation in today's world must appreciate that a corporate conviction can result in staggering consequences and that everything must be done to avoid it. The corporate sentencing guidelines have substantially enhanced the penalties a company will be required to pay in the event of a conviction. Just as Willie Sutton went after banks because that was where the money was, prosecutors know that they can obtain staggering financial penalties by going after companies. White-collar prosecution units are now profit centers for the government. We are no longer talking about thousands of dollars in penalties, but hundreds of millions of dollars. In lieu of an indictment, the government now will often allow your client to enter a deferred prosecution agreement. If you pay hundreds of millions of dollars, admit wrongdoing, and agree to a wide range of compliance and personnel changes, including the appointment of an outside monitor, you may escape an indictment.

In a very real sense, corporations have fewer rights than individuals. As a defender of corporate clients, it is the rare exception when you can exercise the constitutional right to a trial. Even if you ultimately win at trial, there is a good chance that your client will not be around to enjoy the victory. The public accounting firm Arthur Andersen won an appeal reversing its conviction, but there was virtually no one left to celebrate. After its indictment, a death spiral began, which eventually resulted in the end of one of the nation's premier accounting firms. Under the Sarbanes-Oxley Act of 2002, the audit committees of public corporations now hire outside auditors. I cannot imagine any audit committee hiring an outside auditor that is under indictment. Therefore, defending a corporation in today's climate requires every bit of skill, creativity, and perseverance to convince the prosecutor to give your client a no-prosecution or deferred prosecution agreement in lieu of an indictment.

A *deferred prosecution agreement* simply means that while charges are filed with the court, the government agrees to drop these charges down the road if the company lives up to its end of the bargain. While a deferred prosecution agreement carries with it significant risks, if worked out properly with appropriate provisions and conditions, devastating risks are minimized and the companies usually survive and, indeed, prosper. Under the current climate, I often find myself telling my corporate clients that they "should rise above principle and make a deal." While prosecutors always see themselves as wearing white hats, some do not realize that at times they are engaging in legalized extortion. Even if a company believes it is innocent, it cannot, absent unique circumstance, afford to fight the charges to the bitter end. Often, winning at trial is a Pyrrhic victory because the company will be destroyed in the process. It is doubtful that any law firm in the world has handled more corporate criminal cases than Skadden, Arps. In Washington alone I have more than a hundred lawyers in my group dedicated to this area of practice, and the firm has many other lawyers throughout the country doing similar work. Recently Skadden has successfully represented Enron, Healthsouth, and KPMG, to name only a very few. What is often forgotten is that by helping to save a corporate entity, you are not saving bricks and mortar, but you are saving the jobs of thousands of innocent people whose families depend on the company's survival. Many innocent employees and their families were seriously damaged, indeed destroyed, by the Arthur Andersen debacle.

While I am intensely proud of the successes my colleagues and I have had avoiding the prosecution of clients, I am at heart a fighter and prefer to duke it out rather than compromise. Therefore, at times I feel enormously frustrated that I can't say to the government, "I will see you in court." With all of the problems facing lawyers who represent individuals, at least sometimes they can say that, and a surprising number of times they win.

One reason why the government loses cases is because of the complexity inherent in the prosecution of white-collar crime. Many prosecutors focus more on getting all the evidence they have before the jury rather than making it simple and understandable. If there is one lesson beyond all others I have learned in my forty-plus years of practice, it is to keep it simple. The single biggest mistake trial lawyers make, whether they are prosecutors or defense lawyers, is that they overtry their cases. As I've said before, the rule I follow is overprepare but undertry. All trial lawyers, no matter which side they are on, should spend as much time simplifying their case as they do in putting it together in the first place.

Another reason why the government loses white-collar cases is that prosecutors must often rely on insiders who are wrongdoers and have made favorable deals for a lower sentence. When I first started defending while-collar defendants in the 1970s, they were not facing the draconian sentences one faces today. Generally, judges would consider one's background, the absence of a criminal record, and good works in the community. I often told individual clients, without making guarantees, that if they pled to a white-collar offense, they might get probation or at worst a year or two of incarceration. To those who went to trial, I would say that if convicted, you probably will not get probation, but if the judge believes you put on an honest case and didn't commit perjury on the stand, you might get a few years at a minimum-security prison. No defense lawyer can say that today.

On Thursday, May 25, 2006, a jury in Houston, Texas, convicted former Enron Chairman Ken Lay and former CEO Jeffrey Skilling of multiple fraud, conspiracy, and related counts. We had represented the company, Enron, throughout the many investigations by the DOJ, SEC, and Congress. Since Enron was billed by the media as the corporate criminal case of all time and as the poster child of corporate wrongdoing, I was particularly pleased that we were successful in convincing the Department of Justice not to charge the company.

During the course of our representation of Enron, I had several discussions with Ken Lay. Frankly, I liked him. I recall one occasion in particular when we were flying from Houston to Washington. It was early in the case and we had a few hours to get to know each other on a more personal basis. I vividly recall that he had a dinner scheduled with the first President Bush and was concerned about whether he should go. While not yet indicted, he was a target of the government's investigation and the subject of much adverse press. He asked me what I thought about his going to the dinner. I suggested he not go as it would put the former president on the spot. Ken said he had reached the same conclusion because he was concerned that his attendance might embarrass the former president. His sensitivity was not lost on me and, over time and after many other conversations both personal and professional, I concluded that he was a decent man. The verdict did not change my mind.

At the time of their convictions, Mr. Lay was sixty-four and Mr. Skilling, fifty-two. Both men were facing extremely long sentences, and in Mr. Lay's case his could have been a death sentence because of his age. I recall thinking that because of his deep religious faith, he might be able to survive in prison. On the morning of July 5, 2006, I received a call from Marty Klepper, a partner and close friend at Skadden. Marty had worked on Enron matters for a number of years. Marty told me that Ken Lay had been found dead earlier that morning in Aspen, Colorado. Within hours, the news wires were burning up with news of his death. It was reported that Lay died of coronary heart disease. While there was some talk that his death may have been the result of suicide, the autopsy report showed that he had several severely clogged arteries and had suffered two prior heart attacks. Since he died before sentencing and appeal, the conviction was vacated. What a tragic end for a guy who was on the top. All of his undisputed good works and charitable contributions will likely be forgotten.

The nearly unanimous passage of the Sarbanes-Oxley Act on July 25,

2002, by both houses of Congress, and its prompt signature into law by President Bush on July 30, 2002, reflected a broad public consensus that enhanced criminal and civil enforcement measures are required to curb corporate abuses in the upper echelons of the nation's top corporations. Nearly four years after its passage, Sarbanes-Oxley continues to have significant implications for public companies, their directors, officers, and stockholders, not the least of which are its criminal prohibitions and the strengthening of existing criminal penalties for various types of fraud and other offenses. Sarbanes-Oxley changed the criminal law both by adding and amending substantive law and by increasing the penalties for white-collar criminal offenses. Sarbanes-Oxley includes four categories of new criminal provisions, relating to document retention, whistleblower retaliation, securities fraud, and corporate officer certification of a company's public filings. In addition, Sarbanes-Oxley increased the maximum penalties for fraud offenses four-fold and directed the United States Sentencing Commission to stiffen the provisions of the United States Sentencing Guidelines relating to white-collar offenses.

While it has made my job more difficult, and while I am troubled about the penalty provisions, I must confess that Sarbanes-Oxley has been a positive force for good. There is more corporate accountability than in the past and it has forced executives and directors of companies to focus more on their obligations to the public.

Today, under the federal sentencing guidelines, white-collar defendants who are convicted can, and do, get long jail sentences. In my opinion, someone convicted of a white-collar offense, absent special circumstances, should not be given the same sentence as a murderer or rapist. Because of these draconian sentences, I believe that many defendants enter guilty pleas even though they do not truly believe they are guilty. They will say whatever is necessary to get the plea deal because they do not want to run the risk of what in effect is a life sentence.

Usually, a defendant who cuts a plea deal is required as part of his agreement to testify against others. I also have no doubt that much untruthful testimony is sworn to in courts as a result of the threat of a draconian sentence. Let us assume, for example, a defendant I am representing is married and has small children and I tell him that if he agrees to plea to one count and testify against others, I can get him a five-year sentence, but if we go to trial and he loses, he may get twenty-five years in jail. Don't you think such a person will start thinking about how he can help the government, and will, because of self-interest and concern about his family, shape his testimony and give the prosecution what it wants? Isn't it awfully tempting for a defendant in trouble to make a deal and say what he has to say in order to protect himself and his family? There is a lot of pressure to cooperate and, in my view, to revise history to the prosecutor's liking.

I am confident that no federal prosecutor, at least none that I know, would use perjured testimony to win a case. Also, I don't know of any defense lawyer who would knowingly allow a client to perjure himself and allow an innocent person to be convicted as a result of his client's false testimony. But who knows, in any given case, what really is the truth? Isn't it likely that the prospect of a twenty-five-year sentence can over time cause one to remember things not previously recalled or cause an individual to say things to please a prosecutor who holds the key to the jail cell? The instinct to survive is stronger than the instinct to be a truth teller. To be guilty of white-collar offenses such as fraud or bribery, one must have a certain intent or knowledge. I have little doubt that many defendants are convicted on the testimony of a cooperating witness who is under enormous pressure, on the nuanced issues of knowledge or intent.

Some recent examples of draconian sentences are Bernie Ebbers, CEO of WorldCom, convicted of conspiracy and fraud, sentenced to twenty-five years to life; John Rigas, chairman and CEO of Adelphia, convicted of conspiracy and fraud charges, sentenced to fifteen years; Dennis Kozlowski, CEO of Tyco, convicted in state court on grand larceny and fraud charges, sentenced to a minimum sentence of more than eight years to a maximum of twenty-five years, now serving hard time in the state prison system; and, on October 23, 2006, Jeffrey Skilling, the former CEO of Enron, given a sentence of twenty-four years and four months on his conviction in the Enron case. In January 2007, after his third trial, Walter Forbes, former Cendant chairman, was sentenced to twelve years and seven months in prison and ordered to pay the staggering sum of $3.2 billion in retribution for his conviction on conspiracy to commit securities fraud and making false statements.

For all these reasons, doing what I do can be scary, frustrating, and hard. But my representation over the years of both individuals and companies has also been a source of great satisfaction, joy, and pride. I could never give it up. It is how I define myself. The fighter in me and the feel of the adrenalin rush is addictive and will keep me going.

# CHAPTER NINETEEN

# JAIL FOR JUDY

O N NOVEMBER 17, 2004, I attended a hearing before the House Committee on International Relations regarding the Oil-for-Food Program. I was there on behalf of a major international client. We had made several presentations to the committee on behalf of the client to show them that there was nothing to pursue. Unfortunately, many of these hearings take on a circus-like atmosphere where the media and photojournalists seem to take over the room.

A significant part of my practice is to represent clients before these committees. It is hard to take these hearings seriously when all of the logistical arrangements are designed to maximize the press exposure for the members rather than to ascertain the facts in any given matter. For example, at the Oil-for-Food hearing, between the members and the witnesses, there were thirty or more photographers constantly snapping shots from every angle to be used in hometown and national newspapers. Also, there were television outlets present in the hope that the news channels in a member's district would show footage of the member bearing down on a witness with what is usually an unfair rhetorical question. These photo ops are very distracting to the witnesses and undermine the dignity of the proceedings, but often the priority in Congress seems to be getting publicity, which helps in fund-raising and future elections, rather than getting the facts, which are often complex and nuanced.

During a break in the hearing, I saw Judy Miller, the Pulitzer Prize–winning investigative reporter for the *New York Times,* talking with one of the staffers. While I did not know Judy well, we had spoken before on other matters. I greeted her and she said "Bob, I may need a criminal lawyer." I told her I would be glad to help if she needed one. I knew about her problem since it was front-page national news. On October 7, 2004, Chief Judge Thomas Hogan of the United States District Court for the District of Columbia issued an order holding Judy in contempt of court for refusing to comply with a grand jury subpoena requiring her to testify regarding conversations she had had with confidential sources in connection with the outing of Valerie Plame, a CIA employee whose husband, Joseph Wilson, was a critic of President George W. Bush. The most chilling part of the order provided for "suitable confinement." Judy was not jailed immediately, but had been released on bail pending appeal. Matt Cooper of *Time* magazine, who had written a story about Plame, was also held in contempt and, like Judy, was released pending appeal of the contempt order.

Shortly after this conversation, I spoke with my partner Matt Mallow, a first-class corporate lawyer in our New York office. Matt, a personal friend of Judy and her husband, Jason Epstein, a famous editor at Random House and a founder of the *New York Review of Books,* told me that he had received a call from Judy regarding her situation. I told Matt about my conversation with her, and Matt and I agreed that we should represent her. On December 4, 2004, Judy retained our firm as criminal counsel. Judy should have had criminal counsel months before, and counsel who had only her interest in mind. Prior to our retention, she had been represented by the eminent First Amendment lawyer Floyd Abrams, who was also representing Judy's employer, the *New York Times, Time* magazine, and Matthew Cooper of *Time.* We were added to the team and over time would become her primary counsel in connection with the contempt proceeding. I knew we had a tough job ahead because Judy had already been held in contempt and Judge Hogan had made it pretty clear that confinement was going to occur. I asked my partner Saul Pilchen and associate Nathan Dimock to work with me on the case; we immediately set about the task of minimizing the damage to Judy.

Before I get too far ahead of myself, let me give you some context as to how Judy got into this jam.

The triggering event occurred on July 14, 2003, when *Chicago Sun-Times* columnist Robert Novak wrote a piece entitled "The Mission to Niger." The column discussed former Ambassador Joseph Wilson's trip to Niger on a mission for the CIA prior to the Iraq war. Wilson's trip was to determine whether intelligence reports about Iraq's attempt to obtain nuclear materials in Niger were accurate. On his return, former Ambassador Wilson published an opinion piece in the *New York Times* titled "What I Didn't Find in Africa." He wrote, "I have little choice but to conclude that some of the intelligence related to Iraq's nuclear weapons program was twisted to exaggerate the Iraqi threat." While this subject had been written about by other reports, Novak for the first time identified Wilson's wife, Valerie Plame, as an operative of the CIA. He wrote:

> Wilson never worked for the CIA, but his wife, Valerie Plame, is an Agency operative on weapons of mass destruction. Two senior administration officials told me that Wilson's wife suggested sending him to Niger to investigate the Italian report. The CIA says its counter-proliferation officials selected Wilson and asked his wife to contact him.

Novak's reference to the Italian report refers to information received by United States intelligence agencies from the Italian intelligence service of a supposed agreement between Iraq and Niger for the sale of uranium yellowcake, an ingredient necessary for the production of a nuclear bomb. This report was later discredited.

Novak's column created an uproar. In an article entitled "Columnist Blows CIA Agent's Cover," *Newsday* published a story saying that senior administration officials "violated the law and may have endangered her [Mrs. Wilson's] career and possibly the lives of her contacts in foreign countries." The public outcry gathered steam and the intelligence community, wanting to protect its own, went on the warpath.

I have known Bob Novak for several years. If you want to know what is going on in the inner circles of a Republican administration, he is a must read. However, while Novak could have been more careful in his choice of language, I am confident that he would never knowingly break the law by outing a covert agent. Also, I do not believe he would do the administration's dirty work for the sake of doing dirty work. He undoubtedly felt that it was newsworthy to report that Valerie Plame, a CIA employee, played a role in her husband being selected for this assignment. I do not know why he felt it necessary to use the term *operative* in his story, but there are other things that have remained a mystery about the whole situation. If Wilson's wife was an operative of the CIA, who played a role in his selection to go on a sensitive mission, why would Wilson run the risk of his wife being exposed by going public with his allegations against the administration? What was his understanding with the CIA regarding any public disclosure of what he found or didn't find? Did the CIA want Wilson to write the piece because of the agency's well-known dispute with the Vice President's Office?

All of this might have blown over or at least would have been a limited political scandal except that on July 30, 2003, the CIA sent a letter to the Criminal Division of the United States Department of Justice saying that a possible violation of criminal law occurred concerning the unauthorized disclosure of classified information—namely the outing of Valerie Plame.

On September 30, 2003, the Department of Justice publicly announced that it had opened a criminal investigation. On that very same day, President Bush publicly stated, "If there is a leak out of my administration, I want to know who it is. And if the person has violated the law, the person will be taken care of."

While the scandal was gathering steam, it was not until the last day of the year that it went into high gear.

On December 31, 2003, the *Washington Post* reported that Attorney General John Ashcroft recused himself from the Valerie Plame leak investigation and delegated his authority to Patrick Fitzgerald, the United States attorney in Chicago, as special counsel. Fitzgerald had been given the full authority of the attorney general over the investigation.

While I generally am opposed to the delegation of this sort of vast power to a single individual, I do believe that the appointment of a special counsel in this case was appropriate given the fact that the investigation would involve individuals at the highest levels of the administration. While aggressive and tough, Special Counsel Patrick Fitzgerald, a career professional, was no Lawrence Walsh, and I was grateful for that.

On February 15, 2005, the United States Court of Appeals for the District of Columbia Circuit affirmed the District Court's contempt finding against Judy and Matt and rejected their contention that there was a reporter's privilege which permitted them to refuse to identify their confidential sources. Following a denial of the Court of Appeals to reconsider their decision, on May 10, 2005, Judy Miller and Matt Cooper requested that the Supreme Court hear their case. On June 27, 2005, however, the Supreme Court refused to take the case, meaning that the rulings of the lower court denying relief would stand.

A trial lawyer never gives up, and I certainly did not want Judy hurried off to jail without taking one more crack at Judge Hogan. So at 10:15 A.M. on June 27, 2005, only fifteen minutes after the Supreme Court's refusal, we filed a motion in the District Court requesting a scheduling conference. Over the objection of Special Counsel Fitzgerald, the District Court granted our motion for a conference and set it for June 29 at 4:00 P.M.

We were pleased because it meant that we, as newly retained counsel, would have the opportunity of making a presentation to Judge Hogan. While we hoped to convince the court that it would serve no purpose to send Judy to jail, we knew it was a long shot. We did feel we had a reasonable chance of keeping Judy out of the District of Columbia jail, which, because of its overcrowding and other problems, would be extremely harsh and, we believed, unsafe for Judy. In any event, every day the ball was in play was one day that Judy would not have to be in jail.

The purpose of sending someone to jail for contempt is not to punish, but to coerce. In this case, it was to convince her to testify and divulge her source. In a very real sense, the person who goes to jail for contempt has the key to the cell. If you purge yourself of contempt by testifying, you go free. Judy was adamant that she would go to jail to up-hold her journalistic principles.

At the scheduling conference, Judge Hogan set a further hearing for 2:00 P.M., Wednesday, July 6, 2005.

When we arrived at the courthouse on July 6, there was a media mob scene, with photographers and reporters in a fever pitch to get photos and comments. Every now and then the federal courthouse is the center of worldwide attention, and this was one of those times. The press from all over the world was covering the hearing. I grabbed Judy by the arm, bulled our way through the crowd, and entered the courthouse. We entered the courtroom by the side door and proceeded to the counsel table. There was not an empty seat in the courtroom. My daughter Peggy, who is a federal prosecutor in the United States Attorney's Office in Washington, was to meet me in the hall outside the courtroom. This was one of those special events and I thought she would enjoy watching. A few minutes before 2:00 P.M. she had not yet arrived, so I asked a United States marshal friend, who had been a courtroom marshal when I was a federal prosecutor many years before, to look out for her and find her a seat.

Judge Hogan entered the courtroom and took his seat. The crowd quieted and the judge began explaining to the packed courtroom that the purpose of the hearing was "to address the contempt orders that were issued by the court upon Ms. Miller and Mr. Cooper and also *Time* magazine when they refused to testify or produce documents to the subpoena in response to the subpoena issued as part of the special investigation of potential illegal disclosure of the identity of the CIA official, Valerie Plame."

As the hearing got under way, Judy knew that incarceration was likely for both herself and Matt. Undoubtedly, there was some comfort in knowing that they were in this together. This feeling did not last long, as Matt Cooper shocked everyone in the courtroom when he addressed the court:

> "[I]n the matter before us today, Your Honor, until today, the source had merely signed a blanket waiver, the kind widely dis-

tributed to government officials by their superiors, and it is my view that such blanket waivers cannot be considered voluntary.

"To be effective, in my view, a waiver must be specific and personal, and so last night, Your Honor, I went to sleep planning to tell you that I must remain in civil contempt to protect the confidentiality of this source and I went to bed ready to accept the sanction of this court today. This morning I hugged my six-year-old son good-bye and I told him that I didn't expect to see him for some time.

"However, Your Honor, a short time ago, in somewhat dramatic fashion, I received the expressed personal consent from my source, not one of these blanket waivers but expressed personal consent, in which he released me from my pledge of confidentiality to him, and consequently, Your Honor, I am prepared to testify about our conversation so, Your Honor, it's with a bit of surprise, and I must say no small amount of relief, that I will comply with the subpoena."

Judge Hogan responded:

**THE COURT:** Thank you, Mr. Cooper. I appreciate your statement. I don't know if I agree with the definition of what a blanket release is as opposed to a personal release, but if you are willing to testify, that would purge you of the contempt citation and make unnecessary an appropriate sanction, which would include incarceration.

This left Judy all alone. It was now her turn to address the court. She had prepared her own statement in draft and had given it to us to review. We had made only slight revisions. Judy's statement was terrific. As she delivered it, you could hear a pin drop in the courtroom. Her comments were powerful and emotional and effectively contrasted the conflicting principles before the court. Those principles were, on the one hand, the government's right to every person's evidence and, on the other hand, the importance of confidentiality to an independent press. Judy spoke with great passion and conviction and you could tell that everyone in the courtroom, including the judge, was moved. Here is what she said:

"Your Honor, on Independence Day I thought long and hard about what you said to us in court last week. I knew that I would have to stand before you today to explain my motives and state of mind.

"You said that the law must be obeyed by everyone, that no one is above the law, and I want to assure you that I'm not above the law. I do not view myself as above the law and I am here today because I believe in the rule of law and you are right to send me to prison for disobeying your ruling if you choose to do so.

"You also said that citizens could not select which laws to obey. This you said would result in anarchy. I know firsthand that the rule of law is the core of decent government. I saw the heart-breaking results of anarchy while covering America's war in Iraq two years ago.

"For decades I have lived and worked in Middle Eastern and other countries where there is no independent judiciary. I have chronicled what happens on the dark side of the world where the law is an arbitrary foil that serves the powerful in Iraq under Saddam Hussein for instance, in Syria, in Iran, and in the former Soviet Union.

"I do not take our freedom for granted. I never have. I never will. But I also know again from my reporting that the freest and fairest societies are not only those with independent judiciaries but those with [an] independent press that works every day to keep government accountable by publishing what the government—publishing what the government might not want the public to know.

"Your Honor, I know that journalists are not perfect. But Thomas Jefferson put it best. If he had to choose between government and newspapers, he would choose the latter because the latter is the long-term guarantor of the former.

"If journalists cannot be trusted to guarantee confidentiality, then journalists cannot function and there cannot be a free press. I believe that a free press, Your Honor, depends now more than ever on people willing to express their views, particularly those in government.

"From my experience and the experience of investigative journalists like me, I know that many of these people in government will not talk to reporters if we cannot be trusted to protect their identity. The risks are too great. The government is too powerful and the country is too polarized.

"I am very gratified that the *New York Times* understands the importance of such pledges of confidentiality and I am deeply grateful to my paper and to its publisher in particular for supporting my decision in this case.

"But I want to emphasize this is my decision. As difficult as this time is for me and my family, I take great comfort in the strong public and private support I've received from my paper, my colleagues, and my friends who know of my convictions and my determination.

"I know that I do not stand before you alone. I do not make confidentiality pledges lightly. But when I do, I must honor them. If I do not, how can I expect people to accept assurances in the future? When offering to protect a source, journalists seldom know in advance whether the information being provided will turn out to be significant or sufficiently strong to produce a story or of major national importance.

"My motive here is straightforward. A promise of confidentiality, once made, must be respected or the journalist will lose all credibility and the public, in the end, will suffer. This belief is fundamental to my work and therefore to who I am.

"Last week, Your Honor, you said you could not understand a refusal to testify because sources in this case had waived their right of confidentiality. But waivers demanded by a superior as a condition of employment are not voluntary. They are coercive, and should they become common practice, and I fear they are, they will be yet another means by wrongdoers in government to silence people who want to report facts of public import to journalists or to express views that differ from the official orthodoxy. This is what I believe. This is what my supporters know and this is why I stand before you today.

"Your Honor, in this case, in this case I cannot break my word just to stay out of jail. The right of civil disobedience based on personal conscience is fundamental to our system and honored throughout our history.

"For four months in early 2003 I reported on soldiers in Iraq during a very sensitive and dangerous mission. I wrote about people who were truly among the nation's best and bravest, men and women willing to die for their country's freedom. If they can do that, surely I can face prison to defend a free press.

"Your Honor, I do not want to go to jail and I hope you will not send me, but I feel that I have no choice both as a matter of personal conscience and to stand up for the many who share my views and believe in a truly vigorous and independent press. That is why I am ready to accept your ruling.

"Thank you, Your Honor, for letting me address you and for your courtesy and your enormous patience in this proceeding."

When I got up to argue following Judy, I knew I had a difficult task. I never like to make arguments in the alternative because it shows a lack of confidence in your primary argument. Also, you never want to suggest to a court that you really don't expect it to grant the primary relief you are seeking. In this case, however, the likelihood of incarceration was all but certain so I could not take a chance of putting all of my eggs in one basket. Our prehearing research showed that the District of Columbia jail was the most likely place Judy would be incarcerated. This we had to avoid. Accordingly, we decided to make alternative arguments that went as follows: no incarceration at all, but if there would be incarceration, then home detention was appropriate rather than jail, and finally, if jail was required, we wanted incarceration in a facility safer and more suitable than the D.C. jail. My argument was as follows:

"Last week, Your Honor, you talked about Lewis Carroll . . . and Alice in Wonderland and I used to be quite an expert at it because, as the father of three daughters, it was required reading. One of them is here today and she is an assistant United States attorney.

"It has become part of the popular culture. I never dreamed it would make its way into your court but I was pleased that it did. Part of that popular culture is a magnificent exhibit at Disney World. Alice goes down a rabbit hole and she winds up in a place called the upside-down room. Everybody is standing on their head. The furniture is upside down and there is even a goldfish bowl with water and a fish upside down.

"Your Honor, I don't look like Alice. That I will concede but I somehow feel like I am. I'm perplexed as she was. I'm concerned as she was. There are things that just don't fit together for me. What am I talking about?

"I am here asking you not to send Judith Miller to jail. Judith Miller committed no crime. Judith Miller never even wrote an article. I know that's not constitutionally relevant but in terms of putting someone in jail, I think it is something you could consider.

"Perhaps more important, Your Honor, Judith Miller served with the most sensitive unit in Iraq. She was embedded. She was trusted by our government to maintain confidentiality and secrets. She got . . . clearances and she swore she would not breach the confidences that were shared with her.

"And yet I am perplexed like Alice because we are in court today and another part of the government is saying she has to go to jail because she's maintaining confidentiality. Admittedly in a different situation but very similar subject matters.

"Another part of why I am troubled as Alice was Your Honor yourself, during the contempt hearing, said . . . 'I agree with Mr. Abrams that Ms. Miller is acting in good faith doing her duty as a responsible and established reporter.' And then a few pages later you said, 'This is, as I said, an effort not made except in the highest tradition of the press, Ms. Miller not answering the questions.'

"Your Honor, I only present that for purposes of context. Your Honor, as you know, you must make an individualized judgment and determination whether there is any realistic possibility of Ms. Miller revealing her sources. Your Honor, I've been doing this for forty years. I will raise my hand and tell you I have spent a lot of time with Ms. Miller. She is not going to reveal her source. And Mr. Abrams and Mr. Pilchen likewise have spent time. She is not going to reveal her source.

"We don't say that as a challenge to the court. Of course not. But what we are saying is, as Your Honor knows, this is not about punishment. At the stage we are talking about coercion and I respectfully submit to you, Your Honor, that sending her to jail will not coerce her, and also I was pleased to hear Your Honor, in the beginning of this session, indicate that what you are to do under the law is to impose the least amount of coercion.

"Your Honor, there is another point I want to make in support of why I believe the strong evidence is that she will never disclose her confidential sources and I refer you to two letters that we have attached as exhibits. One is from General Petraeus and, Your Honor, everyone knows he is one of the most respected generals in the country. He handles the really serious, sensitive stuff in Baghdad, and Your Honor, we did not solicit this letter.

"This general came forward and here is what he says to Your Honor. He said, 'I find it unlikely that Judith would compromise on those values to include betraying information gained in confidence from her sources. My sense is that she is equally incapable of consciously reporting information that would threaten American national security. Judith is clearly a highly professional journalist, one who has demonstrated to me that she will keep her word.'

"And she said to you, Your Honor, she gave her word. She has not been relieved of that commitment and she will keep it.

"The second letter, if Your Honor please, was submitted again, not solicited, Your Honor, which is rather remarkable that these military men would come forward to support a reporter. I won't mention all of them by name. You have the exhibit before you but in pertinent part this is what they say, 'We feel that it is important to let you know,' referring to you, Your Honor, 'that during four months of combat operations we came to know her well enough to be sure that her principles would never allow her to compromise our trust or our Nation's security. Based on her working with us in this sensitive area, we do not believe she would reveal secrets or confidential sources under any circumstances.'

"So, Your Honor, I know it's a tough thing to ask you, and only you in your heart can answer it, but with all due respect, and there is no one who has more respect for you than I, if you feel in your heart and determine that you believe Judith Miller will not reveal her sources, then I respectfully submit to you that the only thing you can do under the law is to let her go free.

"Your Honor, in the event that you do not so conclude, we ask you to consider a home confinement. I was a little disappointed in my colleague, Mr. Fitzgerald's reference to unpaid vacation. It was unnecessarily harsh. If you take the tools of a reporter away from them, that's where the coercion is.

"Your Honor, again there is no dispute that you must use the least respected means necessary to coerce compliance. That is all established law. You take away her phone. You take away the Internet. You prevent her from meeting with her sources. You have limited visitations. These can be done, Your Honor, in a home setting. . . .

"Finally, Your Honor, and I am almost reluctant to even raise this as an option but I feel I have to and the words are difficult in coming. But if Your Honor feels that you must send Ms. Miller to prison, and we hope to God you don't, we ask that it be at the federal prison in Danbury, Connecticut. . . .

"Your Honor, why there? It is reasonably close to the court. It is reasonably close to where her husband lives. Her husband, and we have submitted material as to why we think that is important. But to be candid with the court, my primary concern was one of safety. That is something I think, with all due respect, that the court should take into serious, serious consideration.

"Also, Your Honor, there are some medical needs. Now let me be very candid with the court. I cannot come before you and in good faith—I explored it. You can be sure I explored it. But I cannot, in good faith, say to the court that because of any medical condition of Ms. Miller, she cannot be incarcerated. That is not the case. I can say to the court that because of some of the medical conditions which we brought to your attention that they can be dealt with easier and more professionally if she were in a home detention setting.

"But Judith Miller was strong enough in body and mind to go to Iraq under conditions which would make most of us quiver so I can hardly come in here today and say she doesn't have the medical wherewithal to go to a prison. My arguments against prison are other. . . .

"We would request . . . if you do sentence her to prison, we would ask that you let her voluntarily submit herself to prison. Let her go through that door and not the one in the back. We ask if Your Honor rejects all of this . . . then we ask you, if Your Honor please, to have her go to the Arlington detention center.

"I would point out again this is not a special treatment situation that we are asking for. . . . The sad fact is, Your Honor, D.C. Jail is overcrowded and that I seriously believe that Ms. Miller's safety would be in jeopardy if she would be there, if she were sent there.

"Your Honor, I am at a real disadvantage in arguing because I don't, on certain things, because I don't know what that grand jury secret testimony is. But I will tell you after forty years in this business I have the nagging feeling, the nagging feeling that Judy Miller may be the only person going to jail in this case. If that were the case, it would be an absolute tragedy."

Let me let you in on a little secret. Trial lawyers are superstitious. We wear a certain tie or go through a silly ritual in the hope that it will bring us luck. I usually wear a purple tie. I find the color purple has certain powers—only kidding (sort of). The reference to Alice in Wonderland, however, has been a key to my success. To bring me luck, I mention my daughters in my arguments before judges and juries and whenever I can, in the context of Alice because she was a favorite literary character of theirs when they were little. I know it is silly but my references to Alice have worked over the years. Usually, my problem is finding an opening to work it in, so I was delighted when Judge Hogan gave me the opening when on June 29, 2005, he said that it was time to resolve the matter and made reference to *Through the Looking-Glass,* by Lewis Carroll, where the walrus said, "The time has come to face where we are." The moment I heard the reference, I smiled and knew the door was opened to engage in my superstitious nature.

My daughter Peggy, who had found her seat, liked my argument before Judge Hogan, and in particular, my reference to Alice. With fond remembrance she recalled the many arguments of mine that she had heard when I was taking a shower—I often practiced my jury arguments while showering. Once when Catherine and Peggy were little, they asked Ellen who Daddy was talking to in the shower. Ellen explained I was a lawyer and I was just practicing my jury argument. Some years later, Sarah, our youngest, heard me arguing away and asked her sisters what was going on. Catherine said, "Sarah, don't you know anything. Daddy is talking to the jury." I am told that Sarah, with a puzzled look, walked away shaking her head.

Following the argument on July 6, Judge Hogan ruled that Judy would be incarcerated for contempt until she purged herself of contempt by testifying. Fortunately, he sent her to a safe facility in Alexandria, Virginia, to serve her time.

When we were retained to represent Judy, the *New York Times* agreed to pay her legal fees and fully supported her decision to go to jail rather than breach her promise of confidentiality to her source. In fact, the publisher of the *New York Times,* Arthur Sulzberger Jr., the scion of the famous publishing family, repeatedly told me he was supportive of Judy. A strong-willed and highly principled reporter, Judy was certainly not a pawn of the *New York Times,* but it is also true that Sulzberger viewed Judy's decision to go to jail as a badge of honor for his newspaper. A few reporters at the *Times* privately joked that he saw this as another Pentagon Papers case. (This was a reference to the 1991 case in which the Defense Department's top-secret study regarding our involvement in Vietnam was leaked to the *New York Times.* Following the leak, the Department of Justice asked the federal court to restrain the publication of the material in the report. This conflict between National Security and the First Amendment was finally decided by the Supreme Court in favor of the newspaper.) Under Sulzberger's direction, the *New York Times* was again taking a very absolute and aggressive position regarding the privilege. They hoped that they could get the courts to reject the earlier Supreme Court decision in *Branzburg v. Hayes,* in which the high court refused to recognize a reporter's privilege. Specifically, the high court ruled that reporters have no First Amendment privilege to refuse to reveal their confidential sources before a grand jury engaged in a good-faith criminal investigation. If that was the *Times* view, it was a serious miscalculation because the underlying facts were not helpful to the cause. This was not a case where a confidential source disclosed government wrongdoing; rather, it was the position of the government that the assertion of the privilege protected a source who was possibly engaged in wrongdoing, namely the outing of a CIA operative. Because of this, the posture of the case as it made its way through the courts was not likely to gather sympathy for the position of the *New York Times.*

When Chief Judge Hogan confirmed his order of contempt and required that Judy be confined, he immediately turned her over to the custody of the United States marshal. Judy and I hugged and kissed good-bye. I had a lump in my throat as I left the courtroom. It is always depressing when your client does not leave the courtroom with you, but we all expected the result. Judy looked small and frail as she was taken into custody and escorted out the back door by the burly marshals, to be confined in the Alexandria detention center. It is a foreboding redbrick building and is, in every respect, a real jail. As Judy observed: "Inside her cell in the Alexandria Detention Center [she] was able to peer through a narrow concrete slit to get an obstructed view of a maple tree and a concrete highway barrier." She also said she "was losing weight and struggling to sleep on two thin mats on a concrete slab." While treated with respect, Judy was not shown any special treatment.

Judy is a very attractive woman with a smile that lights up her face. On my first visit to the jail shortly after her incarceration, she was wearing drab green prison garb, but she looked great and her spirits were just fine.

Saul, Nathan, and I frequently visited Judy. Usually, we met in a very small room with large steel doors on either side. When we went to visit her, we were escorted into the room, the door was locked, and then Judy would be brought in and both doors would be secured. It was a creepy feeling. When we wanted to leave, we had to call a deputy, who would release the latch. As I said, this was a jail and not a country club.

Judy's incarceration became a cause célèbre. Everyone wanted to visit her in jail. She had a steady stream of visitors who were a Who's Who list of leaders in politics and the media. All gave Judy their support and thanked her for what she was doing for the cause of protecting press sources. So many supporters wanted to visit Judy that one of our paralegals, Jacquelyn Pearo, was put in charge of scheduling and coordinating visits. Arthur Sulzberger and other officials at the *New York Times* visited Judy and gave her much-needed moral support. However, the senior management of the *New York Times*, including Sulzberger, did not appear to be as troubled about Judy's incarceration as was I. They were really into the "cause" aspects of the situation, believing that they were striking a blow for press freedom and a federal shield law. In fairness to them, they were confident that Judy would be released in a few months when the grand jury expired at the end of October. I disagreed. Fitzgerald made it clear to me that his investigation would not end on October 28. The notion that Judge Hogan would reject Fitzgerald's request to keep Judy in jail until she revealed her source was preposterous.

Judge Hogan was of the view that Scooter Libby, believed to be one of Judy's sources, had given Judy an appropriate waiver, but Judy felt that the circumstances of the waiver were coercive. Libby's lawyer, Joseph Tate, and Floyd Abrams disagreed on the nature of the waiver. For example, on September 29, 2005, in response to Tate's assertion that there was a voluntary waiver, Abrams wrote to Tate as follows: "In our conversations, however, you did not say that Mr. Libby's written waiver was uncoerced. In fact, you said quite the opposite. You told me that the signed waiver was by its nature coerced and had been required as a condition for Mr. Libby's continued employment at the White House."

I decided to call Joe Tate and discuss it with him directly. I certainly did not want Judy to remain incarcerated if, in fact, Libby had or was willing to give her the kind of waiver she required.

It was at this point in time that significant tension started to develop between me and the *New York Times*. On more than one occasion, I had to make it clear that even though they were paying Judy's fees, my sole obligation was to Judy and not some "cause" or the newspaper as an institution. The senior management of the *New York Times* was opposed to my calling Libby's lawyer because they saw it as a sign of weakness. I thought that was nonsense and said so. Judy was intensely loyal to Sulzberger and the *Times* and felt she had to accede to her employer's preferences.

I would not normally write about tensions within the team, but the *New York Times* disclosed it all for reasons that made little sense to me. Here is what they wrote on October 16, 2005:

> Mr. Freeman [in house counsel at The New York Times] advised Ms. Miller to remain in jail until October 28, when the term of the grand jury would expire and the investigation would presumably end.
>
> Mr. Bennett thought that was a bad strategy; he argued that Mr. Fitzgerald would "almost certainly" empanel a new grand jury, which might mean Ms. Miller would have to spend an additional 18 months behind bars.
>
> Mr. Freeman said he thought Mr. Fitzgerald was bluffing. Mr. Abrams was less sure. But he said Judge Hogan might release Ms. Miller if Mr. Fitzgerald tried to take further action against her.

"At this point," Ms. Miller said, "I realized if and when he did that, objectively things would change, and at that point, I might really be locked in."

After much deliberation, Ms. Miller said she finally told Mr. Bennett to call Mr. Libby's lawyer. After two months in jail, Ms. Miller said, "I owed it to myself to see whether or not Libby had had a change of heart, the special prosecutor had had a change of heart."

Judy was caught in the middle, but we finally convinced her that I should at least be allowed to make a call to Libby's lawyer to ascertain the true state of affairs. When I called Tate, he assured me that Libby had given Judy a waiver.

Judy was still concerned about the voluntary nature of the waiver and did not like the idea of hearing only from lawyers. I sympathized with her on this and called back Tate, asking him if Libby would call Judy directly.

Tate called me back and agreed to such a call. On September 19, 2005, a conference call with Libby, Judy, Mr. Tate, and myself was held in which Libby told Judy that she was free from her promise of confidentiality. Judy accepted his sincerity. Libby followed this up with a written letter waiving confidentiality.

With this voluntary, personal, oral, and written waiver, we had gotten over only the first hurdle in getting Judy released. The second hurdle would be a bigger one.

While Judy was satisfied with Libby's waiver, she did not have a waiver from any other source. While Judy was now prepared to tell the special counsel and the grand jury about her conversation with Libby, she was not prepared to disclose conversations with anyone else. Since Fitzgerald, in an earlier conversation with Abrams, refused to limit the inquiry to only Libby, I felt that this second hurdle might be more difficult to overcome.

Saul, Nathan, and I carefully reviewed Judy's notebooks. Our team went over every entry with Judy. At the end of the day, we concluded that while there were some other references to the Wilson/Plame affair in

Judy's notes, there were no sources identified, nor could Judy recall who made the remarks or when they were made. Since we now knew that it was only Libby who was in play, I thought that a real possibility existed that we could make a deal with Fitzgerald. Again, the *New York Times* was resistant to the idea. Frankly, they saw their interest differently than we saw Judy's. Judy instructed me to go forward and I called Fitzgerald. He was cordial and professional and accepted my representation as to the facts based on our review of the notes. He agreed that the only subject that Judy had to discuss with him and the grand jury was the Wilson-Plame matter and that her discussions regarding that subject would be limited to Libby. Our team was elated as we now knew that Judy would soon be released.

Had Fitzgerald not trusted me to redact the notes and had he not accepted my representation that Judy could only remember discussing the matter with Libby, no deal could have been made. This is just one example of why I tell young lawyers that if you have a reputation as a straight-shooter, you can do a lot of good for your clients. Of course, I was being absolutely straight with Fitzgerald and would never have made the representations if I did not believe them to be absolutely correct.

Arrangements were made for Judy to meet with the special counsel at 9:00 A.M. on September 29, 2005. The purpose of the meeting was to produce the redacted notes and for Judy to discuss her potential testimony before the grand jury. We met in the prison library, which was cramped and depressing.

Fitzgerald was low-key and respectful, and Judy showed no bitterness or anger toward him. She was very cool. She knew he had a job to do and realized that it was her decision to refuse to cooperate until she got the waiver that satisfied her high standards. The meeting went well and Fitzgerald agreed to Judy's release pending her grand jury appearance.

That same afternoon, Fitzgerald and I called United States District Court Judge Royce Lamberth. Fitzgerald and I explained the situation to him. He agreed to see us in chambers. Judge Lamberth often serves as acting chief judge when Judge Hogan is unavailable. We met the judge in chambers and presented to him a joint motion to stay the order of confinement, which would allow for Judy's temporary, but immediate, release. Fitzgerald agreed that after Judy testified the following day before the grand jury, he would file a motion to vacate the order of contempt. Once Judge Lamberth signed the temporary order, we could secure Judy's release. I have learned over the years that the bureaucratic machinery does not always work and I was particularly concerned because two jurisdictions, Washington, D.C., and Virginia, were involved, which complicated the process. Because of this, I asked Fitzgerald to please see to it that the law-enforcement personnel working with him prevent any delays in releasing Judy. Out of abundance of caution, I requested Judge Lamberth to do the same. The judge kindly offered to monitor the situation to be sure Judy was promptly released in accordance with his order.

Mr. Sulzberger had made it clear that he wanted to be at the jail when Judy was released, and I was happy to agree. As the hour for Judy's release approached, I received a call from the U.S. marshal's office advising me that they would only release Judy in my presence. I raced to the jail and on my arrival saw both Mr. Sulzberger and Bill Keller, the executive editor of the *New York Times,* waiting for Judy. It was a bright and sunny day, which seemed fitting for the occasion. At the designated time, a van with darkened windows exited the jail. I was told by a U.S. marshal to follow them to a location off the Alexandria jail grounds. Our car followed the marshals at a close but safe distance, with Sulzberger and Keller behind us. As we approached the transfer point, Sulzberger's chauffeur sped up and got between me and the marshal's van. I was a little concerned about what the marshals would think, as Judy was still a federal prisoner. The van stopped and Sulzberger lept out of his car and ran to the van vigorously knocking on its windows yelling, "Judy, Judy." My concern grew, but fortunately the marshals simply ordered him away. When Judy emerged, it was a joyous occasion. Judy was beaming, her fabulous smile as bright as the day, and there were hugs and kisses all around.

Sulzberger had made arrangements for Judy to stay at the Ritz-Carlton Hotel in Georgetown in advance of her grand jury appearance the next day. I thought this was thoughtful and supportive. However, I also learned that he planned a dinner party for her that night and this concerned me. I told Sulzberger that I didn't think that was a very good idea for several reasons. I explained that Judy was appearing before the grand jury the next morning and needed her rest. Also, we wanted to spend some time preparing her for her testimony. Also, I explained that I didn't want the media, if they found out about it, to report it. I thought that if such a report occurred, it might annoy Judge Hogan as well as Fitzgerald. It just didn't seem the right thing to do under the circumstances.

Sulzberger was not happy with me and made it clear that he was going to do what he wanted. I then spoke to Keller, who seemed to understand my position, and he said he would talk to Sulzberger. A dinner did take place that evening, but it was far more restrained than I suspect was initially planned and ended in time for a few more hours of preparation for Judy's grand jury appearance.

I met Judy in the hotel lobby early the following morning; both Sulzberger and Keller were there. Judy and I agreed that we should spend some time alone together and we stopped for coffee before we made our way to the courthouse.

As would be expected, it was a mob scene at the courthouse and we had to fight our way through the press. Once we got inside, I asked Judy how, as a reporter, she liked being on the receiving end of press attention. She just gave me one of her great smiles.

Sulzberger wanted to be with Judy at the courthouse when she appeared before the grand jury. No one is permitted to enter the grand jury room except the witness. If Judy needed to talk to me, she would have to leave the grand jury room to do so. Judy was thoroughly prepared and proved to be a very good witness. Every hour or so during the grand jury proceeding, there would be a short break and Judy and her lawyers would talk about what occurred and take stock of how things were going. Sulzberger was not satisfied to be there in only a supporting role. He clearly wanted to participate in my discussions with Judy. When I suggested that he should let her lawyers talk with her alone, he let it be known that he did not appreciate being excluded, although he reluctantly accepted the appropriate protocol. Fitzgerald did not like the fact that Sulzberger and Keller were with us. He clearly could have excluded them, but because he wanted to be supportive of Judy, he did not make an issue of it.

Judy did a fine job in the grand jury. She was later required to make two additional appearances to clarify the record and supplement her testimony, and did a great job at these as well.

At this point the *New York Times*, Sulzberger, and Judy were winners. All were getting well-deserved credit for acting in a principled and responsible fashion.

Sulzberger and the *New York Times* had been very supportive of Judy throughout the ordeal and I appreciated and respected them for it. However, following her appearance, things would turn sour. In my opinion, the *New York Times* would snatch defeat out of the jaws of victory. The first thing that happened was that Judy's bosses wanted her to write a story about her grand jury appearance and, in particular, to describe in detail her grand jury testimony. To accompany her first-person story, the *Times* decided it would write a soul-baring saga of the entire matter.

Judy was under explicit instruction to write the one story and to cooperate with the writer of the other. Under pressure from her bosses, Judy instructed me to cooperate with the reporter writing the magnum opus. I thought this was all pretty foolish and was particularly troubled about Judy writing about her grand jury appearances. Initially, Judy, following my instructions, had decided not to write about her grand jury testimony. But when it was made clear to her by her bosses that she was an employee of the *New York Times* and she had to do it, she gave in. When she had resisted, citing my advice, I received a call from Bill Keller, the executive editor, and Jill Abramson, the managing editor, of the *New York Times*. While professional, they made it clear, in very aggressive tones, that Judy had to write it. I explained my reasons why it was a bad idea. I explained that there were legal reasons why it was against her interest to do it. No lawyer wants his client to have multiple statements of the same event in existence. The slightest variation, no matter how trivial or insignificant, can be exploited on cross-examination to make it look like a witness has changed his or her story. Libby's lawyer would get her grand jury testimony, so why have another version floating around? Also, I was very concerned that, even though a witness can disclose his or her own testimony, Judge Hogan and Special Counsel Fitzgerald would be angry at Judy for revealing what, at that time, was secret grand jury testimony.

Would Fitzgerald believe that by describing her testimony in the newspaper, Judy was giving Libby a heads-up as to what she said so he could work around it? I reminded Keller and Abramson that the position of Sulzberger was to help Judy and that I was assured that they would do whatever was in her interest, but that this clearly was not. They cavalierly rejected my arguments. At the end of the conversation, I was told in no uncertain terms that Judy was an employee of the *Times* and that if she wanted to remain one, she had no choice but to write her story. What I did not know at the time was that the storm clouds were gathering—to get rid of Judy. Of course, before any action would be taken, they wanted to use her by getting her story in print.

Judy wrote her story not simply because she was ordered to do so, but because she was loyal to the *New York Times,* where she had worked for twenty-eight years. Judy also felt that the readers of the *New York Times* were entitled to know the reasons behind her spending eighty-five days in jail. Also, she was particularly loyal to Sulzberger, who she believed was totally loyal to her. Unfortunately, she would learn the hard way that this was not the case.

After her release, tension within the *Times* increased and the paper cannibalized itself. Judy, who had been a valued reporter at the *New York Times* for nearly three decades now saw her reporting being called into question by the paper. It was reported that she was difficult to work with, and even the columnist Maureen Dowd (who by the way is Tommy Corcoran's niece) took time off from beating up President Bush to attack Judy in her column.

Instead of declaring victory for both Judy and themselves, which would have been entirely justified, the *Times* engaged in destructive self-flagellation. The goal of the *Times* and Sulzberger was to use Judy's incarceration as an incentive to get the public and Congress to push for a federal shield law protecting reporters from having to reveal their confidential sources. Powerful figures from the media, such as Tom Brokaw, and from Congress, like senators Chris Dodd and Arlen Specter, visited Judy in jail and gave her their support. By now, trying to discredit Judy, they were discrediting the very person who was their best argument for a shield law. Comments like "What is the *New York Times* doing attacking Judy," "Their conduct is disgraceful," and "They obviously used her and then they threw her overboard" were the sentiments I heard time and again as I traveled throughout the city. Even friends of mine at the paper, some of whom did not like Judy, expressed their concerns to me about what was being done to her and how senior management was turning a big win into a disaster for the *New York Times.*

Judy was too proud and principled to let the dispute persist. She did not want to be the story and so she resigned, after working out a favorable separation agreement, which our firm helped her to negotiate. Following her departure from the *Times,* I am told that a staggering number of letters and e-mails were sent to the paper protesting their treatment of Judy and giving her the praise that this brave and principled journalist deserved. I am very proud that she was my client, but even more important, that she is my friend.

While Judy's case was not the best fact situation to argue for shield legislation, it did bring great attention to the issue and hopefully will be one more step in the direction of achieving such legislation.

A shield law is needed to ensure that the press remains independent, and is able to keep government honest. Today, there is great confusion among the press corps as to whether a reporter can promise confidentiality. While most states have shield legislation, the federal government does not. Congress should pass federal legislation so that reporters and their sources know where they stand. In my judgment, this is required by the public interest.

The grand jury before whom Judy and other reporters testified indicted Scooter Libby on October 28, 2005, on five counts of perjury, false statements, and obstruction of justice for lying to the grand jury and FBI agents regarding the leak of Valerie Plame's identity as being employed by the CIA.

On January 30, 2007, Special Prosecutor Fitzgerald called Judy as a witness at Libby's trial along with journalists Matt Cooper and Tim Russert. All of them provided damaging testimony against Libby. On cross-examination of Judy, Bill Jeffress, one of Libby's counsel, went after

Judy in a very aggressive and hostile way. At the time I thought his approach was a mistake because Judy, who had a good relationship with Libby and went to jail for eighty-five days rather than break her promise of confidentiality to him, could have been helpful to Libby on several points if treated differently.

On Tuesday, March 6, a District of Columbia jury convicted Libby on four counts. Following the verdict, the juror Denis Collins spoke to the press and explained the jury's verdict and their reaction to some of the witnesses. It was clear from his remarks that the jury liked Judy, found her credible, and felt that the defense badgered her during her testimony. Trial lawyers should remember that sometimes "honey catches more flies than vinegar." This certainly was true in this case.

President Bush granted clemency to Libby so he would not have to serve jail time. My prediction to Judge Hogan was right, Judy would be the only person in the case to serve time in jail.

# CHAPTER TWENTY

# TO THE YOUNG LAWYERS WHO WILL FOLLOW ME

NOW THAT I AM a gray-haired member of the bar, I feel an obligation to the young to pass on lessons I have learned. So let me make a few observations. I do so in the spirit of an obscure poem, "The Bridge Builder" by Will Allen Dromgoole, which speaks of each generation's responsibilities to its successors. In the poem, an old man crosses for the last time a dangerous chasm. To the surprise of an observer sitting nearby, the old man begins to build a bridge. The observer asks him why he is building the bridge since he will not be crossing this way again. The old man lifts his head and responds as follows:

> "There followeth after me today
> A youth, whose feet must pass this way.
> This chasm, that has been naught to me,
> To that fair-haired youth may a pitfall be.
> He, too, must cross in the twilight dim;
> Good friend, I am building the bridge for him."

The single most important quality a lawyer must have is a reputation for honesty and integrity. Judges and lawyers know who can be trusted and who can't be trusted. As an officer of the court, which every lawyer is, there is a duty to be honest and candid. A lawyer with a reputation for candor and integrity gives much value to his client.

I believe very strongly that a lawyer must live a balanced life. A lawyer is a part of a community, and a family, and must, at least part of the time, use his or her talents and skills for the public good. It is a great privilege to practice law and we must all act accordingly.

Relationships with clients have been a great source of satisfaction to me, but a young lawyer must be careful in dealing with clients. You should never blindly follow a client's instructions. You must, often at the risk of losing clients, tell them that they are wrong and that, as an officer of the court, you cannot do what is asked of you. One very common mistake is for lawyers to go into business with their clients. This is generally a bad idea. You cannot give truly independent and objective advice if you have a personal financial interest in the advice you are giving. Of course, there are business aspects to the law just like any profession, but once it becomes only about business, you have lost the soul of what it means to be a lawyer.

One of the most dangerous things about the law is that it can become all consuming. I could spend twenty-four hours a day working on my cases, to the exclusion of everything else. There is always one more file to read, one more case to analyze, or one more witness to interview. You must resist that temptation. You must always seek balance and proportionality in your life. This will make you a better lawyer.

I look forward to going to work each day. It is not labor for me; it is a love. But after a good day's work I look forward, even more, to going home. You can never allow the practice of law to smother your personal relationships. It cannot replace the companionship of your loved ones. You cannot allow the demands of this profession to destroy, as it can, your relationships with your spouse, your children, your friends, your lovers. Many lawyers of my generation complain that their children grew up without them. One of our country's most distinguished lawyers told me that his relationship with his children has been by long-distance telephone calls. He was proud of the fact that he was at least available to speak with them. What a tragedy!

The greatest joy in my life has been my family. My wife, Ellen, and I have joyously watched our three daughters, Catherine, Peggy, and Sarah, grow into mature, caring, and independent young women. I never allowed the practice of law to interfere with that and I am grateful for what has come of it. Both Catherine and Peggy are now married. My son-in-laws Sophien Bennaceur, Catherine's husband, and Carlos Mejia, Peggy's husband, are now part of our close family. On November 15, 2007, our daughter Peggy gave birth to Ava Ellen Mejia, our first grandchild. It was a glorious day.

Let me fill you in on a secret. If you have balance and fullness in your life, you will be a better lawyer. Wisdom comes from living a full life and experiencing all of its sounds, aromas, and colors. And the greatest thing you can give to a client is wisdom.

Finally, to be happy in this stressful and demanding profession, I suggest that you have a special place—where the tensions and burdens of dealing with other peoples' problems evaporate, or at least are put on hold for a while. For me, it is fly-fishing on a mountain stream or river. It is not that fly-fishing is so important, it is just that when I am doing it, nothing else seems very important. It was John D. Voelker, now deceased, a former judge in Michigan, who made the observation that nothing else seems very important when you are on a trout stream. Judge Voelker may be known to you by his pen name, Robert Traver. In addition to many wonderful books about trout, he wrote *Anatomy of a Murder*, a great book that was later turned into a movie. He also made an observation that really registered with me as a Washington lawyer; he said that trout fishing was "an endless source of delight because trout do not lie or cheat and cannot be bought or impressed by power, but respond only to quietude and humility and endless patience." And, former President Herbert Hoover noted that fishing "is discipline in the equality of men, for all men are equal before fish."

For me, as the preceding pages have shown, the law has been my magic carpet. It has taken me across the oceans. I have visited many countries and have met world leaders and represented a wide variety of interesting people, some famous and others not famous at all, rich and poor, honest and dishonest. I am not ready to put the carpet in storage. I will continue to work as long as I am wanted and can function as I do today. Each day when I go into work, I am excited and hopeful, always wondering where the law will take me next. Who will want my help? What challenging problems await me? What will the demands of justice ask of me? With each ring of the phone, my hopes rise and I wonder where the magic carpet will take me. Maybe it will not take me to a new place at all but back to Brooklyn. Only time will tell.

# ACKNOWLEDGMENTS

In December 2002, my daughter Peggy gave me a journal for Christmas with the following inscription:

> Daddy, I got you this book so you could start writing your story. . . . I, for one, think it is worth writing and I think it is time you started it. You have accomplished a lot in your life. . . . Please document it. . . .

With this encouragement and that of her sisters, Catherine and Sarah, I began writing after the first of the year.

After I finished my memoir, which I did not intend to publish, my daughter Catherine, an in-house lawyer at the William Morris Agency in New York, suggested I share it with Jim Griffin and Mel Berger, agents at William Morris. With their encouragement and help I agreed to publish it. They are the best.

I want to thank my editor Sean Desmond, who skillfully and patiently helped me through the process. Sean is a fabulous editor.

There are many others to thank. I am particularly grateful to my clients who authorized me to tell their stories, and without whom there would be no book.

Carl Rauh and I have been friends and colleagues for more than forty years. He is a great friend and lawyer, and his help has been invaluable.

Many of my other colleagues at Skadden, Arps—Joe Barloon, Hank Barnette, Austin Brown, Mitch Ettinger, Dana Freyer, Alan Kriegel, Saul Pilchen, Anand Raman, Mike Rogan, and Amy Sabrin—made helpful suggestions to the finished product.

Professor Ken Gormley of Duquesne University Law School read the

Clinton chapter and provided valuable insights. I also want to thank author Kitty Kelley for her encouragement and support.

I could never have completed this project without the invaluable help of my wonderful assistant, Judy Sachs; Margaret Heath, head librarian of Skadden's D.C. office, who can find anything anywhere; and legal assistant Brian Stuebner.

Finally, I want to thank my wife, Ellen Gilbert Bennett, one of the world's great readers, for her guidance, advice, and love.

# WORKS CONSULTED

Abley, Mark. "Adventures in the Arms Trade: A Canadian Saga." *The Canadian Forum,* April 1979, p. 6.

Acheson, David C. *Acheson Country: A Memoir.* W. W. Norton & Co. Inc., New York 1993.

Adams, James. *Bull's Eye: The Assassination and Life of Supergun Inventor Gerald Bull.* Crown Publishers, New York, 1992.

Altman, Nancy J. "When Prosecutors Pull the Press's Strings." *Legal Times,* March 8, 1993, p. 27.

Anderson, Jack and Michael Binstein. "When Legal, Political Defenses Collide." *Washington Post,* June 10, 1996, p. D20.

Axelrod, Susan. "3 Ex-Officers Acquitted in Iran Contract Case." *Washington Star,* November 24, 1977, p. D1.

Baker, Peter. *The Breach: Inside the Impeachment and Trial of William Jefferson Clinton.* Scribner, New York, 2000.

Balz, Dan. "Party's Top Soldier Keeps Marching Even As White House Sounds Taps." *Washington Post,* August 11, 1994, p. A18.

"Baseball Executive Seeks Action on Schott." *Cincinnati Post,* November 28, 1992, p. 1A.

Basham, William. "Aid-to-Reds Probe Opens After Judges Dissolve Injunction: In Court." *The Evening Star,* August 16, 1966, p. A1.

Bass, Mike. "Allegations Against Schott Merit Attention." *Cincinnati Post,* October 15, 1991, p. 1C.

———. "Baseball Declines To Say If Schott Being Investigated." *Cincinnati Post,* November 19, 1992, p. 2B.

———. "Baseball Promises To Be Fair." *Cincinnati Post,* December 11, 1992, p. 3B.

———. "Marge Schott: Pressure Mounts from Peers, Public." *Cincinnati Post,* November 30, 1992, p. 1A.

————. "Schott Feels at Ease Among Owners: Meeting Generates No Hassles." *Cincinnati Post,* January 13, 1993, p. 1D.

————. "Schott Goes On Offensive: Reds Owner Cites Unfair Treatment." *Cincinnati Post,* January 23, 1993, p. 1A.

————. "Schott Receives Report: Lawyer Wants Until Jan. 25 to Respond." *Cincinnati Post,* December 31, 1992, p. 1C.

Bass, Mike and Rick Van Sant, "Marge's Partners: No Place for Bigotry." *Cincinnati Post,* December 1, 1992, p. 1A.

"BCCI Was a Stuccoed Sham, Concealing Multiple Fraud By Switching Fictitious Assets from One Front to the Next. " *The Economist,* July 13, 1991, p. 81.

Bernstein, Carl and Bob Woodward. *All the President's Men.* Simon and Schuster, New York, 1974.

Berry, Jason. *Lead Us Not Into Temptation: Catholic Priests and the Sexual Abuse of Children.* University of Illinois Press, Chicago, 2000.

Beschloss, Michael R. and Strobe Talbott. *At the Highest Levels: The Inside Story of the End of the Cold War.* Little Brown & Co., New York, 1993.

"Bishops' Partial Response." *Boston Globe* (op. ed.), June 16, 2002, p. E6.

"Board Is Deeply Disturbed By the Situation in Boston." *Boston Globe,* February 28, 2004, p. A15.

Borklund, C. W. "Bill". "South Africa: A Self-Made Threat to American Security," *The Retired Officer,* March 1979, p. 15.

Bradlee, Ben. C. *A Good Life: Newspapering and Other Adventures.* Simon & Schuster, New York, 1995.

————. "The Man Who Made the Arms." *Boston Globe,* August 27, 1979, p. A20.

————. "Vermont Firm Allegedly Sold Arms Illegally to S. Africa." *Boston Globe,* August 26, 1979, p. A1.

Brenner, Marie. "Lies and Consequences: Sixteen Words That Changed the World," *Vanity Fair,* April 2006, p. 206.

Burke, Hon. Anne M,.et al., "A Report on the Crisis on the Catholic Church in the United States." February 27, 2004.

Burleigh, Nina. *A Very Private Woman: The Life and Unsolved Murder of Presidential Mistress Mary Meyer.* Bantam Books, New York, 1998.

Calame, Byron. "The Miller Mess: Lingering Issues Among the Answers." *New York Times,* October 23, 2005, p. 4:12.

Carroll, Louis. *Through the Looking Glass.* Penguin Classics, New York, 1998.

Castaneda, Ruben. "Georgia to Send Home Diplomat Involved in Car Crash." *Washington Post,* January, 10, 1997, p. A17.

Catholic News Service, "Keating Resigns from Bishops' National Review Board." July 7, 2003, p. 5.

Chemnick, Paul W. (Editor Comment), "The Response of Washington, D.C. Community and Its Criminal Justice System," 37 *George Washington Law Review,* 862, 1969.

Clark, Kim and Marianne Lavelle. "Guilty As Charged!" *U.S. News & World Report,* June 5, 2006, p. 44.

Clarke, Kevin. "Are Our Children Safe Yet?" *U. S. Catholic,* June 1, 2003, p. 18.

Clifford, Clark M. and Richard Holbrooke. *Counsel to the President: A Memoir.* Random House, Inc., New York, 1991.

Clinton, Bill. *My Life.* Random House Inc., New York, 2004.

"Clinton v. Jones." No. 95-1853, *Supreme Court Transcript,* January 13, 1997.

Conason, Joe and Gene Lyons. *The Hunting of the President: The Ten-Year Campaign to Destroy Bill and Hillary Clinton.* St. Martin's Press, New York, 2000.

Congressional Quarterly, Inc. "House of Representatives Casts Historic Vote to Impeach Clinton." *CQ Almanac,* 1998, p. 12-3.

Congressional Quarterly, Inc. "President Clinton Survives Impeachment Trial; His Reputation Does Not." *CQ Almanac,* 1999, p. 13-3.

Cooper, Glenda. "Ex-Diplomat Sought for Lawsuit." *Washington Post,* August 10, 2001, p. A9.

Cooper, Matthew. "The New FOBs: Foes of Bill; The President Hopes to Discredit Conservative Activists Who Are Bent on Bringing Him Down." *U. S. News & World Report,* May, 16, 1994, p. 26.

Cooperman, Alan. "Nearly 4,500 Priests Accused of Abuse, Draft Report Finds: 11,000 Victims, CNN Says, Citing Study of Diocese Data." *Washington Post,* February 17, 2004, p. A2.

Cooperman, Alan and Caryle Murphy. "4% of Priests Were Accused of Sex Abuse." *Washington Post,* February 28, 2004, p. A1.

Corcoran, Thomas G. and Phillip Kopper. "Rendezvous with Democracy: The Memoirs of 'Tommy the Cork.'" Unpublished, 1982.

Crossette, Barbara. "Iraq Agrees to Ease Way for U.N. Monitors." *New York Times,* June 25, 1996, p. A9.

Cue, Eduardo. "3 Acquitted of Fraud in Iranian Navy Contract." *Washington Post,* November 24, 1977, p A6.

———. "Defendant in Iranian Navy Training Trial Says He Recommended Lulejian Company." *Washington Post,* November 22, 1977, p. A14.

———. "Lulejian Firm's Ex-President Denies Hiring 2 Codefendants." *Washington Post,*
November 23, 1977, p. A7.

———. "Told to Conceal Deal From Navy, Witness Testifies." *Washington Post,* November 16, 1977, p. A25.

Daugherty, Paul. "Schott Oblivious to Harm She's Done." *Cincinnati Post,* December 2, 1992, p. 1D.

DeFrank, Thomas M. "Two B'klyn-Bred Lawyers to Duke It Out in Top Court." *New York Daily News,* January 13, 1997, p. 4.

Dennis, Debra. Fired Reds Controller Vows To Press His Case, Cincinnati Post, November 18, 1992, at 12A.

Donovan, John. "Rooted in Red: Schott Travels a Trail of Turmoil As Baseball Team Owner." *Cincinnati Post,* February 4, 1993, p. 4C.

Douglas, Hon. Paul H. (Chairman). "Ethical Standards in Government: Proposals for Improvement of Ethical Standards in the Federal Government, Report of a Special S. Subcomm. on the Establishment of a Commission on Ethics in Government." *Committee on Labor and Public Welfare,* 82nd Congress, 1951.

———. "Ethics in Government." 1952.

Dowd, Maureen. "Woman of Mass Destruction." *New York Times,* October 22, 2005, p. A17.

Drinan, Robert F. "The Mobilization of Shame." 2001.

Dromgoole, Will Allen. "The Bridge Builder." *Masterpieces of Religious Verse,* HarperCollins Publishers, 1948, p. 342.

Eisler, Kim Isaac. "House of 1,000 Lawyers." *Washingtonian,* September 1, 2004, p. 41.

Engleberg, Stephen. "North Implicated in Contra Supply through Portugal." *New York Times,* January 10, 1987, p. 1:1.

Falsani, Cathleen. "Bishops, Lay Group Pursue 'Audit' of Abuse Cases; Tension Subsides After Uproar Over 'Mob' Remarks." *Chicago Sun Times,* June 20, 2003, p. 12.

———. "Burke to Lead Sex Abuse Probe; Set to Take Over As Interim Chairman of Catholic Review Board." *Chicago Sun Times,* June 17, 2003, p. 8.

Frantz, Douglas and David McKean. *Friends in High Places: The Rise and Fall of Clark Clifford.* Little Brown & Co., New York, 1995.

Friedman, Alan, Lionel Barber and Tara Soneshine. "CIA Challenged on BCCI Role." *Financial Times,* July 15, 1991, p. 1.

Friedman, Alan and Tara Soneshine, "'Stonewalling' Accusation by Prosecutor." *Financial Times,* July 19, 1991, p. 7.

Gerth, Jeff. "C.I.A. Reported to Have Used Bank That Regulators Seized." *New York Times,* July 13, 1991, p. 1:1.

Goldstein, Amy. "Crash Victim's Mother Visits Georgian Embassy." *Washington Post,* February 11, 1997, p. B3.

Goodstein, Laurie. "Cardinal Egan Upsets Members of Review Board Studying Abuse." *New York Times,* January 15, 2003, p. B1.

———. "Catholic Review Board Begins Its Interviews on Abuse Crisis." *New York Times,* January 18, 2003, p. A12.

———. "Abuse Scandal Has Ended, Top Bishop Says." *New York Times,* February 28, 2004, p. A1.

Hamilton, Alexander. *The Federalist Papers.* "No. 78: The Judiciary Department." Signet Classics, New York, 2003.

Harris, John F. *The Survivor: Bill Clinton in the White House.* Random House, Inc., New York, 2005.

Harwood, Richard. "17 Arrested in HUAC Hearing Uproar: Congressmen Assail Corcoran for Injunction." *Washington Post,* August 17, 1966, p. A1.

Hemingway, Sam. "Fourth Arms Shipment Investigated." *Burlington Free Press,* January 21, 1979, p. 1A.

———. "'Hot Shells' Program Probes Alleged Sale to South Africa." *Burlington Free Press,* January 16, 1980, p. 1D.

———. "Jury Probes S. Africa Arms Sales." *Burlington Free Press,* December 7, 1978, p. 1A.

———. "Space Research Official Defends South Africa Ties." *Burlington Free Press,* October 22, 1979, p. 1A.

Hemingway, Sam and William Scott Malone, "CIA Role in Weapons Smuggling Alleged." *Burlington Free Press,* November 4, 1979, p. 1A.

———. "Defense Department Broke Rules in Deal With Space Research." *Burlington Free Press,* September 12, 1979, p. 1A.

———. "House Subcommittee Considers Hearings On Space Research." *Burlington Free Press,* October 28, 1979, p. 1A.

————. "Vt. Firm Sold Arms System to S. Africa." *Burlington Free Press,* July 8, 1979, p. 1A.

Hendershott, Anne. *The Politics of Deviance.* Encounter Books, San Francisco, 2002.

Herbers, John. "War Foes Clash With House Unit; 17 Are Arrested." *New York Times,* August 17, 1966, p. 1:1.

Hope, Judy Richards. *Pinstripes and Pearls.* Scribner, New York, 2003.

Horwitz, Tony. "Seized Giant Pipes Bound for Iraq Were for a Big Gun, Britain Says." *Wall Street Journal,* April 19, 1990, p. A11.

Howes, Joshua S. "Panel Seeks Bishops' Compliance." *Chicago Tribune,* July 30, 2003, p. 1.

"Investigation of Senator Harrison A. Willams, Jr." Before the S. Select Committee on Ethics, 97th Congress, 1981.

Investigative Staff. "Betrayal: The Crisis in the Catholic Church." *Boston Globe,* 2001.

"Iran's Leader Blames U.S. for Poor Ties." *New York Times,* May 28, 1997, p. A6.

Janega, James. "Bishops Applaud Pace of Abuse Plan But Critics Say Clerics' Actions Still Fall Short." *Chicago Tribune,* June 22, 2003, p. 6.

Jenkins, Philip. *Pedophiles and Priests.* Oxford University Press, New York, 1996.

Jennings, Bruce and Daniel Callahan. "Representation and Responsibility: Exploring Legislative Ethics, at 68." (See Amy Gutmann & Dennis Thompson, "The Theory of Legislative Ethics." 1985.)

Johnson, Carrie. "Enron's Lay Dies of Heart Attack." *Washington Post,* July 6, 2006, p. A1.

Kamen, Al. "Not a Pretty Picture." *Washington Post,* September 23, 1998, p. A23.

Lardner Jr., George. "Haggling Over History." *Washington Post,* June 13, 1998, p. A1.

————. "U.S., Zapruders Reach Deal on Assassination Film." *Washington Post,* October 17, 1998, p. A12.

Lattin, Don. "Bishops Meet Under Scandal's Shadow: Recent Black Eyes Mar Church's Effort to Regain Credibility." *San Francisco Chronicle,* June 20, 2003, p. A1.

Lehr, Dick. "Free and Clear." *Boston Globe Magazine,* January 22, 2006, p. 24.

Levenson, Michael. "Decision in Police Beating Praised: Hopes Expressed for Conley Return." *Boston Globe,* August 22, 2004, at B1.

Levine, Susan. "Love, Anger at Funeral of Girl, 16." *Washington Post,* January 8, 1997, p. B1.

Likoudis, Paul. *AmChurch Comes Out: The U.S. Bishops, Pedophile Scandals and the Homosexual Agenda.* Roman Catholic Faithful, Inc., 2002.

Lobdell, William and Richard Winton. "L.A. Archdiocese Seeks to Withhold Files in Sex Cases." *Los Angeles Times,* April 2, 2003, p. B1.

———. "Later Deadline for Priest Cases Sought." *Los Angeles Times,* March 13, 2003, p. A1.

Lobdell, William and Larry B. Stammer. "Mahony Criticized By National Review Panel."

*Los Angeles Times,* February, 28, 2004, p. A1.

"Local Fall-out from BCCI." *Financial Times* (op. ed.), July 15, 1991, p. 14.

Locy, Tony. "Judge Defends Decision to Jail Miller." *Associated Press,* April 28, 2006.

Loftus, John Allan. Sexual Abuse in the Church (1989).

———. *Understanding Sexual Misconduct by Clergy.* Pastoral Press, 1994.

Loftus, John Allan and Robert J. Camargo. "Treating the Clergy." *Sexual Abuse: A Journal of Research and Treatment,* 1993, Vol. 6, No. 4.

"London Branches of BCCI Used to Fund International Terrorism." *The Sunday Times* (London), July 21, 1991, p. 1.

Mahoney, Joe. "Probe Into Space Research Concludes." *Burlington Free Press,* May 9, 1981, p. 1B.

———. "Space Research Founder Wants to Change Plea." *Burlington Free Press,* September 25, 1980, p. 1A.

Malone, William Scott, David Halevy and Sam Hemingway. "The Guns of Saddam." *Washington Post,* February 10, 1991, p. C1.

Mann, Thomas E. and Norman J. Ornstein, *The Broken Branch: How Congress Is Failing America and How to Get It Back on Track.* Oxford University Press, New York, 2006.

Marcus, Ruth. "Clinton Asks Unprecedented Immunity." *Washington Post,* August 11, 1994, p. A1.

———. "Starr Urged to Decline Counsel Post." *Washington Post,* August 8, 1994, p. A1.

"The Marge Schott Decision." *Cincinnati Post* (op. ed.), February 4, 1993, p. 10A.

Margolick, David. "Mr. Fitz Goes to Washington." *Vanity Fair,* February 2006, p. 128.

Marsden, William. "Britain Seizes World's Largest Artillery Weapon." *The Gazette* (Montreal), April 12, 1990, p. A1.

———. "Bull Laid to Rest as Question Begs: Was Israel Behind His Murder." *The Gazette* (Montreal), April 1, 1990, p. B6.

———. "Bull Told Israelis Were 'After Him,' Son Says." *The Gazette* (Montreal), April 3, 1990, p. A3.

Mauro, Tony and Sam Vincent Meddis. "Legal Eagle Has His Hands Full: Clients Are Rich, Famous—and a President." *USA Today,* May 20, 1994, p. 4A.

McElwaine, Sandra. "Anna Chennault—A Certain Air of Mystery." *Washington Star,* August 20, 1979, p. D1.

———. "Tommy Corcoran, a Washington Institution: After Nearly a Half-century, He Just Keeps Rolling Along, *Washington Star,* April 30, 1979, p. C1.

McGee, Jim. "No BCCI 'Foot Draggin,' Says Top Justice Official." *Washington Post,* July 25, 1991, p. A1.

McGee, Jim & Mark Potts. "BCCI Papers Challenge Clifford, Altman Testimony." *Washington Post,* September 11, 1991, p. A1.

McGiffert, Carolyn Ekedahl and Melvin A. Goodman. *The Wars of Eduard Shevardnadze.* Pennsylvania State University Press, 1997.

McKean, David. *Tommy the Cork: Washington's Ultimate Insider from Roosevelt to Reagan.* Steerforth Press, New Hampshire, 2003.

Melville, Herman. *Moby-Dick.* Bantam Books, New York, 1981.

"Memorandum from Larry D. Thompson, Deputy Attorney General, to Heads of Department Components." United States Attorneys, January 20, 2003.

"Memorandum from Paul J. McNulty, Deputy Attorney General, to Heads of Department Components." United States Attorneys, December 12, 2006.

Mestel, Rosie. "Church's Defense Called Valid—To a Point." *Los Angeles Times,* July 4, 2002, p. A1.

Metreveli, Roin. *Georgia.* Publisher's International, 1995.

Michael, Robert T., John H. Gagnon, Edward O. Laumann and Gina Kolata, *Sex in America.* Little Brown & Co., New York, 1994.

Miller, Bill. "Georgian Diplomat Is Sent Home." *Washington Post,* July 1, 2000, p. B7.

———. "Georgian Diplomat to Go Home Soon." *Washington Post,* June 7, 2000, p. B4.

———. "U.S. Officially Asks Georgia to Waive Diplomat's Immunity." *Washington Post,* February 12, 1997, p. B1.

Miller, Judith. "My Four Hours Testifying in the Federal Grand Jury Room." *New York Times,* October 16, 2005, p. 1:31.

Mintz, John. "Starr's Probe Expansion Draws Support, Criticism." *Washington Post,* January 23, 1998, p. A20.

Mintz, Morton. "Attorney Corcoran Faces Ethics Probe." *Washington Post,* December 21, 1979, p. A1.

Mnookin, Seth. "Unreliable Sources: Judith Miller and the *New York Times*" *Vanity Fair,* January 2006, p. 132.

Moncrief, Charlie. *Wildcatters: The True Story of How Conspiracy, Greed and the IRS Almost Destroyed a Legendary Texas Oil Family.* Regnery Publishing, Inc., Washington, D.C., 2002.

Moloney, Sharon. "Schott Says She's Sorry." *Cincinnati Post,* November 21, 1992, p. 1A.

Moloney, Sharon and Mike Bass. "Schott to Meet Jewish, Black Leaders." *Cincinnati Post,* November 19, 1992, p. 14A.

Mozingo, Joe and John Spano. "$660-million Settlement in Priest Abuses." *Los Angeles Times,* July 15, 2007, p. A1.

Munn, Michelle. "Bishops' Panel Meets Amid Dissent." *Los Angeles Times,* July 31, 2002, p. A11.

Nelson, Lars-Erik. "Conservatives Are Sole Winners in Bizarre Case." *New York Daily News,* January 13, 1997, p. 4.

Novak, Michael and Jana Novak. *Tell Me Why.* Simon and Schuster, New York, 1999.

Novak, Robert. "The Mission to Niger." *Chicago Sun Times,* July 14, 2003, p. 31.

Oliphant, Thomas. "Righting a Wrong in the Conley Case." *Boston Globe,* August 24, 2004, p. A15.

———. "Time to Drop the Conley Case." *Boston Globe,* July 26, 2005, p. A17.

"Open Session Hearings," Before the S. Select Committee on Ethics, 101 Congress, 1990–1991.

Page, Susan. "Those Bennett Brothers of D.C. Potent Forces, Often in Opposite Directions." *Newsday,* May 22, 1994, p. A19.

Paolucci, Dominic A. "Abuse of Power: The Day of the Prosecutor." Unpublished, 1978.

Paulson, Michael. "Abuse Crisis Exploited, Prelates Say." *Boston Globe,* June 20, 2003, p. A1.

———. "Abuse Study Says 4% of Priests in US Accused: Figure Is Higher Than Church Officials Expected." *Boston Globe,* February 17, 2004, p. A1.

———. "Bishop Urges Fast Conclusion to Boston Suits: Conference Head Seeks Healing. *Boston Globe,* June 22, 2003, p. A25.

———. "Bishops' Watchdog to Meet Church Heads" *Boston Globe,* January 23, 2003, p. B2.

———. "Church Hierarchy Faulted by Lay Panel on Abuse: 700 Priests Removed by Bishops in 2 Years." *Boston Globe,* February 28, 2004, p. A1.

———. "A Church Seeks Healing: Pope Accepts Law's Resignation in Rome." *Boston Globe,* December 14, 2002, p. A1.

———. "Keating to Quit Board on Sex Abuse, Stands By His Criticism of Some Bishops' Secrecy." *Boston Globe,* June 16, 2003, p. A1.

———. "Keating's Test of Faith: Oklahoman Talks Tough as He Seeks to Reform Church." *Boston Globe,* September 29, 2002, p. A1.

———. "Lay Panel Sets Wide Review of Church: Keating Panel to Examine Sexuality, Role of Celibacy." *Boston Globe,* January 18, 2003, p. A1.

———. "Remarks, Resignation Put Bishops in Spotlight." *Boston Globe,* June 19, 2003, p. A1.

Paulson, Michael and Michael Rezendes. "Bishop Raps Critics of Abuse Policy: Calls for Unity, Warns Against 'False' Prophets." *Boston Globe,* November 12, 2002, p A1.

Pear, Robert. "The Story Thus Far: Assembling Some of the Pieces of the Puzzle." *New York Times,* December 14, 1986, p. 4:1.

Peterson, Bill. "NL Invites Schott Accuser to Meetings." *Cincinnati Post,* January 8, 1993, p. 3B.

Phelps, Timothy M. and Knut Royce. "Columnist Blows CIA Agent's Cover." *Newsday,* July 22, 2003, p. A4.

Pincus, Walter. "Iran-Contra Probe Focuses on Meese." *Washington Post,* August 6, 1992, p. A1.

———. "'Mock Trial' of Weinberger Is Staged by Independent Counsel's Prosecutors." *Washington Post,* December 15, 1992, p. A5.

Plante, Thomas G. *Bless Me Father for I Have Sinned: Perspectives on Sexual Abuse Committed by Roman Catholic Priests.* (See Chapter 2: John Allan Loftus, "Sexuality in Priesthood: Noli me tangere") Praeger Publishers, Connecticut, 1999.

Potts, Mark. "BCCI Stock Deal: Was Profit Proper?" *Washington Post,* September 19, 1991, p. A1.

Potts, Mark and Robert J. McCartney. "BCCI Indicted on Fraud Charges." *Washington Post,* July 30, 1991, p. A1.

"Prosecutors Studying Arms Firm's Dealings." *The Gazette* (Montreal), May 10, 1979, p. A3.

Gurwin, Larry. "Who Really Owns First American Bank?" *Regardie's* magazine, May 1990, p. 66.

Rezendes, Michael. "Church Editorial Admonishes Okla[homa ] Governor's Comments." *Boston Globe,* August 10, 2002, p. A10.

Riechmann, Deb. "Suit Challenges Zapruder Film Purchase." *Washington Post,* November 24, 1998, p. A17.

Robinson, Timothy S. "Watergate Legacy Still Plagues Attorneys, Clients." *Washington Post,* January 14, 1980, p. C1.

Rossetti, Stephen J. *Slayer of the Soul: Child Sexual Abuse and the Catholic Church.* Twenty-Third Publications, Connecticut, 1990.

————. *A Tragic Grace: The Catholic Church and Child Sexual Abuse.* Liturgical Press, Minnesota, 1996.

Rudman, Warren B. *Combat: Twelve Years in the U.S. Senate.* Random House, Inc., New York, 1996.

Satinover, Jeffrey. *Homosexuality and the Politics of Truth.* Baker Books, Michigan, 1996.

Schmidt, Robert. "Testing the Limits of Diplomatic Immunity." *Legal Times,* May 18, 1998, p. 1.

Seper, Jerry. "Libby Gets 30 Months, $250,000 Fine." *Washington Times,* June 6, 2007, p. A1.

Sherr, Lynn and Nancy Kramer. "Above the Law." *20/20,* ABC News, January 17, 1997.

Silverburg, Jay. "Cagle, Hooper, Paolucci Not Guilty: Retired Naval Officers Cleared of Conspiracy Charges." *The Pensacola Journal,* November 24, 1977, p. 1A.

Snider, Steve and Louis Berney. "Federal Grand Jury to Be Told Vermont Firm Broke Arms Ban." *Rutland Daily Herald,* December 6, 1978, p. 1.

Stammer, Larry B. "Abuse Panel Chief Critical to End." *Los Angeles Times,* June 17, 2003, p. A1.

————. "Bishops Change Tone on Abuse." *Los Angeles Times,* November 12, 2002, p. A1.

————. "Bishops Meet in Somber Gathering." *Los Angeles Times,* June 20, 2003, p. A24.

————. "Bishops Ratify Policy on Abuse." *Los Angeles Times,* November 14, 2002, p. A1.

————. "Bishops Urged to Rethink Policy of Expelling Abusive Priests." *Los Angeles Times,* May 7, 2003, p. A24.

Stammer, Larry B. and David Holley. "Bishops to Retain Policy on Abuse." *Los Angeles Times,* October 19, 2002, p. A1.

Stevens, William K. "Militant at Wounded Knee Is Shot as Fighting Erupts." *New York Times,* April 18, 1973, p. 1:1.

Taylor, Guy. "Georgia Diplomat Freed Years Early." *Washington Times,* March 1, 2002, p. A1.

Thompson, Dennis F. *Ethics in Congress: From Individual to Institutional Corruption.* Brookings Institution Press, 1995.

Toobin, Jeffrey. *A Vast Conspiracy: The Real Story of the Sex Scandal That Nearly Brought Down a President.* Random House, Inc., New York, 1999.

Torry, Saundra. "Arguing the Strategy for the Clifford-Altman Defense." *Washington Post,* August 10, 1992, p. F5.

Truell, Peter. "BCCI Used Letters of Credit to Guarantee Property Lending, New Documents Show." *Wall Street Journal,* August 23, 1991, p. B3.

————. "Fed Seeks Bar on 3 Ex-Officers of BCCI, Pharaon; Bank's CIA Ties Are Probed." *Wall Street Journal,* July 15, 1991, p. A4.

————. "Hatch Several Times Met BCCI Holder Alleged to Be Key Front-Man for Bank." *Wall Street Journal,* November 21, 1991, p. A16.

Truell, Peter and Larry Gurwin, *False Profits: The Inside Story of BCCI, the World's Most Corrupt Financial Empire.* Houghton Mifflin, New York, 1992.

*Time,* "Club Business: A Member Faces Expulsion." March 15, 1982.

————. "Hasty Exit: Williams Forgoes a Vote." March 22, 1982.

————. "Marge's Mouth." December 7, 1992.

"United States v. Bigesby." No. 1103-69, Hearing Transcript, D.D.C. November 17, 1969.

"United States v. Coleman." No. 1103-69, Indictment, July 15, 1969.

"United States v. Coleman." No. 1103-69, Trial Transcript, D.D.C., February 24–26, 1970.

"United States v. Conley." Criminal No. 97-10213, Motion Hearing Transcript, D. Mass. July 23, 2003.

"United States v. Crump." No. 930-64, Trial Transcript, D.D.C., July 20–30, 1965.

"United States v. Paolucci." No. 77-175-A, Trial Transcript, E.D. Va., November 15–23, 1977.

"United States v. Space Research Corp." No. 80-4-1, Plea Transcript, D. Vt., Mar. 25, 1980.

"United States v. Weinberger." Affidavit of Colin L. Powell, April 21, 1992.

"United States v. Weinberger." No. 92-235, Memorandum Opinion and Pretrial Order No. 6, D.D.C. Sept. 29, 1992.

Van Natta Jr., Don, Adam Liptak and Clifford J. Levy. "The Miller Case: A Notebook, a Cause, a Jail Cell and a Deal." *New York Times*, October 16, 2005, p. 1:1.

Van Sant, Rick. "Jackson to Owners: It's Not Just Schott." *Cincinnati Post*, December 8, 1992, p. 1A.

Walsh, Lawrence E. *Firewall: The Iran-Contra Conspiracy and Cover-Up.* W.W. Norton & Co., New York, 1997.

Walsh, Sharon. "The Case That Bit Back." *Washington Post*, August 18, 1993, p. C1.

———. "Clifford, Altman Settle BCCI Case; Partners to Forfeit $5 Million, Keep Nearly $15 Million." *Washington Post,* February 4, 1998, p. A1.

———. "N.Y. Sets BCCI Trial Ahead of Federal Case." *Washington Post*, August 6, 1992, p. B13.

Watanabe, Teresa. "U.S. Bishops Adopt Policy on Sexual Abuse." *Los Angeles Times,* June 15, 2002, p. A1.

Weigel, George. *The Courage To Be Catholic: Crisis, Reform, and the Future of the Church.* Basic Books, New York, 2002.

Weinberger, Casper W. and Gretchen Roberts. *In the Arena: A Memoir of the 20th Century. Regnery Publishing, Inc.,* Washington, D.C., 2001.

Wilkey, Malcolm Richard. (Chairman), *To Serve with Honor: Report of the President's Commission on Federal Ethics Law Reform.* Government's Printing Office, March, 1989.

Wilson, IV, Joseph C. "What I Didn't Find in Africa." *New York Times,* July 6, 2003, p. 4:9.

Winship, Frederick. "da Vinci Notebook to be Auctioned in NY." *United Press International,* June 23, 1994.

Winton, Richard. "D.A. Subpoenas Files on 14 Priests in Sex Scandal." *Los Angeles Times,* April 25, 2003, p. B4.

———. "L.A. Archdiocese Hit with Class-Action Suit." *Los Angeles Times,* July 17, 2002, p. B5.

Woodward, Bob & Scott Armstrong. *The Brethren: Inside the Supreme Court.* Simon & Schuster, New York, 1979.

"Zapruder v. United States." Hearing Transcript, D.C. Circuit, May 25–26, 1999.

"In re Zapruder Film Arbitration." Affidavit of Stephen Johnson, January 7, 1999.

# INDEX